Social Policy in the African Context

This book is part of the CODESRIA Book Series.

Social Policy in the African Context

Edited by
Jimi O. Adesina

Council for the Development of Social Science Research in Africa
DAKAR

South African Research Chair in Social Policy
PRETORIA

© CODESRIA 2021
Council for the Development of Social Science Research in Africa
Avenue Cheikh Anta Diop, Angle Canal IV
BP 3304 Dakar, 18524, Senegal
Website: www.codesria.org

ISBN: 978-2-38234-045-5

All rights reserved. No part of this publication may be reproduced or transmitted in any form or by any means, electronic or mechanical, including photocopy, recording or any information storage or retrieval system without prior permission from CODESRIA.

Typesetting: Stefanie Krieg-Elliott
Cover Design: Genevieve Simpson

Distributed in Africa by CODESRIA
Distributed elsewhere by African Books Collective, Oxford, UK
Website: www.africanbookscollective.com

The Council for the Development of Social Science Research in Africa (CODESRIA) is an independent organisation whose principal objectives are to facilitate research, promote research-based publishing and create multiple forums for critical thinking and exchange of views among African researchers. All these are aimed at reducing the fragmentation of research in the continent through the creation of thematic research networks that cut across linguistic and regional boundaries.

CODESRIA publishes *Africa Development*, the longest standing Africa based social science journal; Afrika Zamani, a journal of history; the *African Sociological Review*; *Africa Review of Books* and the *Journal of Higher Education in Africa*. The Council also co-publishes *Identity, Culture and Politics: An Afro-Asian Dialogue; and the Afro-Arab Selections for Social Sciences*. The results of its research and other activities are also disseminated through its Working Paper Series, Book Series, Policy Briefs and the CODESRIA Bulletin. All CODESRIA publications are accessible online at www.codesria.org.

CODESRIA would like to express its gratitude to the Swedish International Development Cooperation Agency (SIDA), the Carnegie Corporation of New York (CCNY), Andrew W. Mellon Foundation, the Open Society Foundations (OSFs), UNESCO, Oumou Dilly Foundation, Ford Foundation and the Government of Senegal for supporting its research, training and publication programmes.

Contents

Dedication vii

Preface ix

Notes on Contributors xiii

1. Social Policy in the African Context: An Introduction
   Jimi Adesina 1

2. Reclaiming Transformative Social Policy for Inclusive Development
   Tade Akin Aina 13

3. Rethinking Social Policy in Africa – A Transformative Approach
   Katja Hujo 29

4. Nati on-Building and the Nationalist Discourse: Revisiting Social Policy in Ghana and Zambia in the First Decade of Independence
   Ndangwa Noyoo and Emmanuel Boon 45

5. Gender, Poverty and Land in Africa: A Transformative Social Policy Perspective
   Newman Tekwa 65

6. Informal Social Protection, Group Membership and Agriculture: Male and Female Wheat Farmers in Ethiopia
   Kristie Drucza and Dagmawit Giref Sahile 91

7. Do Temporal Myopia and Asymmetric Information Matter in the Demand for Social Insurance?
   Walid Merouani, Nacer-Eddine Hammouda and Claire El Moudde ... 121

8. Interest, Resources and Policy Networks: Understanding the Adoption of Social Protection Policies in Kenya
   Marion Ouma and Jimi Adesina 147

9. Non-State Actors and Social Policy in Africa: Issues and Perspectives for Agenda 2063
   Jonathan Makuwira 165

10. Excavating Communal Mutual Support Praxis in Two Townships in South Africa: Preliminary Notes for Social Policy Learning
    Kolawole Omomowo and Jimi Adesina 179

11. The Nigerian Social Health Insurance System: Reconceptualising the Approach to Meeting Universal Coverage
    Augustine I. Omoruan 197

12. Land Reform as Social Policy: Exploring the Redistribution and Social Protection Outcomes in Goromonzi District (Zimbabwe)
    Clement Chipenda 213

13. The Male Breadwinner Myth: The South African Case
    Marlize Rabe 241

14. Does How We Measure and Explain Income Inequality Make a Difference for Social Policy? A Case Study of Kenya
    Boaz Munga 259

Index 283

Dedication

For Thandika Mkandawire, In Memoriam
A friend, mentor, an inspiration, and a veritable *Mwalimu*

Preface

Over the last three decades or so, a select number of scholars operating under the auspices of CODESRIA, and later UNRISD, have dedicated their energies and time to rescuing social policy from a major policy and intellectual assault. The assault manifested itself in the form of a reductionist neoliberal approach to the idea of social policy, which primarily questioned the role of the state in development. This assault framed the discourse on development, centring it almost exclusively on market forces that controlled the allocation of public goods. From this perspective, the state had a limited role in ensuring 'the well-being and minimum welfare of its various constituents'. This role reduced social policy to a mere 'social protection' function and so emptied it of its broad meaning and content within a development context.

The attack on social policy in the African context has persisted. This is especially the case as neoclassical economics has held sway and found various guises to explain the various crises of development, the brutal inequalities these crises have sustained and the marginalisation of some constituencies of society they have caused. The situation worsened once poverty was 'discovered' and became trendy, and the resulting Poverty Reduction Strategy Papers framework was advanced as a means of addressing poverty's often debilitating effects. In this framework, social policy was rephrased into the language of safety nets, as merely providing subsidies, and was assigned the role of easing the pain of poverty. Governments have been coerced, cajoled or simply made to comply to this framework by adopting neoliberal 'solutions' that have promised that the effects on the poor can and will be minimised through social assistance handouts. Shaping the debate as one between growth and equity, the proponents of the limited state, and cash assistance, seem to have won in the last few decades, especially since the emphasis on retrenching the state was given a new lease of life under the Washington Consensus.

Three of the scholars involved in rescuing social policy—Jimi Adesina, Tade A. Aina and Katja Hujo—are part of this study on *Social Policy in the African Context*. The fourth, Thandika Mkandawire, who passed away just over a year ago, gave one of the keynote addresses at the conference at which these papers were first presented and discussed, in Pretoria, in 2017. While Tade A. Aina worked with Thandika at CODESRIA in the 1990s, and authored two pioneering studies in this rescue mission, Jimi Adesina and Katja Hujo helped to elaborate the discussion further through UNRISD, and later, after Jimi Adesina occupied the DSI/NRF SARChI Chair in Social Policy at the University of South Africa (Unisa). It is therefore not a coincidence that he convened the conference in 2017 and edited this volume. Jimi Adesina is a long-standing member of CODESRIA whose work has expanded from his initial focus on labour and labour policy in the explanation of the African crisis to his current focus on social policy. The Chair he occupies at Unisa has been at the forefront of research on social policy and in training students for this at advanced levels. Some of these researchers are contributors to this volume.

The passing on of Thandika may have undermined the speed with which this rescue mission is being conducted. But it certainly has not stopped the desire and conviction to document the historic relevance and undeniable importance of social policy in development. Through his illustrious intellectual career, the conceptual clarity he brought to it, the strength of his methodological grounding and the historical depth of his understanding of socioeconomic processes globally and in Africa, Thandika left a rich but unfinished research agenda. The scholars he worked with and the institutions he belonged to and was associated with, have no option but to dive deeper, tenaciously pursue and finish the research agenda he so ably initiated.

This research agenda is organised around the notion of transformative social policy. It is built around a set of assumptions that depart radically from the neoliberal anchors around which the dominant mainstream practice and thinking on social policy have been organised. As the chapters in this volume show, periodic handouts in the forms of cash transfers do not make social policy. Rather, social protection is treated as a neoliberal decoy aimed at diverting social policy from its transformative agenda and shifting it towards an ahistorical framework and anti-development agenda. For the last three decades, and to borrow Tade Aina's words in this volume, 'Notions and practices of social policy are often fragmented, residual, sectoralist and at times reductionist.' Yet in its very transformative character, social policy, he argues, ought to be 'integrated, holistic, congruent and constitutive'.

The chapters in this volume cover the range of constituent elements that, if read together, suggest a rethinking in academia and policy circles that would make for sound social policy. These elements are summarised in the introductory chapter and given greater elaboration in the next two keynote chapters. The subsequent chapters elaborate the dimensions of social policy using the conceptualisation envisioned in the transformative framework. They focus on land, agriculture and the health sector, while other chapters use specific spatial entry points (such as urban contexts) to examine how elements of social policy work. The chapters weigh the varied levels of effectiveness of whatever approach is used. Above all, most of the chapters are careful to ensure that they address a central issue of transformative social policy. The desire to ensure that the interventions not only contribute to development but also address issues of poverty, equity and marginalisation is notable in these chapters. In other words, there is a general social justice ethos undergirding the vision of social policy that the contributors to this study aim to advance.

The terrain of justice, however, is murky, more so when the key institutions mandated to ensure justice are themselves weak, incapacitated or under attack. While there are broad global commitments to all forms of justice and the equity that social justice promises, very few global institutions walk the talk of equity and justice in reality. This has worked to generate enormous doubt in global commitments for fairness, equity and justice, and this doubt has cascaded to regional and local institutions. The state in Africa has come under particular focus, and its role in policy-making in general and social policy in particular deserves more than a passing mention.

In Africa, doubts about the willingness, capacity and commitment of the state to further social justice goals have grown over the decades. This was framed as 'the national question' in the immediate decade after independence. Deliberations on the nature of the state, on state–society relations and subsequently on their role in development dominated the discussion. These discussions highlighted, but did not sufficiently elaborate on, the issue of policy sovereignty. In any case, this was also a moment when policy spaces were dominated by external actors, many of whom had arrived in Africa as 'stickholders'.

During the Structural Adjustment Programmes and their various subsequent iterations, existing spaces of policy sovereignty were attacked and occupied by foreign merchants and marabouts of development. So vicious was this attack that government officials waited for a node from Washington DC and other capitals in the global North to take simple decisions on issues of national concern. In other cases, multilateral and bilateral donors discussed in advance and approved lists of key officials to occupy pertinent positions in key government ministries. Christened the 'dream team' in several countries, their presence and instruction to report directly to partners abroad confirmed the extent to which African governments had ceded policy space to external actors.

To date, much of the continent has not recovered the space for autonomous policy-making. To be sure, this challenge for policy-making in Africa has a long history and the continent has suffered enormous damage because of its inability to secure this space. This therefore raises the issue of policy sovereignty as key to reflections on policy in general and social policy in particular. At the end of the day, the main issue at the heart of policy processes in Africa remains that of creating spaces for sovereign policy-making and linking them to similar experiences in the global South, creating a South–South framework for social policy thought and intervention. It is indeed our aim in CODESRIA that a major initiative be mounted to discuss policy processes in Africa with the aim of seeking to grow, within the continent, spaces of policy sovereignty.

Godwin R. Murunga
Executive Secretary, CODESRIA
25 June 2021

Notes on Contributors

Jimi Adesina is Professor and the DSI/NRF SARChI Chair in Social Policy at the College of Graduate Studies, University of South Africa (Unisa) in South Africa. A past President of the South African Sociological Association (2004–2006), Professor Adesina was elected to the Academy of Science of South Africa (ASSAf) in 2005. He served on the Board of the UN Research Institute for Social Development, Geneva (2013–2019) and on the Board of RC19 of the International Sociological Association (2014 to 2018). His research interests include Sociology, Social Policy and the Political Economy of Africa's Development. He has published widely in these areas.

Tade Akin Aina was a Professor of Sociology at the University of Lagos. He is Head of Research at the MasterCard Foundation. Previously, Prof Akin Aina served as the Deputy Executive Secretary of CODESRIA; Ford Foundation Resident Representative in Nairobi; Programme Director, Higher Education in Africa at the Carnegie Corporation in New York; and Executive Director of the Partnership for African Social Governance and Research based in Nairobi. He obtained his doctorate from the University of Sussex and studied Sociology at the University of Lagos and the London School of Economics. He also served on the Kenya Human Rights Commission. He was co-editor of Globalization and Social Policy in Africa (2004) and Giving to Help, Helping to Give: The Context and Politics of African Philanthropy (2013) among many other publications.

Emmanuel Boon is the founder of the International Centre for Enterprise and Sustainable Development (ICED), an NGO dedicated to promoting sustainable development in sub-Saharan Africa. He obtained a BA Hons in Economics and Geography from the University of Ghana in 1979, a Master's in Industrial Location and Development from Vrije Universiteit Brussels (VUB) in Belgium, an MBA from the University of Antwerp in 1983, a PhD in Economic Sciences from VUB in 1986, and an Honorary Doctorate Degree from Sumy State University in 1998. He lectured at University of Ghana Business School and VUB till 2017. He is a Visiting Professor to several universities and has published several scientific papers and books. He was the President of UNESCO's International Commission for developing 'Theme 6.150—Wildlife Conservation and Management in Africa'. He is crowned as the Development Chief of Ghana's Lambussie Traditional Area in the Upper West Region and a Development Linguist of the Wli community in the Volta Region.

Clement Chipenda, PhD, is a Research Fellow with the SARChI Chair in Social Policy, College of Graduate Studies, University of South Africa (Unisa). Currently he is a Visiting Research Fellow with the Collaborative Research Centre (CRC) 1342: Global Dynamics of Social Policy, at the University of Bremen, Germany. He is a member of the Network of Young African Researchers in Agriculture (YARA) and of Anthropology Southern Africa. His research interests are in agrarian political economy, land reform, social policy, youth development, gender and rural development. His has published several book chapters and journal articles, including in the *Canadian Journal of African Studies, Africa Review, African Identities, Journal of Comparative Family Studies* and *African Journal of Economic and Management Studies*.

Kristie Drucza is currently based in Ethiopia where she manages a research incubator that uses innovative methods to study inclusion—Includovate. Dr Drucza has an MA in gender and applied anthropology and participatory development from the Australian National University, and a PhD from Deakin University that explores social inclusion and social protection in Nepal. Her research interests include building inclusive institutions, markets and states, protecting the poor and the excluded, women's economic empowerment, and the inter-relationship between agency and structures of power.

Nacer-Eddine Hammouda holds a Bachelor's degree in Mathematics. For his Master's degree, he trained as an economic statistician. From January 1983 onwards he held several posts at Algeria's National Statistical Organisation (ONS), focusing on social statistics and household surveys. Mr Hammouda is currently in a doctoral programme, while continuing to practice within the ONS as a methodologist. He joined the Center for Research in Development Economics (CREAD) from July 2001, where he participated in several research teams working on labour market, migration, social economy and human development issues. At CREAD, he conducted several surveys on various forms of migration, and has worked in collaboration with other national and international institutions.

Katja Hujo is Senior Research Coordinator in the Social Policy and Development Programme at UNRISD. She studied Economics and Political Science at Eberhard-Karls-University in Tübingen, Freie Universität Berlin (FUB) and the National University of Córdoba, Argentina, and holds a PhD in Economics from FUB. Katja's academic work focuses on social policy, poverty and inequality, as well as socioeconomic development. She is co-ordinator and lead author of the latest UNRISD flagship report, *Policy Innovations for Transformative Change – Implementing the 2030 Agenda for Sustainable Development* (2016) and co-ordinated the international conference on *Overcoming Inequalities in a Fractured World: Between Elite Power and Social Mobilization* (2018). Her latest edited volume, *The Politics of Domestic Resource Mobilization for Social Development,* was published by Palgrave MacMillan in July 2020.

Jonathan Makuwira is Professor of Development Studies and the current Deputy Vice Chancellor of Malawi University of Science and Technology (MUST). He is also a Research Associate in the Department of Development Studies at Nelson Mandela University (NMU), South Africa, where he taught between 2014 and 2017, and a Visiting Fellow at Airlangga University, Indonesia. His distinguished academic career has seen him teach International Development at RMIT University, Comparative Indigenous Studies at Central Queensland University and Peace Studies at University of New England, all in Australia. He is the author of more than forty-five journal articles and thirty book chapters. He is the author and co-editor of the following books: *Rethinking Multilateralism in Foreign Aid: Beyond the Neoliberal Hegemony* (2020, Routledge); *Non-Governmental Development Organisations and the Poverty Reduction Agenda: The Moral Crusaders* (2014, Routledge).

Walid Merouani holds a PhD in Economics from the University of Caen-Normandy and a PhD in Economics and Applied Statistics from the High School of Statistics and Applied Economics (Algiers). Since 2011, he has investigated and written articles on issues of pension, social protection and behavioural economics. Merouani works at several research centres, in France, Luxembourg and Algeria. Currently he is working on the impact of Covid-19 and the low oil price on households, labourers, female workers and vulnerable groups in the MENA region, and is preparing a social protection strategy to mitigate the negative impacts.

Claire El Moudden holds a PhD in Economics from the University of Caen-Normandy, France, and works on pension and social protection issues in France and Maghreb countries. She is the co-author of *Économie des Retraites* and author of *Redistribution Équitable et Régimes de Retraite*, and has published on these issues in peer-reviewed journals. Currently, Claire is a lecturer in Economics and Management at the University of Caen-Normandy.

Boaz Munga is a Senior Policy Analyst at the Kenya Institute for Public Policy Research and Analysis (KIPPRA) and has been a researcher for more than fifteen years. He holds a MA in Economics from the University of Nairobi in Kenya. Mr. Munga has built a reputation for highly developed problem-solving skills and analytical thinking in socioeconomic analyses. He has extensive knowledge and experience in the applications of research methods in diverse socioeconomic analyses, including labour issues and redistributive public policy issues. Mr. Munga has published several book chapters, discussion papers and research blogs accessible on the Internet.

Ndangwa Noyoo is an Associate Professor and former head of the Department of Social Development at the University of Cape Town. He previously worked at the University of Johannesburg in the Department of Social Work as an Associate Professor. He was also employed by the South African government in the Department of Social Development as a Chief Director/Social Policy Specialist, and by the University of Witwatersrand, Johannesburg's Department of Social Work as a Senior Lecturer and Deputy Head of Department. He holds a PhD from the University of the Witwatersrand, Johannesburg, an MPhil in Development Studies from Cambridge University, and a Bachelor's in Social Work (BSW) from the University of Zambia. He was a postdoctoral fellow at the Fondation Maison des Sciences de l'Homme (FMSH), Paris, France.

Kolawole Emmanuel Omomowo is a Senior Lecturer at the Department of Sociology, University of Namibia, where he teaches sociological theory. His research is broadly focused on social policy, particularly on the intersection between poverty, as a level of social wellbeing, and the purpose and dimensions of microcredit consumption using the political economy theoretical framework.

Augustine I. Omoruan, PhD. is a lecturer at the Department of General Studies (Sociology Unit), Ladoke Akintola University of Technology, Ogbomoso, Nigeria. Dr Omoruan completed his PhD thesis, 'The Design and Implementation Policy of the National Health Insurance Scheme: A Study of Oyo State' at the University of South Africa (Unisa). His research and academic interests include health sociology, social policy and development studies. He has published articles in local and international journals.

Marion Ouma completed her doctorate studies in Sociology under the South Africa Research Chair in Social Policy at the University of South Africa in 2019. She has a Bachelor's and Master's degree from the University of Nairobi and previously worked at various national and international NGOs. Her research interests include sociology, social policy, social protection, policymaking and the political economy of Africa's development. She has published in *Critical Social Policy* and has a book chapter in *The African Political Economy* edited by Samuel Oloruntoba and Toyin Falola.

Marlize Rabe is a Professor and head of the Department of Sociology at the University of the Western Cape. She mainly does qualitative research on family issues relating to gender and intergenerational relationships. Recently, she has published on how family policies can be more inclusive in South Africa, and how the state, families and the non-profit sector, including faith-based organisations, are linked to issues of care. She is a co-editor of the forthcoming book, Stuck in the Margins? Young people and faith-based organisations in South African and Nordic localities. She is a former Vice-President of the South African Sociological Association and a former co-editor of the journals *South African Review of Sociology* and *Gender Questions*, and is currently an associate editor of *Journal of Family Issues*.

Dagmawit Giref Sahile is currently a PhD student at Justus Liebig University, Giessen in Germany focusing on the marketing system and household decisions in small-ruminant value chains with implications for animal welfare, using quantitative methods. Ms. Sahile has a BSc in Agricultural Economics and an MSc in agricultural business and value chain management from Haramya University, Ethiopia. Her research interests include the analysis of the market value chain, econometric modelling, animal welfare and gender equality in agriculture.

Newman Tekwa is a doctoral student under the SARChI Chair in Social Policy, University of South Africa, (Unisa). He is an alumnus of the Agrarian Studies Training Institute (ASTI 2017), a tri-continental network bringing together interdisciplinary young scholars from Africa and Latin America working on agrarian studies. In 2018 he received the Sam Moyo Research Fellowship Grant. In 2019 Newman was selected as an alumnus to The Journal of Peasant Studies (JPS) Annual Summer Write-shop in Critical Studies, held in Beijing, China, jointly organised by YARA, PLAAS and the China Agricultural University (CAU).

1

Social Policy in the African Context: An Introduction

Jimi Adesina

Social Policy: Contending Visions

The 'counter-revolution' in Development Economics that emerged in the 1980s brought in its wake a 'counter-revolution' in Social Policy. In its origin, the 'counter-revolution' could be understood as a revolt against the normative underpinnings of the 'welfare state'—something marked by Frederick von Hayek's *The Road to Serfdom* ([1944] 2007). By the 1980s in the North, this involved efforts at retrenching the state and restructuring welfare provision. In the South, and especially in the African context, this involved a comprehensive reconstitution of the way the state 'thinks' and 'acts' in relation to the economy and its citizens. From the idea of a state which 'thinks' in terms of a comprehensive obligation for securing long-term national wellbeing and development, what emerged was a 'night watchman' state, more recently recast in the language of the 'capable state'—one more focused on securing the space for private investors than on the wellbeing of its citizens. Economic policy was increasingly disconnected from social policy, with a public policy orientation that is averse to socialised provisioning, solidaristic risk pooling, (inter-class) redistribution and universalism. Social policy became largely residual.

Social policy has always been shaped by two broad contending forces. On the one hand, we have those who see its objectives as mopping up the diswelfares of the market and institutional failures. On the other hand, there are those who see social policy as having an encompassing reach and coverage, integrated with economic policy and underpinned by norms of equality and solidarity. The former view takes a residual approach, with the market as the first port of call in social provisioning and public welfare as a port of last resort focused on the deserving poor who are not able to meet their own social provisioning. The latter addresses diswelfares in the ways development and design production activities are pursued and in response to needs at various stages of the life-cycle.

Over the last thirty years, in response to Africa's development challenges and diswelfares that its citizens face, a more residual take on social policy has become largely hegemonic, with powerful external and local actors using the continent as the site of a range of social experiments. Much of this has been driven by an anti-development thinking, which imagines the solution to poverty as largely a matter of 'just give money to the poor'—even as the 'poor' are defined in highly restrictive fashion to cover the smaller proportion of the population who experience severe entitlement failure—or as a direct distribution of earnings from mineral wealth to citizens (a question of 'oil to cash'). Missing from such propositions is a structural approach to understanding the bases of entitlement failure, poverty and inequality. There is a general refusal to engage with the maladjustment of Africa's economies, deepening their structural weaknesses. The economies are no less subject to the vagaries of external forces in the second decade of the twenty-first century than they were in the eighth decade of the twentieth. The social dislocations and citizens' diswelfares, even in the context of improved growth on the back of the commodity super boom, have not reduced commensurately. In most instances, the diswelfares have deepened. Wealth-based measures of inequality have worsened in much of the continent, and the poverty rate (measured at USD 3.10 PPP/day) is above 70 per cent of the population in several countries.

The hegemonic public policy regime is sustained by an alliance of domestic and external actors. If we understand the relations between state and citizens as a web of rights and obligations, the retreat of the state from socialised and universal social provisioning undermines the legitimacy of the state, reinforces its more coercive face in its engagements with citizens and undermines social cohesion. Leaving citizens to fend for themselves in the marketplace makes them subject to the vagaries of the market. Neither is there evidence that reducing social policy to social assistance, which is narrowly focused on the deserving poor in increasingly dualistic social policy regimes, eliminates poverty or ensures quality services for the poor.

Beyond this, of course, is the lack of appreciation that social policy (or even social protection) is not simply about the relief of poverty. Progressive social policy is fundamentally about ensuring human flourishing. It does this by enhancing the productive capacity of citizens through public investment in education, healthcare, housing, etc.; reconciling 'the burden of reproduction with that of other social tasks' (Mkandawire 2011); protecting people from the vagaries of life throughout the life-cycle; attending to the distributive outcome of economic performance; and advancing social cohesion (and achieving the nation-building objectives so vital in the African context). It does all these more efficiently through a 'prophylactic' approach, preventing vulnerability rather than waiting to address it after people have fallen through the cracks.

Whether in the more progressive welfare regimes in the North or the post-colonial experiences of the global South, and Africa more so, successful advancement in human wellbeing has always involved the integration of social and economic policies and constructing social policy regimes focused on its multiple tasks. Public provisioning of education, healthcare and housing, as social investment on the basis of solidarity and advancing equality, supports economic development. Economic development grounded in the same norms of solidarity and advancing equality ensures the resources necessary for the extension of social policy. The objectives of social policy measures are not only prophylactic but transformative of the economy, social relations, social institutions and deepening democracy. This approach to social policy is defined as Transformative Social Policy (TSP). It is a take on social policy that framed several of the presentations at the conference from which the chapters in this book emanate.

Contributions to this Volume

The Social Policy in Africa International Conference in November 2017 in Pretoria, South Africa, was a flagship activity of the South African Research Chair in Social Policy, based at the College of Graduate Studies, University of South Africa (Unisa). The partner organisations for the conference were the United Nations Research Institute for Social Development (UNRISD), Geneva, and the Council for the Development of Social Science Research in Africa (CODESRIA), Dakar, Senegal. The conference brought together some 100 researchers to discuss the thematic focus, Social Policy in Africa's Development Context.

This edited volume offers thirteen of the papers presented at the conference, with the first two chapters being made up of two of the keynote lectures delivered at the conference. Chapters 2 and 3 explore different dimensions of the transformative social policy framework. The antecedence of the concept of transformative social policy, as Aina notes in Chapter 2, goes back to the work initiated in CODESRIA in the 1990s by Thandika Mkandawire, which sought to rethink social policy from a development perspective. At CODESRIA, this took the form of a 'Greenbook',[1] the *Globalization and Social Policy* research programme (Aina 1997), and an edited volume (Aina et al. 2004). Aina's chapter explores the theme of how to reclaim transformative social policy for inclusive development in twenty-first century Africa. The conference, he notes, came at a time of renewed aspirations in Africa for 'freeing the … continent from [the burden] of poverty, disease, hunger and oppression.' Aina highlights the deployment of social policy and its transformative potentials in early post-independence Africa's development efforts, which Noyoo and Boon also explore further in this collection. In addition to advancing its value in the structural transformation of economy and society, Aina highlights the deployment of social policy in nation-building efforts.

Beyond its deployment in Africa's post-independence phase, social policy in the contemporary African context should go beyond the current 'fragmented, residual, sectoralist and at times, reductionist' design and language of social protection. Social policy, he argues, should be 'integrated, holistic, congruent and constitutive'. As a component of development efforts, it should emphasise the essence of development (itself a journey rather than a destination) in the sustained improvement of human wellbeing. Beyond improvements in living conditions, development should be about widening the democratic space, human freedom and choice.

In Chapter 3, Katja Hujo addresses the second and more substantive phase in the development of the idea of transformative social policy. After he moved from CODESRIA to UNRISD in 1998, as the institute's director, Mkandawire launched the *Social Policy in a Development Context* research programme (Mkandawire 2001). Hujo's chapter is concerned with rethinking social policy in the African context from the perspective of its transformative role and power. Like Aina, Hujo highlights the 'transformative role of social policy in opposition to the residual or secondary role' that is accorded to social policy in the mainstream academic and international 'development' community. While there was a 'social turn' in international development discourse from the 1990s onward—initiated by the 'social dimensions of adjustment' to the current debate on inequality—Hujo emphasises the residual take on social policy in this 'social turn'. The 'turn' was in the context of the policy failures, mass entitlement failures and rising inequalities that accompanied the neoliberal project of using the countries of the global South (and Africa in particular) as open laboratories for a socioeconomic experiment in public policy. International opposition to the neoliberal experiment was most evident at the 1995 Copenhagen World Summit for Social Development, where 'a more integrated approach linking poverty reduction with social inclusion and employment creation as an alternative to the neoliberal model' was suggested.

Hujo frames transformative social policy as an alternative to the neoliberal social policy framework, focusing on its role in enacting transformative change. While the latter deploys social-policy instruments 'to alleviate the worst forms of poverty' and its symptoms, the former is concerned with addressing the 'root causes of poverty, inequality and unsustainability'. TSP deploys social policy as a complement to economic policy 'to guarantee market stability, productivity and innovation, social reproduction, equal opportunities and more equal outcomes across class, gender, ethnicity, age or location, state legitimacy, social cohesion and integration.' In rethinking social policy in the African context, Hujo argues for building the discourse around four axes: a combined rights-based entitlement and productivist take on social policy; the sustainable financing of social policy; integrating environmental challenges and inequality in framing social policy; and the politics of social policymaking.

In Chapter 4, Noyoo and Boon explore the transformative role of different social-policy instruments in the first post-independence decade in Ghana and Zambia, with a special focus on education, health and employment. They look at, in particular, the nation-building impact of social-policy design within the framework of national development aspirations. Both countries, the authors note, inherited a multi-ethnic landscape, with fractious claims for ethnic autonomy — Barotseland in Zambia and the Asante Region in Ghana. Social policy, the authors argue, played a central role in attenuating ethnic factionalism and enhancing nation-building in Zambia and Ghana. Rather than using state-building to legitimise ethnic balkanisation, the efforts in the first post-independence decade involved using education and employment policies, in particular, to anchor the nation-building project. The massive expansion of access to education and healthcare served the functions of improving the well-being of people in both countries, enhancing their productive capacity and meeting the objective of economic development. What Noyoo and Boon demonstrate is how this deployment of the multiple tasks of social policy fell away in both countries in their post-nationalist phase. Both authors make a plea for a return to a more focused and integrated use of social policy in the context of the twenty-first century.

Addressing transformative social policy directly, Chapter 5 by Newman Tekwa examines TSP as an evaluative framework. It was a component of the flagship research project at the SARChI Chair in Social Policy, titled the *Social Policy Dimensions of Land and Agrarian Reform*. The research project focused on the Fast-Track Land Reform Programme (FTLRP) in Zimbabwe. While the FTLRP delivered on the redistributive aspect of social policy and provided the basis for enhancing the productive capacity of its beneficiaries, its implications for the transformation of social relations, in particular, gender relations, is the focus of Tekwa's contribution. A major task of social policy, as Mkandawire (2011: 150–151) argues, is 'the reconciliation of the burden of reproduction with that of other social tasks'. The social reproduction component of social policy is important for the transformation of gender relations. However, with the weakening of public infrastructure investment in Zimbabwe, a corollary of the economic crisis, women's care burden increased. Women in male-headed households spent more time than men on unremunerated household chores. In particular, women in the A1 schemes (small-scale land allotments) 'reported an extraordinarily longer working day of more than 12 hours' relative to women in the A2 schemes (medium-sized land allotments). Ownership of time-saving household consumer items and the outsourcing of household chores to hired help reflected the internal class dimensions of the care burden among women in the two schemes. Whatever the redistributive and production impact of the FTLRP, its evaluation from the perspective of social reproduction demonstrates a major blind spot.

In Chapter 6, Drucza and Sahile offer a different slant on the gender dynamics in social protection, with a study among wheat farmers in Ethiopia. The authors explore, as part of a larger study, membership of 'traditional' burial and credit and saving associations relative to membership of government-initiated co-operative associations, thus unveiling the dynamics of how people secure their wellbeing. Generally, membership of informal/traditional associations among female-headed households declined between 2009/10 and 2012/13 while their membership of more formal, government-inspired cooperatives and 'teams' grew over the same period. Significantly, the study observed a decline in the membership of religion-based self-help groups and associations. The trend in male-headed households was in the same direction, although the rate of change in association membership varied slightly. The authors suggest that shifts in membership may reflect the relative benefits that members receive from the groups or associations. It is also significant that the government-inspired co-operatives and associations are designed to enhance the productive capacity of its members.

Chapter 7, by Merouani, Hammouda and El Moudden, is concerned with an entirely different social policy issue—the factors that explain people's preference for the social insurance take-up. This study is based on a survey of the private sector in Algiers. First, the survey sought to establish the respondents' knowledge of social insurance. Second, it tried to assess the extent to which the respondents were 'forward looking' in their preference for an immediate payment of benefits or one spread over many more years into the future. Firm size and levels of education and income were positively correlated with better knowledge of how the social insurance system worked, especially for retirement plans. Paradoxically, income level was inversely correlated with being forward looking—salaried employees were more patient regarding the monthly payment of benefits than were employers and self-employed participants in the survey. The authors' econometric analysis of the data supports the descriptive findings. 'Demand for social insurance is low in Algeria' the authors note, 'because people do not take the future into consideration' and knowledge of the social insurance schemes and how they work remains very low.

In Chapter 8, Ouma and Adesina explore a central dimension of social policymaking in the African context, the spread of cash transfer-based social assistance schemes. While many of the studies on the adoption of social assistance have been concerned with the design and implementation of these schemes, especially in relation to national ownership and scaling up, a more limited number focus on the dynamics of policy influence in the context of 'policy merchandising' (Adesina 2011). The bulk of the studies that have explored the politics of the spread of cash transfer schemes have operated within the framework of 'political settlement' (Hickey and Bukenya 2016; Hickey et al. 2018; Lavers and Hickey 2016; Pruce and Hickey 2017). The 'political settlement' framework has an ontological reading of African politics similar to that of the neo-patrimonialism school: primarily, that African politics is enmeshed in a 'patron-client' relationship, the essence of which is about buying allegiance to ensure the political survival of the 'political elite' or 'big men' who run African politics. Often the mechanisms of the settlement between factions of the political elite or between the political elite and the citizens are assumed rather than demonstrated. A fundamental problem with the clientelist take on African politics (where the elite buy the allegiance of the citizens) is that it has taken much grit and effort to get the African 'political elite' to take ownership of the cash transfer schemes. In focusing on endogenous claims, the political settlement framing of the spread of the social assistance schemes underplays the clientelist politics of donors, the dynamics of policy merchandising, and the constitution of 'policy networks to ensure the enforcement of donor policy preferences. In this chapter, Ouma and Adesina offer an alternative explanation of the dynamics of social assistance policy adoption, using the cases of two schemes in Kenya: the Cash Transfer for Orphans and Vulnerable Children (CT-OVC) and the Hunger Safety Net Programme (HSNP). The chapter outlines the role of (donor) interest and resource deployment in the constitution of the policy network. The chapter explores the mechanism of generating policy influence and infusing ideas into the national policymaking machinery of a country.

In Chapter 9, Makuwira explores the role of non-state actors in African policymaking. He locates the exponential growth of non-governmental organisations within the context of two effects of the neoliberal ascendancy. The first is the rolling back of the economic and social provisioning roles of the state, and the second is the primacy of market-based provisioning. Makuwira situates his discussion in the AU's Agenda 2063, looking at social policymaking in southern African countries. In spite of the numerous limitations and the variations in policy regimes in the region, Makuwira argues, non-state actors are essential to policymaking and implementation in Africa. Governments need to create enabling environments for the functioning of non-state actors and create a mutually beneficial relationship between the two entities. Non-state actors, on the other hand, need to understand that while they can play a complementary role to that of the state, aligning themselves with national development aspirations, they cannot replace the state.

Chapter 10 focuses on a different dimension of non-state forms of how people try to secure their wellbeing. Omomowo and Adesina explore mutual support institutions and practices in two urban townships in South Africa as the basis for social-policy learning in the African context. The mutual-support practices covered in the study range from proto-social insurance schemes, such as burial societies and rotating savings and credit schemes, to community-based mutual support during celebrations and funerals. As indicated in the chapter, people join the self-help groups 'to achieve what they would not have been able to achieve alone'. Social solidarity, trust, mutual obligation and reciprocity are vital to the functioning of the mutual-support social institutions. If Titmuss (1956) highlighted social, fiscal and occupational welfare as dimensions of the 'social division' of welfare, the study suggests that we should add 'community welfare' to the dimensions of how humans secure wellbeing. If the antecedents of mutual support institutions and practices stretch back to the 'cattle lending' and community solidarity practices of the precolonial era, their contemporary forms and practices represent the nibble response to the precarity of the prevailing capitalist environment. The normative underpinning of the mutual support institutions provides the basis for the design of locally sensitive and responsive social-policy architecture beyond the residual neoliberal take on social-policy design.

The next two chapters cover sectoral aspects of social policy that range from health insurance and land reform. In Chapter 11, Omoruan offers an analysis of the national social health insurance scheme that was launched in Nigeria in 2005. Ostensibly, the objective of the Nigerian Social Health Insurance Scheme included bringing quality healthcare within reach of all Nigerians and reducing out-of-pocket health expenditure. In contrast to the universal, publicly provided healthcare that prevailed in the country up to the late 1970s, the NHIS introduced an individual health insurance scheme in line with neoliberal thinking on injecting market transactional logic into as many domains of social provisioning as was feasible. Contrary to the promises of the NHIS, coverage remains extremely low (at 3 per cent of the population), the scheme is fragmentary with multiple healthcare plans, and has low levels of risk-pooling. The prospect of expanding coverage remains limited due to premiums being unaffordable to most of the country's residents.

In Chapter 12, Clement Chipenda explores land reform as a social policy instrument. In the OECD-centric debate on social policy, land reform hardly features. This is bewildering considering that the concern of social policy is to secure and enhance human wellbeing and that the objectives of social policy include redistribution and enhancing people's productive capacity and social protection, among others. These objectives are self-consciously behind most land and agrarian reform programmes. Chipenda's chapter reports the findings of a study of the post-2000 land reform programme in Zimbabwe in the country's Goromonzi District. The chapter discusses the new agrarian structure in the aftermath of the land reform programme and explores the social-policy outcomes of the reform. The land reform programme has been significantly redistributive, and—in comparison with the residents of the adjoining communal areas—has placed a larger acreage of land assets in the hands of the beneficiaries. Chipenda illustrates the ex-ante protection that access to the land offered its beneficiaries in terms of relative food security, and a more intangible sense of the rural homestead, or *musha*. Chipenda highlights the phenomenon of livestock as 'social insurance' and as a resource that protects owners of livestock against external shocks. A reconceptualisation of land reform as a social-policy instrument contributes to the bodies of knowledge in the areas of land reform and social policy.

In Chapter 13, Marlize Rabe explores the myth of the male breadwinner in South Africa within the context of high levels of unemployment in the country. While the prevailing social norms expect men to be income-earners and breadwinners in their households, and women to be responsible for a considerable share of paid and unpaid care of the families, the labour market exposes these norms as myths. In addition, the social assistance regime privileges women as recipients, if not the beneficiaries, of the social grants system. The combination of high rates of unemployment and the modalities of social grants suggests that men are becoming financial liabilities within the households. To remedy the situation, Rabe argues, is not simply a matter of creating employment opportunities to allow men to recapture their roles as breadwinners. Rather, what is required is a transformative social policy approach that enables dual-earner households and encourages men to take up more equitable care responsibility within the household.

In the final chapter, Boaz Munga explores whether how we measure and explain income inequality makes a difference for social policy. Using two nationally representative income surveys from Kenya, Munga applies different measurements of inequality to the data sets—from the Gini index to the Atkinson measure and decile ratios—with a number of very interesting results. Whereas the fact that income inequality is sensitive to the Atkinson measure is widely accepted, Munga notes, the Gini index is more sensitive to changes in the middle sections rather than the extreme ends of the income distribution profile. If the focus is on the upper segments of the income distribution profile, the data, Munga suggests, will show that rural inequality worsened while urban inequality showed some improvement. If inequality is decomposed on the basis of locality, Munga argues that inequality within urban and rural areas accounts for over three-quarters of inequality. If decomposed on the basis of education, a significant share of inequality is identified among educated people. The implications for social-policy design are significant. Policy efforts to reduce rural/urban inequality will have little traction since inequality is largely within rather than between spatial locations. Further, improving access to education alone will have limited impact on inequality without complementary efforts. This study's conclusions highlight the futility of fragmented and segregated social-policy design and call for a comprehensive social-policy architecture, with interlocking social-policy instruments; they underscore the need for a transformative social-policy framework.

Conclusion

The chapters in this edited volume reflect the range of papers presented at the 2017 Social Policy in Africa conference jointly sponsored by the SARChI Chair in Social Policy, UNRISD and CODESRIA. Several of the papers support a transformative social policy framework as a handle on policymaking, as an analytical and heuristic device, and as an evaluative device. TSP stands in sharp contrast to the prevailing neoliberal-inspired fragmented and stratified social-policy architecture that underpins the 'social protection' discourse currently paraded and merchandised across the continent. Unlike the neoliberal-inspired take on social policy, TSP is concerned with addressing the root causes of poverty and vulnerability rather than their symptoms. Rather than a residual take on social policy intended to mop up market and institutional failures, TSP is concerned with social policy that works in tandem with economic policy, underpinned by shared norms and values, and seeks to enhance productive capacity while paying attention to how the proceeds of economic growth are shared. Hujo's four-axial framing of rethinking social policy for twenty-first-century Africa becomes important, in this regard. A central concern is with building social cohesion or, in the African context, with the nation-building project, as put forward by Aina and Noyoo and Boon.

The need to pay attention to gender relations even in traditional social-welfare systems and in policy instruments that work quite well in addressing other tasks of social policy is clearly demonstrated in the chapter by Tekwa. Social-policy regimes and instruments are never gender-neutral. The important message of their chapters is the imperative of embedding gender sensitivity in social-policy designs.

While framed in gender terms, Drucza and Sahile's chapter demonstrates the significance of production capacity-enhancing public efforts in people's preferences for social-protection associations. While often seen as instruments for political control, the significance of the efforts of the government of Ethiopia in promoting co-operatives and production-enhancing teams is not simply about tapping into the productive aims of public investment but promoting a prophylactic social-protection objective (Alemu and Adesina 2015). A substantive argument by the authors is that people's choice to join or leave a self-help group and association may reflect the benefits that accrue from membership of the association or group.

The significance of the chapter by Merouani, Hammouda and El Moudden is in highlighting the role of knowledge and preferences in social-insurance uptake. A robust social-welfare regime combines social insurance with social provisions funded directly from the fiscus. An important element in the success of social-insurance schemes is knowledge of those schemes and initial preferences of potential members. This highlights the role of public education and design that policymakers need to take into consideration. A combination of a publicly funded universal social pension and a social-insurance-funded tier in pension not only helps in securing adequate income in old age but in securing the commitment of the better-offs in society to the universal pension scheme. An inference from the study is that income security is better secured through a national pension scheme rather a provident scheme. This has to be within the comprehensive and integrated social-policy framework that TSP suggests.

The significance of Ouma and Adesina's chapter is in drawing attention to the dynamics of social policymaking in much of Middle Africa, where 'donors' and multilateral organisations engage in excessive policy merchandising. The nature of social policymaking that helps to deepen democratic culture involves the autonomous interest articulation and contestation of public policy space. By contrast, the Kenya case demonstrates the extent to which donor policy preferences, interest, the deployment of resources and the construction of a 'policy network' are furthering the neocolonial subordination of local policy processes to the preferences of external actors. Makuwira's chapter offers some insights into the role of non-state actors in policy contestation, although the focus is more on non-governmental organisations (often donor-sponsored and -funded) rather than endogenously grounded, membership-based social movements.

The examinations of the social policy domain by sector—health and land reform—by Omoruan and Chipenda offer insights into the role of the market in social policymaking and the tapping of multiple tasks of social policy. The neoliberal logic of the push for the social health insurance approach to delivering quality healthcare services, as Omoruan's chapter shows, is a glaring failure. The Nigerian health insurance scheme is fragmented and unaffordable for the overwhelming proportion of the population. Chipenda's chapter on land reform points to a neglected but important policy instrument. Land reform simultaneously addresses multiple aims of social policy—in enhancing the productive capacity of the beneficiaries, in providing protection ex-ante, and in redistribution. The challenge for Zimbabwe is the imperative of getting social and economic policy to work in tandem. Without paying attention to economic policy, the potential for social policy to deliver on the welfare of its beneficiaries will be undermined.

The chapters by Rabe and Munga address different dimensions of a transformative approach to social policy. In the context of the labour market and the modalities for delivering social assistance in South Africa, the myth of the male breadwinner is glaring. However, the answer to the labour market challenges of unemployment and precarious employment lies not in the reconstitution of the male breadwinner model but in efforts to enhance a dual-earner household model and greater male involvement in the household care work. It requires combining productive (labour market) and social reproduction (care work). In a distinct way, Munga's chapter reiterates the importance of a comprehensive and interlocking social policy approach to addressing inequality. How we measure and define inequality has relevance for the efficacy of a social policy approach in addressing inequality.

Note

1. In CODESRIA-speak, a 'Greenbook' is the literature-scoping and research-issue mapping exercise published in the institution's working paper series. The working paper is normally commissioned to initiate a new research programme. The colloquial name derives from the colour of the cover of the working paper.

References

Adesina, J. O., 2011, Beyond the Social Protection Paradigm: Social Policy in Africa's Development, *Canadian Journal of Development Studies–Revue Canadienne d'Études du Developpement*, Vol. 32, No. 4, pp. 454–470.

Aina, T. A., 1997, Globalization and Social Policy in Africa: Issues and Research Directions, Working Paper No. 6/96, Dakar: CODESRIA.

Aina, T. A., Chachage, C. S. L. and Annan-Yao, E., eds, 2004, *Globalization and Social Policy in Africa*, Dakar: CODESRIA.

Alemu, A. E. and Adesina, J., 2015, Effects of Cooperatives and Contracts on Rural Income and Production in the Dairy Supply Chains: Evidence from Northern Ethiopia, *African Journal of Agricultural and Resource Economics*, Vol. 10, No. 311-2016-5640, pp. 312–317.

Fischer, A. M., 2018, *Poverty as Ideology: Rescuing Social Justice from Global Development Agendas*, London: Zed Books.

Hayek, F. A., 2007 [1944], *The Road to Serfdom—Text and Documents: The Definitive Edition*, Chicago: The University of Chicago Press.

Hickey, S. and Bukenya, B., 2016, The Politics of Promoting Social Cash Transfers in Uganda, WIDER Working Paper 2016/118, Helsinki: UNU–WIDER.

Hickey, S., Lavers, T., Niño-Zarazúa, M. and Seekings, J., 2018, The Negotiated Politics of Social Protection in Sub-Saharan Africa, WIDER Working Paper 2018/34, Helsinki: UNU–WIDER.

Lavers, T. and Hickey, S., 2016, Conceptualising the Politics of Social Protection Expansion in Low-Income Countries: The Intersection of Transnational Ideas and Domestic Politics, *International Journal of Social Welfare*, Vol. 25, No. 4, pp. 388–398.

Mkandawire, T., 2001, Social Policy in a Development Context, Social Policy and Development Paper No. 25, Geneva: UNRISD.

Mkandawire, T., 2011, Welfare Regime and Economic Development: Bridging the Conceptual Gap, in Fitzgerald, E. V. K., Heyer, J. and Thorp, R. eds, *Overcoming the Persistence of Inequality and Poverty*, Basingstoke: Palgrave Macmillan, pp. 149–171.

Pruce, K. and Hickey, S., 2017, The Politics of Promoting Social Protection in Zambia, WIDER Working Paper 2016/156, Helsinki: UNU–WIDER.

Titmuss, R. M., 1956, *The Social Division of Welfare*, Liverpool: Liverpool University Press.

2

Reclaiming Transformative Social Policy for Inclusive Development

Tade Akin Aina

Introduction

This chapter was initially presented as a keynote address at the 2017 conference on Social Policy in Africa. It is no accident that the three partners involved in organising the conference — namely, the Council for the Development of Social Science Research in Africa (CODESRIA), UNRISD and the South African Research Chair in Social Policy — constituted the initial strike force in the thinking and rethinking of the notion of a transformative social policy in Africa. We were all part of the team assembled by Professor Thandika Mkandawire[1] in that effort and experiment in the early 1990s at CODESRIA, in Dakar, Senegal. Our project sought to interrogate and engage with Africa's development and to analyse social policy from a developmental perspective, for the purpose of not only understanding and interpreting Africa for ourselves and others, but also confronting what I call an emancipatory agenda to free the African continent from poverty, disease, hunger and oppression.

The conference came at a time when we were seeing remarkable restlessness and tensions in the taken-for-granted practices and principles of democratic governance and development that had characterised the past three decades of our political, economic and cultural lives. The restlessness, tensions and rapid changes also applied worldwide (Van Beek and Wnuk-Lipinski 2016; Mason 2015). As we encounter these upheavals in global institutions and politics, the new turn in identity politics leading to more stringent questioning of the basis of national societies and the prevalence of violent extremisms and populist irredentist politics in conditions of growing inequality, Africa needs to move towards sustainable, inclusive and democratic development more than ever before. This will require reclaiming a transformative social policy that is integrated into sustainable economic development policies, the re-building of democratic institutions and the renewal of citizenship and social contracts that enhance people's individual and collective rights, self-confidence, integrity and social integration.

This calls for a recognition and advancement of the larger roles of transformative social policy not only in the economy but also as it relates to important social and political issues, such as inclusion, legitimation, democratisation, citizenship and rights, and social and state reconstruction. Indeed, the question of social reconstruction is one that African states—except those emerging from conflicts—have not taken as seriously as they should.[2] Yet everywhere one turns one cannot but see the economic, social and political devastation that over four decades of neoliberal policies, environmental crises and disasters, civil wars and conflicts have created. The good news is that African countries are overcoming most of these catastrophes. This recovery was clearly underlined in the United Nations Africa Human Development Report 2016, which stated that 'Africa has shown one of best improvement in HDI (Human Development Indicators) between 1990 and 2014 but also has the lowest average levels of human development compared to other regions in the world' (UNDP 2016: 21). The point here is while it is not all doom and gloom, we must avoid what Thandika Mkandawire termed 'Afro-euphoria' and rather focus on what we have learned from those experiences and on rethinking and repossessing democratic development through transformative social policy. The conference provided an opportunity to reflect on our African condition and our development process through the alternative lens of social and human development and the integration of transformative social policy.

In this chapter I aim to bring the study and practice of social policy together with perhaps Africa's singular economic, political and policy preoccupation, that elusive process and phenomenon characterised as Development. Over the past six decades we have seen an immense preoccupation with development, both by the countries seeking it and those who presumably have achieved it. What we have not seen enough of, in spite of the immense amount of money, time and effort invested in it, is the significant transformation that 'development' promises the individual and collective wellbeing of vast numbers of people all over the world and in Africa in particular. Perhaps the missing link, which the African nationalist leaders recognised but were unable to carry out during their time, is the integration of what we now call transformative social policy into our development process. Scholars such as Amartya Sen, in *Development as Freedom* (1999), were clear about this relationship. Development without investment in building human capabilities and capacities through intentional transformative social policy is nothing but a mirage.

In the rest of the chapter, I intend to show the nature and reason for the preoccupation with development and how transformative social policy (though it was not called that originally) was part of the approach used by the African nationalists in their initial project. I will also touch on the role of social policy in nation-building and social cohesion and conclude with what are some of the emerging issues in reclaiming transformative social policy for inclusive development in contemporary Africa. But before I do this, it is important to outline the key arguments that shape this chapter around transformative social policy and inclusive development. These are:

1. That to be useful in the attainment of an emancipatory and transformational development agenda in Africa, we need a more holistic, inclusive and integrated notion of social policy beyond the fragmented, reductionist and residual notions that are often tied to single-sector or single-issue considerations.
2. That a more useful approach to understanding social policy is to situate it within the historical, political and epistemological contexts out of which the social policies have emerged and to look at the way these policies have related to or connected with national, international and global dynamics and relations.
3. That social policies, like all policies, are neither neutral nor innocent. They embody values, norms, interests and visions of society and the public good. They therefore cannot be divorced from social justice or social justice perspectives that engage with equity, sustainability and equality; and
4. That social policies are only practically and politically viable when there are agents, champions, social and political movements, policy actors and institutions who carry, promote, reinforce and/or anchor them.

Clarifying the Notions of Social Policy and Inclusive Development

The two notions of interest here are similar in many ways. They both address the wellbeing—individual and collective—of peoples and citizens in defined entities. They are both heavily contested, often defined by context, history and place. Because they address structure, agency and process, and means and ends, they are seemingly a perpetual work in progress. By this I mean that human wellbeing is not static, it has no definite end point; addressing and enhancing it therefore is dynamic and ongoing.

Social Policy

The notion of, and the various attempts to define, social policy are rife with tensions and contradictions that result from different perspectives and positions located in political ideologies and theoretical traditions that have mainly emerged from western thought and practices (Aina 1997, 1999, 2004, 2009; Adesina 2007, 2009, 2010; Mkandawire 2001, 2004; Dani and De Haan 2008a; De Haan 2010, 2013).

In Africa, in particular, many factors affect the understanding of social policy. First, there has been insufficient attention and understanding of the early nationalist experiments in countries like Tanzania, Ghana, Algeria, Egypt, Nigeria,

Zambia and others where there was a predominance of development planning that integrated more or less significant social policy and social development elements.

Second, most recent experiments with social policy in Africa focused on social protection and oftentimes did not sufficiently integrate issues and constituencies that concern race, gender, sexuality and the inclusion of minority ethnic, religious and social groups and regions. When they did, the emphasis remained on social protection rather than on social policy. Thus, a whole research and management industry grew around social protection rather than social policy (Devereux and Getu 2013; Pruce and Hickey 2016; Seekings 2017; Awortwi and Aiyede 2017).[3]

Notions and practices of social policy are often fragmented, residual, sectoralist and at times reductionist. Some of these policies focused on housing, education, public health and cash transfers as single issues unconnected to the overall development process (Aina 1999) or to other sectors of the economy and society. They were also not defined as integrated and holistic strategies to advance citizens' wellbeing and development. Some of the reasons for this have to do with the requirements of service delivery and the administrative and disciplinary vehicles available for it. There were also the deliberate efforts in policy and research to divest social provisioning from development in some quarters.

In my view, social policy is integrated, holistic, congruent and constitutive. It is connected to the different elements of a development process based on an articulated vision and goals for society. I have in earlier work defined it as 'systematic and deliberate interventions in social and economic life for the purpose of ensuring the basic needs and wellbeing of the peoples of a society' (Aina 1997: 17). It is also the expression and definition of socially desirable goals in accordance with the rights of citizens and the objectives of human development through legislation, institutions, administrative programmes and practices and attendant structures of incentives and sanctions. Social policy is broader than the more technical and professional domain of social work and welfare and the current professionalisation of social protection. It aims to promote access to and remove obstacles from citizens' enjoyment of basic needs and wellbeing.

As pointed out above, social policy is therefore not a neutral notion. It is intrinsically tied up with world views, some social vision and mission and a perspective on development. Social policy is thus about the making of a better world through intentional systematic policymaking, where equity and productivity are valued, where equality of opportunities is promoted and where the marginalised and the excluded can find freedom, inclusion and emancipation from the structural and other sources that reproduce their negative condition. (Aina 2009: 30–31; Dani and De Haan 2010: 4).

This notion of social policy resonates strongly with the position advanced by Jimi Adesina (2010) and Thandika Mkandawire (2007) on transformative social policy. For Adesina, 'Transformative social policy relates not only to the transformation of an economy or protection from destitution, but also to the transformation of social relations as well.' For him, it is based on norms of equality and solidarity, grounded in a specific national vision and embodies the functions of production, protection, reproduction, redistribution, social cohesion and nation-building (Adesina 2010: 10). Mkandawire (2007) also made it very clear that: 'Social policy consists of major transformative instruments many of which are simply unavoidable for any meaningful policy of "catch-up" and development.' He went on to identify four instrumental values of social policy, namely, 1) legitimation and embedding of the development project; 2) accumulation and investment; 3) human resource development; and 4) labour market relations (Mkandawire 2007: 10). Social policy as used in our sense thus contains holistic, integrative, constitutive and congruent elements, which other scholars such as Arjan de Haan have confirmed (De Haan 2013: 2–3).

Inclusive Development

The notion, process and practice of development evoke complexity as much as they evoke confusion, which is only increased by the international array of researchers, technocrats, technicians and practitioners for whom development constitutes a livelihood and ideological space. The contestations, confusion, ambiguities and territoriality that characterise development have led to a multiplicity of prefixes that have produced names like human development, social development, sustainable development, equitable development, etc. We now live in an era of inclusive growth and development, which seeks to correct excessive and unacceptable structural inequalities that exclude large numbers of people from participating and enjoying the wellbeing and benefits of productive humankind.

Dani and De Haan (2010: 3–4), in discussing inclusive growth, have argued for the notion of 'inclusive states'. For them:

> Inclusive states are those whose policies are directed towards addressing the needs of all their citizens and creating equal opportunities for all. Citizens of such states have a say in the decisions about which services are provided, how these services are delivered and where they can exercise democratic rights.

It is not out of place to see inclusive states as core to the process of inclusive development. Inclusive development is a phenomenon which recognises that societal efforts to build productive wealth and improve the wellbeing and lives of people are often not a perfect process, as many people are left out, either intentionally or by omission. Most of the time, many are structurally excluded through what has been termed 'structural inequality'. This is '… a condition that arises out of attributing an unequal status to a category of people, a relationship that is perpetuated and reinforced by a confluence of unequal relations in roles, functions, decision rights and opportunities' (Dani and De Haan 2010: 3).

Inclusive development seeks to address structural inequality, citizenship, rights and development. It therefore involves intentional systematic interventions to correct the exclusion of people, through the building and/or creation of institutions, policies, legislations and values that deliberately enhance the integration and inclusion of people whose circumstances, through birth, location, culture, creed, gender and/or religion, have denied them the benefits of social and economic growth.

Many of the discussions around inclusive development today suffer from the same problems as the use of the residual notion, in which inclusion is an add-on to an already formed political and economic structure that lacks inclusion in its design. The residual notion of inclusive development therefore sees inclusion as a residual element, a palliative or/and alleviation of the condition of social and economic exclusion that remains unaddressed both in design and structure. Transformative social policy seeks to transcend this limited notion of inclusive development.

Because of the abundant and varied literature and opinions on the idea of development, my preference here is to reiterate my position from an earlier work of mine on the issue:

> I have always seen development as liberation from want, undue suffering and distress, and as an issue of priorities about how societies and peoples make choices, create spaces and places for the attainment of collective and individual well-being, and provide the opportunities for these within the context of justice and equity. (Aina 2003: 77).

Further on in that paper, I state that:

> We need to be clear that development is about the possibilities, and unintended and sometimes unpredictable outcomes of the intentional search and collective construction of human beings and their societies and communities for their material and other well-being. I want to add that there are no guarantees that positive outcomes will always be attained, which is why the factor of intentionality is very important. It is also why as a notion and process it is valid that it retains the objective of improving human well-being that transcends the merely economic. In that sense, development is not an ideal, but a gigantic and perpetual work-in-progress that communities, societies and some states undertake. (Aina 2003: 81)

This, for me is inclusive development, an integrative and sometimes emancipatory and equitable notion and process. And transformative social policy is one of its multiple engines. So, why are we still talking about reclaiming it today in the twenty-first century? This is because what constitutes the notion and practice of inclusive development was once one of the instruments of the nationalist construction of African nations and states, but has since been lost over three decades of structural adjustment policies and the rejection of an integrative, socially just and emancipatory approach to development.

We must also remember that inclusive development is incomplete if it is not organically linked with democracy. Again, like development, democracy is a highly contested notion that has been appropriated by many ruling groups in modern times to legitimise their rule, ideology or/and interests. From my point of view, I see democracy from the larger perspective of growth, development, change and transformation and as part of a larger social project. As I stated elsewhere:

> This (the democratisation) project is in substance an emancipatory project that through social values, the creation and growth of relevant charters and institutions, and the use of laws and other practices, seeks to promote the significance of the conditions of equality, justice, representation, participation and due process in the ways individuals and groups interact not only with each other, but also with institutions of government and the state … The democratisation project has however either been subverted and undermined by various forces and players in 20th Century Africa or never allowed to grow and develop so as to expand the full possibilities of many African societies and polities. Those who have subverted the project range from nationalists who either were never democrats or were unable to accommodate diversity and pluralism, to military rulers and power drunk potentates, as well as agents of international institutions and donor organisations … (Aina 2003: 85)

We can see that transformative social policy has strong linkages with both inclusive development and the democratisation project, both as an instrument and as a constitutive element. It featured as an aspect of the nationalist project in Africa immediately after independence. Let us turn briefly to this.

Social Policy and the African Nationalists' Social Project

Literally, the founders of modern African nations, the nationalists, have had a bad press. This negative depiction has applied to governance, development and politics and even, in certain cases, culture. In my view, it stems from a fundamental misunderstanding of the nationalist project. Again, I want to quote from an earlier publication which states that:

> … Thandika Mkandawire has asked us to reconsider our concentration on their failures and appreciate some of their achievements. He believes that after independence, African leaders made significant progress in development by investing in education for all, by improving healthcare facilities and infrastructure, and by making a serious drive towards import substitution. Given this kind of endeavour, he believes that they cannot be accused of having sought high office for personal gain (Aina 2003: 84).

The inquiry around social policy and development in Africa provides an opportunity for an empirical and theoretical re-engagement with the role of the nationalists. Let us start with a brief look at their social project. I am using the singular 'project', to characterise a multiplicity of different but carefully interwoven endeavours.

The key postcolonial project for the early nationalist leaders after the Second World War and in the era of Africa's decolonisation can be summarised under struggles for freedom and independence, efforts at state- and nation-building, and a formal commitment to economic transformation and growth that was more or less precisely defined as 'development'. The formulation of this project can be seen in the writings and speeches of the nationalist leaders in the 1950s, 1960s and 1970s (Obeng 2009; Lema, Mbilinyi and Rajani 2004). However, the independence or decolonisation project in Africa remains an unfinished business, as reiterated in important contemporary pan-African documents, such as the African Union Commission's 2015 vision, *Agenda 2063: The Africa We Want* (AU Commission 2015). Democratisation, human rights, peace and security and environmental sustainability, are stated as key global and regional concerns, but the aims of the African project remain fundamentally unchanged yet unfulfilled over the past five decades.

Freedom and Independence

The freedom and emancipation element of the nationalist project is located in the specific African history of slavery, colonisation and independence and anti-apartheid struggles. It is a politically sensitive issue. It defined the nature and search for African solidarity in the fight for decolonisation and against apartheid in South Africa and has remained very fresh in African memories — apartheid came to a formal end in South Africa only in 1994. Emancipation has been both a major part of the project and an imperative in pan-African politics. It has been tied with development goals and the thinking around important economic strategies, such as regional integration and intra-African trade. It has also defined African analyses of global power relations and regional unequal development. It is often seen in the discourses around pan-Africanism, solidarity and unity. It constituted one of the key founding principles of the Organisation of African Unity, which later became the African Union.

Nation- and state-building were the second element of the African project. The nationalists had inherited entities built on arbitrary boundaries and made up of diverse and wide varieties of nationalities, ethnic communities and linguistic groups united only by the force of colonial domination. Nation-building came along with new forms of state-building that transcended the colonial project. Here the efforts included attempts at inscribing new forms of identity and notions of citizenship on previously colonial subjects. The new nations battled from their very inception with internal and external forces that moved in the direction of further fragmentation and self-determination movements that were often driven by armed conflicts and insurrection. Nation-building was a process that was contested in many cases by civil wars, sectional insurrections, attempts at secession and conflicts. It was and has been a costly process, and along with modern state-building continues to be an important work in progress. Interestingly, the nation- and state-building projects were never coterminous with the building of liberal democracy. In fact, they rejected or ignored liberal democratic practices and paths a few years after independence, which led to the era of one-party states, authoritarian rule and military dictatorships that thrived on the continent throughout the 1970s to the late 1990s. In the early stages, however, nation-building was characterised by tremendous investments in human, physical and social infrastructure. Schools, health institutions, parliament buildings, airports, stadia and bridges to connect people were built. There were investments in monuments and museums, and in political parties and elections to create institutions, a national presence and identities of citizenship. Some countries, such as Tanzania and Senegal, to some extent also invested in developing and strengthening national languages, such as Swahili and Wolof, which helped to create a sense of oneness and built bridges across several sub-nationalities and language groups.

But the most important part of the African independence project was the wholescale belief in and adoption of 'development' by the nationalist leaders. And whether it was Nyerere, Jomo Kenyatta, Kwame Nkrumah (Nkrumah 1961; Lema et al. 2004), Obafemi Awolowo (Awolowo 1967), Kenneth Kaunda, Houphouët-Boigny, Gamal Nasser or Nnamdi Azikiwe, the African nationalist leaders were modernisers. In an uncompromising Cold War era and with the imperatives of nation-building and emancipation confronting them, they sought modern development. There were exceptions, like Mobutu Sese Seko of Zaire who explicitly promoted nativist and 'return-to-precolonial-culture' ideologies, but they were neither dominant nor in the majority. For the rest, it did not matter whether it was socialist or capitalist, left or right. The vision, aspiration and endgame was development. Again, social policy was woven into the very fabric of these early models. It was a combination of the search for economic growth, industrial and rural transformation and nation-building. With the archives now opening up, the opportunity abounds for research on this era.

Let us briefly examine how the integration of social and economic policies during the nationalist era contributed to nation-building. This approach is not limited to African countries. Arjan de Haan, in studies of the social policies of emerging economies as they related to growth and welfare, provided evidence for India and China (De Haan 2008b, 2010, 2013). For the nationalist era in Africa, however, the analysis of this phenomenon is effectively viewed within state-society and state-economy relations (Aina 1997: 45–53).

The nationalist era must first be understood as emerging from a colonial era that was restrictive, discriminatory, exploitative and exclusionary where the colonial subjects and 'natives' were concerned. Most colonial subjects had not been incorporated into the economy and society in any beneficial manner.

After independence, the nationalist elites, in correcting this legacy, included the indigenes in the post-colonial state as part of their nation-building project. New jobs were created in the civil service, education, health, industry, services, the civil and armed forces and in the fledgling state-owned economic enterprises. In many countries, co-operatives were created and expanded, and trade unions that were often pro-government were formed or enlarged. Social services were established, such as in health, education and agriculture (such as extension services, marketing boards, research stations, etc.). There were also state subsidies to encourage commodity exports and import-substitution industrialisation. As pointed out by Laakso and Olukoshi (1996: 15), the international environment up to the late 1970s, dominated by systems of national welfarism, communist and socialist states in the West and East, favoured this kind of investment and state-driven expansionism.

The strategy of incorporation also had a legitimation component, described by Mkandawire (2007). It involved differential processes of class formation and elite-building in agriculture, in rural areas in places like Côte d'Ivoire and Kenya, and in industry, bureaucracy, transportation, retail and wholesale trade in urban areas across the continent. Legitimation involved creating new landowners, workers, teachers, nurses, bureaucrats and others whose interests were served by the new nationalist governments. It also involved new forms of affirmative action, like the 'federal character' system in Nigeria and the norm of rotating political appointments in the Union of Tanzania.

But with the economic crises of the late 1960s and 1970s, the fiscal bases for the legitimation strategy began to be eroded. The adjustment era ushered in the initial delegitimisation of not only the nationalists and successive African leaders but also of the African state and any type of state-driven intervention. The onslaught of structural adjustment programmes, the onset of the neo-liberal era and globalisation, the assault on and delegitimisation of African states, government and political leadership, together with the emergence of new intellectual rationalisations by the academic establishment in economics, the social sciences and the development industry, created massive disruptions in ideas, institutions, practices, disciplines and processes that were to be in place for more than four decades. Policymaking power and the intellectual production of evidence and approaches to policymaking shifted from national levels and national higher education institutions to global, multilateral and bilateral supported agencies, networks and their nodes in Africa (Adesina 2010). This led to the dominance of what Adesina termed an erosion of vision in social policymaking, the rise in the influence of single-issue INGOs and the prevalence of 'policy-merchandising' (Adesina 2011).

Indeed, the nature, language and system of social policymaking and thought in Africa changed over this period, becoming residual, reductionist and sectoralist. It is during this time, which lasted for about four decades, that the notion of transformative social policy came to challenge thinking, foundations, evidence and practice.

At this point, it is perhaps necessary to point out that transformative social policy has emerged in a world that is much changed since the nationalist era of 1960 to 1970. Although the foundational elements of constitutive, integrated, holistic policies based on sound political and social vision remain, along with a multiplicity of functions that cover production, reproduction, protection, legitimation and cohesion, massive changes have occurred in technologies, the global system, the nature of jobs and work and in the politics and orientation of new generations of human actors. Let us examine some of them. They include:

- Significant changes in African population growth and its composition. Africa had an estimated population of 284,887,148 million in 1960. By 2017 it was estimated at 1,256,268,025. Its rate of urbanisation and its urban population have increased since 1960 and its population is much younger than in 1960-1970.[4]

- Changes in the education status of Africans across the education pipeline, in terms of enrolments in institutions and the number of institutions across the board.

- Shifts in the nature of political regimes—the first-generation nationalist parties gave way to second-generation one-party rule and authoritarian politics, including military regimes. In turn, these evolved into third-generation multi-party electoral democracies and politics with different degrees of democratic spaces.

- Changes in the emergence, growth and strength of what is known as civil society at national and international levels and in modes of organising, mobilising and demand-making.

- Transformations in the actual role of the African state, state capacity and size and concomitant state effectiveness. Along with new technologies, a greater space for business and national and local civil-society organisations (CSOs) and INGOs, as well as new complexes of plurality and polycentricity of stakeholders and voices, have emerged.

- The pervasiveness of business- and market-driven models, ideas, language and practices permeating all sectors of society, including higher education, government, the armed forces, CSOs, etc.

- Reshaped global, national and local economies with a greater integration of financial markets, the growth and delivery of services, knowledge of labour regimes and transborder contracting.

- Changes in technologies, the organisation and management of knowledge and knowledge systems. This has seen the emergence of artificial intelligence (AI), machine learning, digital and new biotechnologies with implications for labour markets, the organisation of work and the delivery of services.

- Emergence of explicitly formulated global agendas, such as the MDGs, SDGS, global health programmes, global climate change programmes with new conventions, global architectures but remaining under the controls and financing of multilateral institutions, the UN systems, the IFIs, bilaterals and a few powerful private foundations with global reach and ambitions.
- Transformed forms, patterns and directions of migrations with concomitant changes in the range and volume of remittances. This global mobility also has implications for labour trafficking, child and sex trafficking and the trafficking of narcotics on a greater scale. It also has implications for the internationalisation of criminal gangs, money laundering, transnational policing and citizen safety.
- Intensification and growth of new forms of conflicts and violence, communal and populist politics, resistance movements, insurrectionary and extremist militant groups with multi-local and transnational presence.

All of these changes and cross-cutting dynamics have implications for the promotion, advancement, structuring and mobilisation of what we call transformative social policy. They open up new opportunities, present non-traditional forms of constraints and define new research agendas, research uptakes, policy engagement, dissemination and communications.

Emerging Issues in Transformative Social Policy and Inclusive Development

From the discussion above, it is clear that doing transformative social policy today is different from the era of the nationalists. We need to be cognisant of the changes and their implications. In closing, it is important to explore a few emerging issues and the current situation we face in our world today. Many of these issues are wide open for detailed and in-depth research.

The first emerging issue is the rise of global social policymaking and its implications for the contraction of local and national policymaking spaces. I see two sets of global policymaking as important. The first has to do with agenda-setting around global goals, such as the 2030 Development Agenda and the SDGs. These are big-ticket items with international funding baskets, convenings and monitoring, evaluation and learning aspects. The global development industry is now mobilised around the SDGs, and national and local goals such as the various Vision 2020s and 2030s are being aligned around these ventures. Even regional goals, such as the African Union Agenda 2063, are seeking alignment.

Another current in global social policymaking has to do with initiatives led by some private foundations but made up of alliances with bilaterals and the UN system. These are single- or narrow-issue initiatives, such as The Global Fund to fight AIDS, Tuberculosis and Malaria. There are others around climate change, polio and other health issues. Each of them has the capacity to re-orient national social policy priorities. Some might argue that because these projects for the public good, they add value to national interventions. But a casual empirical scan shows that they capture local attention and capacity, and in some cases are not local priorities, but they are pursued by national and local stakeholders who only follow the money.

The second set of issues relates to emerging devolved governance structures in many African countries and their implication for the effective delivery of transformative social policy interventions. Devolved governance as we know emphasises administrative devolution with little or no fiscal devolution. The results for service delivery have not been too impressive on the whole. What does this phenomenon mean for transformative social policy delivery?

A third issue has to do with the growing importance of international remittances in Africa. How is this affecting access to transformative social policy interventions, say, in education, sanitation and health? Even at the individual household level, do we have evidence of the proportion and patterns of payments for access to social policy delivery from the beneficiaries of these remittances?

Finally, I want to touch on the very difficult terrain of nation-building and social cohesion. Devolution provides some differentiation in governance and governing in African countries. What difference to social cohesion and citizenship-building does a more active set of transformative social policy interventions make? What lessons are we learning from different kinds of state arrangements, devolved governance and political settlements in terms of transformative social policy interventions?

My understanding is that along with the role of changing technologies, new forms of accountability and social and political actions, these issues are going to be important as we seek to understand and shape transformative social policy interventions in inclusive development in Africa.

Acknowledgements

I would like to thank the organisers of this conference for their kind invitation to present the keynote address. I want to thank in particular, Professor Jimi Adesina of the South African Research Chair in Social Policy, at the University of South Africa, UNISA, and the worthy partners who have put this event together, namely CODESRIA, UNISA, UNRISD and the National Research Foundation of the Republic of South Africa.

Notes

1. Prof. Mkandawire delivered the opening keynote address at the conference.
2. I have made the argument for social reconstruction and the role of social policy in doing this in Aina, T., 1999, West and Central Africa: Social Policy for Reconstruction and Development, in Morales-Gomez, D., ed., *Transnational Social Policies: The New Development Challenges of Globalisation*, Ottawa and London, UK: IDRC and Earthscan Books.

3. The social-protection industry has grown rapidly since 2010 and has received a tremendous infusion of resources for knowledge production and direct development intervention. Authors such as Adesina 2011, De Haan 2011 and Hickey and Seekings 2017 have sought to locate the political, ideological and practical origins and dynamics of this growth of the approach. A key institutional player in research on this theme is the United Nations University, World Institute for Development Economics Research, WIDER.
4. See: Population of Africa (2017), www.worldometers.info/world-population/Africa-population/.

References

Adesina, J., ed., 2007, *Social Policy in Sub-Saharan Africa In Search of Inclusive Development*, Basingstoke: Palgrave Macmillan.

Adesina, J., 2009, Social Policy in Sub-Saharan Africa: A Glance in the Rear-View Mirror, *International Journal of Social Welfare*, Vol. 18: S37–S51.

Adesina, J., 2010, Rethinking the Social Protection Paradigm: Social Policy in Africa's Development, paper prepared for the conference Promoting Resilience through Social Protection in Sub-Saharan Africa, European Report on Development, Dakar, Senegal, 28–30 June 2010.

Adesina, J., 2011, Beyond the Social Protection Paradigm: Social Policy in Africa's Development, International Conference on Social Protection for Social Justice, 13-15 April 2011, UK: Institute of Development Studies.

African Union (AU) Commission, 2015, *Agenda 2063: The Africa We Want*, September 2015. Available online at https://www.un.org/en/africa/osaa/pdf/au/agenda2063.pdf.

Aina, T. A., 1994, Things Need Not Fall Apart: Social Policy in Africa, in International Development Research Centre (IDRC) Reports, Vol. 21, No .4., Special Issue on Social Policy, p. 9.

Aina, T. A., 1997, *Globalisation and Social Policy in Africa: Issues and Research Directions*, CODESRIA, Working Paper Series 6/96, Dakar: CODESRIA.

Aina, T. A., 1999, West and Central Africa: Social Policy for Reconstruction and Development, in Morales-Gomez, D., ed., *Trans-National Social Policies: The New Development Challenges of Globalisation*, Ottawa and London: IDRC and Earthscan Books.

Aina, T. A., 2003, Scales of suffering, Orders of Emancipation: Critical Issues in Democratic Development in Africa, *African Sociological Review*, Vol. 7, No. 1, pp. 73–93.

Aina, T. A., 2004, Introduction: How Do We Understand Globalisation and Social policy in Africa?, in Aina, T. A., Chachage S. L. and Yao, E. A., eds, *Globalisation and Social Policy in Africa,* Dakar: CODESRIA.

Aina, T. A., 2009. Reflections on Social Policy and Social Justice in Africa, in Bujra, A., ed., *Mijadala: A Discourse on Social Policy, Governance and Development Issues in Kenya*, Nairobi: Development Policy Management Forum.

Aina, T. A., 2010, Beyond Reforms: The Politics of Higher Education Transformation in Africa, *African Studies Review,* Vol. 53, No 1, pp. 21–40.

Awolowo, O., 1967, *Path to Nigerian Freedom*, London, UK: Faber Books.

Awortwi, O. and Aiyede, E. R., eds, 2017, *Politics, Public Policy and Social Protection in Africa: Evidence from Cash Transfer Programmes*, London: Routledge.

Dani, A. A and De Haan A., 2008a, *Inclusive States: Social Policy and Structural Inequalities,* Washington DC: The World Bank Group.

Dani A. A. and De Haan, A., 2008b, Social Policy in a Development Context: Structural Inequalities and Inclusive Institutions, in Dani A. A. and De Haan, A. eds, *Inclusive States: Social Policy and Structural Inequalities*, Washington DC: The World Bank Group, pp. 1-37

De Haan, A., 2010, *Towards a New Poverty Agenda in Asia: Social Policies and Economic Transformation,* New York: Sage Publications.

De Haan, A., 2011, The Rise of Social Protection in Development: Progress and Pitfalls, paper for International Conference on Social Protection for Social Justice, 13–15 April 2011, London, UK: Institute of Development Studies.

De Haan, A., 2013, *The Social Policies of Emerging Economies: Growth and Welfare in China and India*, International Policy Centre for Inclusive Growth, Working Paper No. 110, Brasilia: IPC-IG.

Devereux S. and Getu. M., eds, 2013, *Informal and Formal Social Protection Systems in Sub-Saharan Africa*, Kampala: OSSREA and Fountain Publishers.

Hickey, S. and Bukenya B., 2016, The Politics of Promoting Social Cash Transfers in Uganda, WIDER Working Paper 2016/118, Helsinki: UNU–WIDER.

Hickey, S. and Seekings J., 2017, The Global Politics of Social Protection, WIDER Working Paper 2017/115, Helsinki: UNU–WIDER.

Laakso, L. and Olukoshi, A. O., 1996, The Crisis of the Post-Colonial Nation-State Project in Africa, in Olukoshi A.O. and Laakso L, eds, *Challenges to the Nation-State in Africa,* Uppsala and Helsinki: Nordic African Institute and Institute of Development Studies (NORAD).

Lema, E., Mbilinyi, M. and Rajani, R., eds, 2004, *Nyerere on Education*, Dar-es Salaam: Haki Elimu.

Mason, P., 2015, *Postcapitalism: A Guide to Our Future,* Harmondsworth: Penguin Books.

Mkandawire, T., 2001, Social Policy in a Development Context, Paper No. 7, Geneva: UNRISD. Available online at https://www.unrisd.org/80256B3C005BCCF9/search/C83739F8E9A9AA0980256B5E003C5225.

Mkandawire, T., ed., 2004, *Social Policy in a Development Context*, Basingstoke: Palgrave Macmillan.

Mkandawire, T., 2007, Transformative social policy and innovation in developing countries, *The European Journal of Development Research*, Vol. 19, pp. 13–29.

Nkrumah K., 1961, *I Speak of Freedom*, New York: Frederick Praeger.

Nkrumah K., 1963, Opening of the Institute of African studies Legon, 25 October 1963, in Nyerere, J, 2004, in Lema, E., Mbilinyi, M. and Rajani, R., eds, 2004, *Nyerere on Education*, Dar-es Salaam: Haki Elimu.

Nyong'o, P. A., 2002, *The Study of African Politics: A Critical Appreciation of a Heritage*, Kenya: Heinrich Böll Foundation.

Obeng, S., ed., 2009, *Selected Speeches of Kwame Nkrumah*, Vol. 2., Centenary Edition, Accra: Afram Publications.

Pruce, K. and Hickey, S., 2016, The Politics of Promoting Social Protection in Zambia, WIDER Working Paper 2016/156, Helsinki: UNU-WIDER.

Seekings, J., 2017, 'Affordability' and the political economy of social protection in contemporary Africa, WIDER Working Paper 2017/43, Helsinki: UNU-WIDER.

Sen, A., 1999, *Development as Freedom*, Oxford: Oxford University Press.

United Nations Development Programme (UNDP), 2016, *Africa Human Development Report 2016: Accelerating Gender Equality and Women's Empowerment in Africa*, New York: United Nations Publications.

Van Beek, U. and Wnuk-Lipinski, E., eds, 2011, *Democracy under Stress: The Global Crisis and Beyond*, Stellenbosch: Sun Press.

3

Rethinking Social Policy in Africa: A Transformative Approach[1]

Katja Hujo

Introduction

More than a decade ago, former UNRISD (United Nations Research Institute for Social Development) director Thandika Mkandawire developed the concept of transformative social policy (TSP), the understanding that social policy, beyond its obvious protective function, also plays productive, reproductive and redistributive roles (Mkandawire 2004; UNRISD 2006). This approach, which soon guided the entire social policy research and policy work at UNRISD, was in many regards a game changer. It encouraged a focus on the real challenges that social policy faces in a development context, characterised by the need to foster structural transformation, dynamic accumulation processes and sociopolitical change. It triggered a multi-disciplinary inquiry to which economists could contribute alongside sociologists, gender experts, political scientists, legal scholars, historians and anthropologists. It connected the development literature with the social policy literature, helping to overcome the Western bias in social policy scholarship, and the social policy blindness of development theory. And it helped to do away with the myth that social policy was largely an instrument for rich countries, but not suited for lower-income countries lacking the basic preconditions for issues such as formal wage employment, effective state bureaucracy or fiscal space.

In this chapter, I would like to emphasise this transformative role of social policy, in opposition to the residual or secondary role that it was assigned in mainstream academia and anti-poverty programmes (Nitsch 1997; Titmuss 1974). I will talk about the social turn in development thinking and practice we have witnessed in the last two to three decades, and its limitations. I will then zoom in on the African context, trying to answer the questions—What has shaped social policies in the region? Who are the models and actors behind policies? Are they transformative? Finally, I would like to discuss what rethinking social policy in Africa could imply, and which lines of thinking could inspire a new approach to social policy in the region and beyond. The four axes of this new thinking, which ground social policy in a broader discourse of sustainable social development, are:

1. The combination of a rights-based and productivist approach to social policy.
2. The integration of questions of sustainable financing into social policy.
3. The opening up to other relevant questions, such as environmental challenges and the rise in inequality.
4. The analysis of the politics of social policymaking.

The 'Social Turn' and its Limitations

We are all familiar with the arguments that reduced the remit of social policy to a residual role. In the 70s and 80s, neoclassical and monetarist economists became increasingly influential, associating social policies with fiscal crisis, inflation and negative impacts on efficiency. This contrasted starkly with the preceding Keynesian paradigm that saw a mutually beneficial relationship between economic development and universal social policies for achieving a stable accumulation process via active demand management and a smoothing of the business cycle. Keynes's discovery of an economic equilibrium with underemployment, not full employment as assumed by the classical–neoclassical school, meant that the state had to intervene by institutionalising policies that would guarantee the income of the unemployed and stabilise demand through different means. The same logic was applied to periods of income loss across the life-cycle as the result of social contingencies (childhood, maternity, sickness, work accidents and disability, old age, etc.). These were not seen as individual risks, but as certainties—from an aggregate macroeconomic perspective—that needed systemic responses rather than individual risk management strategies, such as those proposed by the World Bank Risk Management Framework (World Bank 2001; Hujo 2005; Adesina 2010).

While the Keynesian policy approach (which also had problems in terms of its practical application, in particular the neglect of monetary constraints such as inflation) was not fully applied in the developing world, given a variety of limitations to it, there was a developmental period in the post-war era that led to significant progress in economic and social development dimensions in different regions, and which for many still serves as a benchmark for what is possible.

In contrast to the Keynesian model, interestingly, the neoliberal approach was fully and radically applied in the developing world after the collapse of the previous model, to a much greater extent than in the Western hemisphere, where social-democratic and conservative, continental-European welfare regimes, to use the Esping-Anderson classification (Esping-Anderson 1990), demonstrated greater path dependency, resisting the dismantling of state-led development for a longer period.

The policy recommendations and conditionalities of the neoliberal turn in development and social policy were expenditure cuts, privatisation of social protection systems and a general shift towards social funds, safety nets and market-based schemes. Trade as well as financial and capital markets were liberalised and deregulated at a global scale, but the expected economic miracles did not materialise, the social costs of stabilisation and structural adjustment policies (SAPs) were huge, and the discussion about what role social policy had to play within the development process remained contested (Mkandawire and Soludo 1999; Adesina 2004, 2010).

Similar to the Keynesian approach, there was an attempt to establish a positive relationship between social and economic policies within the market-liberal framework. However, this attempt can be criticised on the grounds of its partly contested theoretical assumptions, such as the pre-Keynesian view of the need for a savings fund to be accumulated to finance investment, which is often referred to in the case of insurance schemes based on capitalisation. This supposed synergy, creating pension accounts to stimulate savings and financial sector development, was for example used by the World Bank in its global campaign for privatising public pension schemes based on the Chilean Model (World Bank 1994).[2] Furthermore, the neoliberal approach tended to focus almost exclusively on microeconomic and structural issues like productivity, efficiency or human capital promotion, while neglecting the importance of the macroeconomic constellation as expressed in the external accounts (including external debt) and the competitiveness of the exchange rate (for which post-war Germany and Japan, and more recently China, are telling examples).

Two developments in the over four decades of neoliberal practices had a major impact on the policy debate: the mentioned disappointing results of the model in terms of social development, as well as the wave of economic and financial crises that started in the late 1980s, continued in the 1990s and culminated in the global economic and financial crisis in 2008 (Hujo 2005).

According to Polanyi's double movement theory, after the laissez-faire and free market euphoria came the counter-movement demanding protection against adverse market effects (Polanyi 1944).[3] UNRISD has labelled this latest comeback of social policy in the international development discourse, the 'social turn', defined in its 2016 flagship report as a 'combination of shifts in ideas and policies that has reasserted social issues in development agendas' (UNRISD 2016: 34). The need to re-establish a comprehensive definition of social policy had been articulated in the late 1980s, but the social turn got its real drive internationally through the World Summit for Social Development of 1995, held in Copenhagen. In the words of my former colleague, Peter Utting, the UN was finally reclaiming the terrain of social policy from the international financial institutions (IFIs) (UNRISD 2016: 35).

The Copenhagen summit suggested a more integrated approach, which would link poverty reduction with social inclusion and employment creation as an alternative to the neoliberal model. Participants also rejected the trickle-down assumptions that link liberalisation to a virtuous circle of growth, employment generation and poverty reduction, as well as the notion that the key social function of governments should be restricted to the provision of safety nets.

Since the turn of the millennium, in particular the need for a more proactive approach to eradicate poverty, reduce inequality and protect people against the risks associated with market economies, and social contingencies across the lifecycle, has gained currency. Global social policy agendas that were designed in that period, such as the Millennium Development Goals, Education and Health for all initiatives, or the ILO Social Protection Floor Recommendation No. 202, are further examples of this growing recognition (UNRISD 2016).

In practice, however, the social turn had severe shortcomings. Several of the key instruments and interventions promoted by the international donor community did very little against the drivers of social exclusion and economic stagnation (which was the result of designing policies based on a protective or welfarist approach, neglecting production and other functions of social policy). Far from being transformative, they have reproduced the problems they were meant to address. This was mainly the result of endorsing rather than questioning mainstream orthodox economic recipes and ignoring unequal power relations.

Two examples of this are the Poverty Reduction Strategy Papers (PRSP), promoted by the World Bank, and public-private partnerships (PPPs), which are still prominent as a means of implementation of the 2030 Agenda for Sustainable Development. While the former have treated social programmes as an afterthought to conventional Washington consensus policies, which continue to undermine growth and employment creation, PPPs have often tended to be more expensive than public investments, while failing to meet expectations in terms of service delivery and development outcomes (Jomo et al. 2016).

A third and prominent example of the shortcomings of the contemporary social turn is the uncritical promotion of conditional cash transfer (CCTs) and public works programmes, which often narrowly target specific populations or provide minimal benefits for a limited time period without providing a long-term solution to chronic poverty and the absence of comprehensive social protection systems. I will briefly come back to this instrument in the next part of my speech.

Social Policy in the African Context

Social policy varies according to the political and economic models that prevail in a specific country and during a specific historical period, an observation that was confirmed by several speakers presenting country case studies during the Social Policy in the African Context conference. And while there is a certain path dependency, or continuity, associated with welfare regimes, social policy also evolves in response to different external and internal challenges and risks, or opportunities (Hujo and Yi 2016).

The global economic crisis that started in 2008 clearly highlighted the new global political and economic context in which these risks and challenges unfold: globalisation and financialisation; persistent poverty and rising inequality; technological progress coupled with a growing technological divide; post-industrial demographic change; and the rise of the service sector, characterised by the sharp contrast between sophisticated services relying on new technologies and highly skilled labour, and a growing number of poor service providers struggling for a livelihood in the informal economy. These changes are interlinked and have reinforcing and contradictory impacts on society—in the areas of global and national finance for development; employment, productivity and wages; vulnerability and poverty; inequality and the environment.

Turning to social policy in Africa, these policies have to be understood, then, in terms of their specific history and country context, and according to whether they respond successfully or less successfully to the new challenges and risks I have outlined. Africa, like Latin America, has been a laboratory of development models and donor practices, especially after the global debt crisis of the early 1980s paved the way for a stronger integration of African economies into global markets. To define social policy models or welfare regimes in Africa is a difficult task, not only because the traditional approaches developed in the classical literatures are often not suitable and new classifications not entirely satisfactory, but also because the continent's more recent history has seen an increasing hybridisation of models and fragmentation of approaches, rather than a consolidation of a social model that could easily be linked to a dominant mode of production, such as a market, family or state economy.

As we heard the day before, social policy approaches in Africa were shaped by colonial history, when rudimentary social policy systems or sometimes non-systems were introduced following the respective European models. These were aligned with the requirements of a specific pattern of incorporation in the colonial economy—for example, cash crop economies in western Africa versus labour-reserve economies in southern Africa, as Prof. Mkandawire has shown in his seminal works about colonial heritage and welfare and tax regimes in Africa (Mkandawire 2010, 2020). What I find especially interesting in this work is that contestation and rupture were crucial to adapt these models to new state visions in the post-independence eras, post-conflict situations or periods of political transition, for example after the end of apartheid regimes, rectifying old injustices and adapting schemes to current challenges.

Secondly, social policy approaches in sub-Saharan Africa were influenced by factors such as economic crises, donor influence and generalised institutional crisis driven by the SAPs, which had resulted in economic polarisation, fragmented social identities and a backlash against the post-independence modernisation project, as analysed aptly by Yusuf Bangura in several of his works (for example, Bangura 1994). This crisis in the public sector was then meant to be fixed through public management approaches and good governance reforms in the 1990s, but the neglect of social relations and an enabling environment for institutional reform led to widespread failure of this agenda, and the necessary resources and administrative capacities to expand what had started as a universal approach in many countries after independence could not be maintained (Bangura and Larbi 2006).

The traditional social policy definition (see, for example UNRISD 2010, Chapter 5) comprises social insurance schemes, social assistance programmes and labour market policies (in addition to the social services that were the primary focus of post-independence African states), which are either directly financed and provisioned through the state, or at least regulated by the state (for example by mandating contributions from social partners) and delivered through social insurance agencies. However, this conception of social policy could not be successfully emulated in the African context for several reasons:

Firstly, the coverage of formal contributory insurance remained low in contexts of high economic informality; secondly, it declined even more when public sector workers were retrenched in large numbers during structural adjustment; and thirdly, in the case of public services such as education and health, which had started off ambitiously in many countries in the post-independence period, their subsequent privatisation and dismantling resulted in fragmented, unequal and underfunded systems, with negative impacts on access and quality. In some countries where public mining companies had funded generous social services in mining communities, for example in the Zambian Copper Belt, the privatisation of these companies also led to a decline in these services, as municipalities or national governments lacked the funds to maintain the previous social infrastructure and the companies focused on their core business rather than taking over state functions, favouring soft instruments such as the newly promoted Corporate Social Responsibility (CSR) programmes.[4]

The results of these social policy responses to a changing global context and recurrent crises have been mixed. Poverty, while reduced in some countries, has not been eliminated, and inequality has actually increased in developed and developing countries. Poverty in absolute numbers has increased in sub-Saharan Africa, and in many countries in the region the majority of the population still lives in poverty and precariousness. I repeat: after several decades of development, national development plans, the implementation of the MDGs and the disbursement of millions of dollars of Official Development Assistance (ODA), poverty is still the reality for the majority of African people. This tells us something about the explanatory power of the theories promoted and the recipes deployed in the region and the developing world in general.

In sum, the social systems that were meant to be built over several generations in tandem with economic development and in a synergistic way stalled, or more correctly, were aborted prematurely, with the state losing its steering and co-ordinating function in both social and economic policy. This loss of steering capacity meant reacting to and accommodating the exigencies of a globalised market economy, represented by donors, IFIs, Multinational Corporations (MNCs) and large investors, rather than negotiating with and responding to the claims of ordinary citizens and national interest groups to move forward a home-grown, long-term development vision.

This loss of policy space and state capacity, but also the worsening of state–citizen relations, and the fact that democratic regimes often appeared to be 'choiceless' or 'disempowered' (Mkandawire 2006) in the face of external constraints and interferences, goes indeed a long way to explain the bad governance, patronage, rent-seeking and corruption that have haunted the continent.

I would like to zoom in once more on the topic of social protection, in particular social assistance policies in this context. Simplifying the reality of social policy in Africa into two main models (see, for example, Niño-Zarazúa et al. 2011)[5] we can identify:

1. A smaller number of countries that are viewed as international role models, such as the more comprehensive systems in southern Africa (South Africa, Namibia, Botswana, Lesotho or Swaziland) and Mauritius, with tax-financed social transfers determined by age categories (older persons, children), relatively high coverage of contributory social insurance schemes, and relatively high coverage of public services (although dualist models with a strong presence of public service providers prevail in most cases);
2. A larger number of mostly lower-income countries where formal social insurance is very limited, social services are fragmented and commercialised, and myriad anti-poverty, emergency (such as food aid) and targeted social transfer programmes or projects are often financed by external donors and implemented by technical cooperation, NGOs or UN agencies.

In terms of policy trends and emerging discourses, although the social turn of the 1990s in combination with the international commodity boom, strong growth rates in Africa and scaled-up donor investment could have provided a big push for social policies, the picture remains uncertain for a variety of reasons in both country groups (see also Adesina 2004).[6]

Firstly, the framing of social policy by dominant actors such as external donors and governments, despite the rediscovery of the importance of the 'social', is not in line with the Transformative Social Policy (TSP) concept or with the UNRISD definition of transformative change as attacking the root causes of poverty, inequality and unsustainability, instead of the symptoms (UNRISD 2016: 38–40). Social policy is seen as an instrument of protection against risks and shocks, or as an instrument to alleviate the worst forms of poverty, but it is not seen as a necessary complement to economic policy to guarantee market stability, productivity and innovation, social reproduction, equal opportunities and more equal outcomes across class, gender, ethnicity, age or location, state legitimacy, social cohesion and integration.

Secondly, there seem to exist at least two obstacles on the way to switching from these residual visions to a transformative social policy model:

1. The first obstacle can be located in the understanding and design of social policy itself. Small pilots, targeted projects and programmes, inadequate social insurance and low-quality social services cannot play the role of automatic stabilisers or nation-wide human capital investments; their redistributive potential is minimal, as is their impact on social reproduction, while their effect on social cohesion, state legitimacy and nation-building has proven to be negative (Adesina 2010; UNRISD 2010; Bangura 1994).
2. The second obstacle is related to the linkage between economic and social policy. In fact, as long as economic policy is based on the market-liberal approach and the default position (markets as self-regulating entities), social policy is constrained by permanent austerity while also overburdened, limiting its transformative potential. The latter occurs as social policy cannot take up all the functions economic policy could play but is not allowed to play in mainstream policy models, such as industrial and trade policies, active monetary and fiscal policies, and regulations that hold at bay wealth concentration, rent-seeking, and the exploitation of people and nature. Economic and social policies have to work in tandem, but in a coherent and balanced way.

Rethinking Social Policy in Africa: Four Ideas

In the last part of this speech, I would like to briefly sketch four ideas for rethinking social policy in Africa and beyond.

We have already discussed the need for a productivist approach to social policy, but certain aspects of this approach have also been criticised, especially the linking of entitlements with formal employment, as this excludes all those in the informal economy or engaged in unpaid care and domestic work, leading to a stratification that is reflected, for example, in labour aristocracies or gender inequalities. Advocating for delinking social rights from employment became popular, as the expansion of tax-financed social assistance schemes and debates on basic income demonstrate.

There are, however, many good reasons to maintain the link between labour and capital through social insurance—for example, to keep employers responsible for financing social insurance schemes and social services, and to emphasise the productive contribution of informal workers, which can enhance their bargaining position in claiming support from business and the state (Alfers et al. 2017).

Researchers from WIEGO (Women in Informal Employment Globalizing and Organizing) and UNRISD have argued that an either-or approach between a productivist and a rights-based approach to social policy is counterproductive, as both need to be pursued simultaneously (for example Alfers et al. 2017; Heintz and Lund 2012; UNRISD 2013).

The human rights-based approach (HBA) adds value to social policy in many regards:[7]

1. First of all, we should see the linkage between the HBA and social policy as a two-way relationship: human rights improve social policies, in terms of design, implementation and monitoring, and social policies are instruments to realise human rights.
2. The HBA emphasises the value of universal policy approaches, while also paying attention to the fact that different groups might require specific support or affirmative action to fully access and enjoy their rights.
3. The HBA is naturally linked to empowerment, meaningful participation, agency and democratisation—it requires political mobilisation and active citizenship to claim rights, to participate in the design of systems and to hold governments and other powerful actors to account on delivery of transfers and quality services.
4. The HBA is linked to the broader political, social and economic context, as the principle of progressive realisation guarantees that poor and disadvantaged people are not excluded from growth dynamics, and that governments prioritise investments in social development, therefore avoiding rising inequalities and social disintegration.

Integrating Questions of Sustainable Financing into Social Policy

Soon after the Copenhagen Social Summit, UNRISD started to look into the potential funding sources for social policies, the various implications of changing from state to private funding in social insurance and for public services, the international governance of financial flows (aid and taxation), and the prospects and limitations of mobilising resources at the grassroots level (through popular instruments such as microcredit and remittances) (UNRISD 2000).

Today, in a context of mounting uncertainty with regard to aid flows, and with many rich economies in crisis, the mobilisation of domestic resources is increasingly important for achieving development goals. This is highlighted in the Addis Ababa Action Agenda for Finance for Development as a key means of implementing the Sustainable Development Goals (SDGs) (UN 2015a, 2015b; UNRISD 2016). While more attention to financing challenges is laudable, what is often neglected are the productive, redistributive, reproductive and protective implications of different financing instruments (which are explored in the 2010 Poverty report) (UNRISD 2010), the consequences of power imbalances between actors engaged in fiscal and revenue bargains, the political factors that impact on the potential to mobilise resources, as well as constraints emerging from the international context.

The 2016 UNRISD flagship report delves more deeply into the questions of sustainable financing and domestic resource mobilisation (UNRISD 2016: Chapter 6), as does the UNRISD Politics of Domestic Resource Mobilization for Social Development project (Hujo 2020). A broader definition of sustainable financing (beyond the conventional definition of macro stability and debt service capacity) would, for example:

- rule out a prolonged recourse to austerity policies, which are socially and politically unsustainable (and ultimately unsustainable with regard to growth and employment) and in violation of human rights standards;
- bring to the fore questions about the quality of revenues, measured in terms of their transformative impact on production and employment, redistribution, gender equality, sustainable use of natural resources, and inclusion;
- and suggest that financing and expenditure policies need to be designed in an integrated way, based on principles of efficiency, equity, fairness, social justice and human rights, while ensuring political processes related to financial issues are inclusive and participatory.

Other aspects stressed in the project are the political nature of resource mobilisation as well as the governance challenges associated with implementing financing policies. Domestic resource mobilisation, whether through taxation or capture of mineral rents, is a political process of contestation and bargaining over who pays and who benefits.[8]

Taxation is probably the high road of revenue mobilisation, and fortunately, many countries, including lower-income countries, are more open to discuss options beyond the neoliberal recipes of flat rates and Value Added Tax (VAT). UNRISD research has revealed a range of factors that are conducive to increasing tax capacity and equity. These include political leadership and bargaining power vis-à-vis elites and big corporations, the design and marketing of reforms (including information campaigns), technological innovations (to improve tax enforcement and administrative efficiency), inclusive and transparent bargaining processes, a positive growth context, the extension of citizenship rights, and electoral competition (UNRISD 2016).

Many countries, including many in Africa, rely on revenues from natural resource sectors, such as mining or agriculture. When policy reforms related to rent capture or rent distribution from extractive industries (EI) or natural resource sectors have been linked with social policy, countries have benefitted more from EI, as seen in Bolivia and Mongolia. However, increasing social spending, while a necessary condition, is not sufficient. Mineral-led development also hinges on macroeconomic policies and productive strategies that foster diversification while safeguarding stability and environmental protection.

Broader Questions, such as Rising Inequality and Environmental Problems

One of the greatest challenges of our current time is the rise in inequality, within and between countries, and vertical and horizontal inequalities related to income and group differences (UNRISD 2019). In his keynote address, Prof. Mkandawire mentioned that it is almost impossible to change income distribution, especially functional income distribution in peaceful times. Big jumps towards greater equality have been observed in post-war and post-revolutionary settings, and sometimes after destructive economic crises. These are not scenarios we would like to see in the future. The question then remains how to achieve greater equality in opportunities and outcomes in normal times. Again, the economic models operating in countries determine to a great extent who benefits from growth processes, and to what extent redistribution happens through tax and social policies, or other regulations for investors and wealth owners.

Social policy is maybe more powerful in addressing horizontal inequalities, such as those between different social groups, but the challenge is not to throw out the baby with the bathwater but to integrate affirmative action and interventions targeted at specific groups into a universal framework that benefits and is supported by all people, in order to maintain the necessary linkages between classes, generations, gender or national groups, etc., to promote a sense of national identity and social cohesion.

Climate change and environmental sustainability are of course at the top of the international agenda since states launched the 2030 Agenda for Sustainable Development in 2015. Sustainability is not a new subject, but historical memory is again short. The 1970s and 1980s featured emancipatory ecological movements from below in a variety of countries, which included a different vision of the economy and society, before the topic was captured by corporate and political elites who brought in a business mindset and the commodification of nature as the solution, as Prof. Tade Aina has described.

What does the environmental challenge mean for transformative social policy? In UNRISD, eco-social policies have been analysed as an integrated approach to this challenge, but social policies that have a clear environmental dimension are still rare, and often fall into the public works or CCT category—for example, the Indian MNREGA employment scheme or the Brazilian Bolsa Verde programme.[9] We need more debate and analysis on how to harness social policies for environmental sustainability, for example with regard to social services and infrastructure, labour market policies and social security.

Consider the Politics of Social Policymaking: Who Drives Transformative Change?

Some scholars classify development theories into optimistic and pessimistic approaches. It quickly becomes clear that structuralist ideas, such as dependency theory, but also a range of other heterodox approaches, are rather pessimistic regarding the prospects for achieving progressive transformation. More optimistic is neoliberal thinking (in which markets by themselves result in optimal outcomes) or those approaches that build on agency, individual capabilities and capacities, or the power of political leadership and enlightened elites.

I think that the truth is once more in the middle, and I am glad that this conference has taken structural constraints, historical legacies, world market conditions and patterns of incorporation into the global economy seriously. But we should also discuss the power of ideas, the lasting impact of a generation of African leaders who did not shy away from substantive thinking and long-term visions, and the importance of non-state actors, civil society, voters, interest groups, social partners etc. in influencing and monitoring policy processes, discourses, social innovations and behaviour of corporations.

What the sociopolitical basis of a new twenty-first century eco-social compact could be in a world of increasing fractures and inequalities, nationalist populism and opting out of elites and middle classes from redistributive approaches and the notion of the commons, is the key question of a new UNRISD research project currently being developed (UNRISD 2019), so hopefully this can be a topic for collaboration and future discussions within the TSP network.

Notes

1. This chapter is based on a keynote speech given at the 2017 Social Policy in Africa International Conference, November 2017, Pretoria, South Africa.
2. For a critique, see Hujo 2004, 2014.
3. For contemporary perspectives on the double movement approach, see for example Fraser 2013, Block 2008.
4. The dismantling of social services previously provided by mining companies without replacement by public services contrasts with the European experience, where the mining sector (and other key industrial sectors and companies) has been a pioneer in social provisioning and insurance programmes, which over time have been universalised through state programmes, see Hujo 2012, p. 320; on the Zambia case, see for example Negi 2011; for a critique on CSR, see UNRISD 2010, Chapter 9 – Business, Power and Poverty Reduction.

5. UNRISD 2010, Chapter 5 categorises countries into developmentalist-industrialised, dualist, agrarian-informal and universal models. The described two models in sub-Saharan Africa fall broadly into the categories of dualist and agrarian-informal contexts. Dualist structures are typically found in middle-income countries with stalled industrialisation and high inequality. Prominent examples are Argentina, Brazil and South Africa.
6. For a more nuanced analysis of the new trends and innovations in the Global South, see UNRISD 2016, Chapter 2.
7. For different examples see the special issue edited by Hujo and Behrendt on the human right to social security, Hujo and Behrendt 2017.
8. This is the conceptual framing of an UNRISD research project on the politics of domestic resource mobilisation, see www.unrisd.org/pdrm for a list of project publications and Hujo 2020.
9. For a critical appraisal of these policies see UNRISD 2016.

References

Adesina, J., 2004, In Search of Inclusive Development: Introduction, in Adesina, J., ed., *Social Policy in Sub-Saharan African Context: In Search of Inclusive Development*, Basingstoke: UNRISD/Palgrave Macmillan, pp. 1–53.

Adesina, J., 2010, Rethinking the Social Protection Paradigm: Social Policy in Africa's Development, paper prepared for the conference Promoting Resilience through Social Protection in Sub-Saharan Africa, European Report on Development, Dakar, Senegal, 28–30 June 2010.

Alfers, L., Lund F. and Moussié, R., 2017, Approaches to Social Protection for Informal Workers: Aligning Productivist and Human Rights-Based Approaches, *International Social Security Review*, Special Issue: The Human Right to Social Security (guest editors Hujo K. and Behrendt C.), Vol. 70, No. 4, pp. 67–85.

Bangura, Y., 1994, Economic Restructuring, Coping Strategies and Social Change: Implications for Institutional Development in Africa, UNRISD Discussion Paper No. 52, Geneva: UNRISD.

Bangura, Y. and Larbi G.A., eds, *Public Sector Reforms in Developing Countries: Capacity Challenges to Improve Services*, Basingstoke: UNRISD/Palgrave MacMillan.

Block, F., 2008, Polanyi's Double Movement and the Reconstruction of Critical Theory, *Revue Interventions Économiques*, No. 38, pp. 1–13.

Esping-Andersen, G., 1990, *The Three Worlds of Welfare Capitalism*, Cambridge, UK: Polity Press.

Fraser, N., 2013. A Triple Movement?, *New Left Review* 81, May–June, pp. 119–132.

Heintz, J. and Lund F., 2012, Welfare Regimes and Social Policy: A Review of The Role of Labour and Employment, UNRISD Research Paper No. 4., Geneva: UNRISD.

Hujo, K., 2004, *Soziale Sicherung im Kontext von Stabilisierung und Strukturanpassung: Die Reform der Rentenversicherung in Argentinien* (Social Security in the Context of Stabilisation and Structural Adjustment: The Pension Reform in Argentina), Frankfurt: Peter Lang.

Hujo, K., 2005, *Wirtschaftskrisen und sozioökonomische (Un-)sicherheit in Lateinamerika* (Economic crises and socio-economic (in-)security in Latin America,) in Fritz, B. and Hujo, K., eds, *Ökonomie unter den Bedingungen Lateinamerikas: Erkundungen zu Geld und Kredit, Sozialpolitik und Umwelt, Schriftenreihe des Instituts für Iberoamerika-Kunde*, Hamburg, Vol. 61, Frankfurt/Madrid: Vervuert Verlagsgesellschaft, pp.153–172.

Hujo, K., 2012, Conclusions: Harnessing the Potential of Mineral Rents for Social Development—Options and Constraints, in Hujo, K., ed., *Mineral Rents and the Financing of Social Policy: Opportunities and Challenges*, Basingstoke: UNRISD/Palgrave Macmillan , pp. 318-331.

Hujo, K., 2014, Reforming Pensions in Developing and Transition Countries: Trends, Debates and Impacts, in Hujo K., ed., *Reforming Pensions in Developing and Transition Countries*, Basingstoke: UNRISD/Palgrave Macmillan, pp. 3–40.

Hujo, K. and Behrendt C., eds, 2017, *International Social Security Review*, Special Issue: The Human Right to Social Security, Vol. 70, No. 4.

Hujo, K. and Ilcheong Y., 2016, Introduction. Social Policy and Inclusive Development, in *Social Policy and Inclusive Development*, UNRISD Classics Vol. I, Geneva: UNRISD.

Hujo, K., ed., 2020, *The Politics of Domestic Resource Mobilisation for Social Development*, Basingstoke: UNRISD/Palgrave Macmillan.

Jomo K.S., Chowdhury, A., Sharma K. and Platz, D., 2016, Public-Private Partnerships and the 2030 Agenda for Sustainable Development: Fit for Purpose, DESA Working Paper No. 148, New York: UN DESA. Available online at http://www.un.org/esa/desa/papers/2016/wp148_2016.pdf. Accessed 17 May 2016.

Mkandawire, T., 2004, Social Policy in a Development Context: Introduction, in Mkandawire, T., ed., *Social Policy in a Development Contex*t, Basingstoke: UNRISD/Palgrave Macmillan, pp. 1–33.

Mkandawire, T., 2006, Disempowering New Democracies and the Persistence of Poverty, Programme on Democracy, Governance and Human Rights, Paper No. 21, Geneva: UNRISD.

Mkandawire, T., 2010, On Tax Efforts and Colonial Heritage in Africa, *Journal of Development Studies*, Vol. 46, No. 10, pp. 1647–1669. Available online at http://eprints.lse.ac.uk/31211/. Accessed 23 February 2016.

Mkandawire, T., 2020, Colonial Legacies and Social Expenditure in Africa: An Empirical Exercise, in Hujo, K., ed., *The Politics of Domestic Resource Mobilization for Social Development*, Basingstoke: UNRISD/Palgrave MacMillan, pp. 139–172.

Mkandawire, T. and Soludo, C., 1999, *Notre continent, notre avenir: perspectives africaines sur l'ajustement structurel*, Dakar: CODESRIA.

Negi, R., 2011, The Micropolitics of Mining and Development In Zambia: Insights from the Northwestern Province, *African Studies Quarterly*, Vol. 12, No. 2, pp. 27–44.

Niño-Zarazúa, M., Barrientos, A., Hickey S. and Hulme, D., 2011, Social Protection in Sub-Saharan Africa: Getting the Politics Right, *World Development*, Vol. 40, No. 1, pp. 163–176.

Nitsch, M., 1997, *Dimensionen von Sozialversicherung Reformen: Lateinamerika, Deutschland und darüber hinaus, Lateinamerika, Analysen-Daten-Dokumentation*, No. 36, Hamburg: Institut für Iberoamerika-kunde, pp. 15–32.

Polanyi, K., 1944 / 1978, *The Great Transformation*, German translation, Berlin: Suhrkamp Taschenbuch Wissenschaft.

Titmuss, R. M., 1974, *Social Policy: An Introduction*, Abel-Smith, B. and Titmuss, K., eds, New York: Pantheon Press.

United Nations (UN), 2015a, *Addis Ababa Action Agenda*, Third International Conference on Financing for Development, New York: UN Publications, Available online at http://www.un.org/esa/ffd/wp-content/uploads/2015/08/AAAA_Outcome.pdf. Accessed 6 May 2016.

United Nations (UN), 2015b, *Transforming Our World: The 2030 Agenda for Sustainable Development*, A/RES/70/1, New York: UN Publications. Available online at https://sustainabledevelopment.un.org/post2015/transformingourworld. Accessed 21 January 2016.

United Nations Research Institute for Social Development (UNRISD), 2000, *Visible Hands: Taking Responsibility for Social Development*, Geneva: UNRISD.

United Nations Research Institute for Social Development (UNRISD), 2006, *Transformative Social Policy: Lessons from UNRISD Research*, Research and Policy Brief No. 5, Geneva: UNRISD.

United Nations Research Institute for Social Development (UNRISD), 2010, *Combating Poverty and Inequality: Structural Change, Social Policy and Politics*, Geneva: UNRISD.

United Nations Research Institute for Social Development (UNRISD), 2013, *Social Policy and Employment: Rebuilding the Connections*, UNRISD Beyond 2015 Brief No. 3, February 2013, Geneva: UNRISD.

United Nations Research Institute for Social Development (UNRISD), 2016, *Policy Innovations for Transformative Change*, UNRISD Flagship Report 2016, Geneva: UNRISD.

United Nations Research Institute for Social Development (UNRISD), 2019, *Overcoming Inequalities in the Context of the 2030 Agenda for Sustainable Development*. Issue Brief No. 10. Geneva: UNRISD.

World Bank, 1994, *Averting the Old-Age Crisis. Policies to Protect the Old and Promote Growth*, Washington, DC and New York: World Bank Publications and Oxford University Press.

World Bank, 2001, *Social Protection Sector Strategy: From Safety Net to Springboard*, Washington DC: World Bank Publications.

4

Nation-Building and the Nationalist Discourse: Revisiting Social Policy in Ghana and Zambia in the First Decade of Independence

Ndangwa Noyoo and Emmanuel Boon

Introduction

When Africans rose up against colonialism and demanded self-rule, the motivating factor was the need to be treated as citizens in their own countries and as people who had citizenry entitlements. This urgency and militancy stemmed from the Africans' recognition that they had been excluded from the development processes unfolding in their own lands. Africans were effectively treated as second-class citizens in their own countries by foreign colonisers who originated from Western Europe. In this regard, colonialism was premised on the Europeans' brutal subjugation and exploitation of Africans and the significant plunder of Africa's natural resources. Also, it is important to note that Africans in the colonial setting were not only oppressed and barred from accessing life chances by racist and discriminatory policies and legislation, but they were also disenfranchised and could not vote for any political representative to take care of their interests. It is due to this state of human wretchedness that nationalist movements were formed to overthrow colonial rule and create independent and socially just states. In effect, the fight for independence was also a fight for social rights and human rights, which the colonialists had never extended to Africans. Poignantly, the fight against colonial domination was in fact a fight for citizenship. That is why the clarion call for freedom of the nationalists was simplified in the phrase, One-Person, One-Vote. This was supposed to translate into the enfranchisement of Africans so that they would be able to access life chances, such as good healthcare, education, housing, clean and potable water, proper sanitation and employment. These life chances, or social rights, were also the famed 'fruits of independence' that the African masses were promised by their nationalist leaders.

From Ghana to Zambia, most nationalist leaders were preoccupied with 'seeking the political kingdom so that everything could be added' to their poor, illiterate, ignorant and diseased citizens—as Kwame Nkrumah, the founding president of Ghana, had asserted while paraphrasing the Scriptures (Ibhawoh 2020). Therefore, when Africans won their independence, it was not coincidental that most of them sought to create developmental states in which the state occupied a central role, as Mkandawire (2001) argues. The state presided over the development of comprehensive social policies and expanded welfare systems that dovetailed social rights with human rights. More importantly, such states were able to marshal resources for creating equitable social and economic systems in sub-Saharan Africa (SSA) (Mkandawire 2004). For example, they were able to have social anchoring—which prevented them from using their autonomy in a predatory manner and enabled them to gain the adhesion of key actors (Mkandawire 2001). It is important to note that, at the time, the nationalist discourse informed economic and social policy thinking in most of post-colonial Africa. The nationalist discourse hinged on two concerns across the ideological divide, namely economic growth and national unity. The eradication of ignorance, poverty and disease were central to the nationalist agenda, and economic growth was seen as a means for achieving these objectives. Given the many ethnic groups in all African countries, with some even embroiled in ethnic rivalries, social policy helped to cement both social and political cohesion, thereby crystallising the state's legitimacy in Africa (Mkandawire 2004; Adesina 2007). Aina (2004) locates this role of social policy in the legitimising model, which is underpinned by a strong social policy initiative that is tied to the constructionist approach to economic development, involving the building of physical, social and human infrastructure. Therefore, public spending on education and healthcare simultaneously played the instrumental role of enhancing production and the normative role of social cohesion in enhancing functional citizenship (Mkandawire 2001; Aina 2004; Adesina 2007).

It is worth noting that in the 1960s and 1970s, ideology played a crucial role in determining the content and pace of social policy in certain countries. For example, Tanzania under Julius Nyerere and Zambia under Kenneth Kaunda espoused Ujamaa and Humanism respectively, as guiding ideologies to inform social policy interventions. Ujamaa and Humanism were derivatives of Democratic African Socialism and were also underpinned by Indigenous Knowledge Systems (IKS). Therefore, indigenous knowledge relating to ideas around family-hood and the care of orphans, children, older persons and vulnerable groups informed social policy interventions during this era. African social policy models were encouraged whereas Western notions and theories were eschewed. In this regard, this chapter, using case studies from Ghana and Zambia, argues for a return to a broader vision of social policy in Africa because this type of social policy is 'important for its long-term efficacy, development, and inclusive social citizenship. Therefore, reconnecting social policy to the wider development objectives and the nation-building project is essential for sustainable social policy outcomes, as it is for sustainable economic development' (Adesina 2007: 42).

Another objective of this chapter hinges on the understanding that there 'is a need to re-think social policy expenditure not as a gratuitous favour done to citizens but as investments in development and nation-building or social cohesion (Adesina 2007: 42). To achieve these two objectives, this chapter revisits the first decade of independence in Ghana and Zambia, so as to draw lessons that could inform present-day social policy responses in the two countries.

The first decade of independence in Ghana and Zambia was an important period for social policy because in both countries it played multiple developmental and transformative roles. Social policy was also premised on a strong normative foundation. However, this social policy thrust was not carried forth into later years and there are stark disparities in socio-economic outcomes and the living standards of the people in both countries between the first decade of independence and latter decades. Thus, this chapter argues that social policy during the first decade of independence in the two countries was emancipatory and not palliative.

However, after this period, successive governments in both countries seem to have mainly been preoccupied with the implementation of piecemeal social policy interventions compared to the bold and comprehensive social policy of the first decade of independence. In addition, social policies in the two countries during this period fostered national unity despite the existence of strong ethnic identities. In order to draw lessons for formulating and implementing sound social policies and social protection programmes in Ghana and Zambia in contemporary times, we discuss the first decade of independence in the two countries in this chapter to stimulate further discourse on the subject in sub-Saharan Africa (SSA). The chapter relied on available literature to investigate the contribution of social policy to the process of nation-building in Ghana and Zambia. In the first part of the chapter, we define key concepts that underpin this discussion. In the second part, we focus on the two case studies. Lastly, we end the chapter with a number of recommendations.

Review of Key Concepts

This section briefly reviews three inter-related concepts — nation-building, social policy and social protection — to establish the background for the discussion in the chapter.

Understanding Nation-Building

Nation-building in much of Africa started in the post-independence period as a reaction against the divide-and-rule tactics of the colonialists. Echoing Utz (2005), we note that nation-building is the most common form of a process of collective identity formation with a view to legitimising public power within a given territory. This is an essentially indigenous process which often not only projects a meaningful future, but also draws on existing traditions, institutions and customs, and redefines them as national characteristics in order to support a nation's claim to sovereignty and uniqueness. A successful nation-building process produces a cultural projection of the nation containing a certain set of assumptions, values and beliefs that can function as the legitimising foundation of a state structure (Utz 2005). Furthermore, Attafuah (2009) looks at nation-building in two ways. First, he refers to nation-building's broad efforts to promote political and economic reforms with the objective of transforming a society emerging from conflict into one at peace with itself and its neighbours. In this broad sense, it entails the simultaneous use of strategies of mass reorientation, including propaganda and major infrastructural developments, to foster social harmony and economic growth. Second, he takes nation-building as the process of constructing or structuring a national identity through the use of state power (Attafuah 2009). The aim here is to foster a shared and coherent national identity, orientation and unification among the people of a state in order to ensure its long-term political stability and viability. According to Attafuah, this second definition also emphasises the development of the social sector comprising education, health and family welfare, water supply, sanitation, housing, social welfare, nutrition, rural development and minimum basic services (Attafuah 2009).

Although Ghana and Zambia have made some progress in nation-building, like many SSA countries, they still face enormous challenges that need to be addressed. In Ghana, the existing strong ethno-cultural suspicions, such as those between the Asante and Ewe, constitute fundamental challenges to nation-building in the country. Ethnocentrism or ethnic prejudice, grounded in the belief that one's ethnic group is superior to another, is a serious impediment to nation-building and national development efforts in Ghana. In addition, conflicts between ethnic groups in the northern parts of the country and those in the south equally hinder nation-building and development efforts. The fact that the development of the resource-endowed south has been made possible by and with the critical supply of cheap labour from the resource-deprived north makes the problem more acute (Grebe 2015).

In Zambia, the Barotseland question remains unanswered, with successive Zambian governments choosing to criminalise this issue and refusing to treat it as a political and national question. Barotseland was amalgamated with Northern Rhodesia to form the new independent state of Zambia in 1964. The fusion of

Barotseland and Northern Rhodesia into a unitary Zambian state was facilitated by a treaty known as the Barotseland Agreement of 1964. This treaty contained certain pre-conditions, one of which was for Barotseland to exist in Zambia semi-autonomously, probably akin to Scotland's existence in the United Kingdom.

However, in 1969 the Barotseland Agreement was abrogated by the first president of Zambia, Kenneth Kaunda, and the governing party at the time, the United National Independence Party (UNIP). The Lozi, or people of Barotseland, have since then been complaining of marginalisation and discrimination. To date, they have been treated with suspicion by the rest of Zambia and labelled as 'separatists' or 'secessionists' (Flint 2003; Maundeni, Bwalya and Kwerepe 2015). Also, several individuals from Barotseland have been either incarcerated on 'sedition' or 'treason' charges and awaiting trial or are already serving jail terms related to the former 'crimes' (Noyoo 2016). Needless to say, the origins of these conflicts are traceable to the colonial and post-colonial political economy, the systems of resource mobilisation for economic production, and the unfair distribution of educational and development facilities and opportunities.

Unpacking Social Policy

According to Mkandawire (2004: 1), social policy is a collective intervention in the economy to influence access to and the incidence of adequate and secure livelihoods and income. In this regard, we agree with his assertion that social policy has always played redistributive, protection and transformative or developmental roles. Indeed, as he points out, in the context of development, there can be no doubt that the transformative role of social policy needs to receive greater attention than it is usually accorded in developed countries and much more than it does in the current 'safety nets' (Mkandawire 2004). We will augment this conceptualisation of social policy with that of Adesina (2007: 1–2), which states the following:

> For the purpose of our analysis, we define social policy as the collective public efforts at effecting and protecting the social well-being of the people within a given territory. Beyond immediate protection from social destitution, social policy might cover education and health-care provision, habitat, food security, sanitation, guarantee some measure of labour market protection, and so on. The idea of a tolerable, minimum level of livelihood and decency is intuitive and socially constructed; and normative (ideological) rather than technical.

In addition, social policy involves two aspects. First, it refers to the actual policies and programmes of governments that affect people's welfare. Second, it connotes an academic field of inquiry concerned with the description, explanation and evaluation of policies. Of the different ways of influencing human wellbeing through social policy, the direct method is the most common (Midgley, Tracy and Livermore 2000). The rationale for social policy formulation rests on an assumption of change and, in this respect, positive change. Social policy must then be perceived as a change agent. It also recognises the factor of deliberate planning, because the different instruments that support its operationalisation are usually deliberately thought out and then tested for efficacy. It is this notion that makes social policy both an intellectual and practical activity.

Nonetheless, social policy's mandate will be context-driven, with socio-economic, political and cultural forces (of a particular country) having a bearing on how it is conceptualised and then utilised. The process of formulating and implementing social policy goes a long way in translating the development objectives of a given society into actual well-being (Noyoo 2010). Crucially, this results in citizens accessing certain services and other life chances that enable them to build their capabilities.

Shedding Light on Social Protection

In this discussion, we argue that nation-building, social policy, social protection and welfare are closely interconnected. With that being said, Garcia and Gruat (2003) define social protection as having security in the face of vulnerabilities and contingencies, and that it is about having access to healthcare and working in safety. The main objective of social protection policy is to confront poverty and insulate the population from risks and shocks caused by unforeseen natural and socio-economic changes. In other words, social protection is an integral component of any strategic effort to reduce the incidence and severity of poverty. Social protection basically aims to improve the livelihoods of ordinary citizens irrespective of their status in society.

The International Labour Organisation (ILO) (2014) regards social protection as measures put in place to provide benefits, whether in cash or in kind, to secure protection, due to insufficient income caused by sickness, disability, maternity, employment injury, unemployment, old age or death of a family member; lack of access or unaffordable access to health care; insufficient family support, particularly for children and adult dependants; general poverty and social exclusion. Abebrese (2011) believes that social protection is the basis of a secure life that is of an acceptable standard. However, the World Bank (2001) suggests that social protection is not just about providing benefits, but also about creating opportunities for people to upgrade themselves. It therefore defines social protection as policies and programmes designed to reduce poverty and vulnerability by promoting an efficient labour market, diminishing people's exposure to risks, and enhancing their capacity to manage economic and social risks, such as unemployment, exclusion, sickness, disability and old age (World Bank, 2010). In this chapter, we take social protection as a facet of a comprehensive social policy.

Case Study 1: Ghana

Social Policy in the First Republic: 1954–1966

The development of social policy and formal social security systems was very limited during colonial rule in Ghana. The colonial policy focused on agricultural development, leaving social support to kin and community (Grebe 2015). After independence, these forms of social protection were principally championed by churches and missionaries and supported by secular welfare organisations, including international Non-Governmental Organisations (NGOs) that delivered foreign aid from the 1960s onwards (Tomlinson 2013). Tomlinson (2013) also observes that 'peasant export' economies like Ghana developed more pro-poor institutions than did settler economies under colonialism, and that these institutions affected the evolution of policy and welfare state-building after independence.

On 6 March 1957, Ghana became the first country in SSA to attain political independence from Britain. At the time, a substantial proportion of Ghana's population relied on subsistence agriculture. From 1954 to 1966, Kwame Nkrumah, the founding president of Ghana, governed the country with the Convention People's Party (CPP). Nkrumah's personality was very instrumental in influencing the socio-economic development trajectory that Ghana took after independence. At the outset:

> Nkrumah inherited a fragmented country besieged by an insidious colonial legacy, such as Eurocentric economic, judicial and educational systems, law enforcement and military institutions, civil service administrative superstructure, infectious diseases and uneven socio-economic development. Other aspects of the colonial legacy included illiteracy, ignorance, superstitious and undemocratic and violent behaviour of the embittered parochial and ethnic based political parties. All these were more difficult to combat than the anti-colonial struggle (Botwe-Asamoah 2005, pp. x–xi).

At that time, Ghana, like other states of Asia and Africa at their dates of independence, faced a similar economic and political situation as foreign private enterprises dominated many of the monetised sectors of their national economies and, in so doing, controlled the utilisation of significant portions of the countries' natural, physical-capital, human and financial resources. Over 90 per cent of the country's import trade was in the hands of foreign firms; two British banks shared about 90 per cent of all banking business; expatriate companies held 96 per cent of total timber concessions; foreign investors owned all functioning gold mines and controlled about half of the annual diamond production; general insurance was entirely in the hands of expatriate firms; and foreign companies earned the bulk of total receipts in the small manufacturing sector (Esseks 1971: 59).

After independence, Ghana transited from an informal social protection system to a formal one. The immediate attention of the first post-independent government of Ghana focused on redressing the socio-economic disparities in the country and designing social welfare policies to improve the living conditions of the population. The colonial informal system of social protection in Ghana gradually gave way to formal systems, which largely became the responsibility of the government. It expanded coverage of social insurance much more than in most SSA countries and was one of the only African countries to introduce— at least nationally— unemployment benefits. We argue in this chapter that social policy was implied in the government's economic development agenda during this period. Aryeetey and Goldstein (2000: 13) observe that:

> Although the government focused its attention primarily on economic development and did not articulate a clear set of social policy objectives, public interventions and expenditure patterns nevertheless suggested some social orientation during this period. There was a sustained upward trend in the social sector's share of government spending in Ghana between 1960 and 1965.

Therefore, massive developmental projects of national priority were implemented during this period. The government had inherited huge reserves of funds from the colonial administration, much of which were accrued from cocoa exports. Nkrumah embarked on mass industrialisation in the country as part of the state-directed economic growth strategy of the country.

In 1963, the government introduced a seven-year development plan, the first economic plan of post-independent Ghana. The plan was comprehensive and considered the needs and resources of the country. It focused on agricultural modernisation as the backbone of industrial expansion, which was expected to lead the country towards a self-sustaining economic status. The major objectives of the government were to achieve sustainable economic growth and improvements in the living standards of the urban and rural populations.

The government promoted the establishment of key industries for producing goods that had previously been imported (import substitution) during the colonial era. This strategy was instituted within a broader framework of central planning aimed at using the collective resources of the state in the best interest of all the people. According to Killick (2009), this system was operated in a dualistic manner, with traditional labour-intensive production techniques co-existing with modern capital-intensive techniques in almost all sectors of the economy. The government boosted output level in the country by providing opportunities for employment, but at a high level of productivity. These strategies led to high, national per-capita income accompanied by a low level of national debt.

The seven-year development plan also envisaged the massive development of services and amenities, such as social services, transport, communication, electricity and water supply, on a unique scale. The provision of education and training of the country's human capital was another nation-building priority. Free education for primary and middle schools was introduced in 1961 to ensure that children of school-going age were enrolled in school and received basic education. Additionally, the Pan-African Education Programme of Free Education under Nkrumah's government provided free education from elementary to university levels. This led to large-scale school enrolment during the first decade of independence in Ghana, especially in the northern part of the country. As part of the programme, the government offered scholarships to children whose parents were engaged in cocoa production in the country.

Several secondary schools, training colleges and universities were established and numerous educational programmes were introduced during the first decade of Ghana's independence. In addition, the Ghana Education Trust (GET) pioneered the establishment of many secondary schools and training colleges in the country. The GET also sought to equip schools with qualified teachers, which culminated in the establishment of sixteen teacher training colleges under the GET. In 1961 the then University College of the Gold Coast was renamed the University of Ghana. The following year saw the establishment of the Cape Coast University, which was mandated to further train teachers who would run training colleges, technical and vocational institutes and secondary schools, among others. Middle schools also benefited from the scholarship programme, in addition to the free distribution of exercise books which began in 1963.

A major development in the social protection arena was the creation of a range of provident funds from the 1960s onwards. The Social Security Act of 1965 was implemented to provide older citizens in the country with a Provident Fund Scheme with a lump sum as a benefit package for the elderly, invalids and survivors (of accidents). Under this Act, there was a compulsory deduction from workers' wages and salaries, which was paid into the Trust as a source of income security for the workers in old age, disability, incapacity, survivorship and unemployment or child-rearing. The Act mandated employers to pay 15 per cent of their workers' salaries to the Trust, whereas the workers paid 7.5 per cent from 1965 to July 1966. The rate changed on 1 August 1966, when workers and employers were required to pay 5 per cent and 12.5 per cent respectively. This amendment was not popular among both workers and employers, and they requested a reduction. Despite this, the Trust served as a source of income for retired workers and their families in times of death or illness. It also helped employers to reduce labour turnover and served the purpose of a reward package that honoured older employees.

Nkrumah was also an ardent champion of Pan-Africanism. His vision relating to Africa's emancipation from colonial domination was clear. In his speech on Independence Day, he asserted: 'Our independence is meaningless unless it is linked up with the total liberation of Africa.' This meant that the social investment made by the Ghanaian government was also extended to the liberation struggles of countries that were still under colonial oppression. To this end, Ghana provided sanctuary and different forms of support to nationalist movements in many SSA countries.

Despite investments in the economic and social infrastructures, the country began experiencing economic difficulties by the mid-1960s (Monga and Lin 2008). The Gross National Product (GNP) per head declined, shortages of consumable products were common, inflation skyrocketed, living conditions deteriorated and the government's popularity waned. It was overthrown through a coup d'état.

Towards the end of his rule, Nkrumah had shown autocratic tendencies and other habits which were inimical to good governance and transparency. But this should not take away the good and solid work that was undertaken by Nkrumah and his government to raise the living standard of Ghanaians. Botwe-Asamoah (2005) reminds us that in spite of the hostile and violent environment in Ghana during the First Republic, the level of national unity, the rapid cultural and socio-economic transformation and industrial development achieved in the country within a very short span by Nkrumah's government is one of the most remarkable periods of post-independence social policy achievements and nation-building in African history. After Nkrumah, many governments followed and for the better part of its post-colonial history, Ghana was ruled by military dictators. Arguably, none of these governments returned to the social policy of the First Republic, which had helped to foster national unity and stimulated the creation of a new nation.

Case Study 2: Zambia

Social Policy in the First Republic: 1964–1972

As in other SSA countries, colonial social policy in Zambia was largely determined by its mission, which was residualist in approach. Colonial Zambia was premised on the racist ideology known as the Colour-bar system, which classified people according to race: people of mixed-race origin or 'Coloureds' were a notch lower than Europeans; Asians or Indians were below mixed-race people; and Africans were the last on this racial ladder of social stratification. Colonial Zambia's welfare system favoured Europeans over other races. Colonial social policy was driven by racial discrimination, social exclusion and elitism. Zambia's colonisation was facilitated by the discovery of rich mineral deposits. Thus, Europeans came to Zambia to exploit these minerals, especially copper, which is still Zambia's economic mainstay. The mining industry was key in creating a welfare state for the white settler population, to the exclusion of the local population. This was typified by a racialised formal labour market in which the white working class had won for themselves a fairly extensive set of welfare rights (Mkandawire 2004).

One of the two nationalist movements that had fought against colonial rule, the United National Independence Party (UNIP), emerged victorious after the polls of 1964. The party was voted into power overwhelmingly by the African majority due to its militancy and ideological stance. UNIP was very sensitive to the question of African liberation, black economic empowerment and the general advancement of Zambians (Noyoo 2010). These were its clarion calls during the fight for independence and it would remain committed to these ideals until it was voted out of power in 1991 (although these ideals had become more rhetorical by then). UNIP formed its first cabinet under Kenneth Kaunda as prime minister, who inherited a country of 3.5 million people, less than 0.5 per cent of whom had even full primary education (Tordoff and Molteno 1974). At independence, there were only 109 graduates, who had all been trained outside the country. Zambia itself had no university.

When Zambia gained independence it had a prosperous mining-based mono-economy. Its main export, copper, was in high demand and fetched huge profits from export sales. These were hitherto either externalised or invested in the welfare of the European settlers. Prior to independence, the wealth of the country was not in the hands of the indigenous people. By 1969, Zambia was classified a middle-income country, with one of the highest GDPs in Africa: three times that of Kenya, twice that of Egypt, and higher than Brazil, Malaysia, Turkey and South Korea (Fraser and Lungu 2006). The new government was focused on positive social and economic development and therefore introduced an ambitious and fast-paced programme of building economic and social development infrastructure. By raising the standard of living, attaining a more equitable redistribution of wealth, humanising social security (in particular free health services and expanded educational facilities), and promoting trade, industry and agriculture in the interests of the people (Tordoff and Molteno 1974: 14), the government attempted to erase the colonial legacy of racial discrimination and segregation, to maintain individual liberties and achieve African Democratic Socialism. To this end, it built hundreds of primary and secondary schools as well as teacher training, technical, agricultural and nursing colleges, and finally the University of Zambia in 1966. This was the first time that Zambia had its own university. In addition, the government signed technical agreements with countries that had constituted the former Eastern bloc to train young Zambians in mainly science and technical fields.

Planning was critical to the transformation of the new post-colonial Zambian society and was linked to Zambia's social policy. Hence, in 1964, the Emergency Development Plan (EDP) was launched, and in 1965 the Transitional Development Plan (TDP) was put into motion. Later, in 1966, the First National Development Plan (FNDP) replaced the former plans. These plans were also political blueprints which guided state actions in the country's social and economic domains. Nevertheless, these development initiatives were hamstrung. This is because the structure of the Zambian economy was tilted towards the production of primary commodities and dominated by copper, with unskilled and cheap labour supporting the production process. The country lacked technical know-how, and its geographic position and poor infrastructure made it unattractive to foreign investors (Mwanawina 1993).

Lack of patriotism in the civil service also incapacitated the state. The civil service, which was the implementer of the government's policies and programmes, clashed with the ideals of the governing party and the aspirations of the mass of the people relating to the notion of a 'better life for all'. This was because the majority of the civil servants were British expatriates who previously had been recruited by the colonial authorities to implement colonial policies and programmes. Civil servants were also drawn from a small settler population that had emigrated from Southern Rhodesia and South Africa. Thus, many civil servants did not identify themselves with the vision of the new government.

The government counteracted the expatriates' obstructionist stance by accelerating the indigenisation of the civil service, which was referred to as Zambianisation. This indigenisation was later extended to other sectors as well. Zambianisation also sought to distribute wealth more fairly, end exclusiveness and racial privilege, and open opportunities to Zambians, who had been denied all the elements of a good life—education, health, responsibility and a fair return for labour (Kaunda and Morris 1966). On 19 April 1968, the government announced the Mulungushi Reforms whereby it declared its intention to acquire an equity holding (of 51 per cent) in a number of key foreign-owned firms in the retail, transportation and manufacturing sectors. A year later, in 1969, the Matero Economic Reforms were announced. These resulted in the government purchasing a 51 per cent share of the mining companies. And so the nationalisation of the commanding heights of the economy was achieved.

Nationalisation was deemed necessary by the UNIP government and Kaunda because Zambia's economy had been almost totally owned by foreigners. Thereafter, foreign businesses were not keen to play key roles in the development of the country, and from this period onwards, the state dominated the economy. State-led industrial development was possible because it channelled the copper revenues towards industrial transformation and rural development. The government relied on both monetary and fiscal policies to promote growth in the manufacturing sector. The import substitution strategy was adopted and its main thrust was the introduction of various parastatals through which the local manufacturing sector was protected by high tariffs and an over-valued exchange rate, as the United Nations Development Programme (UNDP) (2003) argues.

It can be contended that social policy played a significant role in nation-building and social cohesion initiatives in the first decade of independence. As noted earlier, ethnic challenges abounded at the time, with various ethnic groups pursuing narrow ethnic agendas. But despite the abrogation of the Barotseland Agreement 1964 by the UNIP government and some Lozis seeking a separate state, there were equally many Lozi nationalists who had supported UNIP and Kaunda and who had played key roles in cementing the unitary character of Zambia. These individuals had occupied senior government positions in the first post-independence cabinet. This cabinet has actually proved to be the most ethnically diverse cabinet in the whole of Zambia's post-colonial history (Noyoo 2016). Therefore, many urban Lozis did not see the need for a separate state.

Another way social policy reinforced the national character was through public sector employment. Individuals were employed in the civil service and then deployed to various parts of Zambia. There was a deliberate government policy to send civil servants from different ethnic groups to those parts of Zambia from where they did not originate. Thus, nurses, police officers, teachers and other civil servants were sent to work in regions with ethnic groups different to their own. This policy worked so well that, after the first decade of independence, there were many interethnic marriages resulting in mixed offspring. To date, this legacy endures. In this regard, employment opportunities through the process of Zambianisation practically served the dual purposes of nation-building and social cohesion.

Furthermore, during this period, social policy was aimed at improving social services to promote social equity and narrow the gap between the rich and the poor. The guiding principle for social policy formulation and implementation was the ideology of Humanism (Masiye, Tembo, Chisanga and Mwanza 1998). Social policy was also extended to subsidies for food and transport (through newly created parastatals), and price controls on essential commodities and agricultural requirements, such as fertiliser, pesticides and seeds.

However, nationalisation and import substitution strategies proved very costly in the long run as Zambia failed to diversify the economy beyond copper mining. Import substitution industries were inefficient and uncompetitive—they had high input costs, high monopoly prices, heavy reliance on government subsidies and a lack of technological dynamism. In addition, Zambia's support for the liberation movements of Southern Africa and the closure of the border after the Unilateral Declaration of Independence (UDI) by Rhodesia seriously affected its development plans (Zimba 2003). Also, the world oil crisis of 1973 and subsequent recession led to plummeting copper prices and the downward spiral of the country's economy.

The mining sector experienced a steep decline following the first oil crisis, and the second one in 1979 cemented the country's precarious standing. Zambia

Consolidated Copper Mines (ZCCM), which had emerged from the nationalised mines, was the government's 'cash cow'. Yet years of neglect resulted in production falling from 750,000 tons a year to 250,000 tons a year. By the late 1980s, massive urgent capital investments were required to replace plant and machinery (Fraser and Lungu 2006). Furthermore, extensive state intervention had given rise to bureaucratisation, corruption and uncertainty which discouraged productive private investment and foreign trade initiatives (Zimba 2003). Ultimately, the weakness of the centralised welfare state, a one-sided industrialisation strategy based on copper mining with declining commodity prices, and the neglect of the agricultural sector and infrastructure such as transport, water, energy and health, transformed Zambia into one of the poorest countries in Africa by the late 1980s (UNDP 2003).

What is worth noting as well is that, in December 1972, Kenneth Kaunda declared Zambia a one-party state. Thereafter, all opposition parties were banned and Kaunda assumed more power. He presided over a bloated party structure and became more and more autocratic with each passing year. He ruled Zambia by decree and many policy decisions that were mostly wrong-headed were conjured up by him. The intelligence and other security wings were used to persecute, hound, intimidate and arrest Kaunda's opponents. Anyone who did not agree with Kaunda and UNIP was labelled an 'enemy of the state'. Kaunda relied on the State of Emergency, which was renewed annually, to detain his opponents without recourse to fair trial. Kaunda and UNIP mismanaged Zambia's economy and paved the way for the World Bank and International Monetary Fund (IMF) to compel Zambia to implement the Structural Adjustment Programme (SAP) because the UNIP government had borrowed heavily after it had mismanaged the economy. By the time Kaunda and UNIP were voted out power in 1991, social policy was no longer comprehensive and transformative but sought to create 'safety nets'. Unfortunately, the social policy of the First Republic was never revisited by successive governments. To this day, Zambia's social policy remains inchoate and untransformative.

Social Policy Lessons from Ghana's and Zambia's First Republics

Colonial rule in Ghana and Zambia did not provide effective social policies for developing their indigenous people, but sought only to use them as cheap labour in the mines, factories and on the farms. However, during the first decade of independence in Ghana, it may be argued that social policy during the Nkrumah era was embedded in economic policy that sought broader welfare outcomes. The economic policy of Ghana in the first decade of independence reflected implicit socio-economic priorities, such as reducing the politically unacceptable levels of unemployment and producing the human skills required for development (Mkandawire 2006a). Economic growth was regarded as a springboard for national social development in Ghana. In the case of Zambia, we can say that most elements of social policy were explicit and expressed in direct government provision of social welfare through broad-based education and health services, subsidies and benefits, social security and pensions, labour market interventions, land reform, progressive taxation and other redistributive policies (Mkandawire 2006a: 1).

However, what is clear in both cases was that central planning and ideologies had played significant roles in determining the pace of national development. In both countries, the state was central in driving social policy objectives. Social policy was not left to the vagaries of the market as in the latter period of the era of Jerry Rawlings in Ghana and Frederick Chiluba in Zambia, when there was a strong push for the implementation of the Structural Adjustment Programme (SAP) of the World Bank and the International Monetary Fund (IMF). What is significant in both cases is that in the first decade of independence, social policy and other policy instruments were used to create new societies altogether.

Furthermore, it can be argued that the social policies of Ghana and Zambia during the first decade of independence were transformative and focused on tackling the structural inequality and inequities that had been engendered by colonial rule. A strong thrust for universal education and healthcare was evident in both countries, as was human resource development. But after the first decade of independence, social policy in both countries was not able to regain its nation-building role. We concur with Kpessa, Béland and Lecours (2011: 2117) who observe: 'Sub-Saharan nationalists used social policy as a transformative tool for the purposes of mobilisation and solidarity-building as well as national identity formation and nation-building in a manner consistent with the overall objectives of socio-economic and political development.' As Aina (2004) asserts, social policy was expressed through the building of social infrastructure. By building schools, clinics, hospitals, roads and universities, and sinking boreholes for clean water, and enabling all citizens (irrespective of ethnic background and socio-economic class) to access such life chances, governments in both countries made it easier for many individuals to 'buy into' the national identity. People felt validated and included in the nation. Social cohesion was also fostered through the immunisation of children under the age of five against communicable diseases. Mothers from low-income classes and different ethnic groups would be found at health centres and clinics where they would mingle with people they rarely interacted with in their communities. This was the same with schools, in which children from different ethnic groups were enrolled and provided with quality education.

We contend that the recent surge in social protection endeavours across Africa should not be touted as the best approach to raising the quality of life of people but should be seen as only one facet of a comprehensive and transformative social policy. For example, cash transfer schemes should not be seen as a panacea to poverty and social exclusion in Africa. It may be argued that if the current social policy agendas in most SSA countries had been implemented during the first decade of independence, the progress that was achieved then would not have been possible. One key reason for this observation is that, unlike the transformative social policy at independence that built people's capabilities and created clear pathways out of poverty, ignorance and disease for citizens, there is no guarantee that cash transfers will effectively do this, mainly because they are merely ameliorative. In contrast, the social policies of the First Republics of Ghana and Zambia discussed in this chapter were fundamentally long-term and futuristic in content and outlook.

Concluding Remarks and Way Forward

We concur with Adesina (2010) that there is an urgent need for a transformative social policy approach in Ghana and Zambia considering the high levels of poverty and inequality in the two countries. Such an agenda could embrace the multiple roles of redistribution, protection, reproduction, social cohesion and nation-building. Economic development that is supported by this type of social policy would combine growth with structural transformation of the economies and social relations in the two countries, buttressed by the norms of equity, equality and social solidarity. Moving forward, social policy in Ghana and Zambia should deal with four major concerns: distribution, protection, production and reproduction. It should be concerned with the redistributive effects of economic policy, protecting people from the vagaries of the market and the changing circumstances of age; enhancing the productive potential of members of society; and reconciling the burden of reproduction with that of other social tasks, as well as sharing the burden of reproduction (Mkandawire 2006b).

Taking into account the aforementioned, we argue that social policy in Ghana and Zambia needs to return to its historic mission of nation-building. Indeed, nation-building seriously requires the creation of a universal national identity and a sense of common destiny for the people in all parts of the two countries. This is essentially an enterprise of persuading, manipulating, moulding, cementing and bonding diverse peoples into a nation with a common emotional relationship to the state and modernising and improving their material and socio-economic circumstances, as Attafuah (2009) eloquently argues. This form of nation-building thus requires the subordination of all competing ethno-cultural, primordial loyalties to an emergent nationhood and supra ethnic identity (Grebe 2015). As Attafuah (2009: 1) argues, 'nation-building is not an event but a process; it is not a revolution, but it is no fancy needle-work either'. According to Gambari (2009), nation-building involves the following aspects: it is about building a political entity which corresponds to a given territory, based on some generally accepted rules, norms and principles, and a common citizenship; it is also about building institutions that symbolise the political entity, institutions such as a bureaucracy, an economy, the judiciary, universities, a civil service and civil society organisations; it is about building a common sense of purpose, a sense of shared destiny, and a collective imagination of belonging. In other words, nation-building is about building the tangible and intangible threads that hold a political entity together and gives it a sense of purpose. In conclusion, all-inclusive social policies certainly have a central role to play in promoting effective nation-building processes in Ghana and Zambia and, generally speaking, in most SSA countries.

References

Abebrese, J., 2011, *Social Protection in Ghana: An Overview of Existing Programmes and Their Prospects and Challenges*. Available online at http://library.fes.de/pdf-files/bueros/ghana/10497.pdf.

Adesina, J. O., 2007, In search of Inclusive Development: Introduction, in Adesina, J., ed., *Social Policy in Sub-Saharan African Context: In Search of Inclusive Development*, Basingstoke: Palgrave Macmillan, pp. 1–53.

Adesina, J., 2010, Rethinking the Social Protection Paradigm: Social Policy in Africa's Development, Paper prepared for the conference Promoting Resilience through Social Protection in Sub-Saharan Africa, European Report on Development, Dakar, Senegal, 28–30 June 2010. Available online at http://erd.eui.eu/media/BackgroundPapers/Adesina.pdf.

Aina, A., 2004, Introduction, in Aina, A., Chachage, C. S. L. and Annan-Yao, E., eds, *Globalisation and Social Policy in Africa*, Dakar: CODESRIA, pp. 1–20.

Aryeetey, E. and Goldstein, M, 2000, Ghana: Social Policy Reform in Africa, in Morales-Gomez, D. A., Tschirgi, N. and Moher J. L., eds, *Reforming Social Policy: Changing Perspectives on Sustainable Human Development*, Ottawa: International Development Research Centre (IDRC), pp. 9– 44.

Attafuah, K. A., 2009, *Ethnic Diversity, Democratisation and Nation-Building in Ghana*. Available online at https://thefutureofafrica.wordpress.com/2009/10/16/ethnic-diversity-democratisation-and-nation-building-in-ghana/.

Botwe-Asamoah, K., 2005, *Kwame Nkrumah's Politico-cultural Thought and Policies: An African-Centred Paradigm for the Second Phase of the African Revolution*, New York: Routledge.

Esseks, J. D., 1971, Political Independence and Economic Decolonisation: The Case of Ghana under Nkrumah, *The Western Quarterly*, Vol. 24, No. 1, pp. 59–64.

Flint, L. S., 2003, State-Building in Central Southern Africa: Citizenship and Subjectivity in Barotseland and Caprivi, *The International Journal of African Historical Studies*, Vol. 36, No. 2, pp. 393–428.

Frazer, A. and Lungu, J., 2006, *For Whom the Windfalls? Winners & Losers in the Privatisation of Zambia's Copper Mines*. Available online at https://www.banktrack.org/download/for_whom_the_windfalls_/report_for_whom_the_wind_falls.pdf

Gambari, I. A., 2009, *The Challenges of Nations Building: The Case of Nigeria*, Address at the First Year Anniversary Lecture, Mustapha Akanbi Foundation, Abuja 7 February 2008. Available online at http://www.mafng.org/anniversary/challenges_nation_building_nigeria.htm.

Garcia, A. and Gruat, J. V., 2003, *Social Protection: A Life Cycle Continuous Investment*, Geneva: International Labour Organization (ILO).

Grebe, E., 2015, The Evolution of Social Protection Policy in Ghana's 'Fourth Republic': Contributory Social Insurance Reform and Limited Social Assistance for the 'Extreme Poor' Under NPP and NDC Governments, 2000–2014, CSSR Working Paper No. 63, Cape Town: Centre for Social Science Research (CSSR).

Ibhawoh, B., 2020, Seeking the Political Kingdom: Universal Human Rights and the Anti-colonial Movement in Africa, in Moses A. D., Duranti, M. and Burke, R., eds, *Decolonization, Self-Determination, and the Rise of Global Human Rights Politics*, Cambridge: Cambridge University Press, pp. 35-53. DOI: 10.1017/9781108783170.003.

Kaunda, K. D. and Morris, C. M., 1966, *A Humanist in Africa*, London: Longman Greens.

Killick, T., 2009, *Development Economics in Action: A Study of Economic Policies in Ghana* (2nd ed), New York: Routledge.

Kpessa, M., Béland, D. and Lecours, A., 2011, Nationalism, Development, and Social Policy: The Politics of Nation-Building in Sub-Saharan Africa, *Ethnic and Racial Studies*, Vol. 3, No. 12, pp. 2115–2133.

International Labour Organization (ILO), 2014, World Social Protection Report 2014/2015: Building Economic Recovery, Inclusive Development and Social Justice, Geneva: ILO.

Masiye, G. P. C., Tembo, R., Chisanga, B. and Mwanza, A., 1998, Social Policy and Research Environment in Zambia, *Journal of Social Development in Africa*, Vol. 13, No. 2, pp. 34–43.

Maundeni, Z., Bwalya, E. and Kwerepe, P., 2015, The Rise of Barotse Separatist Nationalism in Zambia: Can Its Associated Violence Be Prevented? *Journal of Politics and Law*, Vol. 8, No. 4, pp. 263–276.

Midgley, J., Tracy, M. B. and Livermore, M., 2000, Introduction, in Midgley, J., Tracy M. B. and Livermore M., eds, *The Handbook of Social Policy*, Thousand Oaks, CA: SAGE Publications, pp. 3–10.

Mkandawire, T., 2001, Thinking About Developmental States in Africa, *Cambridge Journal of Economics*, Vol. 25, No. 3, pp. 289–313.

Mkandawire, T., 2004, Social Policy in a Development Context: Introduction, in Mkandawire, T., ed., *Social Policy in a Development Context*, Basingstoke: UNRISD/Palgrave Macmillan, pp. 1–36.

Mkandawire, T., 2006a, *Targeting and Universalism in Poverty Reduction*, Social Policy and Development, Paper No. 23, Geneva: UNRISD.

Mkandawire, T., 2006b, Transformative Social Policy: Lessons from UNRISD Research, Policy Brief No. 5, Geneva: UNRISD.

Monga, C. and Lin, J. Y., 2015, *The Oxford Handbook of Africa and Economics, Volume II, Policies and Practices*, Oxford: Oxford University Press.

Mwanawina, I., 1993, Zambia, in Adepoju A., ed., *The Impact of Structural Adjustment on the Population of Africa*, London: James Currey Limited, pp. 69–77.

Noyoo, N., 2010, *Social Policy and Human Development in Zambia*, London: Adonis & Abbey.

Noyoo, N., 2016, *Barotseland's Amalgamation with Zambia: A Political Conundrum*, Pretoria: Kwarts.

Tomlinson, B., 2013, *Working with Civil Society in Foreign Aid Possibilities for South–South Co-operation?*, Beijing: UNDP.

Tordoff, W. and Molteno, R., 1974, Introduction, in Tordoff, W., ed, *Politics in Zambia*, Manchester: Manchester University Press, pp. 1–39.

Utz, R., 2005, State-Building, Nation-Building, and Constitutional Politics in Post-Conflict Situations: Conceptual Clarifications and an Appraisal of Different Approaches, *Max Planck Yearbook of United Nations Law*, Vol. 9, No. 1, pp. 579–613. Available online at http://www.mpil.de/files/pdf2/mpunyb_bogdandyua_9_579_613.pdf.

United Nations Development Programme (UNDP), 2003, *Zambia Human Development Report*, Lusaka: UNDP.

World Bank, 2010, *Ghana—Improving the Targeting of Social Programs*, a World Bank Study, edited by Wodon, Q. Available online at http://documents.worldbank.org/curated/en/684851468201829917/Ghana-Improving-the-targeting-of-social-programs.

Zimba, B., 2003, Development Policy and Economic Change in Zambia: A Re-Assessment, *DPMN Bulletin*, Vol. 10, No. 2, pp. 1–4.

5

Gender, Poverty and Land in Africa: A Transformative Social Policy Perspective

Newman Tekwa

Introduction

The dream of industrialisation and growth of the service sector in most African countries faded away with economic liberalisation (Tsikata 2009: 18). The outbreak of the COVID-19 pandemic further exacerbated the compromised position of the African manufacturing and service sectors to absorb the massive number of new job-seekers entering the labour market annually. The African Development Bank (AfDB) estimated that the African Gross Domestic Product (GDP) would contract by between 1.7 per cent and 3.4 per cent in 2020 due to the economic impact of COVID-19 on African economies (AfDB 2020: 34). Consequently, they predicted, between 24.7 and 30 million jobs would be lost, severely affecting groups most vulnerable to structural problems within the labour market, such as women and the youth (AfDB 2020: 34).

It is within this present context that the continent's agrarian sector remains critical for socio-economic progress post-COVID-19. With the right mix of investment policies, African rural areas—long seen as poverty traps—are poised to emerge as lands of economic opportunity for growth, job creation and welfare (FAO 2017: 86). With this new focus on rural areas and their potential for economic growth pegged to food production and related sectors, it is envisaged that millions of people in developing countries who are about to enter the labour force in the coming decades need not flee rural areas but stay and thrive in the countryside (FAO 2017: 94). By relocating to the cities, they are likely to join the ranks of the urban poor instead of finding pathways out of poverty.

Transforming these once- and often-ignored economies and setting up supportive public policies and investment to create employment in the countryside represents today's strategic intervention (Marock and Grawitzky 2014: 57). As such, land and agrarian reforms, as engines for transformative and equitable growth, remain relevant to the development agenda of many developing countries geared to generate new farm and off-farm economic opportunities and related input supply and agriculture-related services (Jayne, Yeboah and Henry 2017: 21; UNCTAD 2018: 22).

Within all these policy efforts, a gender perspective reveals that the dominant view in much of the gender, poverty and land literature in Africa, as elsewhere, is that unequal land rights are a key factor in eradicating gendered inequalities and women's poverty (Wanyeki 2003; Butegwa 1991). Land-tenure studies have demonstrated how inequalities between women and men in ownership, control and access to land have resulted in gendered livelihood outcomes (Davison 1988; Butegwa 1991; Wanyeki 2003; Whitehead and Tsikata 2003). Bina Agarwal, for example, has been extremely successful in arguing for the need of effective and independent rights in land for women to improve welfare, equity and empowerment (1994: 1460–1464).

Also highlighted in this literature are gendered inequalities in other factors of production, such as capital, credit, technologies and labour, as economists have tried to make sense of women's lower productivity compared to that of men while farming on the same-sized plots with the same crop (Tsikata 2009: 20). While it is true that access to land remains a struggle for women, this literature mimics neoliberal discourses of individual tenure and misses the gendered processes of poverty and inequality relating to asymmetries in the extent to which men and women allocate the labour at their disposal between earning a living and caring for the family (Kabeer 2015: 194; Sen 1984, cited in Gasper and Van Staveren 2003: 2). Feminist research has long brought attention to the restrictive burden of care that is a function of poverty status, location (rural/urban) and household status in relation to land (Tsikata 2009: 24). While care work is critical for sustaining consumption for poor women, it limits their 'freedoms' of engaging not only in economic activities but also politics, social exchanges and leisure (Sen 2008; Gasper and Van Staveren 2003).

Within the context of gendered political demands for land and agrarian reforms, much emphasis is being placed on women's rights to land through land-tenure reforms with less attention paid to the gender inequalities that underlie women's invisible work. Without state intervention to assist in balancing the burden of unpaid reproductive work in the home and productive work in the fields, women obtain access to land which they cannot productively work without negative implications on their social, physical and emotional wellbeing. Empirical evidence emerging from our research at the South African Research Chair in Social Policy indicates that the same land reforms that comparatively increased women's access to land in Zimbabwe inadvertently increased women's social reproductive burden.

After giving a literature overview, the rest of the paper is structured as follows. A conceptualisation of labour power from a social reproductive perspective is discussed, followed by the conceptual framework that informed the research, Transformative Social Policy. The methods of data collection and analysis are described, followed by an analysis of the statistics from the study. Finally, conclusions and recommendations from the results are presented.

Literature Overview

Several recent contributions within a rapidly growing literature on gender, poverty and land in Africa south of the Sahara have emphasised the importance of examining gender in land-tenure systems (Chigbu 2019; Njieassam 2019; Whitehead and Tsikata 2003; Davison 1988; Yngstrom 2002; Gray and Kevane 1999) and livelihoods (Whitehead and Kabeer 2001; Mutopo 2011; Jacobs 2004; Adams, Sibanda and Turner 1999; Verma 2007). Tsikata (2009) highlighted the importance of linking gender, land and labour relations in an attempt to understand livelihood outcomes for women in sub-Saharan Africa (SSA). A particularly innovative recent development, Transformative Social Policy (UNRISD 2006; Adesina 2009; Mkandawire 2004; Yi 2015; Hujo 2014), attempts to bridge the analytical gaps generated by the failure of both labour and land-tenure studies in integrating reproductive work in their analyses, not only from a gender and livelihoods perspective but also in terms of socio-economic outcomes like poverty, inequality and the welfare of women in relation to men. While research on the burden of care and its implications for women's livelihoods is increasingly becoming topical, insufficient research has analysed it in relation to land and agrarian reforms from a social-policy perspective.

Social Reproductive Theory

Marx's analysis of capitalism identified 'labour power' or the 'capacity to labour' as the special commodity that capitalists need to set their system in motion and that 'labour power' has the peculiar property of being a source of value (Bhattacharya 2013: 1). It is through the use of labour power that one can create commodities and value in a capitalist system (Bhattacharya 2013: 1). This transformative but incomplete insight by Marx has been seized by late Marxist feminists, such as Lise Vogel, Martha Gimenez, Johanna Brenner and, more recently, Susan Ferguson and David McNally, who have developed it further, questioning how labour power, critical to the capitalist economy, is produced as workers do not spring from the ground to arrive at the marketplace, fresh and ready to sell their labour to capitalists (McNally and Ferguson 2015: 2). They have challenged the rationale choice theories and assumptions underpinning certain strands of mainstream economics that viewed labour power as 'natural'—simply presumed to be present, a given factor of capitalist production, a product of natural, biologically determined, regenerative process (McNally and Ferguson 2015; Himmelweit 2002; Budlender 2002; Razavi 2007). They argued that labour power is produced and reproduced outside capitalist production, in a kinship-based site called family, arguing for labour as a 'produced' input of the capitalist economic system of production (Grown, Elson and Cagatay 2000; Bhattacharya 2013: 2).

Social reproduction theory shows that the 'production of goods and services and the production of life are part of one integrated process thus providing analytical linkages between the 'two spheres' of a single system (Bhattacharya 2013: 7; McNally and Ferguson 2015: 3). This necessitates conceptualising capitalism as an integrated system or capitalist totality, in which the production of goods and services is scaffolded by social reproduction, helping to understand the significance of political struggles in either sphere and the need for uniting them (Bhattacharya 2013: 7; McNally and Ferguson 2015: 3). It is the socialisation of labour power that reveals how its reproduction is made possible through a set of gendered and sexualised social relations in the so-called private sphere (UNRISD 2010; Razavi 2011; Folbre 2012). The theoretical importance of the social reproduction approach lies in its ability to explicate the interconnections of the work we do to reproduce ourselves on the one hand, and waged work on the other, thus presenting a completely differentiated yet nonetheless unified understanding of social reality (McNally and Ferguson 2015: 4). The authors continued to argue that social reproduction demystifies labour power, posing questions about the conditions of its production and reproduction and theorising the concrete sites of that reproduction and associated social relations (McNally and Ferguson 2015: 2–3). This requires an analysis of the influence of gender ideology in social reproduction.

Gender Ideology and Social Reproduction

Gender relations are defined as sets of social norms, values, rules and conventions that informally or formally regulate practical daily relationships between women and men (Akram-Lodhi 2009: 79). One aspect of gender relations transcends common gender-based cultural differences to assess the systemic and structured asymmetries of social power between women and men (Acker 1992). As argued by Collins (1998), ignoring gender as a signifier of power relationships is a failure to understand the 'how' and 'why' of structures of inequality and exploitation (Collins 1998: 150). Reinforcing the same argument, Ridgeway (2009) states that although difference need not imply inequality, the socially constructed systemic and structural asymmetries based on dominant gender ideologies tend to emphasise those aspects of life that differ between women and men, in a way conflating the 'biological' and the 'social' to arrive at a 'natural' gendered allocation of tasks (Ridgeway 2009: 149). The material impact of gender ideology, as a belief system that privileges men over women, lies in its division of labour within the household, where women usually have a distinct role in performing the caring, maintenance and service activities that comprise household production (Sen 1984, cited in Gasper and Van Staveren 2003: 2). At the very minimum, these activities often consist of the biologically necessary tasks of food preparation, child and familial care, sanitation and family reproduction (Akram-Lodhi 2009: 79). This allocation consequently affects the division of labour between paid work in a commodity-producing economy and the caring labour engaged in household production, segmenting the labour market based on gender as we know it (Akram-Lodhi 2009: 79–80).

Women, 'Reproductive Labour Tax' and Poverty

The constraint on women's labour emanating from the gendered division of household tasks is reflected in the gendered output gap between potential and actual production (Tsikata 2009: 20). Ingrid Palmer (1995) has termed this the 'reproductive labour tax'—the constraint on women's agency that is imposed by care and household maintenance activities (Palmer 1995: 81). Such critical insights have illuminated the gendered processes of poverty relating to the asymmetries in the extent to which women and men are able to delegate their own labour or enjoy command of the labour of others (Kabeer 2015: 194).

While households must allocate the labour at their disposal between earning a living and caring for the family, in much of the world women bear a disproportionate share of the unpaid work of caring for the family (Kabeer 2015:194; Sen 1984 cited in Gasper and Van Staveren 2003: 2). This 'reproductive labour tax', from which men are largely exempt, leaves women with less time to earn an income, making them economically dependent to a greater or lesser extent on male earning—the male-breadwinner model (Lewis 1992; Sen 1984, cited in Gasper and Van Staveren 2003: 2). As such, gender asymmetries are evident in the ability to translate labour efforts into income in the marketplace. In areas of strict exclusion, women do either unpaid family labour or home-based forms of economic activity in which they relinquish control over production processes and the proceeds of their labour to male household members (Kabeer 2015: 194). The 'reproductive labour tax' may be further exacerbated by social institutions that oblige women to provide labour on their husband's farms before they can labour on their own, curtailing the returns they enjoy form their efforts, as is prevalent in most African rural societies (Apusigah 2009: 56).

Social reproduction theory positions women at the intersection between production and reproduction, between making a living and caring for the family (Folbre 1994). To explore this gendered process and how gendered poverty is reproduced and perpetuated, including the feminisation of poverty, we need to look at where working women and men are in the global workforce and at the nature of today's global economy, studying the totality of women's work (Chen, Vanek, Lund, Heintz, Jhabvala and Bonner 2005: 21).

Feminist economic analysis reveals that women's participation in the labour market is contingent on other demands on their time, especially unpaid work in the household and communities. Understanding the relationship between women's work and poverty therefore requires a comprehensive view of formal and informal paid work, subsistence productions, unpaid work in family enterprises and unpaid work for household members. Studies of only one aspect of women's work rather than its entirety fail to take cognisance of the ways in which women's unpaid care work in the household and community constrains their ability to access or continue in paid employment, illuminating the hidden costs of shifting the provision of care to households (Chen et al. 2005: 23).

There is much to be learnt from the Nordic countries on how they have simultaneously and successfully managed to attain low levels of inequality and gendered poverty. Particular reference can be made to Sweden, whose social policies, in the rubric of reconciling work and family, have included investment in social-service infrastructure, such as publicly funded child and elderly care (UNRISD 2006: 1). Such gender-aware initiatives released many Swedish women into the labour market, thus producing a vastly different gender profile (Adesina 2011: 466).

This paper explores the extent to which feminist theoretical insights into welfare-state regimes can provide valuable lessons for social policy in development contexts. As Mkandawire (2004) observed, so few of these insights have found their way into the field of social policy in development contexts (Mkandawire 2004: 3). Yet the history and current use of social policy can be useful in the study of social policy in developing countries, including explicating relationships between gender, poverty and inequality (Mkandawire 2004: 3). This takes us to a review of the Transformative Social Policy, the conceptual framework that informs this paper.

Conceptual Framework: Transformative Social Policy

The Transformative Social Policy (TSP) approach defines social policy as 'collective public efforts aimed at affecting and protecting the wellbeing of people in a given territory' (Adesina 2009: 38), or collective interventions in the economy to influence access to and the incidence of adequate and secure livelihood and income (Mkandawire 2004: 1). Transformative Social Policy emanates from the UNRISD flagship research report, Social Policy in a Development Context. Apart from highlighting the multiple productive, redistributive, social protection and social cohesion/nation-building functions of social policy, the report emphasises the social reproductive aspect of TSP and its potential to affect and transform gendered forms of inequality and social discrimination (Adesina 2009; Mkandawire 2004; Yi 2015; Hujo 2014). Transformative social policies are the instruments that can reconcile the burden of family and household care with other social tasks (Prasad, Hypher and Gerecke 2013; Adesina 2011: 455; Mkandawire 2011). Specific measures include investment in social infrastructure and basic services, such as public care centres for children and the elderly, education, health, drinking water, sanitation and energy provision, with the specific goal of reducing the workload of women (UNRISD 2010).

Conceptualising Social Reproduction (SR)

While social reproduction has been broadly defined, in this paper it is conceptualised as the daily reproduction of households in the acquisition and provision of basic needs, such as food, shelter, clothing, health and education, among others (Naidu and Ossome 2016: 52). Included in this conceptualisation are biological reproduction, everyday survival, the accumulation of education and skills to participate in the capitalist economy, and inculcating the necessary value systems referred to as 'labour power' (Bhattacharya 2013; Ferguson and McNally 2015) or human capacity (Braunstein 2015). Hence, social reproduction functions to produce and reproduce the working classes (Bhattacharya 2013; McNally and Ferguson 2015).

As labour power is a reproduced means of production (Mkandawire 2004: 17; Bhattacharya 2013: 1; Braunstein 2015: 3) within contemporary capitalist economies, social reproduction hinges on three institutions, viz households/families/communities, markets and the state (Naidu and Ossome 2016: 50; Braunstein 2015: 1; Orloff 1993: 312; O'Connor 2013). Women's involvement in the regeneration, maintenance and reproduction of a current and future class of workers, particularly their capacity to bear children, has resulted in a disproportionate burden of social reproduction falling on their shoulders (Bhattacharya 2013: 1; Braunstein 2015: 3).

In operationalising social reproduction, the paper adopts a feminist Marxist notion of social reproduction in which the labour force is reproduced both in the long run, in terms of preparing the next generation to enter the labour force, as well as in the short run, in the daily care activities given to workers to enable them to resume their productive work (Folbre 1994). This conceptualisation encompasses all direct and indirect care services that support unpaid (care) work in the home or community. Unpaid 'care' work includes caring for children, the elderly and the sick (Fälth and Blackden 2010). It also includes washing, cooking, shopping, cleaning and helping other families with their chores (Fälth and Blackden 2010). Unpaid work includes the collection of food, fuel and water and other sources of energy, informal unpaid work and family labour in agriculture (Fälth and Blackden 2010). Though not intended to be exhaustive of all aspects of unpaid care work and unpaid work, this summary highlights some important aspects and quick entry points for the analysis.

Figure 5.1 represents the social reproduction function, in which the household, a key location for social reproduction in Razavi's (2007) care diamond, is the entry point into a system to which the state, market and communities may contribute in the daily maintenance of the labour force and longer-term investment in terms of time and money (Braunstein 2015: 9). As illustrated in the diagram, there are three inputs into the social reproduction (time, commodities and infrastructure), which all combine to produce human capacity and welfare. Time refers to the quantitative measurement of non-market hours spent or devoted to unpaid work in the home (UNRISD 2012). Particularly important from a gender perspective is the distribution of this time between men, women, the state and the market. Commodities are defined as the goods and services that pass through the market even though households may receive in-kind services that they do not directly pay for but which are paid for by others—either the government or other non-state actors (Braunstein 2015: 13). As highlighted by Braunstein (2015), the mode of delivery of these commodities, whether private, public or family, is particularly important as it affects the gender content of reproductive labour (Braunstein 2015: 11–13). Public infrastructure refers to facilities that affect the time intensity of reproductive work, such as roads, electricity, water, sanitation, health and education (Agénor and Agénor 2009). I adopt this conceptualisation to analyse the gendered welfare outcomes of the latest land reform in Zimbabwe within the broader gender, poverty and land debates in Africa.

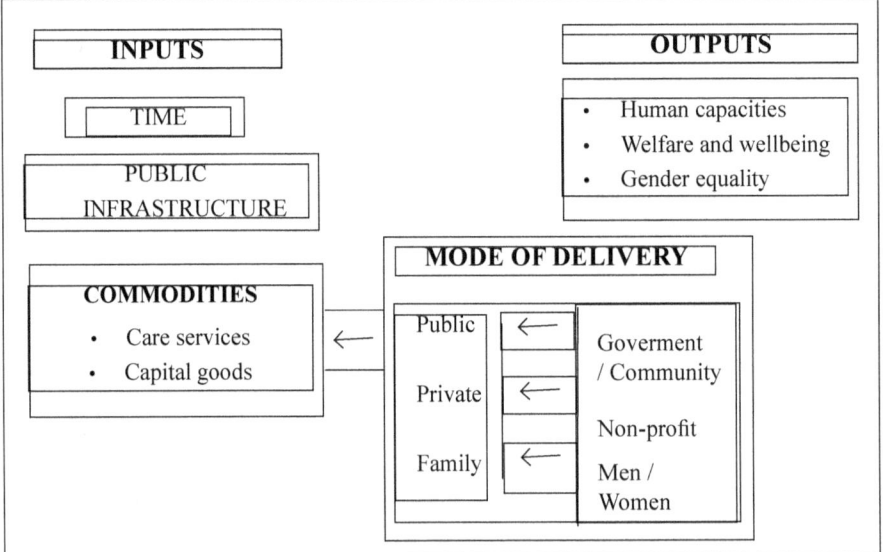

Figure 5.1: The Social Reproductive Function
Adapted from Braunstein (2015: 11)

Commodities are financed by income from work, public and/or private transfers and include paid direct and indirect care services and capital goods that aid social reproduction, such as stoves, refrigerators and washing machines (Braunstein 2015: 13).

Methodology

The research findings presented in this paper are derived from a study conducted in Chiredzi District, Zimbabwe, in 2016. The study site is 365 kilometres southeast of Harare, in Masvingo Province. The district is classified under Natural Farming Regions IV and V,[1] which are characterised by aridity and erratic rainfall patterns, with a mean annual rainfall of 450 – 600 millimetres and a mean annual evaporation exceeding 1,800 millimetres because of very hot temperatures (Mutanga, Ramoelo and Gonah 2013). However, the combination of high temperatures, plenty of sunshine and access to fresh water for irrigation from Lake Mutirikwi and other dams makes the region favourable for sugarcane production at a commercial level. Prior to the Fast Track Land Reform Programme (FTLRP) the rest of the district where smallholder farmers derived their livelihoods was arid with little access to irrigation (Mutanga, Ramoelo and Gonah 2013).

Sampling Techniques and Data Collection Tools

Data was gathered through an ethnographic field study, over a period of eight months from 27 March 2016 to 4 November 2016, using structured questionnaires, in-depth interviews, focus group discussions and key informant interviews within an explanatory sequential mixed-methods research design. Chiredzi District comprises thirty-two rural wards—seventeen communal, ten A1 and five A2 wards.[2] The study adopted an embedded case-study approach with study units purposively selected from each category: Ward 21 Mkwasine farming areas for A2 wards; Ward 20 Maware for A1 wards; and Ward 25 Muteyo for communal wards. Ward 21 represents the largest block of resettled A2 sugarcane farms in Chiredzi District, following the acquisition of the entire former Mkwasine Sugarcane Estate and its white settler out-grower sections by the government during the FTLRP. An area of 6,230 hectares was redistributed to 431 land beneficiaries, of which 24.3 per cent were women. In Ward 20, government water reforms since 2000 enabled land beneficiaries in this ward to access water for irrigation from the forty-kilometre canal that used to supply irrigation to the former Mkwasine Estate, now supplying A2 sugarcane land beneficiaries in Mkwasine. Ward 25, a nearby communal area, served as a proxy control or counterfactual group to assess the gender, poverty and welfare outcomes of the FTLRP.

A stratified random sampling technique was used to select the survey respondents for the preliminary quantitative study from the three study units.

Ward agricultural extension registers were used as sampling frames, and farmers were further stratified according to their marital status. The sampling procedure ensured that all categories of women — married, widowed, divorced/separated/single — were represented, though not proportionately. The sample of 105 survey participants comprised thirty-two medium-scale A2 land beneficiaries, thirty-three small-scale A1 land beneficiaries, and forty communal non-land beneficiaries. Empirical evidence suggests that many of the land beneficiaries in Chiredzi came from surrounding communal areas within the district or province. Based on these findings, a sub-sample of forty non-land beneficiary participants drawn from a nearby communal area was considered large enough to provide a reliable counterfactual. To give weight to the perspectives of women in the study, female participants constituted 62.5 per cent, 54.5 per cent, and 55.1 per cent (married, widowed, divorced/separated/single) within the A2, A1 and communal study areas, respectively.

The questionnaires, piloted before being administered, were used to collect information on the basic demographic data of household heads, such as gender, age, marital status, family size, education level, formal agricultural training, origin and on/off-farm residency. The first section of the survey questionnaire focusing on the redistributive outcomes of the FTLRP collected data on household cultivable land size and land tenure issues. The second section focusing on the productive outcomes of the FTLRP gathered data on ownership of productive and non-productive assets and farm investment, access to agricultural inputs, training, irrigation, labour, credit, markets and land tenure issues. The third section, on social protection, collected data on household incomes and expenditure, household food security and type of housing. The last section, on social reproduction, gathered data on access to social services and infrastructure and household time-use survey with a particular focus on women. The same questionnaire was used for land beneficiaries and non-beneficiaries in line with Jalan and Ravallion's (2003) suggestion that in evaluative assessments it is important that the same questionnaire be administered to both experimental and control groups for comparison purposes (Jalan and Ravallion 2003).

The qualitative component of the study comprised thirty follow-up in-depth interviews equally divided between A1 and A2 study areas and drawn from the preliminary quantitative study. To enhance the validity and reliability of the study findings, these two study components shared similar research questions, with the latter delving deeper to capture micro-level, individual, lived experiences of female land-reform beneficiaries. To give prominence to women's voices, perspectives and experiences, two-thirds of the respondents in the qualitative study were female-headed households with varied marital statuses. This was complemented with two focus group discussions for each gender conducted within the A1 farming areas and thirteen key informant interviews.

Analytical Methods

The study used both qualitative and quantitative data analysis methods in which the data from the two studies were analysed separately. Thematic analysis, involving the generation of codes, then categories, meanings and eventually themes, was employed to analyse qualitative data with the aid of ATLAS.ti software. On the other hand, descriptive univariate, bivariate and multivariate analyses and cross-tabulations were performed using Pearson χ^2 tests for statistical significance for categorical variables with the aid of SPSS (Statistical Package for the Social Sciences). Findings from each study were then integrated at the write-up stage.

Discussion of Results

In the paper I argue that attempts to address gendered poverty through land and agrarian reforms without taking cognisance of the location of women at the intersection between production and reproduction, that is, making a living and caring, run the risk of having an insignificant impact on, if not exacerbating, gendered poverty and inequality (Kabeer 2015: 201). As land and agrarian questions remain the cornerstone of all other dimensions, including gender, poverty and inequality, for autonomous, democratic, equitable and sustainable development in Africa, it has been argued that political demands for land and agrarian reforms should address the gender inequalities that underlie women's invisible work (Ossome and Naidu 2016: 53). Presented in Tables 5.1 and 5.2 are findings from the quantitative component of the research. Table 5.1 shows correlations of selected social reproductive variables in relation to available household cultivable land size.

The premise is anchored on the redistributive outcomes of the FTLRP that resulted in increased household cultivable land size for resettled households relative to non-land-reform households located in the communal areas (Mkodzongi and Lawrence 2019: 1; Tekwa and Adesina 2018: 54; Moyo 2011: 944). The social reproductive variables correlated with household cultivable land size included access to social services, time-use and ownership of commodities critical for social reproduction. Availability of services included access to protected sources of clean drinking water, sanitation, childcare facilities and access to healthcare. Time-use surveys included amount of time spent on water collection, wood collection, household chores and field activities. Commodities included ownership of household gadgets, such as electric stoves, fridges, washing machines and hiring of paid helps. Also presented in Table 5.1 are correlations between household cultivable land size and time poverty, spousal sharing of household tasks and married women's perception of balanced sharing of reproductive work with their spouses.

Table 5.1: Correlations of Household Cultivable Land Size and Selected Social Reproductive Variables

Social Reproductive Variables	Pearson χ2-Square Coefficients		Social Reproductive Variable	Pearson χ2-Square Coefficients		Social Reproductive Variable	Pearson χ2-Square Coefficients	
	Value	Sig. Level		Value	Sig. Level		Value	Sig. Level
1. Availability of services						**2. Commodities**		
Protected water source (500m)	-.408	0.05				Electric stove	.027	0.05
Access to sanitation	-.154	–				Fridge	.037	0.01
Childcare facilities (3km)	-.081	–				Washing machine	.142	0.01
Healthcare facility (5km)	-.081	–				Employ maid	.014	0.01
3. Time								
Water collection	.117	0.05						
Wood collection	.156	0.05						
Household chores	.960	0.01						
Field activities	.348	0.01						
4. Analysis								
Time poverty	.320	0.05	Spouse sharing	.148	0.05	Balanced sharing	.030	0.05

Table 5.2: Time Spent on Reproductive Work by Gender of Household Head

Social Reproduction Variable		Mkwasine A2 Farms						Maware A1 Farms						Muteyo Communal Areas					
		Male		Female		Total		Male		Female		Total		Male		Female		Total	
Time		No	%	No	%	No	%	No	%	No	%	No	%	No	%	No	%	No	%
Time spent on housework	< 3 hrs	5	15.6	11	34.4	16	50.0	2	6.1	6	18.2	8	24.2	9	22.5	10	25.0	19	47.5
	4–6 hrs	5	15.6	2	6.3	7	21.9	5	15.2	2	6.1	7	21.2	9	22.5	6	15.0	15	37.5
	< 6 hrs	5	15.6	4	12.5	9	28.1	13	39.4	5	15.2	18	54.5	3	7.5	3	7.5	6	15.0
Time spent in the fields	0–3 hrs	6	18.8	5	15.6	11	34.4	2	6.1	0	0.0	2	6.1	0	0.0	0	0.0	0	0.0
	4–6 hrs	6	18.8	9	28.1	15	46.9	6	18.2	9	27.3	15	45.5	8	20.0	6	15.0	14	35.0
	< 6 hrs	3	9.4	3	9.4	6	18.8	12	36.4	4	12.1	16	48.5	13	32.5	13	32.5	26	65.0
% Women reporting	>12 hr day	8	25.0	7	21.9	15	46.9	25	75.8	8	24.2	33	100.	16	40.0	16	40.0	32	80.0

Access to protected drinking water

	Distance (km)				Collection Time (hours)				Mode of Transport				Day/Frequency of Collection			
	< 0.5	1.0	> 1.0	Taped	< 0.5	1 hr	> 1hr	Taped	Head	W/barrow	Cart	Vehicle	Once	Twice	> 2	Tape
A2	0.0	0.0	0.0	100.0	0.0	0.0	0.0	100.0	0.0	0.0	0.0	0.0	0.0	0.0	0.0	100.0
A1	3.0	0.0	97.0	0.0	3.0	0.0	97.0	0.0	78.8	9.1	3.0	6.1	9.1	6.1	84.8	0.0
Com	95.0	2.5	0.0	2.5	92.5	5.0	0.0	2.5	75.0	22.5	0.0	0.0	30.0	32.5	35.0	2.5

Table 5.2 provides a further analysis of time spent on reproductive work by gender of household head across the three study sites, namely: A2 medium-scale farms, A1 small-scale farms, and the communal areas. Also presented in Table 5.2 are the average time spent to make a single round trip of fetching water, the frequency of journeys to a water source per day and the modes of transport used by different households in transporting household drinking water from the source to the point of consumption. These variables were critical in making a comparison between female- and male-headed households and across study sites, that is, resettled communal areas as explained in the preceding discussion. The results of data analysis are presented in the following section, starting with descriptive statistics from $\chi 2$-square tests on the correlations between household cultivable land size (a proxy for land reform) and selected social reproductive variables.

Social Reproductive Work and Non-Market Time

Table 5.1 shows a positive Pearson d $\chi 2$-Square value of .960 with a 0.05 significance level between household cultivable land size and time spent on household chores. This indicates that as household land size increases, time spent on household chores congruently increases. Among the many household tasks selected, a positive chi-square value of .117 with a 0.05 significance level exists between household cultivable land size and time spent collecting water, indicating that women in resettlement areas are spending more time collecting water. This association between household cultivable land size and time spent collecting water confirms other studies, which suggest that, in many African rural contexts, water and firewood collection consume a greater proportion of women's time (Folbre 2012:17). The findings depicted in Table 5.2 indicate that the percentage of women spending six or more hours on housework — reproductive labour tax — is more than twice as high in resettled areas in comparison to the control group, with 54.5 per cent and 28.1 per cent for A1 and A2 areas compared to 15.0 per cent for the communal area. Within the resettled areas, the percentage is double in A1 areas relative to A2 farming areas, a phenomenon which requires further investigation. A gendered analysis reveals that women in male-headed households (MHHs) expend more unremunerated time in social reproduction compared to female-headed households (FHHs), with 39.4 per cent in relation to 15.6 per cent, and 15.2 per cent in relation to 12.5 per cent in A1 and A2 areas, respectively.

A review of women, work and poverty by Chen et al. (2005) made reference to the totality of women's work, obtained by the cumulative time women spend on reproductive and productive work in the home, and which is a contributor to the feminisation of poverty (Chen et al. 2005: 20). Juxtaposing the time women spend on housework and in the field reflects the double burden of productive and reproductive roles for women, as illustrated in Table 5.2. Despite spending more time on housework as shown above, 48.5 per cent of women in A1 farming areas reported spending more than six hours in the field compared to 18.8 per cent in A2 farming areas. The lower percentage in the A2 farming areas is attributed to their ability to hire farm labour. Noteworthy is a gendered distribution of time spent in the field in A1 farming areas in which the percentage of women spending six or more hours in the field in MHHs is three times higher, at 36.4 per cent, in relation to 12.1 per cent for women in FHHs. The analysis presented in Table 5.2 reveals that all women in A1 reported an extraordinarily longer working day of more than twelve hours in comparison to 46.9 per cent of women in the A2 areas. These high percentages of time poverty have negative implications for the welfare of women in these areas compared to that of men, since all people require a minimum of leisure time to maintain their physical and mental wellbeing. Such associations support conclusions reached elsewhere that gender-blind land and agrarian reforms often increased the work burdens for women (Jacobs 1993, 1996, 2009, 2013; Cross and Hornby 2002). The following are some insights drawn from the qualitative component of the study with women land beneficiaries:

> As a woman, I work both in the household and on the farm. We do not have a maid to assist with household chores. I am expected to work both in the field and in the home. As a result, I may fail to find time for my own personal activities. (In-depth interview, Married A1 land beneficiary, 14 May 2016)

> In my household, there are no household tasks l can say they are for my husband; he will assist if he can. Most of the work I do on my own. In these farming areas with irrigation, there is always a lot of work. I cannot finish all the work but have to leave some for the next day. (In-depth interview, polygamous married A1 land beneficiary, 5 May 2016)

In support of the above findings, research has indicated endemic time poverty in low-income countries, a pattern shaped by inequalities of class, race, ethnicity and gender (Folbre 2012: 17). Combined house and farm work absorb quantitatively considerable time and energy for women with corresponding negative implications not only on their individual and household welfare but also economic wellbeing.

Time is a limited resource, which individuals — including women — divide between labour and leisure, productive and reproductive activities, including paid and unpaid work (Ferrant, Pesando and Nowacka 2014: 1). Within the framework, social reproductive work is a responsibility that constrains adults' allocation of time and constitutes significant investment of time to which men, women, children and networks of kin or community may all be important contributors (Braunstein 2015:11). Gender inequity in total work time spent on social reproduction is important in analysing the gendered pattern of unpaid work and its impact on women's poverty in relation to men. This is particularly important since the extent to which society and policymakers address issues concerning reproductive work has important implications for gender equality: it either expands the capabilities and choice of women and men or confines women to traditional roles associated with femininity and motherhood (Razavi 2007). In most cases, particularly in developing country contexts, the unequal distribution of reproductive work between men and women within the household translates into unequal opportunities in terms of time to participate fully in productive work (Ferrant et al. 2014: 3). This has implications for women's economic wellbeing in relation to that of men. As such, the reduction of time spent by women on housework is one policy objective for gender equality in tackling women's poverty in relation to that of men (Fälth and Blackden 2010). The evidence presented above exposes states' failure to institute land and agrarian reforms at levels sufficient for social reproduction, and their likely impact resulting on the reproduction of gendered poverty and inequality (Naidu and Ossome 2015; Kabeer 2015: 195).

Public Infrastructure

The provision of physical and social infrastructure is a critical component for social reproduction. A negative chi-square correlation value was found between household cultivable land size and all the selected social service provision indicators, namely availability of a protected water source within 500 metres, access to household sanitation (toilet), availability of child and healthcare facilities within distances of three kilometres and five kilometres respectively. Pearson correlation values of -408 and -154 were found between household cultivable land size and the availability of water and sanitation, respectively. Such inverse correlation values suggest that, as household cultivable land size increases, the provision of public infrastructure decreases, pointing to a deficient infrastructure provision within resettled areas compared to communal areas. Time-use surveys show how women, men, girls and boys spent their time each day or week, an important technique to measure how individuals' total working time allocations include leisure (Rai, Hoskyns and Thomas 2010: 11). The analysis presented in Table 5.2 shows the effect of poor provision of social infrastructure (health and education) and physical infrastructure (water and electricity) on the time devoted by women in resettlement areas to unpaid care work. Such analyses provide insights into aspects of development not yet fully explored (Chen et al. 2005). The study revealed that 97 per cent of the female respondents in the A1 small-scale farming areas indicated that the nearest source of water was more than a kilometre away, a round trip which took them more than an hour. In addition, 84.8 per cent of these female respondents made more than two trips of water collection per day, with 78.8 per cent using their head as a mode of transporting water for home use. This provides insights into the time and energy demands on women for a single social reproductive task, the collection of water for household consumption.

The social service provision in the fast-track areas presented above is in stark contrast to that in the control group, the communal areas. Although 75 per cent indicated they used their head as the mode of transporting domestic water, 95 per cent indicated that there was a clean, safe water source less than 500 metres away, with 92.5 per cent taking thirty minutes or less to make one round trip to collect water. This suggests that women in the communal areas expend less time and effort for this and possibly other social reproductive tasks. Such social reproductive insights highlight the extent to which levels of service provision affect not only the welfare of women in different geographical contexts (Sen 2008) but also the time constraints imposed by reproductive work on women, leaving little time to engage in productive work that would improve their economic fortunes.

I argue that land and agrarian reforms without the concomitant provision of public and social infrastructure does little to transform gendered poverty and inequality within agrarian societies. Lack of social service provision represents one major gendered shortfall of the FTLRP in Zimbabwe. The programme saw the introduction of large numbers of people, together with domestic animals, into areas that were hitherto sparsely settled, frequently remote and underdeveloped. This was without attention paid to the increased concomitant need for physical, social and economic infrastructure Women in fast-track areas are increasingly off-setting the shortfall that results from the deficient provision of social infrastructure. The Phase One Resettlement Programme (pre-2000 land reforms) was characterised by sufficient infrastructure provision with domestic water supplies provided at a rate of one borehole, with an installed hand pump, per every twenty-five families (Gonese and Mukora 2003: 13). Such a level of social infrastructure is critical in reducing the social reproductive burden on women within resettlement areas.

Ownership of Time-Saving Household Consumer Commodities

A positive correlation was found between household cultivable land size and ownership of selected household time-saving commodities, namely electric stoves, fridges and washing machines, and the ability to acquire the services of paid help. Ownership of time-saving household commodities increased with larger sizes of available household cultivable land. These commodities, as inputs to the social reproduction function system, were financed by income from work (employment) and public and/or private transfers (Braunstein 2016: 11). This study showed that access to large tracts of land through land reform provided a source of income for the purchase of time-saving household goods, with a direct impact on the amount of time spent by women on unremunerated social reproductive work (Folbre 2012; Braunstein 2016). Ownership of time-saving household gadgets was high in the resettled areas, particularly A2 areas, with 90.6 per cent of households reporting ownership of electric stoves and refrigerators.

Some households, particularly FHHs in the A2 farming areas, had moved up the socioeconomic ladder as a result of their purchase of higher status commodities, such as washing machines. This explains the reduced amount of time spent on reproductive work by women in the A2 farming areas relative to other study sites (see Table 5.2). However, ownership of time-saving household commodities by resettled farmers could not offset the time constraints imposed by deficiencies in the provision of public services, such as child and health care, water supply and sanitation. Study participants reflected this in the incidence of time poverty reported across all study sites. A positive Pearson chi-square value of .320 with a 0.05 significance level indicated a close association between increasing household land size and female time poverty. As a comparison, in South Africa, rural electrification and investment in time-saving technologies have been associated with a decrease in time spent on housework, leading to a 9 per cent increase in female labour force participation in rural areas (Dinkelman 2011).

Outsourcing Unremunerated Reproductive Work

The option to outsource unpaid care activities, such as cooking, cleaning and fetching water, has been found to be an unaffordable luxury for most households in low-income countries, where women need to carry out these activities for their household's daily wellbeing (Ferrant, Pesando and Nowacka 2014: 5). However, enhanced household incomes enable households to outsource many or a part of these activities through engaging the services of housemaids, thus freeing more time for women to engage in paid work activities. From a gender perspective, this is less transformative, as it represents one class of women shifting their social reproductive burden onto another class of the same gender, as most paid helps are women. In Table 5.1, a positive Pearson correlation value exists between hiring paid help and household cultivable land size. Access to land through the FTLRP enabled households, particularly within the A2 farming areas, to outsource unremunerated reproductive activities, with a consequent decline in the amount of time spent on housework by women in the A2 farming areas. Below are some lived experiences of resettled women land beneficiaries drawn from the qualitative component of the study:

> Earliest in the morning l attend to my garden, after which we go and work in the husband's field, then cook for the family and return to work on our fields as wives. We can only have time to chat late in the night provided we are not tired. Our husband does not assist with looking after children. It is our duty as mothers and other grown-up female children to assist us. (In-depth interview, polygamous married female A1 land beneficiary, 13 May 2016)>

Combined house and farm work absorb quantitatively considerable time and energy for women with corresponding negative implications for the time they could devote to rest and leisure.

Male Participation in Reproductive Work

A positive correlation was found between household cultivable land size and spouses sharing reproductive work, with a Pearson chi-square value of .148 (see Table 5.1). This suggests that husbands in resettlement areas are taking part in social reproductive work. However, focus group discussions with men revealed the need to tackle the gendered social norms that prevail in resettlement areas:

> After coming from the field men would sleep on the mat waiting for the wife to bring food. Very few men would take the baby whilst the mother is cooking. Some men would even hurry the wife forgetting that they were all working in the field and tired as well. The only people to help her might be elderly girls who may take away the crying baby not the husband. (Male focus group discussion, 23 October 2016)

> We encourage men to share household work with their wives. (Key informant interview, A1 Agricultural Extension Officer, 30 May 2016)

On the other hand, social relations and institutions in many African societies oblige women to provide labour on their husband's plots before they can work on their own, thus increasing the time they spend on productive work (Yngstrom 2002: 29; Amanor-Wilks 2009: 32; Tsikata and Amanor-Wilks 2009: 3) as highlighted in in-depth interviews with women in MHHs:

> Earliest in the morning I attend to my garden, after which we go and work in the husband's field, then cook for the family and return to work on our fields as wives. (In-depth interview: polygamous married female, A1 land beneficiary, 13 May 2016)

> I must finish the work he had assigned before attending to my own field. If he finds me there without finishing the work a conflict would arise. (In-depth interview: polygamous married female, A1 land beneficiary, 5 May 2016)

This suggests that women in MHHs are most likely to experience acute time poverty, with possible negative implications not only on their individual wellbeing but also economic welfare, compared to those in FHHs.

Outcomes of Inadequate Social and Physical Infrastructure

A 'social reproductive crisis' exists within resettlement areas, particularly A1 small-scale areas, due to deficiencies in the provision of social infrastructure. Images of women working in the fields with babies on their lap or back are not uncommon. As a result, within resettlement areas the distinguishing line between productive and reproductive work is increasingly blurring for most women, as these tasks are inseparable. The contradiction for women to balance the burden of unpaid reproductive work in the home and productive work—whether in formal workplaces or in the fields — asserts gender as one unresolved contemporary agrarian question. As such, Naidu and Ossome (2016) argue, since the reproduction of rural households is dependent on land and women's labour, a condition which leads to continued immiseration of most women, deficient service provision deepens the contradictions of achieving gender equality, as most land and agrarian reforms fail to address the gender inequities that underlie women's invisible work (Naidu and Ossome 2016: 53). Consequently, the mere redistribution of land to women runs the risk of exacerbating existing gender inequality.

Conclusion and Recommendations

As land and agrarian reforms are re-emerging as important policy agendas for rural development, poverty alleviation and social transformation post-COVID-19, I argue that land reforms that rely on individualistic ontologies, concerned only with tenure security or land redistribution, are insufficient for social transformation (see also Razavi 2003). The interrogation of gender inequity within reproductive labour reveals the crisis emanating from the intersection of subsistence economies and gendered labour regimes that are highly predicated on free, exploitative labour, the bulk of which is shouldered by rural women daily. The situation is exacerbated by the acute lack of provision of social and physical infrastructure in many of these contexts, which is an obstacle to agrarian transformation in Africa, as elsewhere. Social reproductive work consumes much of women's time, which they could otherwise use for economic gain but which instead traps them in the reproductive household economy.

Secondly, I argue that even though gender can be accounted for (normatively, through guarantees of women's rights to land, such as the 30 per cent quota for land beneficiaries being reserved for women in the FTLRP in Zimbabwe), this incorporation should not proceed in isolation (Naidu and Ossome 2016: 70). Women might have land, which they can not actually cultivate due to the failure and insufficiency of state social provisioning. It may not be possible for women to escape the trap of poverty and immiseration simply because they have access to land. Failure to address the problem of reproductive labour (the agrarian question of gendered labour) renders land and agrarian reforms incomplete, and serves to make the question of social reproduction the most important contemporary and unresolved agrarian question in Africa.

The following forms part of my recommendation to policymakers in Africa:

1. **State intervention in social reproduction**

    In managing the contradictions associated with social reproduction, African states can draw lessons from social policy in the Nordic countries, and intervene to prevent or mitigate cost-shifting by capitalists through appropriate legislation or underwriting some or most of the social reproductive costs. Paradoxically, most states in Africa, as in many other developing contexts, and emanating from neoliberal residual social policy, have increasingly intervened only to the extent of correcting market failures or failures of family provisioning by providing meagre support to ultra- or 'deserving' poor or households (Adesina 2011: 460; Braedley 2006: 216). By adopting residualist social policies, African states limit themselves to attempts at reducing poverty rather than focusing on the objectives of economic growth and systematically gutting the welfare state. Consequently, social policies have been more sensitive to the needs of the capitalist economy, resulting in escalating gendered poverty and inequality in the past three decades of neoliberalism.

2. **Public social infrastructure provision**

   As the household or family remains a major site for social reproduction in most agrarian societies, state support in terms of public social and physical infrastructure remains critical in lessening the social reproductive burdens on households, particularly on women. Most land reforms are characterised by an insufficient provision of social services. The increased social reproductive burden takes up much of the time women can devote to productive work to enhance their economic wellbeing. In the study areas, the scale of the FTLRP saw the resettlement of large numbers of people with little or no provision of physical, social and economic infrastructure (Gonese and Mukora, 2003: 13), posing a contradiction to the aim of creating a path to agrarian transformation. Fast-track policymakers and planners can learn from the pre-2000 Phase One Land Reforms, in which the provision of infrastructure complemented the settlement of incoming communities to ensure that they could access, within reasonable reach, the necessary social services. The programme was hailed worldwide as one of the most successful land reforms (Gonese and Mukora 2003: 3). The key implication of the social reproductive approach is the need for investment in a social and physical infrastructure that reduces the structural constraints on women's time.

3. **Male participation in social reproductive work**

   Some feminists have argued that future gender equality rests on promoting the parental sharing ideal through encouraging men's care (Gornick and Meyers 2003; Fraser 1994). In the context of welfare states, policies that encourage and incentivise fathers to share caring responsibilities, such as granting paternal leave and fathers' quotas—time set for father's childcare—facilitate men's capacity to take solo care of young children while the mother returns to work. The involvement of fathers in caring work is likened to a better gender division of care work and better welfare outcomes for women (Mathieu 2016: 580). Within agrarian societies men can be incentivised and encouraged to take part in social reproductive work thus easing the social reproductive burden on women and enabling them to balance their time between earning and caring.

Notes

1. Zimbabwe is divided into five agro-ecological regions, known as natural farming regions, on the basis of rainfall, soil quality and vegetation, among other factors. The quality of the land resource and annual precipitation declines from Natural Region (NR) I to NR V.

2. Model A1 farms are the smaller farms, allocated five arable hectares in wetter regions and ten arable hectares in drier regions. Land reserved for communal grazing is seven hectares minimum per household. Model A2 farms are larger and range in size, with larger farms at the higher end of Natural Farming Regions 1 to 5. An average for sugarcane plots is twenty hectares (Sukume, Moyo and Matondi 2004: 3–4).

References

Acker, J., 1992, Gendered Institutions: From Sex Roles to Gendered Institutions, *Contemporary Sociology*, Vol. 21, pp. 565–69, cited in Martin, P. Y., 2004, Gender as Social Institution, *Social Forces*, Vol. 82, No 4, pp. 1249–1273.

Adams, M., Sibanda, S. and Turner, S., 1999, Land Tenure Reform and Rural Livelihoods in Southern Africa, *Natural Resource Perspectives*, Vol. 39, London: Overseas Development Institute.

Adesina, J., 2009, Social Policy in Sub-Saharan Africa: A Glance in the Rear-View Mirror, *International Journal of Social Welfare*, Vol. 18, No. 1, pp. 37–51.

Adesina, J., 2011, Beyond the Social Protection Paradigm: Social Policy in Africa's Development, *Canadian Journal of Development Studies Studies–Revue Canadienne d'Études du Developpement*, Vol. 32, No. 4, pp. 454–470.

African Development Bank (AfDB), 2020, African Economic Outlook 2020, Supplement Amid COVID-19, Abidjan: Côte d›Ivoire.

Agarwal, B., 1994, *A Field of One's Own: Gender and Land Rights in Asia*, Cambridge, UK: Cambridge University Press.

Agénor, P-R. and Agénor, M., 2009, Infrastructure, Women's Time Allocation, and Economic Development, Economics, The University of Manchester Centre for Growth and Business Cycle Research Discussion Paper Series, No. 116, Manchester: The University of Manchester.

Akram-Lodhi, A., 2009, The Macroeconomics of Human Insecurity, in Leckie, J., ed., 2010, *Development in an Insecure World: The Relevancy of Millennium Development Goals*, London, UK and New York: Routledge, pp. 71–90.

Amanor-Wilks, D-E., 2009, Land, Labour and Gendered Livelihoods in a 'Peasant' and a 'Settler' Economy, *Feminist Africa*, Issue 12, pp. 31–50.

Apusigah, A.A., 2009, The Gendered Politics of Farm Household Production and the Shaping of Women's Livelihoods in Northern Ghana, *Feminist Africa*, Issue 12, pp. 51–68.

Berniell, M. I. and Sanchez-Paramo, C., 2011, Overview of Time-Use Data Used for the Analysis of Gender Differences in Time Use Patterns, Background paper for the WDR 2012.

Bhattacharya, T., 2013, What is Social Reproduction Theory?, SocialistWorker. org. Available online at https://socialistworker.org/2013/09/10/what-is-social-reproduction-theory.

Braedley, S., 2006, Someone to Watch Over You: Gender, Class and Social Reproduction, in Bezanson, K. and Luxton, M., eds, *Social Reproduction: Feminist Political Economy Challenges Neo-liberalism*, Montreal: McGill-Queens University Press, pp. 215–230.

Braunstein, E., 2015, Economic Growth and Social Reproduction: Gender Inequality as a Cause and Consequence, Discussion paper for Progress of World's Women 2015–2016, No.5, Geneva: UN Women.

Budlender, D., 2002, *Why Should We Care About Unpaid Care Work? A Guidebook*, Harare: UNIFEM Southern African Region Office.

Butegwa, F., 1991, Women's Legal Right of Access to Agricultural Resources in Africa: A Preliminary Inquiry, Third World Legal Studies Special Edition, cited in Tsikata, D., 2009, Gender, Land and Labour Relations and Livelihoods in Sub-Saharan Africa in the Era of Economic Liberalisation: Towards a Research Agenda, *Feminist Africa*, Issue 12, pp. 11–30.

Chen, M., Vanek, J., Lund, F., Heintz, J., Jhabvala, R. and Bonner, C., 2005, Progress of the World's Women 2005: Women, Work and Poverty, New York: UNIFEM.

Chigbu, U. E., 2019, Anatomy of Women's Landlessness in the Patrilineal Customary Land Tenure Systems of Sub-Saharan Africa and a Policy Pathway, *Land Use Policy*, Vol. 86, pp. 126–135.

Collins, P. H., 1998, *Fighting Words: Black Women and the Search for Justice*, Minneapolis: University of Minnesota Press.

Cross, C. and Hornby, D., 2002, Opportunities and Obstacles to Women's Land Access in South Africa, research report for the Promoting Women's Access to Land Programme, Johannesburg: University of the Witwatersrand, Johannesburg.

Davison, J., 1988, 'Who Owns What?' Land Registration and Tension in Gender Relations of Production in Kenya, in Davison, J., ed., *Agriculture, Women and Land*, Boulder: Westview Press.

Dinkelman, T., 2011, The Effect of Rural Electrification on Employment: New Evidence from South Africa, *American Economic Review*, Vol. 101, No. 7, pp. 3078–3108.

Fälth, A. and Blackden, M., 2010, Gender. Equality and Unpaid Care Work, UNDP/BDP Brief.

Ferrant, G., Pesando, M. L. and Nowacka, K., 2014, Unpaid Care Work: The Missing Link in the Analysis of Gender Gaps in Labour Outcomes, Paris: OECD Development Centre.

Folbre, N., 1994, *Who Pays for the Kids? Gender and the Structures of Constraint*, London, UK: Routledge.

Folbre, N., 2012, The Care Economy in Africa: Subsistence Production and Unpaid Care, Plenary paper prepared for presentation at the African Economic Research Consortium (AERC) Biannual Research Workshop, 2–5 December 2012, Arusha, Tanzania.

Food and Agriculture Organization (FAO), 2017, *The Future of Food and Agriculture: Trends and Challenges*, Rome: Food and Agriculture Organization of the United Nations.

Fraser, N., 1994, After the Family Wage: Gender Equity and the Welfare State, *Political Theory*, Vol. 22, pp. 591–618.

Gasper, D. R. and Van Staveren, I. P., 2003, Development as Freedom — and as What Else?, *Feminist Economics*, Vol. 9, No. 2–3, pp. 137–161.

Gray, L. and Kevane, M., 1999, Diminished Access, Diverted Exclusion: Women and Land Tenure in Sub-Saharan Africa, *African Studies Review*, Vol. 42, No. 2, pp. 15–39.

Gonese, F. T. and Mukora, C. M., 2003, *Beneficiary Selection, Infrastructure Provision and Beneficiary Support*, Centre for Applied Social Sciences, University of Zimbabwe, and Land Tenure Center, University of Wisconsin–Madison.

Gornick, J. and Meyers, M., 2003, *Families that Work*, New York: Russell Sage Foundation.

Grown, C., Elson, D. and Cagatay, N., 2000, 'Introduction', *World Development*, Vol. 28, No. 7, pp. 1145–1156.

Himmelweit, S., 2002, Making Visible the Hidden Economy: The Case for Gender-Impact Analysis of Economic Policy, *Feminist Economics*, Vol. 8, No. 1, pp. 49–70.

Hujo, K., 2014, Social Policy for Inclusive Development and Productive Transformation, Expert Meeting on Social Inclusion Programmes and their Impact on Sustainable and Inclusive Development and Growth, 27–28 November 2014, Geneva: UNRISD.

Jacobs, S., 1993, Gender and Land Reforms Consumption, Production and Some Contradictions, in Costa, J. A., ed., *GCB—Gender and Consumer Behaviour*, Vol. 2, Salt Lake City: Association for Consumer Research, pp. 133-146. Available online at http://www.acrwebsite.org/volumes/15590/gender/v02/GCB-02.

Jacobs, S., 1996, Structures and Processes: Land, Families, and Gender Relations, *Gender and Development*, Vol. 4, No. 2, pp. 35–42.

Jacobs, S., 2004, Livelihoods, Security and Needs: Gender Relations and Land Reform in South Africa, *Journal of International Women's Studies*, Vol. 6, No. 1, pp. 1–19.

Jacobs, S., 2009, Gender and Land Reforms: Comparative Perspectives, *Geography Compass*, Vol. 3, No. 5, pp. 1675–1687.

Jacobs, S., 2013, *Gender and Agrarian Reforms*, New York: Routledge.

Jalan, J. and Ravallion, M., 2003, Estimating the Benefit Incidence of an Antipoverty Program by Propensity Score Matching, *Journal of Business Economics Statistics*, Vol. 21, No. 1, pp. 19–30.

Jayne, T. S., Yeboah, F. K. and Henry, C., 2017, The Future of Work in African Agriculture: Trends and Drivers of Change, Research Department Working Paper No. 25, December 2017, Geneva: International Labour Office.

Kabeer, N., 2015, Gender, Poverty, and Inequality: A Brief History of Feminist Contributions in the Field of International Development, *Gender and Development*, Vol. 23, No. 2, pp. 189–205.

Lewis, J., 1992, Gender and the Development of Welfare Regimes, *Journal of European Social Policy*, Vol. 2, pp. 59–73.

Marock, C. and Grawitzky, R., 2014, Employment Policy Implementation Mechanisms in South Africa, Employment Policy Department, EMPLOYMENT Working Paper No. 159, International Labour Organization, Geneva: International Labour Office.

Mathieu, S., 2016, From Defamilialization to the Demotherization of Care Work, *Social Politics*, Vol. 23, No. 4, pp. 576–591.

McNally, D. and Fergusson, S., 2015, Social Reproduction Beyond Intersectionality: An Interview, *Viewpoint Magazine*. Available online at https://viewpointmag.com/2015/10/31/social-reproduction-beyond-intersectionality-an-interview-with-sue-ferguson-and-david-mcnally/

Mkandawire, T., 2004, Social policy in a Development Context: Introduction, in Mkandawire, T., ed., *Social Policy in a Development Context*, Basingstoke: UNRISD/Palgrave Macmillan, pp. 1–33.

Mkandawire, T., 2011, Welfare Regimes and Economic Development: Bridging the Conceptual Gap, in Fitzgerald, V., Heyer J. and Thorp, R., *Overcoming the Persistence of Poverty and Inequality*, Basingstoke: Palgrave Macmillan.

Mkodzongi, G and Lawrence, P., 2019, The Fast-Track Land Reform and Agrarian Change in Zimbabwe, *Review of African Political Economy*, Vol. 46, No. 159, pp. 1–13.

Moyo, S., 2011, Changing Agrarian Relations after Redistributive Land Reform in Zimbabwe, *Journal of Peasant Studies*, Vol. 38, No. 5, pp. 939–966.

Mutanga, S., Ramoelo, A. and Gonah, T., 2013, Trend Analysis of Sugarcane Production in Post-Resettlement Areas of Mkwasine, Zimbabwe, Using Hyper-Temporal Imagery, *Advances in Remote Sensing*, Vol. 2, pp. 29–34.

Mutopo, P., 2011, Women's Struggles to Access and Control Land and Livelihoods after Fast Track Land Reform in Mwenezi District, Zimbabwe, *Journal of Peasant Studies*, Vol. 38, No. 5, pp. 1021–46.

Naidu, S. C. and Ossome, L., 2016, Social Reproduction and the Agrarian Question of Women's Labour in India, *Agrarian South: Journal of Political Economy*, Vol. 5, No. 1, pp. 50–76.

Njieassam, E. E., 2019, Gender Inequality and Land Rights: The Situation of Indigenous Women in Cameroon, *Potchefstroom Electronic Law Journal*, Vol. 22, pp. 1–33. DOI: https://doi.org/10.17159/1727-3781/2019/v22i0a4907

O'Connor, J. S., 2013, Gender, Citizenship and Welfare State Regimes in the Early Twenty-First Century: 'Incomplete Revolution' and/or Gender Equality 'Lost in Translation', in Kennett, P., ed., *A Handbook of Comparative Social Policy*, Cheltenham: Edward Elgar Publishing, pp. 137–161.

Organisation for Economic Co-operation and Development (OECD), 2004, Unpaid Care Work: The Missing Link in the Analysis of Gender Gaps in Labour Outcomes, Issues Paper, Paris: OECD.

Orloff, A. S., 1993, Gender and the Social Rights of Citizenship: The Comparative Analysis of Gender Relations and Welfare States, *American Sociological Review*, Vol. 58, pp. 303–28.

Palmer, I., 1995, Public Finance from a Gender Perspective, *World Development*, Vol. 23, No. 11, pp. 1981–6.

Prasad, N., Hypher, N. and Gerecke, M,. 2013, Transformative Social Policy in Small States, Research Paper 2013–3, Geneva: UNRISD.

Rai, S. M., Hoskyns, C. and Thomas, D., 2010, Depletion and Social Reproduction, Working Paper 274/11 for Centre for the Study of Globalisation and Regionalisation (CSGR), Department of Politics and International Studies, University of Warwick.

Razavi, S., ed., 2003, *Agrarian Change, Gender and Land rights*, Oxford: Blackwell Publishing Ltd.

Razavi, S., 2007, The Political and Social Economy of Care in a Development Context: Conceptual Issues, Research Questions and Policy Options, Programme on Gender and Development, Paper Number 3, Geneva: UNRISD.

Razavi, S., 2011, Rethinking Care in a Development Context: An Introduction, *Development and Change*, Vol. 42, No. 4, pp. 873–903.

Ridgeway, C. L., 2009, Framed Before We Know It: How Gender Shapes Social Relations, *Gender and Society*, Vol. 23 No. 2, pp 145–160.

Sen, G., 2008, Poverty as a Gendered Experience: The Policy Implications, Poverty in Focus, *Gender Equality*, Vol. 13, pp. 6–7, International Poverty Centre.

Sukume, C., Moyo, S. and Matondi, P., 2004, Agricultural Sector and Agrarian Development Strategy, Unpublished paper prepared for the World Bank, Harare:

Africa Institute for Agrarian Studies (AIAS).

Tekwa, N. and Adesina, J., 2018, Gender, Poverty and Inequality in the Aftermath of Zimbabwe's Land Reform: A Transformative Social Policy Perspective, *Journal of International Women's Studies*, Vol. 19, No. 5, pp. 45–62.

Tsikata, D., 2009, Gender, Land and Labour Relations and Livelihoods in Sub-Saharan Africa in the Era of Liberalisation: Towards a Research Agenda, *Feminist Africa*, Issue 12, pp. 11–30.

Tsikata, D. and Amanor-Wilks, D-E., 2009, Editorial: Land and Labour in Gendered Livelihood Trajectories, *Feminist Africa*, Issue 12, pp. 11–30.

United Nations Conference on Trade and Development (UNCTAD), 2018, Economic Development in Africa Report 2018, Migration for Structural Change, New York and Geneva: United Nations.

United National Research Institute for Social Development (UNRISD), 2006, Transformative Social Policy: Lessons from UNRISD Research, UNRISD Research and Policy Brief 5, Geneva: UNRISD. Available online at http://www.unrisd.org.

United National Research Institute for Social Development (UNRISD), 2010, *Combating poverty and inequality: Structural change, social policy and politics*, Geneva: UNRISD.

United National Research Institute for Social Development (UNRISD), 2012, Social Dimensions of Green Economy, UNRISD Research and Policy Brief, Geneva: UNRISD.

Verma, R., 2007, 'Without Land You Are Nobody': Critical Dimensions of Women's Access to Land and Relations in Tenure in East Africa, IDRC Scoping Study for East Africa on Women's Access and Rights to Land and Gender Relations in Tenure, Ottawa: IDRC.

Wanyeki, L. M., 2003, *Women and Land in Africa: Culture, Religion and Women's Rights*, London, UK: Zed Books.

Whitehead, A. and Kabeer, N., 2001, Living with Uncertainty: Gender, Livelihoods and Pro-Poor Growth in Rural Sub-Saharan Africa, IDS Working Paper 134, Brighton, UK: Institute of Development Studies.

Whitehead, A. and Tsikata, D., 2003, Policy Discourses on Women's Land Rights in Sub-Saharan Africa: The Implications of the Re-Turn to the Customary, *Journal of Agrarian Change*, Vol. 3, Issue 1–2, pp. 67–122.

Yi, I., 2015, New Challenges and New Directions in Social Policy, Expert Group Meeting on the priority theme of the 53rd and 54th sessions of the Commission for Social Development: Strengthening Social Development in the Contemporary World, Geneva: UNRISD.

Yngstrom, I., 2002, Women, Wives and Land Rights in Africa: Situating Gender Beyond the Household in the Debate Over Land Policy and Changing Tenure Systems, *Oxford Development Studies*, Vol. 30, No.1, pp. 21–40.

6

Informal Social Protection, Group Membership and Agriculture: Male and Female Wheat Farmers in Ethiopia

Kristie Drucza and Dagmawit Giref Sahile

Introduction

Farmers are social beings and not just economic actors. Social organisations are important to rural farmers, who can live remote, isolated or solitary lives. These organisations provide the means to understand the functioning of community norms, build trust, create social cohesion and gain access to stronger and broader social networks. A few of the attributes that groups provide are care and support, structure, information, entertainment and networks. Social mobilisation (the process of actively engaging and motivating citizens into groups that meet regularly for a variety of purposes) is a fairly recent phenomenon in Ethiopia, although traditional or informal groups have existed for some time. However, in Ethiopia, 'group extension and mass mobilisation approaches give little attention to the existing gender inequality and may unintentionally perpetuate the existing inequality' (Leta et al. 2017).

This chapter examines group membership for female- and male-headed households and for spouses, by using panel data from 2011 and 2014. In line with the Women's Empowerment in Agriculture Index (WEAI), 'group membership is deliberately not restricted to formal agriculture-related groups [in the survey question, Table 6.2] because other types of civic or social groups provide important sources of networks and social capital that are empowering in themselves and may also be an important source of agricultural information or inputs' (Meinzen-Dick et al. 2014). The literature on group membership in Ethiopia uses the following categories: formal (registered with the government); semi-formal (a transitional group which may be registered or have the functioning of a registered group but not be registered); and informal (unregistered and local) (Teshome et al. 2014).

Between 1974 and 1987, Ethiopia's Derg regime suppressed almost all forms of collective organisation unless they were associated with customary institutions, such as an *Edir* (voluntary self-help group) and an *Equb* (an alternative to microfinance) (Rahmato 2002). Voluntarism is central to traditional African life, regardless of authoritarian governments (Bratton 1989; Rahmato 2002). Informal groups have always been important aspects of Ethiopian life, and in 2004, 80 per cent of households were members of at least one *Edir* (Dercon and Bold 2004).

Agricultural production occurs on farms and within homes and in communities. Consequently, social relations play a central role in shaping a farming lifestyle. In Ethiopia, the Ethiopian People's Revolutionary Democratic Front (EPRDF)-led government understands this to a certain degree and uses formal groups such as co-operatives to pass on agricultural knowledge and to distribute credit and other inputs, such as seed and fertiliser (Abate et al. 2015). In 2009, co-operatives provided 60 per cent of the credit for fertiliser, 38 per cent of improved seed and 12.5 per cent of agrochemicals (Gebremedhin et al. 2009). In addition, the government also runs groups known as government teams, which pass on agricultural information and other policy initiatives.

The degree of social capital that exists in a community can improve the performance of formal and informal groups (Paldam and Svendsen 2000; Bhuyan 2007). Social capital has a multiplying effect and offers mutual benefits to communities and individuals (Streeten 2002). For Bourdieu and Wacquant (1992), social capital is 'the sum of the resources, actual or virtual, that accrue to a group by virtue of possessing a durable network of more or less institutionalised relationships of mutual acquaintance and recognition.' Social capital can produce benefits for individuals, households and societies (Fukuyama 2001), ranging from protection from shocks, increased income (Krishna 2001; Mogues 2005), improved governance and democracy (Putnam et al. 1993; Paxton 2002) and economic growth (Knack and Keefer 1997; Zak and Knack 1998). Social capital can be one benefit gained from group membership and it has a range of knock-on benefits.

Different types of social capital accrue different benefits. Bonding social capital exists between close family members, friends and neighbours, whereas bridging social capital exists between more distant associates and colleagues. Meanwhile, linking social capital involves horizontal linkages to people with influence or with power (Woolcock 2002: 23). Krishna and Uphoff (2002: 86–88) add further categories: structural social capital facilitates mutually beneficial collective action and external, visible networks through its associations, whereas cognitive social capital involves shared norms, values, attitudes and beliefs that predispose people towards mutually beneficial collective action, is internal and relates to how people think and act. Moreover, in rural Ethiopia women participate more actively in women-only groups than in mixed groups (Lemma et al. 2019). Different farmers need varying degrees of different types of social capital and group set-up depending on their existing stock, their location, life circumstances, etc.

The benefits of group membership and how social capital works in Ethiopia are patchy given the reach of *Edir*. Ruben and Hera (2012) found that in Sidhama the performance (productive and economic) of a co-operative can be enhanced by intra-community bonding social capital. Thus, the closer the community or the more stocks of social capital it has, the more likely it will benefit from formal group membership. Francesconi and Heerink (2010) found that marketing co-operative members have higher commercialisation rates than non-members. Similarly, Getnet and Anullo (2012) identified a relationship between improved rural livelihoods and co-operative membership, demonstrating that government-run co-operatives in Ethiopia generate similar membership benefits to non-government co-operatives in other countries. Government-facilitated groups play an important role in agricultural development and improving livelihoods.

Outside of social capital, group membership can also offer social protection. Social protection is an umbrella term for policies or assistance that involve in-kind help or cash transfers, insurance or employment-related assistance, which protects citizens against unacceptable vulnerability and poverty. Social protection is used to assist 'individuals, households and communities to reduce their vulnerability by managing risks better' (World Bank 2001: 4). Thus, social protection can contribute to one's social capital by providing benefits and giving one access to new networks. Additionally, social protection can be invaluable to farmers facing climate, food or other shocks. Informal social protection helps community members band together to tackle adversity, especially where the state is absent.

Formal social protection is provided by the state or the market and can reduce hunger, increase agriculture productivity, manage risks and build assets (Stavropoulou, Holmes and Jones 2017: 73). Meanwhile, informal social protection in Ethiopia refers to 'assets and/or financial transfers made to protect the livelihoods and to some extent the standard of living of poor families and communities, governed mainly by the principle of reciprocity and exchange and customary laws of social institutions' (Teshome 2013: 99). There is a gap in the research around women's co-operatives, which needs to be filled, particularly in studying what works and what doesn't, and how the co-operatives and their members can be supported on the long road to self-reliance (Hiriyur and Chettri 2020: 38). The role of informal social protection in a farmer's life is under-researched and invisible in policy and programming (Vinci et al. 2014; Devereux and Getu 2013; Stavropoulou et al. 2017).

Dunn (1988) argues that the basic principle underlying all co-operative action is that, through joint efforts, individuals may collectively achieve objectives that are unattainable by individual action. Presumably this means that if group membership does not deliver benefits, then the members will leave and join other higher performing groups (Bernard and Spielman 2009). However, Ethiopia's central state control (see Markakis 2011) may make membership of certain government-supported groups mandatory. Unless membership in government groups is voluntary, citizens may feel unable to leave—even if the group is underperforming. Moreover, the social capital that accrues from government-led groups may be different to that of non-government groups. Ethiopia-specific information on group dynamics and benefits (outside of increased income and access to inputs) is missing in the agriculture literature.

The question this chapter asks is whether all groups are equal in terms of the social capital and protection offered to members, and thus explores whether the changes observed in group membership are positive for farmers. The data presented in this study reveals that informal groups matter to farmers but their value may be decreasing.

In 2009, membership of groups for the heads of wheat-growing households was plentiful in terms of informal group membership, but limited in terms of formal group membership. By 2012, formal group membership had increased but at the expense of informal group membership. Nevertheless, formal and informal groups still play a role for farmers, but how farmers understand the value of each group and which group they choose to join requires further investigation.

This chapter is structured to contextualise the data to Ethiopia, outline the methodology and survey question, introduce the theory of social capital and informal social protection and present the results, followed by a discussion and conclusion.

The Socioeconomic Context of Ethiopia

Ethiopia is the oldest independent country in Africa and was never colonised, apart from a brief Italian occupation between 1936 and 1941. The Derg regime that replaced the monarchy in 1974, and which grossly abused human rights, was overthrown by the Ethiopian People's Revolutionary Democratic Front (EPRDF) in 1991. This ruling political coalition has tried various strategies to unify the heterogeneous country and has ambitions to turn Ethiopia into a middle-income country by 2025.

Ethiopia is a development success story, in some ways. GDP growth was 9 per cent (2018/19) and poverty fell from 44 per cent in 2000 to 24 per cent in 2016. Eighty per cent of Ethiopia's 99.4 million people are employed in the agricultural sector and the World Bank attributes Ethiopia's poverty reduction to agricultural growth. Agriculture's contribution to GDP in 2016 was 37.23 per cent.[1] Nutritional gains have also been witnessed: the prevalence of stunting was reduced from 58 per cent in 2000 to 44 per cent in 2011 and the prevalence of undernourishment fell from 75 per cent between 1990 and 1992 to 35 per cent between 2012 and 2014 (World Bank 2016). Ethiopia has also made improvements in terms of gender equality, especially in gender parity in primary education, seats held by women in Parliament (30 per cent in the 2010 elections up from 22 per cent) and declines in maternal mortality (from 670/100,000 in 2005 to 353/100,000 in 2015) (AfDB 2011).

Despite many successes, however, Ethiopia still faces challenges. The 2015 Human Development Report ranked Ethiopia among the poorest group of countries in the world (174 out of 188 countries). Food insecurity is a defining characteristic of poverty, with up to 10 million people dependent on humanitarian assistance (AfDB 2011). Forty-eight per cent of reproductive-aged women have no formal education (CSA 2014), highlighting the relevance of, and need for, gender programming. According to the 2014 Gender Inequality Index (GII), which measures gender-based inequalities in three dimensions — reproductive health, empowerment and economic activity (UNDP 2015) — Ethiopia had a value of 0.558, ranking it 129 out of 155 countries. This is a lower score than Rwanda (80) and Uganda (122), which are comparable countries to Ethiopia in terms of growth and development trajectories. Repeated droughts and natural disasters have created further development challenges.

Ethiopia's Growth and Transformation Plan II (GTP II) pursues an aggressive, technical approach to increasing agricultural production as a major component of the country's economic growth strategy. One component involves mobilising farmers into groups and sharing agricultural extension information en masse. In Ethiopia, the *kebele* (lowest tier of government) is sub-divided into *nius kebele* (sub-*kebele*) and, further down, into cluster households known as *mengistawi budin* (government groups/teams) (Markakis 2011). A 'government team' is a collection of thirty households on average that implement a range of government activities, including mobilising household labour for community projects and sharing information (World Bank 2010). Each team has a leader in charge of mobilising the members for specific tasks and the leader is also responsible for keeping his/her superiors informed about village activities; this information reaches all the way up to the Prime Minister's Office (Tobias and Kjetil 2012).

There are two types of government teams/groups, *mengistawi budin* (government teams/groups) and *limat budin* (development teams/groups), but sometimes the terms are used interchangeably (World Bank 2010). At the local level, government teams are expected to mobilise people for the local implementation of government policy, and development teams are expected to plan and implement small local development projects and implement the 'One-in-Five' model (Markakis 2011). This model, stipulated by the Ministry of Agriculture (2011), expects each development group to have several sub-development groups (SDGs) that are organised with five members. This One-in-Five model is well known across the country; most extension knowledge, inputs and modern methods are passed to the model farmer, who is then expected to be a role model for other farmers and help them learn about new farming methods. However, this model has been criticised as a form of politicisation of village life and agricultural extension (Berhanu and Poulton 2014; Ketsela 2006a and b; Gudina 2003: 187; Rahmato 2009; Kelemework and Kassa 2006; Segers et al. 2009; Gebremedhin et al. 2006).

The EPRDF-led government mentions these groups in its policies but uses different labels. The GTP II emphasises increasing women's membership in a 'women's army', which is believed to be a government team solely for women, which focuses on health-related information and sharing information about other EPRDF policies. Whether this means there are two government teams (one for men and one for women) or whether women are expected to participate in the regular government team of both genders as well as the female-only government team, is unclear. The benefits associated with membership of government teams are under-researched but anecdotally are reported to be policy transfer, agriculture and health awareness-raising and general information exchange.

According to Vaughan and Tronvoll (2003: 60), the number of formal and informal organisations dramatically increased under the EPRDF-led government, especially in the area of 'religious affiliation and activity'. This was a significant change in government policy, which Teshome (2013: 116) explains 'shifted the responsibility for social protection from the state to the communities'. When the Derg regime ended, the number of local women's NGOs dramatically increased until 2009. The Charities and Societies Proclamation and the Anti-terrorism Proclamation passed in 2009 reduced the number of registered NGOs, from 2,275 in 2009 to 1,701 in 2011, by minimising their ability to secure external finance (Oxfam 2016). The background to this decision was related to securing greater state control over service delivery and rights awareness (Markakis 2011).[2] This change implies that the state realised it had to play a primary role in providing protection and services at the local level (which is a good thing), and hence the increase in government teams.

Methodology

The data used for this study was derived from a farm-household survey in Ethiopia conducted between April to June 2011 (n1,978) and March to May 2014 (n1,918) to capture 2009/10 and 2012/13 production seasons recorded by the International Maize and Wheat Improvement Center (CIMMYT) in collaboration with the Ethiopian Institute of Agricultural Research (EIAR). A stratified two-stage random sampling technique was employed. Stratification was made by Agro-ecological Zone (AEZ) and by Regional State (being Amhara, Oromia, SNNPR and Tigray). Randomisation took place at the *kebele* and household level. For each sampled *kebele*, supervisors randomly selected fifteen to eighteen (on average, sixteen) sample households from the *kebele* household list to secure the targeted 2,000 sample households in total. For more details of the sampling procedure, see Shiferaw et al. 2014: 273). Table 6.1 outlines the sample size by sex and year.

Table 6.1: Female-headed and Male-headed Household Respondents across Years

Sex of Household Head	Total 2009/10	Total 2013/14
Female	154	143
%	7.8	8.08
Male	1,824	1,775
%	92.2	91.92
Total	1,978	1,918

Source: The Wheat Adoption and Impact Survey 2009/10 and 2013/14 (CIMMYT and EIAR).

Farmers were asked questions relating to a range of topics, including plot-level crop production, wheat varieties used, associated agronomic practices, and production and utilisation, along with some village, household and welfare characteristics. This study is informed by data-mining activities associated with social capital-related questions (Table 6.2). The difference between formal and informal groups in Ethiopia is registration with the government. Analytical tools used to mine the two datasets included descriptive statistics, estimation of mean, proportions, production of charts and test statistics (t-tests and chi-square).

Table 6.2: Survey Question – What type of formal and informal institution/group has the husband or wife been a member of in the last three years?

Options Given	Nature of Group*
1. Input supply/farmer co-ops/union[3]	Formal
2. Crop/seed producer and marketing group/co-ops[4]	Formal
3. Local administration[5]	Formal
4. Farmers' association[6]	Formal
5. Women's association[7]	Semi-formal/formal
6. Youth association[8]	Semi-formal/formal
7. Church/mosque association/congregation (*mahiber*)[9]	Informal
8. Saving and credit group[10]	Semi-formal/formal
9. Government team (*mengistawi budin*)[11]	Formal
10. Water user's association[12]	Semi-formal
11. *Edir* (sometimes spelt *Idir*)[13]	Informal/semi-formal
12. *Equb* (sometimes spelt *Iqub*)[14]	Informal/semi-formal
14. Other, specify……….	

Source: The Wheat Adoption and Impact Survey 2009/10 and 2013/14 (CIMMYT and EIAR)
* Please note, this column was not included in the survey but is included here for the readers' benefit.

The limitations of the study include the sampling method, which was not designed to have a representative sample by sex or region and this limits comparative analysis. It was also not primarily interested in social capital or group membership, although this comprised a small section of the survey. Consequently, the definitions of group membership names were not included in the survey instrument, leaving room for varied interpretation by enumerators and respondents. This may have resulted in some inconsistencies. Moreover, there appears to be duplication in one of the categories used: *Equb* is a savings group as well as a credit group, and both categories are given in the survey instrument (Table 6.2); thus some over-reporting is expected. Similarly, government teams/groups could have been interpreted as development groups by some respondents (the One-in-Five model). Thus, the two categories may have been conflated into one result.

Moreover, the sample has 41 per cent of respondents recording that they are a model farmer. Given the One-in-Five model, this should only be 20 per cent in a randomly sampled survey and this hints at either political interference in the research or that people over-report their closeness to the government. The latter point has relevance to the results because it implies that government team membership may also be over-reported.

Additionally, the male head of a household answered the social capital question for their spouse. Some husbands may have known about their wife's social movements and some wives may have been present during the interview, but many husbands may have answered this question unintentionally incorrectly. Moreover, the survey did not define 'female-headed household'. We define it as a woman heading a household single-handedly, without a permanent spouse or partner. While the national average of female-headed household is 26.1 per cent, this figure is believed to be inaccurate as many abandoned or divorced women do not report their single status to the government. Similarly, unless enumerators provide a definition of female-headed households, some women may answer as if they have a spouse so as to avoid the shame associated with abandonment, being a mistress or being unmarried. Therefore, female-headed households in the sample would be self-confessed single or widowed women who are recorded as such on government administration lists. Better definitions in the instrument would improve analysis.

The Theory of Social Capital

Social capital is a broad concept encompassing governments, private initiatives, local associations (community-based organisations), networks or social associations, credit groups, water user associations and various kinds of community or development organisations (Khan 2006: 161). It is a much-debated concept, with some scholars arguing that social capital is a precondition for civil society, and others that it is the product of civil society formation (see Coleman 1988,

1990; Dasgupta and Serageldin 2000; Helliwell and Putnam 2000; Narayan 1999; Putnam et al. 1993; Putnam 1995; Widner and Mundt 1998). Civil society is different from social capital (Edwards 2000). Civil society is the arena in which people come together to pursue the interests they hold in common. Social capital is what makes people co-operate and produces mutual benefits (Uphoff 2000). Bailey (2012: 2) states that 'true social capital is a dialectical exercise built on trust and reciprocity'.

Regardless of how social capital is defined and categorised, it is seen as a good thing. For Putnam (1995), life is 'easier in a country with substantial stock of social capital'. According to Durkheim (1897: 210), a cohesive society has stocks of social capital and 'mutual moral support, which instead of throwing the individual onto his own resources, leads him to share in the collective energy and support.'

However, people do not benefit equally from social capital (Kilby 2005). Social capital can be culturally specific (Torkelsson and Tassau 2008). There can be a gender and social class bias in the utilisation of social networks (Pawar s2006; Bailey 2012). Women benefit from group membership in different ways to men (Teshome et al. 2014). Ethiopian women join informal *Edir* groups to access credit but find the emotional support provided by *Edir* is unparalleled by other types of groups (Teshome et al. 2014: 2). Additionally, women explained that participation in an *Edir* helped them to develop their self-confidence and to raise their voice publicly on a range of issues, such as marriage, poverty and politics (Teshome et al. 2014: 6). People who are poor are often a part of, and dependent upon, other people's social capital (Mosse 2010: 1158). Moreover, 'poverty erodes trust and reciprocity because of the intense competition for scarce resources' (Rahmato 2004), and thus poor people find it harder to accrue social capital. This might suggest that women and the poor benefit differently from government teams/groups than other members.

Moreover, not all social capital is equal. Bonding social capital would be built by informal groups involving close family members, friends and neighbours. For example, *Edirs* usually involve a select group of people who live in close proximity. Bridging social capital arises from groups like co-operatives or inter-village savings and credit groups facilitated by NGOs. Linking social capital involves horizontal linkages to people with influence or in power (Woolcock 1998: 23). By this definition, government-led teams/groups would increase linking social capital, maybe a little bridging social capital but not much bonding social capital. They may also facilitate structural forms of social capital that enable mutually beneficial collective action. The EPRDF could be trying to build a certain kind of cognitive capital (shared norms, values, attitudes and beliefs) through government teams/groups, such as nationalistic sentiments.

What kinds of social capital does Ethiopia need? Levine (1965) argues that Ethiopian society has 'weak horizontal ties' and a 'hierarchical-individualistic structure'. Crummey (1980: 123–124) concurs, suggesting that hierarchical patron-client ties override any horizontal ties. Thus, the kinds of social capital that should be strengthened in Ethiopia are cognitive and bonding, forms of social capital that generate horizontal ties. Yet, positionality is important — excluded groups may prefer linking social capital for the access it provides. This line of questioning suggests that another theory, such as citizenship theory, may be required along with additional data to identify whether excluded citizens benefit more from encounters with the state (vertical citizenship), regardless of hypothesised coercion[15], than other forms of citizenship, such as the horizontal view of citizenship, which views the relationship between citizens to be as important as the vertical relationship between the individual and the state (Kabeer 2005: 23; Cornwall, Robins and Von Lieres 2008).

The role of the government in building social capital is uncertain because social capital is usually associated with non-government entities. Edgerton et al. (2008) suggest that governance and the way power and wealth are shared, especially in oppressive societies, limit the degree of social capital accrued. Therefore, a key question remains: are government teams/groups as beneficial to individual farmers as voluntary membership in local groups, such as *Edir* and *Equb*?

Informal Social Protection

An important contribution to the theory of social capital comes from the social protection literature that examines the differences between formal and informal forms of social protection. Whether formal or informal, social protection offers a safety net function that reduces the severity of crises and shocks. Also known as traditional or community-based social protection, informal social protection mechanisms distribute risk within a community and fill some of the gaps left by formal interventions (Norton and Foster 2001). Mpedi (2008) finds that informal social protection is guided by customary principles, culture and religion and helps people feel connected to their community.

However, the definition of informal social protection is somewhat disputed in the literature. For Oduro (2010), informal social protection relates to its lack of legal status; yet others argue that informal social protection depends on the provider (for example, the state provides formal social protection and the family and community provide informal social protection). Meanwhile, Teshome (2013: 100) identifies five components of informal social protection: traditional savings and credit; burial societies; the extended family; child support; and asset transfers. Stavropoulou et al. (2017), on the other hand, define four: collective rules and mechanisms (such as informal loans, sharecropping and *dabare*[16]); reciprocity networks or gift exchange arrangements (which include remittances and labour-sharing); semi-formal support mechanisms (which include burial societies and rotating savings and credit); and religious-based support. Out of this list the survey instrument includes semi-formal and religious-based support. Thus, informal social protection and certain types of social capital are mutually reinforcing.

While the literature debates the relevance and merit of informal social protection, the important social function played by informal social protection is agreed. Informal social protection plays a role in social cohesion, trust and reciprocity, as well as offering support during hard times. One study estimates that informal labour-sharing practices increase agriculture productivity by almost 20 per cent (Mekonnen and Dorfman 2013). Dercon et al. (2006) found *Edirs* can also offer short-term loans to use during sickness and other shocks, such as a poor harvest or livestock death, which can have an instrumental effect on a farmer's longer-term food security by ensuring the farmer will not have to sell off assets to cope with shocks. Informal social protection originally pre-dates nation states.

The inclusiveness, equity, cost and ability of informal mechanisms to adapt to modern circumstances is questioned. Informal forms of protection can too quickly become a means of social control and a mechanism that reinforces unhelpful norms and inequality (Platteau 1991; Dercon 2003; Kasente et al. 2002; Verpooten and Verschraegen 2010). Kasente et al. (2002) discuss the way any additional unpaid work generated from informal social protection often becomes the responsibility of women, who already have a disproportionately higher workload than men. Covariate shocks affect whole communities and thus the propensity to cope via informal social protection alone diminishes with repeat crises as whole communities are depleted (Croppenstedt et al. 2017). Teshome (2013: 103) argues that informal social protection mechanisms are useful but declining in their value in Ethiopia as 'they need to work on becoming more relevant to the changing situation'.

Regardless, new initiatives should take care not to undermine informal forms of social protection especially if state- and market-based protection mechanisms are underdeveloped or unreliable (Browne 2013). Bhattamishra and Barrett (2010) explain the way external interventions can reduce inter-household co-operation, increase competition and change the position/status of households. State support and development projects should take care not to change the structure of social networks, fragment, weaken and undermine these informal forms of protection without properly replacing the assistance or support they provide, for this would leave a gap in how communities cope and function. Moreover, a study on women's co-operatives and COVID-19 'has highlighted that collective models are a sustainable means of providing social and economic security to informal workers, especially during the crisis' (Hiriyur and Chettri 2020: 36). Consequently, government investment in co-operatives, whether formal or otherwise, will assist in a number of economic and social ways that are only superficially understood.

The idea of informal forms of assistance leaving 'a gap' in coping mechanisms is contested by some scholars. Devereux et al. (2008) argue that formal social protection increases incomes for the poor and may rejuvenate informal social protection mechanisms, rather than displace them. Guenther (2007) concurs because the EPRDF-led government's Productive Safety Net Programme (PSNP)[17] regenerated local *Equbs* and the savings culture enabled members to purchase livestock and agriculture inputs. However, Tirivayi et al. (2013) found that the PSNP crowded out informal support systems. The complementarity of formal and informal social protection is disputed in the literature and yet both forms of social protection are needed.

Results

The previous sections have shown that not all forms of social capital, networks or protection are equal, and financial gain is not the only reason groups form and members stay. This section presents the differences in group membership by female-headed households (FHH), male-headed households (MHH) and the spouses of MHH, between the 2009 and 2012 production seasons.

Table 6.3: Female-headed Household Group Membership, 2009/10 and 2012/13

Group Type	Year 2009/10	Year 2012/13
Edir	78	64
Church/mosque associations	44	15
Farmers' associations	25	17
Women's association	16	3
Input supply/farmer's co-op/union	7	27
Saving and credit	9	10
Equb	6	7
Government team	4	36
Youth association	2	1
Local administration	1	3
Crop/seed producer/marketing co-op	1	1
Consumers associations	1	0
Housing associations	1	0
Total	177 (n154)	175 (n143)

Source: The Wheat Adoption and Impact Survey 2009/10 and 2013/14 (CIMMYT and EIAR)

Table 6.3 reveals that FHH have increased their membership in input supply/farmers' co-operatives/unions and government teams, and decreased their membership in farmers' associations, women's associations, church/mosque associations and *Edir*. The top three groups for FHH in 2009 were (in order): *Edir*, church/mosque and farmers' associations, whereas in 2013 the top three groups were: *Edir*, government teams and farmers' associations. See also Figure 6.1 for a visual representation of the most relevant changes.

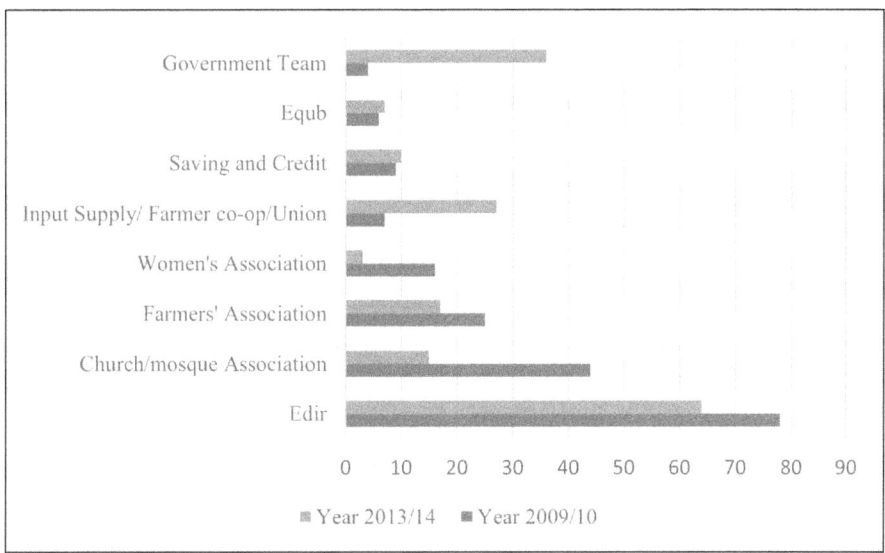

Figure 6.1: Female-headed Household Group Membership

Source: The Wheat Adoption and Impact Survey 2009/10 and 2013/14 (CIMMYT and EIAR)

Table 6.4 reveals the success of the EPRDF-led government's policy to mobilise women to join government teams.[19] Other membership increases for spouses (outside of government teams) include input supply/farmer co-operatives/unions, crop/seed producer/marketing co-operatives, land administration, local administration and women's associations. It is interesting that women joined local security and political membership groups, even though there were only a few observations of this, because these are not typical roles for women. Moreover, the fact that these groups are included in a social capital question by respondents for the 'other' category is revealing as it indicates a merging of civil society, security and politics.

Table 6.4: Spouses' Group Membership 2009/10 and 2012/13

Type of Group	Year 2009/10	Year 2012/13
Edir	948	594
Church/mosque association	339	204
Farmers' association	240	167
Saving and Credit	152	127
Input Supply/farmer co-op/union	88	132
Government team	77	466
Equb	56	34
Women's association	49	54
Youth association	41	13
Local administration	25	75
Crop/seed producer/marketing co-op	11	24
Water user's association	8	1
Not applicable	2	
Labour union	1	0
Health extension	1	0
Housing association	3	0
Informal farmer group	0	1
Local security	0	3
Political member	0	3
Total	1969 (n1824)	1844 (n1775)

Source: The Wheat Adoption and Impact Survey 2009/10 and 2013/14 (CIMMYT and EIAR)

Decreases in membership include farmers' associations, youth associations, church/mosque associations, savings and credit associations, water user's associations, *Edir* and *Equb*. The most dramatic decrease is in *Edir* membership. The most popular groups in 2009 for spouses were *Edir*, church/mosque and farmers' associations, whereas in 2013 it was *Edir*, government teams and church/mosque associations. Figure 6.2 visually highlights the main differences, which are huge, but the reasons behind these changes are unknown.

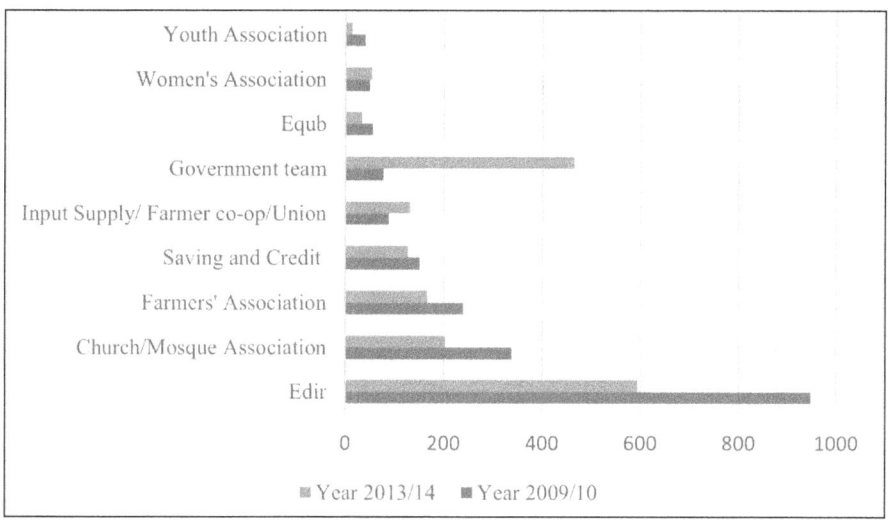

Figure 6.2: Spouses' Group Membership

Source: The Wheat Adoption and Impact Survey 2009/10 and 2013/14 (CIMMYT and EIAR).

Table 6.5: Group Membership for Male-headed Households 2009/10 and 2012/13

Type of Group	2009/10	2012/13
Not applicable	1	13
Input supply/farmer co-op/union	71	141
Crop/seed producer/marketing co-op	16	32
Local administration	34	35
Farmers' association	204	124
Health extension	2	0
Youth association	29	11
Church/mosque association	273	171
Saving and credit	96	143
Government team[18]	47	439
Water user's association	12	3
Edir	901	590
Equb	38	27
Housing association	0	2
Solar association	0	4
Loading and unloading	0	1
Teaching association	0	1
Fishery association	0	1

Local security	0	4
Political member	0	2
School committee	2	0
Consumers association	1	0
Total	1727 (n1824)	1733 (n1775)

Source: The Wheat Adoption and Impact Survey 2009/10 and 2013/14 (CIMMYT and EIAR)

Table 6.5 reveals MHH increased their membership of: input suppl/farmers' co-operatives/unions, crop/seed producer/marketing co-operatives, savings and credit, and government teams. There are also a range of new groups listed in 2012, like solar associations and local security. It is unclear how these new groups function and their membership seems small.

Decreases include: farmers' associations, youth associations, church/mosque associations, water user associations, *Edir* and *Equb*. The most popular groups for men in 2009 were: *Edir*, church/mosque and farmers' associations, whereas in 2013 it was *Edir*, government teams and church/mosque. Figure 6.3 visually shows the similarities in the female results, in that there is an increase in government team membership and a decrease in *Edir* membership.

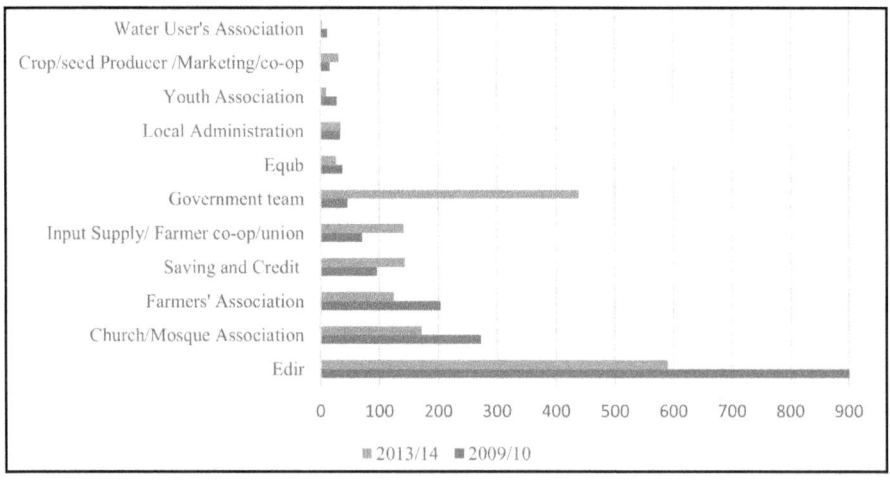

Figure 6.3: Male-headed Household Group Membership

Source: The Wheat Adoption and Impact Survey 2009/10 and 2013/14 (CIMMYT and EIAR)

Discussion

The results reveal a decrease in *Edir*, farmers' associations and church and mosque membership across all respondents' categories, along with a decrease in women's association membership for women. This trend is puzzling, given the strong role that religion plays in an Ethiopian person's life, that national statistics do not reflect this reduction in religious devotion, and the widespread usage of *Edir* and its relevance to traditional Ethiopian urban and rural lifestyles. Farmers' associations may well be replaced by input supply/farmers' co-operatives/unions, so that trend is less puzzling. However, the reduction in women's association membership is unexplainable. There are other knock-on effects on women-only groups that are unlikely to be met to the same degree by mixed groups. Lemma and Tesema (2016) and Lemma et al. (2019) found that women's-only development groups in Ethiopia have had a transformational impact on gender relations, to the extent that they empowered women within the household and in the community. The theory of social capital elucidates that if group membership does not deliver benefits to its members, then the members will leave and join other higher performing groups (Bernard and Spielman 2009). Is the declining membership of these traditional groups at all associated with under-performance?

The changing group membership dynamics may be related to the relevance of government teams to a farmer's survival and livelihood, especially if input of agriculture extension knowledge is distributed through these groups. For example, there are various allegations in the literature that in the government's allocation of seeds, fertilisers and credit, government extension workers give priority to farmers loyal to the EPRDF (Ketsela 2006a: 166; Gudina 2003: 187; Dessalegn 2012: 210, cited in Berhanu and Poulton 2014: 208; Kelemework and Kassa 2006; Segers et al. 2009). This suggests that closeness to the EPRDF-led government has numerous benefits for farmers. Some of these authors view this negatively and argue that access to agricultural inputs has become an instrument of political control and patronage. The fact that some respondents listed political membership and security in a social capital question implies that there may be some truth to these politicisation arguments. In which case, the results may indicate the political nature of relationships in Ethiopia—one matters not as an individual but because of one's affiliation to others outside of traditional kin networks, who have connections to the EPRDF-led government.

Another explanation for the increase in government team/group membership may be associated with the reduction of registered NGOs due to the 2009 Proclamations. As explained in the section on the socioeconomic context of Ethiopia, these proclamations dramatically reduced the number of local NGOs due to a ban on external funding. Development projects implemented by these NGOs sometimes mobilised people into groups. Without this support, farmers have fewer choices and rural people may join government-led groups to access the information and support formerly given by NGOs.

Inclusion in groups is highly beneficial for excluded groups for it enables them to build their own social capital stocks, rather than relying on a patron. Given that women have been excluded from development, government and political spaces for centuries, the benefits accruing to them from government-team membership could outweigh those accruing to men. Contact with the state strengthens linking social capital and may increase women's confidence, sense of citizenship and access to information. This may be the same for the poor and excluded. Contact with the state may offer numerous unexplored benefits to female, excluded and/or impoverished farmers, or it may merely involve swapping one kind of patron with another (Golooba-Mutebi and Hickey 2010). How group membership influences agriculture production and productivity, especially for excluded groups, requires research.

Yet, other questions remain. Do the benefits of government-team membership outweigh the loss of informal groups that offer social protection? Strengthening social groups and networks may be an effective way to achieve increased agriculture innovation, production and productivity. But, this should not come at the cost of a decrease in informal group memberships if such groups offer a form of social protection against shocks and crisis, especially when the state's social protection system is limited to food aid and charity. Does the reduction in informal social protection matter to a farmer's ability to cope with adversity?

It is important to discover what type of social capital the government teams/groups generate in comparison to traditional groups. It is unknown at this time whether moving into state-sponsored groups increases farmers' linking social capital and if this is needed more than the bonding and bridging capital that accrues from informal group membership. Unless government teams/groups matter more to farmers than traditional groups, in terms of the type of social capital generated, the theory of social capital may be an ineffective way to interpret the results. State-society or citizenship theory may offer a more meaningful framework to explore the value of informal groups and especially government-team membership.

To ascertain this would require a better understanding of the social lives of farmers. Damtew et al. (2006) argue that, in Ethiopia, 'kin groups cooperate much more significantly [for parochial confrontation] than in economic matters'. Therefore, the move away from informal support mechanisms and towards government teams and input supply/farmers' co-operatives/unions might reflect the increasing economic concern of farmers and their lack of time to be members of multiple groups. It may indicate the increasing marketisation of social relationships. As Polanyi argues in *The Great Transformation*, markets destroy social embeddedness and socially constituted forms of exchange and distribution and replace them with a cold commercial logic. While Harriss-White (2008: 205) argues that this process usually occurs very slowly over a long timescale, the results in this study show an acceleration of this process, which aligns with the ambitious GTP II. Group membership is a part of a farmer's livelihood strategy and the changes observed in group membership may reflect wider socioeconomic changes. Not enough is known about the social lives of farmers to draw robust conclusions.

If such dramatic change is occurring, how are farmers coping? Informal social protection should not necessarily be the key form of social protection in rural lives because there are inherent weaknesses in these traditional coping mechanisms (Stavropoulou et al. 2017). However, understanding the forms of support farmers need and any gaps or trade-offs would ensure that state-, market- and NGO-led support complements informal mechanisms, rather than undermining traditional coping strategies. The results suggest there is a need for greater alignment between social, economic and agricultural policy.

Conclusion

This chapter presents results from the social capital questions asked in a panel data set from the Wheat Adoption and Impact Survey 2009/2010 and 2013/2014. The results examine informal and formal group membership of male- and female-headed households and spouses of the men in wheat-growing households. The evidence suggests that state-led approaches are only one part of the agricultural development story but that state-led support is increasing. Informal forms of support still complement state-led and private sector-led development, albeit in declining numbers. In isolation, the decline of informal group membership may imply a reduction in cohesion, social capital and trust. However, it could also mean increased connectivity to the EPRDF-led government and increased access to agriculture inputs.

The agriculture survey that generated the data seems insufficiently designed to understand the social lives of farmers. The findings illustrate differences of marital status for women, but the survey does not allow for a similar comparison between the married statuses of men. Similarly, the length of time a person is widowed or single matters to productivity but was not captured. The survey cannot ascertain farmers' reasons for joining groups — necessity, coercion, reputation as a high performer, or whether group membership changes relate to exogenous factors such as development projects. Group membership by sex suggests that the strategies and preferences of female farmers are not that distinct from men's, but given the limitation of the research this issue should be more closely examined through qualitative research methods that aim to understand motives and beliefs. The findings highlight the need for more mixed-methods studies in agriculture that are designed to capture the social as well as economic lives of farmers and the influence, power and role of each group for farmers and the gender differences within.

Traditionally, governments underutilise informal mechanisms for transferring agriculture extension information, especially for women. However, the EPRDF-led government teams/groups may be one of the best ways for female farmers to access inputs and extension information (given existing gendered norms) and this may (or may not) come at the cost of increased surveillance and local politicisation. Whether this new political landscape enables or constrains opportunity structures for farmers is worthy of research, along with how government teams contribute to building social capital.

The group membership of farmers is poorly understood, yet the data suggests that farmers choose to spend their (social) time in various ways and that this possibly has a bearing on their productivity. Moreover, the social lives of farmers, their opportunity structures and market forces are rapidly changing in Ethiopia and how this collectively affects agricultural productivity and wellbeing should be better understood to ensure the government meets its GTP II targets.

Acknowledgements

This research was completed with the financial support of the Federal Ministry for Economic Cooperation and Development, Germany, under the project 'Understanding gender in wheat-based livelihoods for enhanced WHEAT R4D impact in Afghanistan, Pakistan and Ethiopia', implemented by CIMMYT. We would like to thank CIMMYT for the opportunity to conduct this study. Funding support came from BMZ's study, Understanding Gender in Wheat-Based Livelihoods for Enhanced WHEAT R4D impact in Afghanistan, Pakistan and Ethiopia.

Notes

1. Source: https://data.worldbank.org/indicator/NV.AGR.TOTL.ZS?end=2016 andlocations=ETandstart=1981andview=chart Accessed 20 September 2017.
2. Markakis (2011) explains that non-government organisations with an impeccable reputation and which played a useful role in society, especially around human rights, were systematically dismantled.
3. Co-operatives serve as a distribution point for government-supported inputs (machinery leasing and purchasing, technical knowledge, fertilisers, etc.), credit and other financial services. In Ethiopia, co-operatives are formally registered with the Federal Cooperative Agency (see Councils of Ministers Regulation No. 106/2004 and Cooperative Societies Proclamation No. 147/1998).
4. These types of groups are also government-run and supplied with seeds and crops and also involve group-based buying and selling.
5. The local administration is at the *kebele* level (the lowest formal administrative unit). Each *kebele* has an average population of about 5,000 people and the *kebele* executive is powerful with seven members: chairman, vice chairman, health sector co-ordinator, agriculture sector co-ordinator, education sector co-ordinator, justice and security co-ordinator and *hizb aderjajet* (mass mobilisation/organisation co-ordinator). The executive is protected by fifteen security guards (Tobias and Kjetil 2012).

6. Farmers' associations can be similar to co-operatives but are formed for a variety of farming reasons.
7. Women's associations are voluntary associations of women who agree to help each other in a specified way, such as in cash or in kind, in capacity building and by sharing information (Dercon et al. 2005; Habtu 2012). Some may engage in savings and loans or may help organise community events or may help mitigate risks and crisis. The roles vary by group and location. In Ethiopia there is a network of women's associations formally registered with the government and supported by the state-level Ministry of Women and Children Affairs. It is unclear in this survey whether women are members of formal or informal women's associations, as both exist in rural Ethiopia.
8. Based on the National Youth Policy of Ethiopia (2004), youth associations are a voluntary group of young people, usually under twenty-nine years, who meet regularly and sometimes interact with local government or NGOs on matters that concern youth or society. Youth associations can be formal and informal, depending on how they are registered.
9. Church and mosque associations are primarily established for the fulfilment of social or religious obligations (Negash 2003). According to Habtu (2012), *mahibers* can be informal and held in homes and members are also involved in community activities, such as risk-coping, monthly feasts, provision of information, financial services (especially for weddings and funerals) and conflict resolution. Members of *mahiber* are usually followers of the same religion (Orthodox), close friends, relatives and neighbours (Sileshi 2006; Habtu 2012).
10. Savings and credit groups can be formal or informal and meet regularly to deposit small amounts of money and then wait their turn to take out a loan, with the loan amount being determined by the individual and group savings (Dlamini and Brislin 2006). These are similar to *Equb* but may have been formed through external assistance, such as by an NGO.
11. Government teams are a collection of thirty households on average that mobilise people for the implementation of government policy at the local level, including community projects and sharing information (World Bank 2010).
12. A water user's association is usually an informal group that has been elected or volunteers to help manage and make decisions about local water resources and how they should be used and conserved. NGOs usually form these associations.
13. *Edir* is a voluntary self-help association that operates as a funeral society which provides mutual support at times of death, such as financial, material and emotional assistance (Butcher 2007). A high value is attached to funerals in Ethiopia and by participating in an *Edir* one's family members are guaranteed to receive a proper burial (Teshome et al. 2014: 6). *Edirs* are usually sex specific as the sexes perform different roles when it comes to funerals. *Edirs* have existed in Ethiopia for many decades.
14. *Equb* is an informal local institution established voluntarily to collect a specific amount of money (depending on a member's wealth) from the members on a specific date and is redistributed to members on a lottery basis (Habtu 2012; Rahmato and Aklilu 1999). This process continues until the last member receives his/her share (or what he/she has saved so far) and the whole process starts anew (Teshome 2008). Groups are usually homogenous with people from the same workplace, ethnic background, trade, schooling or neighbourhood so that they trust

each other (Sileshi 2006). While *Equb* is an alternative to microfinance, it exists in communities where formal microfinance institutions are established (Butcher 2007). Teshome (2013: 111) argues that *Equbs* are formed 'not only to overcome short term financial difficulties but also to help members start or expand businesses.'

15. Berhanu and Poulton (2014) argue that investment in agricultural extension services by the government has two objectives: the first being economic growth and the second 'to contribute to the securing of political control across Ethiopia's large and diverse countryside, including mobilising support around election time.' Meanwhile, Vaughan and Tronvoll (2002: 62) discuss a widespread belief in Ethiopia that the state is a negative actor and civil society is a positive actor, and that 'political activity is to be avoided'; but the authors question these binary generalisations.

16. Dabare is a traditional practice in Ethiopia whereby well-off villagers lend or give milk-producing livestock to poorer households with children (Addis and Assefa 2013).

17. The PSNP has two streams: a public works stream with over six million beneficiaries, which targets the 'productive poor', and; a direct support scheme for those who cannot work because they are disabled, elderly, ill, etc. The government's target to graduate eighty per cent of public work beneficiaries out of the PSNP by 2014 was unsuccessful because the programme is really about charity for the destitute and to help deliver support during Ethiopia's repeated food shortages.

18. In the data set there seem to be a number of male farmers in 2012 who said they joined the 'government team' before 2009 but in the 2009/10 survey reported that they were not in a government team. Thus, the year joined was removed from the analysis because it is assumed that men were over-reporting their closeness to the government and thus embellished the year they joined. This situation emphasises how important EPRD-government-led networks have become over a three-year period.

19. The GTP II discusses increasing women's participation in development through the promotion of a 'women's army' which is also known as a government heath development/transformation group (Maes et al. 2015).

References

Abate, T., Shiferaw, B., Menkir, A., Wegary, D., Kebede, Y., Tesfaye, K., Kassie, M., Bogale, G., Tadesse, B. and Keno, T., 2015, Factors that Transformed Maize Productivity in Ethiopia, *Food Security*, Vol. 7, pp. 965–981. DOI 10.1007/s12571-015-0488-z.

Addis, E. and Assefa, S., 2013, Social Protection Systems in Pastoral Areas of Ethiopia: The Case of Fentale District, Oromia Region, in Devereux, S. and Getu, M., eds, 2013, *Informal and Formal Social Protection Systems in Sub-Saharan Africa*, Kampala: Fountain Publishers, pp. 177–190.

African Development Bank (AfDB), 2011, Federal Democratic Republic of Ethiopia Country Strategy Paper, 2011–2015, African Development Bank.

Bailey, D. C., 2012, Women and Wasta: The Use of Focus Groups for Understanding Social Capital and Middle Eastern Women, *The Qualitative Report*, Vol. 17, No. 33, pp. 1–18. Available online at http://nsuworks.nova.edu/tqr/vol17/iss33/1.

Berhanu, K. and Poulton, C., 2014, The Political Economy of Agricultural Extension Policy in Ethiopia: Economic Growth and Political Control, *Development Policy Review*, Vol. 32, Issue 2, pp. 199–216.

Bernard, T. and Spielman, D., 2009, Reaching the Rural Poor Through Rural Producer Organisations? A Study of Agricultural Marketing Co-Operatives in Ethiopia, *Food Policy*, Vol. 34, pp. 60–69.

Bhattamishra, R. and Barrett, C.B., 2010, Community-Based Risk Management Arrangements: A Review, *World Development*, Vol. 38, No. 7, pp. 923–932. http://dx.doi.org/10.1016/j. worlddev.2009.12.017.

Bhuyan, S., 2007, The 'People' Factor in Co-Operatives: An Analysis of Members' Attitudes and Behavior, *Canadian Journal of Agricultural Economics*, Vol. 55, No. 3, pp. 275 98.

Bourdieu, P. and Wacquant, L., 1992, *An Invitation to Reflexive Sociology*, London, UK: University of Chicago Press.

Bratton, M., 1989, Beyond the State: Civil Society and Associational Life in Africa, *World Politics*, Vol. 41, No. 3, pp. 407–30.

Browne, E., 2013, Community-Based Social Protection, Governance and Social Development Research Centre Helpdesk Research Report 1020, Birmingham, UK: Governance and Social Development Resource Centre, University of Birmingham.

Butcher, C., 2007, Understanding the Role of Informal Institutions in Social Accountability, World Bank. Available online at http://siteresources.worldbank.org/INTEMPOWERMENT/Resources/Ethiopia_Understanding_Role_of_Institutions.pdf. Accessed 22/09/2017.

Central Statistical Agency (CSA), Ethiopia, Ministry of Health (Ethiopia), World Bank, 2014, Ethiopia Mini Demographic and Health Survey 2014, Addis Ababa: Central Statistical Agency.

Coleman, J., 1988, Social Capital in the Creation of Human Capital, *American Journal of Sociology*, Vol. 94, pp. 95–120.

Coleman, J., 1990, *Foundations of Social Theory*, Cambridge, MA.: Harvard University Press.

Cornwall, A., Robins, S. and Von Lieres, B., 2008, Rethinking 'Citizenship' in the Postcolony, *Third World Quarterly*, Vol. 29, No. 6, pp. 1069–1086.

Croppenstedt, A., Knowles, M. and Lowder, S., 2017, Social Protection and Agriculture: Introduction to The Special Issue, *Global Food Security*. http://dx.doi.org/10.1016/j.gfs.2017.09.006

Crummey, D., 1980, Abyssinian Feudalism, *Past and Present*, Vol. 89, No. 1, pp. 115–138.

Damtew, Y., Tsegy, M., Kenaw, S. and Tegegne, S., 2006, Dinki: Ankober Wereda, North Shewa Zone, Amhara Region, Report of the International Household Survey Network, Addis Ababa and Oxford: Department of Sociology, University of Addis Ababa and the Centre for the Study of African Economies, Oxford University. Available online at http://catalog.ihsn.org/index.php/citations/20585.

Dasgupta, P. and Serageldin I., 2000, *Social Capital: A Multifaceted Perspective*, Washington DC: World Bank Group.

Dlamini, P. and Brislin, N., 2006, Amhara Credit and Savings Institutions: Ethiopia, USAID Amap Financial Services Knowledge Generation—state owned retail banks, microreport #58. Available online at https://www.marketlinks.org/sites/marketlinks.org/files/resource/files/ML4619_mr_58_amhara_credit___savings_institute.pdf.

Dercon, S., 2003, *Insurance Against Poverty*, Policy Brief, Helsinki: United Nations University-WIDER.

Dercon, S., Bold, T., De Weerdt J. and Pankhurst, A., 2004, Extending Insurance? Funeral Associations in Ethiopia and Tanzania, OECD Development Centre Working Paper No. 240, Issey-les-Moulineaux: OECD Development Centre.

Dercon, S., De Weerdt, J., Bold, T. and Pankhurst, A., 2005, Membership Based Indigenous Insurance Associations in Ethiopia and Tanzania, QEH Working Papers 126, Oxford: University of Oxford.

Dercon, S., De Weerdt, J., Bold, T. and Pankhurst, A., 2006, Group-Based Funeral Insurance in Ethiopia and Tanzania, *World Development*, Vol. 34, No. 4, pp. 685–703.

Dessalegn, T., 2012, *Ye Meles Amlko* [Worshipping Meles], Addis Ababa: Mastewal Printing and Advertising Enterprise.

Devereux, S., Dorward, A., Sabates-Wheeler, R., Poulton, C., Guenther, B. and Al-Hassan, R., 2008, Support to Small Farmer Development, Paper commissioned by FAO and presented in FAO Workshop, Rome, 17–18 January 2008. Available online at http://www.fao.org/fileadmin/templates/esa/Workshop_reports/Social_protection_2008/workshop_0108_social_protection.pdf.

Devereux, S. and Getu, M., 2013, The Conceptualisation and Status of Informal and Formal Social Protection in Sub-Saharan Africa, in: Devereux, S. and Getu, M., eds, *Informal and Formal Social Protection Systems in Sub-Saharan Africa*, Kampala: Fountain Publishers, pp. 1–7.

Dunn, J. R., 1988, Basic Cooperative Principles and Their Relationship to Selected Practices, *Journal of Agricultural Cooperation*, Vol. 3, pp. 1–11.

Durkheim E., 1897, *Suicide: A Study in Sociology*, London: Routledge.

Durlauf, S. N. and Fafchamps, M., 2004, Social Capital, in Aghion, P. and Durlauf, S., eds, *Handbook of Economic Growth* 1st ed., Amsterdam: Elsevier, Vol. 1, chapter 26, pp. 1639–1699.

Edgerton, J. D., Peter, T. and Roberts, L. W., 2008, Back to the Basics: Socio-Economic, Gender, and Regional Disparities in Canada's Educational System, *Canadian Journal of Education*, Vol. 3, No. 4, pp. 861–888.

Edwards, M., 2000, *NGO Rights and Responsibilities: A New Deal for Global Governance*, London: The Foreign Policy Centre in association with NCVO, London.

Francesconi, G. N. and Heerink, N., 2010, Ethiopian Agricultural Cooperatives in an Era of Global Commodity Exchange: Does Organisational Form Matter?, *Journal of African Economies*, Vol. 20, No. 1, pp. 153–177.

Fukuyama, F., 2001, Social Capital, Civil Society and Development, *Third World Quarterly*, Vol. 22, No. 1, pp. 7–20.

Gebremedhin, B., Hoekstra, D and Tegegne, A., 2006, Commercialisation of Ethiopian Agriculture: Extension Service from Input Supplier to Knowledge Broker and Facilitator, Nairobi: International Livestock Research Institute.

Gebremedhin, B., Jaleta, M. and Hoekstra, D., 2009, Smallholders, Institutional Services, and Commercial Transformation in Ethiopia, *Agricultural Economics*, Vol. 40, Issue s1, pp. 773–787.

Getnet, K. and Anullo, T., 2012, Agricultural Co-Operatives and Rural Livelihoods: Evidence from Ethiopia, *Annals of Public and Co-operative Economics*, Vol. 83, pp. 181–98.

Golooba-Mutebi, F. and Hickey, S., 2010, Governing Chronic Poverty under Inclusive Liberalism: The Case of the Northern Uganda Social Action Fund, *Journal of Development Studies*, Vol. 46, No. 7, pp. 1216–1239.

Gudina, M., 2003, *Ethiopia: Competing Ethnic Nationalisms and the Quest for Democracy, 1960–2000*, Addis Ababa: Profile Books.

Guenther, B., 2007, Cash-for-Work, Vulnerability and Social Resilience: A Case Study of the Productive Safety Net Programme in Sidama Zone, Ethiopia, MPhil Dissertation, Brighton, UK: Institute of Development Studies.

Harriss-White, B., 2008, Female and Male Grain Marketing Systems: Analytical and Policy Issues for West Africa and India, in Jackson, C. and Pearson, R., eds, 1998, *Feminist Visions of Development: Gender Analysis and Policy*, London and New York: Routledge.

Helliwell, J. and Putnam, R., 2000, Economic Growth and Social Capital in Italy, in Dasgupta, P. and Serageldin, I., eds, *Social Capital: A Multifaceted Perspective*, Washington DC: World Bank Group, pp. 253–68.

Hiriyur, S. M. and Chettri, N., 2020, Women's Cooperatives and COVID-19: Learning and the Way Forward, Research Paper, Ahmedabad: SEWA Cooperative Federation.

Kabeer, N., 2005, Introduction: The Search for 'Inclusive' Citizenship: Meanings and Expressions in an Inter-connected World, in Kabeer, N., ed., *Inclusive Citizenship: Meanings and Expressions*, London: Zed Books, pp. 1–30.

Kasente, D., Asingwire, N., Banugire, F. and Kyomuhendo, S., 2002, Social Security Systems in Uganda, *Journal of Social Development in Africa*, Vol. 17, No. 2, pp. 159–180.

Kelemework, F. and Kassa, H., 2006, Assessment of the Current Extension System of Ethiopia: A Closer Look at Planning and Implementation', Issue Paper Series No. 2, Addis Ababa: Ethiopian Economic Association/Ethiopian Economic Policy Research Institute.

Ketsela, Y., 2006a, Attendant Issues in the Current Agricultural Extension Program in Ethiopia, in Berhanu, K. and Fantaye, D., eds, *Ethiopia: Rural Development Policies, Trends, Changes and Continuities*, Addis Ababa: Addis Ababa University Press.

Ketsela, Y., 2006b, Post-1991 Agricultural Policies: The Role of the National Extension Program in Addressing the Problem of Food Security, in Attilo, A., Berhanu, K. and Ketsela, Y., eds, *Ethiopia: Politics, Policy Making and Rural Development*, Addis Ababa: Addis Ababa University Press.

Khan, S. R., 2006, Learning from South Asian 'Successes': Tapping Social Capital, *South Asia Economic Journal*, Vol. 7, No. 2, pp. 157–178. DOI 10.1177/139156140600700201.

Kilby, P., 2005, Accountability for Empowerment: Dilemmas Facing Non-Government Organisations, *World Development*, Vol. 34, No. 6, pp. 951–963.

Habtu, K., 2012, Classifying Informal Institutions in Ethiopia Internship, Paper Development Economics Group, Wageningen University.

Knack, S. and Keefer, P., 1997, Does Social Capital Have an Economic Payoff? A Cross-Country Investigation, *Quarterly Journal of Economics*, Vol. 112, No. 4, pp. 1251–1288.

Krishna, A., 2001, Moving from the Stock of Social Capital to the Flow of Benefits: The Role of Agency, *World Development*, Vol. 29, No. 6, pp. 925–943.

Krishna, A. and Uphoff, N., 2002, Mapping and Measuring Social Capital Through Assessment of Collective Action to Conserve and Develop Watersheds in Rajasthan, India, in Grootaert, C. and Van Bastelaer, T., eds, *The Role of Social Capital in Development: An Empirical Assessment*, Cambridge, UK: Cambridge University Press, pp. 85–124.

Lemma, M., Alemu, B., Mekonnen, M. and Wieland, B., 2019, *Community Conversations on Antimicrobial Use and Resistance*, Nairobi: International Livestock Research Institute (ILRI).

Lemma, M., Kinati, W., Mulema, A., Bassa, Z., Tigabe, A., Desta, H., Mekonnen, M. and Asfaw, T., 2018, Report of Community Conversations About Gender Roles in Livestock, Nairobi: International Livestock Research Institute (ILRI).

Lemma and Tesema, 2016, New Approaches and Methods for Addressing Gender Gaps in Extension Services: Experiences and Lessons from LIVES Project in Ethiopia, *Journal of Agricultural Economics, Extension and Rural Development*: Vol. 4, No. 4: pp. 429–435.

Leta G., Kelboro G., Stellmacher T. and Hornidge, A-K., 2017, The Agricultural Extension System in Ethiopia: Operational Setup, Challenges and Opportunities, ZEF Working Paper Series 158, Bonn: Center for Development Research, University of Bonn.

Levine, D., 1965, *Wax and Gold: Tradition and Innovation in Ethiopian Culture*, Chicago: University of Chicago Press.

Maes, K., Closser, S., Vorel, E. and Tesfaye, Y., 2015, A Women's Development Army: Narratives of Community Health Worker Investment and Empowerment in Rural Ethiopia, *Studies in Comparative International Development*, Vol. 50, No. 4, pp. 455–478.

Markakis, J., 2011, *Ethiopia: The Last Two Frontiers*, Woodbridge, UK and Rochester, NY: James Currey.

Meinzen-Dick, R., Behrman, J., Pandolfelli, L., Peterman, A. and Quisumbing, A., 2014, Gender and Social Capital for Agricultural Development, in Quisumbing, A. R., Meinzen-Dick, R., Raney, T. L., Croppenstedt, A., Behrman, J. A. and Peterman, A., eds, *Gender in Agriculture: Closing the Knowledge Gap*, Netherlands: Springer, pp. 235–266. DOI http://dx.doi.org/10.1007/978-94-017-8616-4_10.

Mekonnen, D. K. and Dorfman, J. H., 2013, Learning and Synergy in Social Networks: Productivity Impacts of Informal Labor-sharing Arrangements, *American Economic Journal*, Vol. 100, pp. 35–69. Available online at http://ses.wsu.edu/wp-content/uploads/2014/09/Mekonnen_Dorfman_Labor_Sharing.pdf.

Ministry of Agriculture, 2011, Participatory Extension System Extension Training Materials, Addis Ababa. Extension Directorate, Ethiopia.

Ministry of Finance and Economic Development (MoFED), 2010, Growth and Transformation Plan (GTP) 2010/2011–2014/15, Addis Ababa: Government of Ethiopia.

Mogues, T., 2005, Shocks and Asset Dynamics in Ethiopia, *Economic Development and Cultural Change*, Vol. 60, No. 1, pp. 91–120.

Mosse, D., 2010, A Relational Approach to Durable Poverty, Inequality and Power, *Journal of Development Studies*, Vol. 46, No. 7, pp. 1156–1178.

Mpedi, L. G., 2008, The Role of Religious Values in Extending Social Protection: A South African Perspective, *Acta Theologica*, Vol. 28, No. 1, pp. 105–25.

Narayan, D., 1999, Bonds and Bridges: Social Capital and Poverty, Policy Research Working Paper No. 2167, Washington, DC: World Bank Group.

Norton, A., Conway, T. and Foster, M., 2001, Social Protection Concepts and Approaches: Implications for Policy and Practice in International Development, ODI Working Paper 143, London: Overseas Development Institute.

Oduro, A., 2010, Formal and Informal protections in sub-Saharan Africa, Paper prepared for the workshop Promoting Resilience through Social Protection in sub-Saharan Africa, organised by the European Report on Development, Dakar 28–30 June.

Oxfam, 2016, Putting Citizens' Voice at the Centre of Development: Challenging Shrinking Civic Space across Africa, International Centre for Not-for-Profit Law. Available online at https://www.oxfam.org/sites/www.oxfam.org/files/file_attachments/oxfam-policy-brief-civil-society-nov16_en.pdf date. Accessed 15 December, 2016.

Paldam, M. and Svendsen, G. T., 2000, An Essay on Social Capital: Looking for the Fire Behind the Smoke, *European Journal of Political Economy*, Vol.16, No. 2, pp.339–66.

Pawar, M., 2006, 'Social' 'Capital'? *The Social Science Journal*, Vol. 43, No. 2, pp. 211–226. DOI:10.1016/j.soscij.2006.02.002.

Paxton, P., 2002, Social Capital and Democracy: An Interdependent Relationship, *American Sociological Review*, Vol. 67, No. 2., pp. 254–277.

Platteau, J. P., 1991, Traditional Systems of Social Security and Hunger Insurance: Past Achievements and Modern Challenges, in: Ahmad, E., Drèze, J., Hills, J. and Sen, A., eds, *Social Security in Developing Countries*, Oxford: Clarendon Press, pp. 112–170.

Polanyi, K., 1985, *The Great Transformation: The Political and Economic Origins of Our Time*, Boston: Beacon Press.

Putnam, R., 1995, Bowling Alone: America's Declining Social Capital, *Journal of Democracy*, Vol. 6, No. 1, pp. 65–78.

Putnam, R. D., Leonardi R. and Nanetti R. Y., 1993, *Making Democracy Work: Civic Traditions in Modern Italy*, Princeton, NJ: Princeton University Press.

Rahmato, D., 2002, Civil Society Organizations in Ethiopia, in Zewde, B. and Pausewang, S., eds, *Ethiopia: The Challenge of Democracy from Below*, Stockholm: Elanders Gotab.

Rahmato, D., 2009, *The Peasant and the State: Studies in Agrarian Change in Ethiopia 1950s–2000s*, Addis Ababa: Addis Ababa University Press.

Rahmato, D. and Ayenew, M., 2004, Democratic Assistance to Post-Conflict Ethiopia: Impacts and Limitations, *Ethiopian Journal of the Social Sciences and Humanities*, Vol. 2, No. 2, pp. 100–105.

Rahmato, D. and Kidanu, A., 1999, Consultations with the Poor: A Study to Inform the World Development Report 2000/01 On Poverty and Development, National Report, Ethiopia.

Ruben, R. and Heras, J., 2012, Social Capital, Governance and Performance of Ethiopian Coffee Cooperatives, *Annals of Public and Cooperative Economics*, Vol. 83, No. 4, pp. 463–84.

Segers, K., Dessein, J., Hagberg, S., Develtere, P., Haile, M. and Deckers, J., 2009, Be Like Bees: The Politics of Mobilizing Farmers for Development in Tigray, Ethiopia, *African Affairs*, Vol. 108, No. 430, pp. 91–109.

Sileshi, T., 2006, The Role of Traditional Local Institutions to Improve the Livelihood of Rural Community: The Case of Tachgayint Wereda, Anrs, Addis Ababa University Regional and Local Development Studies.

Stavropoulou, M., Holmes, R. and Jones, N., 2016, Harnessing Informal Institutions to Strengthen Social Protection for the Rural Poor, *Global Food Security*, Vol. 12, pp. 73–79.

Streeten, P., 2002, Reflections on Social and Antisocial Capital, in Isham, J., Kelly T. and Ramaswamy, S., eds, *Social Capital and Economic Development*, Cheltenham: Edward Elgar.

Teshome, A., 2008, Role and Potential Of 'Iqqub' in Ethiopia. Unpublished thesis, Department of Accounting and Finance, Faculty of Business and Economics, Addis Ababa: Addis Ababa University. Available online at https://www.researchgate.net/publication/237218164_role_and_potential_of_per cent27iqqubper cent27_in_ethiopia_a_project_paper_submitted_to_the_school_of_graduate_studies_of_addis_ababa_university_in_partial_fulfillments_of_the_requirements_for_the_degree_of_master_of_

Teshome, A., 2013, Informal and Formal Social Protection in Ethiopia, in Getu, M. and Devereux, S., eds, *Informal and Formal Social Protection Systems in Sub-Saharan Africa*, Kampala: Fountain Publishers and OSSREA, pp. 95–120.

Teshome, E., Zenebe, M., Metaferia, H. and Biadgilign, S., 2014, Participation and Significance of Self-Help Groups for Social Development: Exploring the Community Capacity in Ethiopia, Springer Plus 3:189. Available online at https://www.ncbi.nlm.nih.gov/pmc/articles/PMC4000359/pdf/40064_2013_Article_892.pdf. Accessed on 18 November 2016.

Tirivayi, N., Knowles, M. and Davis, B., 2013, The Interaction Between Social Protection and Agriculture: A Review of Evidence, Rome: Food and Agriculture Organization.

Tobias, H. and Kjetil, T., 2012, *Contested Power in Ethiopia: Traditional Authorities and Multi-Party Elections*, Leiden: Brill Publishers.

Torkelsson, A. and Tassau, B., 2008, Quantifying Women's and Men's Rural Resource Portfolios—Empirical Evidence from Western Shoa in Ethiopia, *The European Journal of Development Research*, Vol. 20, No. 3, pp. 462–481.

United Nations Development Programme (UNDP), 2015, Human Development Report 2015, Work for Human Development: Briefing note for countries on the 2015 Human Development Report, Addis Ababa: UNDP.

Uphoff, N., 2000, Understanding Social Capital: Learning from the Analysis and Experience of Participation, in Dasgupta, P. and Serageldin, I., eds, *Social Capital: A Multifaceted Perspective*, Washington, D.C.: World Bank.

Vaughan, S. and Tronvoll, K., 2003, The Culture of Power in Contemporary Ethiopian Political Life, Sida Studies 10, Stockholm: Swedish International Development Cooperation Agency (SIDA). Available online at http://ehrp.org/wp-content/uploads/2014/05/VaughnandTronvoll-The-Culture-of-Power-in-Contemporary-Ethiopian-Political-Life.pdf.

Verpoorten, R. and Verschraegen, G., 2010, Formal and Informal Social Protection in Sub-Saharan Africa: A Complex Welfare Mix to Reduce Poverty and Inequality, in Suter, C., ed., *Inequality beyond Globalisation: Economic Changes, Social Transformations, and the Dynamics of Inequality*, Berlin: Lit Verlag, pp. 311–334.

Vinci, I., Hani, M. and Djeddah, C., 2014, Local Solutions to Social Protection: The Role of Rural Organisations, *Universitas Forum: International Journal on Human Development and International Cooperation*, Vol. 4, No. 1.

Widner, J. and Mundt, A., 1998, Researching Social Capital in Africa, *Africa*, Vol. 68, No. 1, pp. 1–24.

Woolcock, M., 1998, Social Capital and Economic Development: Toward a Theoretical Synthesis and Policy Framework, *Theory and Society*, Vol. 27, No. 2, pp. 151–208.

Woolcock, M., 2002, Social Capital in Theory and Practice: Where Do We Stand?, in Ramaswamy, S., ed., *Social Capital and Economic Development: Well-being in Developing Countries*, Cheltenham, UK: Edward Elgar.

World Bank, 2001, Dynamic Risk Management and the Poor. Developing a Social Protection Strategy for Africa, African Region Human Development Department, Washington DC: The World Bank Group.

World Bank, 2010, Gender and Governance in Rural Services: Insights from India, Ghana, and Ethiopia, Social Science 376, Washington DC: World Bank Group.

World Bank, 2016, Ethiopia Poverty Assessment. Available online at http://www.worldbank.org/en/topic/poverty/publication/ethiopia-poverty-assessment. Accessed on 27 July 2016.

Negash, W., 2003, The Role of Indigenous Voluntary Associations in Community Based HIV/AIDS Intervention Activities: The Case of iddirs in Addis Ababa, Unpublished Master's thesis, Addis Ababa: Addis Ababa University.

Zak, P. and Knack, S. 1998. 'Trust and Growth' Available online at https://papers.ssrn.com/sol3/papers.cfm?abstract_id=136961.

7

Do Temporal Myopia and Asymmetric Information Matter in the Demand for Social Insurance?

Walid Merouani, Nacer-Eddine Hammouda and Claire El Moudden

Introduction

A low rate of social security coverage is observed in many developing countries (ILO 2010). The governments of these countries attempt to extend social security using different strategies. Some of them use the Beveridge Model, which covers the poor through a non-contributory assistance programme. Other countries aim to extend social security through the Bismarck Model, which creates mechanisms for the collection of premiums and for the payment of benefits (Renena 1998). The Bismarckian strategy seems to be more effective because it does not give rise, theoretically, to funding problems. However, identifying the reasons for low coverage is necessary in order to implement the right strategy for extending social security coverage in specific contexts.

Previous studies have shown the role of sociodemographic factors in understanding the phenomenon of low social insurance coverage (Bellache 2010). This paper goes beyond sociodemographics and introduces behavioural determinants into social security coverage (DDSS survey). We focus on forward-looking behaviour and knowledge about social security, the importance of which for decisions about purchasing insurance has been proved by Samuelson (1937) and Chetty et al. (2013). We will show the impact of these variables on the demand for social security in Algeria.

According to Algeria's Office for National Statistics (ONS Employment Survey 2014), 42 per cent of workers do not have any coverage against potential social risks. This means they will face unsolvable problems if any risks or difficulties arise in the future, such as disease, ageing, etc. The gap in social coverage will lead to a lack of social cohesion and to social inequality in Algerian society in the future.

The Algerian social security system is public and Bismarckian (contributory), which means that workers need to contribute to it in order to get benefits when social risks occur. The system is made up of five insurance funds, which offer insurance against all social risks (sickness, maternity, accidents and injuries at work, disability and death) as well as providing a retirement pension. All categories of workers, including the self-employed, temporary workers and contributing family workers, are eligible for the various insurance funds (Merouani et al. 2014). In fact, the insurance system is compulsory, but the state looks the other way when workers do not demand social insurance in order not to pay contributions. There is no severe punishment against such 'free-riders'. Thus, the problem of social security is a problem of demand, the supply is enough to cover everyone. This chapter uncovers the behavioural determinants of this demand.

Many macro- and microeconomic variables can impact on the demand for social insurance (Bommier et al. 2014; Friedman 1974; Nyman 2001). In our previous study (Merouani, Hammouda and El Moudden 2016), we displayed a set of behavioural and sociodemographic variables that impact significantly on the demand for social insurance. As mentioned above, this chapter focuses on: the impact of forward-looking behaviour (Brown, Ivkovic and Weisbenner 2015; Caire 2002; Kessler 1986; Wang et al. 2009), and the knowledge that individuals have about social security features (Liebman and Luttmer 2011; Mitchell 1988; Chetty 2013) on the demand for social insurance.

Indeed, information concerning social security may be available and straightforward to understand. Individuals who are familiar with social security benefits are more likely to demand them. Forward-looking thinking can also impact on the demand for social insurance. High time-discounting rates (that is, not forward-looking) decrease the demand for social insurance. Individuals are less likely to demand social insurance if they don't think about their old age or retirement. To test this point, we measured these variables among a sample of insured and non-insured workers, using an experimental survey of the Algerian labour market.

The rest of this chapter proceeds as follows. We present the theoretical background on time discounting and the impact of knowledge about social policy on individual behaviour. We then describe our methodology and the survey design. The statistics and summary of results of the survey present the empirical outcomes. We conclude by offering policy recommendations that would make people more willing to participate in social security.

Knowledge about Policy and Individual Forward-Looking Behaviour: A Literature Review

This section gives an overview of the literature on time discounting and the impact of policy knowledge on individual behaviour. These issues have been studied in different ways. Here we explore the literature to seek a useful application to the Algerian social security context.

Demand for Social Insurance: Does Knowing about the Mechanisms of Social Security Matter?

The demand for any good on the market is linked to information that the consumer has about this good and its provider. This is also true for social security services. Individuals buy social insurance if they have sufficient information about the system (how to calculate benefits and contributions). Previous research suggests that individuals are not fully informed about tax and transfer policies (Liebman and Luttmer 2011; Kling et al. 2011). Liebman and Luttmer tested the impact of providing information about social security on individual behaviour. The authors randomised two groups of older workers. The first was informed about social security (via a mailed brochure combined with an invitation to participate in a fifteen-minute online tutorial) and the second was not. One year after the information was provided, the authors did an experimental survey to gauge the impact of the information on individual behaviour regarding the labour market and social security. The results showed that the informed group changed their behaviour in the labour market; they tended to work longer in order to get a bigger old-age pension.

Kling et al. (2011) posit that consumers need information in order to compare the different alternatives on the market and to make an efficient choice. Focusing on the Medicare programme in the US, they gathered two sample groups: the first received information which enabled them to compare different drug-insurance plans; the second was a control group. Again, the information provided had an impact on individual behaviour, increasing the probability of switching to a lower-priced plan.

Chetty et al. (2013) hypothesised that providing information about policies to individuals would enable them to make better economic choices, and tested their theory on the recipients of Earned Income Tax Credit[1] (EITC) in the US. They observed that the EITC rules were not well known by the potential filers. They then supplied information about the EITC and tested if the individuals who were informed would change their behaviour towards this institution (EITC). The study found that tax consultants may be able to influence their clients' earning decisions by providing advice about how to respond to tax incentives.

Starr-McCluer and Sunden (1999) examined how much knowledge workers had about their pension plan in the US. They linked data provided by workers (in the 1989 US Federal Reserve Board's Survey of Consumer Finances) with data provided by employers (in the Pension Provider Survey of the same year) and found that the workers had limited knowledge about their pension.[2]

Mitchell (1988) analysed administrative data and workers' reports about pensions in the US, and found that workers were generally poorly informed about their pension plan. Higher-income workers and those in large firms, the better educated, and those with greater seniority, understood the details of their pension plan better. This myopia about pension plans affects individual choices (whether to participate in a plan or not, and if yes, how much to contribute).

Bernheim (1987) conducted a survey on workers close to retirement to identify their expectations of their social security benefits. He too found that these individuals did not form expectations on the basis of all available information.

Based on these works, we suggest that the low social security demand in Algeria is due to the lack of information that workers have about social security. Our survey analyses the quality of information that people receive.

Forward-Looking Thinking: How Do People Discount the Future?

Intertemporal choices (when people weigh up the costs and benefits of actions at different points in time) and the perceptions that people have about the future play a key role in life-cycle theory. These variables impact individual consumption patterns. They affect the demand for different goods and services, including social insurance. Previous works dealing with the question of forward-looking behaviour used different concepts: temporal myopia, intertemporal choices, time inconsistency and time preferences. Since Samuelson's seminal paper (1937), many authors have discussed this issue, drawing mixed conclusions. Some have found that most people do not discount the future highly (Barsky et al. 1997; Loewenstein 1987; Loewenstein and Prelec 1991, 1992; Loewenstein and Thaler 1989). Others have found the opposite, encountering high levels of time discounting (Warner and Pleeter 2001; Samwick 1998; Hausman 1979; Lawrance 1991).

Brown et al. (2015) analysed the intertemporal choices of Croatian retirees who had to choose between two forms of pension plan. The first would give them a deferred payment and the second offered more immediate payment. Seventy per cent of the respondents chose the latter. The study used the second choice to estimate the time-discounting rate. Participants were asked to choose between placing a received amount of money in a solvent bank for one year or taking the money and doing whatever they wanted with it. Respondents who did not want to put the money in the bank for a year were asked what interest rate they would require to change their minds. The interest rate that they gave constituted the time-discounting rate. The mean interest rate required was 8.7 per cent.

Samwick (1998) used a consumption survey to measure time preference in the United States, using the lifetime model. Brasky et al. (1997) measured individual intertemporal choices in the US using a survey. They found very low time-discounting rates.

Warner and Pleeter (2001) studied military time discounting. The military was forced to downsize and had to choose between two pension plans. The first programme offered annuities; the second offered a lump-sum payment. Most pensioners chose the lump-sum payment. The time-discounting rate estimated in this study varied between 0 and 30 per cent with education, age, sex, and other socioeconomic factors. Wang et al. (2009) conducted an international survey measuring time discounting in pension choice. They used several methods, proposing an alternative of immediate and delayed payments. The findings revealed that people discounted the future in different ways. They tended to disregard the near future decidedly more than the distant future. They also discounted small amounts more than larger ones.

The time-discounting rate varies also with country. Arrondel et al. (2004) analysed the time preference of the French population using a survey. They asked individuals many questions about their daily life, such as: do you drop a book after reading only the few first pages? do you use the freeway instead of the national route to get work? The analysis crossed intertemporal preferences with wealth accumulation. The finding was that more patient individuals (forward-lookers) were wealthier.

Based on the studies discussed above, we built a questionnaire to conduct a survey on the Algerian labour market. We explain our survey in the next section.

Methodology
Sampling

To measure the variables we administered an experimental questionnaire to 654 workers between fifteen and sixty-five years of age, employed in the labour market of Algiers province. The survey focused on the private, non-agricultural sector. We excluded the public sector because all public sector workers are automatically affiliated to the social security system. We also excluded the agricultural sector. The sample was chosen using a quota method based on the ONS 2010 household employment survey. Five control variables were used in order to apply the quota sampling: affiliation to the social security system, gender, age, employment status and sector of activity. We chose these variables because they are determinant in the context of social security (Merouani et al. 2016). Thirty-one per cent of the respondents were affiliated to the social security system. Females represented 15 per cent of the sample. The employment status of the population comprised 10 per cent permanent employees, 42 per cent temporary employees and 48 per cent employers and the self-employed. As in the ONS employment survey,

19 per cent of the population of our sample was employed by the industrial and manufacturing sector, 22 per cent by construction and 59 per cent by the trade and services sectors. Hence the structure of our sample was similar to the structure of the 2010 household employment survey. Our survey was large, measuring many variables. However, this paper will present the measurement of only[3] two key determinants in the demand for social insurance, namely time discounting (forward-looking) and knowledge of the social security system.

Knowledge About Social Security

To quantify how much people knew about social security, we first asked two declarative questions: whether the respondents knew of the existence of the social security system; if the response was affirmative, we asked them if they knew how the social security system worked[4] (as a source of income and expense). We then asked five test questions and calculated the score of social security knowledge according to the number of correct answers.

The first of these questions was whether the social security system is funded by workers' contributions. The respondents chose between three answers: true, false or I don't know. The second question listed areas of life risk[5] (health, medication, fire insurance, disability, accident at work and work injury, unemployment, old age pension and road accident), and we asked respondents to tell us which of these risks was covered by the social security system.

The third question had to do with the nature of the social security system, whether it was a 'pay as you go' or funded system. We explained in our question that a 'pay as you go' system meant that the actual contribution of workers aimed to finance the actual pension retirees. On the other hand, in a funded system, contributions are saved (or invested) until the age of retirement, when they are paid to the workers as a pension. The correct answer was that the social security system is a 'pay as you go' system.

The fourth question asked respondents about how to calculate the old age pension — was it based on a lifetime's income, on the income of the last ten years, on the income of the last five years, on the ten best incomes in their active life, or on the five greatest incomes of their active life? The correct answer was: the five greatest incomes of the active life of salaried workers and the ten greatest incomes for employers and the self-employed.

In the fifth question, we explained that the pension is calculated as a proportion (replacement ratio) of the reference income. The reference income is 2.5 times the mean of the five highest lifetime salaries (the ten highest incomes for non-salaried workers). We asked respondents what the higher replacement ratio would be for their old age pension: 50 per cent, 60 per cent or 80 per cent? The correct answer was 80 per cent.

In all these five questions the respondents could answer simply 'I don't know'. Based on the answers, we calculated a score for social security knowledge. For good knowledge, a respondent had to get 5/5 correct answers. Medium knowledge was indicated by 3/5 or 4/5 correct answers and poor knowledge by 1/5 or 2/5 correct answers. No knowledge was indicated by no correct answers.

This score provided empirically categorical variables that measured the respondents' social security knowledge. The statistics of this variable are given in the next section.

Measuring Forward-Looking Behaviour

After reviewing previous studies (Wang et al. 2009; Brown et al. 2015), we chose the most suitable methods to determine if respondents were forward-looking or not. We posed several questions in our survey. In the first question, respondents were asked to choose between a preference for immediate payment and a more substantial, but deferred payment. That was a more substantial payment as follows:

Amount in Algerian Dinars (DZD)	First Year	Second Year	Third Year	Fourth Year	Fifth Year	Sixth Year	Seventh Year
A	15,000						
B		5,000	5,000	5,000	5,000	5,000	5,000

We asked the same question proposing monthly payments rather than annuities. The responses to the questions indicated to us whether the respondent was patient or not. In the second method we proposed the following alternatives to respondents (as per Wang 2009):

Please consider the following alternatives:

A. a payment of DZD 1,000 now;
B. a payment of DZD X one year from now;
X payment has to be at least DZD ….., such that B is as attractive as A.

Next, the same question was asked but with a changed horizon and amount:
A. a payment of DZD 1,000 now;
B. a payment of DZD X ten years from now;
X payment has to be at least DZD …., such that B is as attractive as A.

A. a payment of DZD 10,000 now;
B. a payment of DZD X one year from now;
X payment has to be at least DZD……, such that B is as attractive as A.

A. a payment of DZD 10,000 now;
B. a payment of DZD X ten years from now;
X payment has to be at least DZD …., such that B is as attractive as A.

To estimate the time-discounting rate from these answers, the relationship between the current value of cash, denoted by P, and its future value, denoted by F, was used. Formally,

$$F = P(1 + R)^t$$

where R is the discount rate and t is the time to be waited. Since both P and t are given in our questions, the inferred discount rate can be obtained by applying the following equation:

$$R = (F/P)^{(1/t)} - 1$$

In addition to these two variables, the survey measured the socioeconomic and demographic characteristics of the respondents. We hypothesised that characteristic variables could impact on the demand for social insurance. We present the interaction of these variables with forward-looking behaviour and knowledge of the social security systems in the following section.

Descriptive Statistics and Summary Results

This section presents the main results of our survey. We give the summary statistics of the main variables of this paper (time-discounting rate and knowledge about social security) as well as the cross table with other sociodemographic variables.

Knowledge About the Social Security System

Our respondents seemed to be ill-informed about the social security system. For the first declarative question, 3 per cent of the respondents were unaware of its existence. These respondents were not asked the test questions. The second question showed that 23 per cent declared that they knew how the social security system worked, 46 per cent declared that they didn't know how it worked and 32 per cent said that they had minimal knowledge about how it functioned. The scores of the test questions showed that only 3 per cent of the respondents had good knowledge, 33 per cent had medium knowledge, 55 per cent had poor knowledge and 7 per cent had no knowledge of social security at all.

Analysing knowledge about social security with respect to age is somewhat messy. According to Mitchell (1988) senior workers in the US were more informed about their pension scheme. In our study, we observed that knowledge about social security was almost the same for all the age categories (see Table 7.1). However, some differences were clear. Medium knowledge increased with age. In contrast, many young and elderly workers had little knowledge about social security, and more young workers than seniors had no knowledge about social security. Therefore, we think age is a determinant variable in the demand for social insurance.

Table 7.1: Knowledge of Social Security by Age (%)

Age by year	15–24	25–34	35–44	45–54	55–64
Good knowledge	5	4	4	4	0
Medium knowledge	27	35	3	35	42
Low knowledge	54	54	58	58	58
No knowledge	14	7	7	3	0
Total	100	100	100	100	100

Source: Author's data, DDSS survey

The comparison of knowledge held by men versus women is presented in Table 7.2. Men seemed to be more informed about social security, which can explain why men were more likely to be insured than women (ONS Employment Survey). Our result does not corroborate with Mitchell (1988) who found that women were more informed about pension plans than men.

Table 7.2: Knowledge about Social Security by Gender (%)

	Men	Women
Good knowledge	3	5
Medium knowledge	35	22
Low knowledge	54	63
No knowledge	7	10
Total	100	100

Source: Author's data, DDSS survey

Level of education should influence knowledge about social security. But even well-educated respondents were not well informed about social security, as seen in Figure 7.1.

Figure 7.1 is quite logical. It seems that education and knowledge about social security are positively correlated. The good- and medium-knowledge categories are constituted by more educated respondents. The no-knowledge category is mostly composed of respondents with a low level of education. Thus, the level of education can improve knowledge about social security. It can also improve the demand for social insurance.

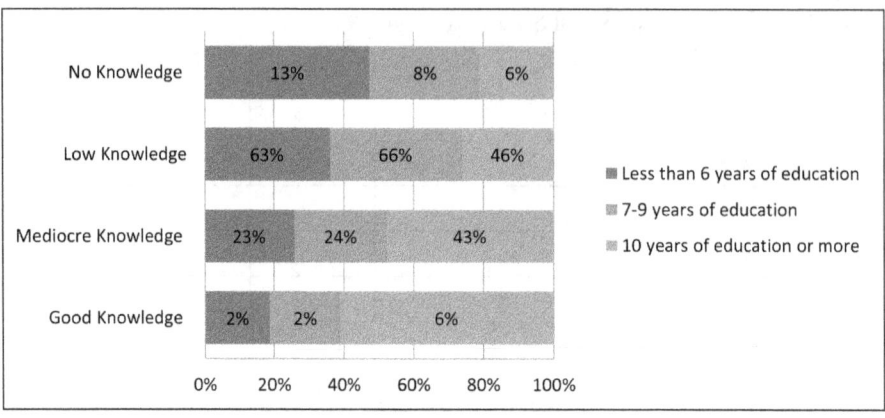

Figure 7.1: Education and Knowledge of Social Security
Source: Author's data, DDSS survey

Table 7.3 shows that higher-income workers are more informed about social security. Our results correspond to Mitchell (1988), showing that the percentage of respondents with good and medium knowledge increases with income. However, poor knowledge also decreases with increased income. The no-knowledge category correlates with low income (less than DZD 18,000) although we did find a small percent of no knowledge among those who earned more than DZD 56,000 a month.

Table 7.3: Knowledge of Social Security and Monthly Income (in Algerian dinars, DZD) (%)

Income in Dinars (DZD)	<18,000	18,001–36,000	36,001–56,000	56,000
Good knowledge	0	3	3	7
Medium knowledge	19	31	35	50
Low knowledge	67	57	56	42
No knowledge	13	8	6	1
Total	100	99	100	100

Source: Author's data. DDSS survey

Table 7.4 shows that workers in the largest firms could be better informed about social security. The percentage of respondents who have good or medium knowledge rises with increased firm size. Otherwise, the percentage of respondents whose have little or no knowledge decreases with increased firm size.

Table 7.4: Knowledge of Social Security by Firm Size (%)

	Self-Employed	1–4 Employees	5–9 Employees	10–49 Employees	More than 50 Employees
Good knowledge	0	6	3	3	2
Medium knowledge	33	30	35	39	50
Low knowledge	56	58	44	57	48
No knowledge	11	5	16	1	0
Total	100	100	100	100	100

Source: Author's data, DDSS Survey

Figure 7.2 reveals the most important of our findings. It provides the key to testing the impact of social security information on the demand for it. The figure shows the difference of knowledge about social security between insured and uninsured respondents. It seems that the insured respondents are more informed than the uninsured. The insured are less represented than the uninsured in the category of low knowledge; a higher proportion of uninsured fall in the low-knowledge category. These results support our hypothesis that people would demand more social insurance if they better understood its benefits and how it worked.

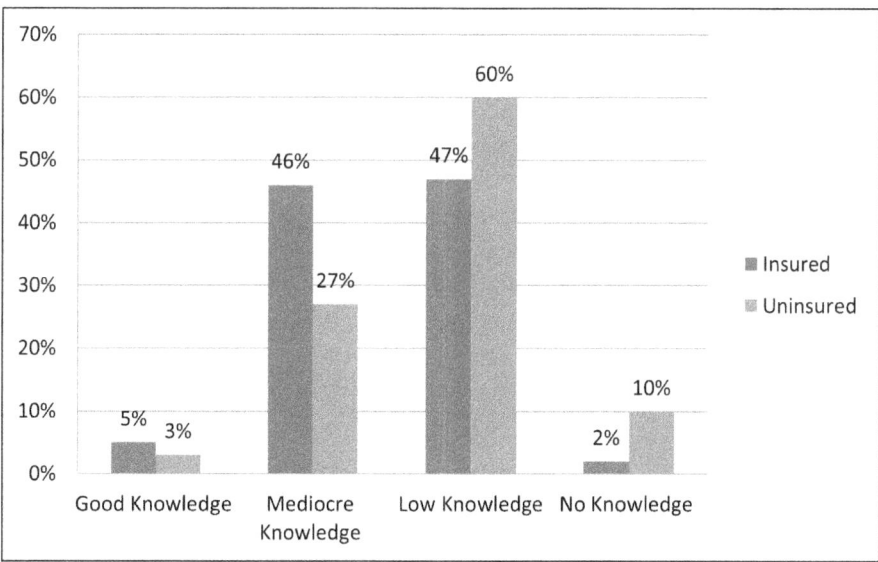

Figure 7.2: Knowledge and Demand for Social Insurance
Source: Author's data, DDSS Survey

Forward-Looking Choices

This subsection presents the summary statistics of intertemporal choice measurement. The results showed that respondents were quite impatient: 29 per cent chose to wait for an annuity (DZD 5,000 for six years = DZD 30,000) than to receive DZD 15,000 immediately; 59 per cent chose the monthly payment (DZD 5,000 every month for six months) over DZD 15,000 immediately. Women seemed to be more patient than men: 40 per cent of women chose to wait for an annuity versus 28 per cent of men; 70 per cent of women chose to wait for monthly payments against 54 per cent for men.

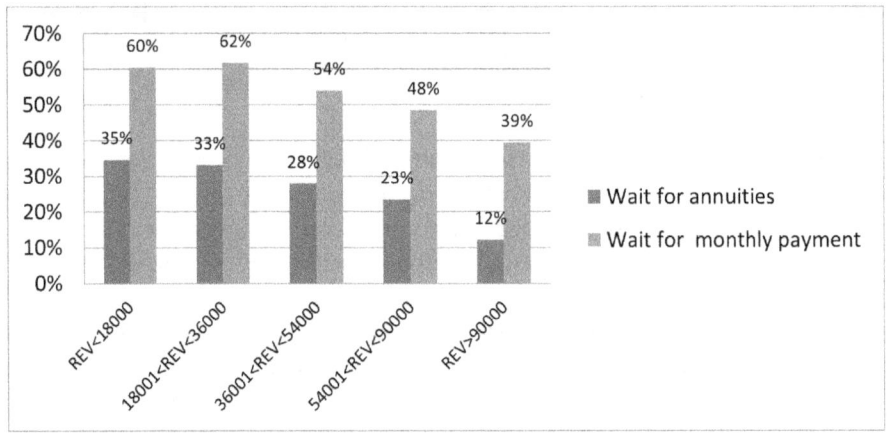

Figure 7.3: Willing to Wait and Income

Source: Author's data, DDSS Survey

The result of willingness to wait according to income (Figure 7.3), shows that the higher the income, the less people were willing to wait: 35 per cent of the respondents with an income less than DZD 18,000 chose to wait for annuities, while 60 per cent chose monthly payments. These percentages decreased the higher the income: only 12 per cent of the respondents who earned more than DZD 90,000 chose to wait for annuities compared with 39 per cent who opted for the monthly payment.

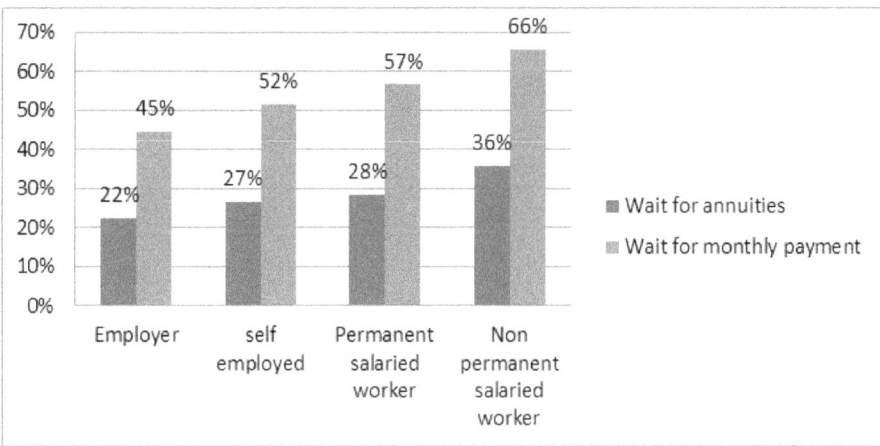

Figure 7.4: Willing to Wait and Employment Status
Source: Author's data, DDSS Survey

Figure 7.4 shows that those willing to wait varied according to employment status. Salaried workers were more patient than the self-employed and employers while only 36 per cent of non-permanent salaried workers chose to wait for annuities (as opposed to 66 per cent preferring a monthly payment).

The questions that we asked in our survey allowed us to calculate the time-discounting rate using the following quasi-hyperbolic model:

$$R = \beta \delta^t X$$

$\delta = \frac{1}{1-i}$ discount factor; i = time-discounting rate; t = number of years; β refers to the degree of present bias; the larger β implies a less present bias; R is equal to 1,000 or 10,000 according to the question; and X is the answer of the respondent.

$$\begin{cases} R = \beta \delta X_1 \\ R = \beta \delta^{10} X_{10} \end{cases}$$

The above equation allows us to measure δ as well as ß. The result gave an average δ of 0,78 and 0,44 for ß. This result is consistent with the literature (for example, Mangot 2007).

Our results also correspond with the literature. The near future and the small amount are more discounted than the far future and highest amount. The discount rate of DZD 1,000 is higher than that of discounting DZD 10,000, while the discounting rate for one year is higher than that of discounting for ten years.

Table 7.5: Time Discounting by Age (%)

	15–24	25–34	35–44	45–54	55 Years or more
P1	45,776	3,919	10,040	3,341	56,464
P2	7,928	2,690	2,757	1,897	5,956
P3	70	52	50	49	67
P4	64	50	50	50	52
	35	31	28	26	36

Source: Author's data, DDSS survey

Table 7.5 presents the different time-discounting rates with respect to age. It seems that the younger and the elderly discount the future more than other age categories. We observed that all time-discounting rates were high for the respondents between fifteen and twenty-four years old. The rate was lower for the intermediate categories, but higher again for respondents who were more than fifty-five years old. These last could underestimate their life expectancy. This result is coherent with the literature (for example, Arrondel et al. 2004; Brown et al. 2015).

Table 7.6: Time Discounting for Men and Women (%)

	Men	Women
P1	18,236	3,724
P2	4,041	2,301
P3	55	56
P4	52	59
	31	30

Source: Author's data, DDSS survey

Table 7.6 compares time-discounting rates between men and women. Men discounted the near future (1 year: P1 and P2) more than women. On the other hand, women discounted the distant future (10 years: P3 and P4) more than men. The same result was found by Arrondel et al. (2004). These results may explain why women are less likely to be enrolled in the pension system. Women in our survey showed a great disregard for the distant future. In the same way, they discounted their old age pension. This supports our hypothesis, which stipulates that the higher the time-discounting rate, the less probability there is of demand for insurance. Otherwise, the hyperbolic discounting rate seems to be the same for men and women.

Very few studies have tested the relationship between marital status and time discounting; Brown et al. (2015) found no significant impact of financial marital status on intertemporal choices We observed in the data (ONS Employment Survey) that married people are more likely to participate in social security systems since their participation allows them to cover their family against social risks. These results are presented in Table 7.7.

Table 7.7: Time Discounting Rate with Respect to Marital Status[6] (%)

	Married	Single
P1	18,691	13,688
P2	3,027	4,295
P3	51	60
P4	49	57
	30	32

Source: Author's data, DDSS survey

Table 7.7 shows that single people discount the future more than married people do. This supports again our hypothesis that time discounting has a negative impact on demand for social insurance.

It is well known that forward-looking behaviour is linked to education level (Peart 2000). Table 7.8 draws the relation between time discounting and education in our survey.

Table 7.8: Time-Discounting Rate with Respect to Education (%)

	Less than 6 Years of Education	7–9 Years of Education	10 Years of Education or more
P1	24,718	2,894	26,089
P2	5,464	1,793	5,220
P3	77	54	52
P4	73	52	49
	42	30	29

Source: Author's data, DDSS survey.

The literature shows that a higher level of education decreases time discounting. Our result appears to follow this logic. Except for discounting small amounts in the near future (P1), the time-discounting rate decreases with education level. P3 is equal to 77 per cent for the respondents who have less than six years of education compared to 52 per cent for those who have more than ten years of education. The time discounting of high amounts over the long term (P3) is about 73 per cent for those who have less than six years of education against 49 per cent for who have more than ten years of education. Obviously, education plays a key role in the demand for social security.

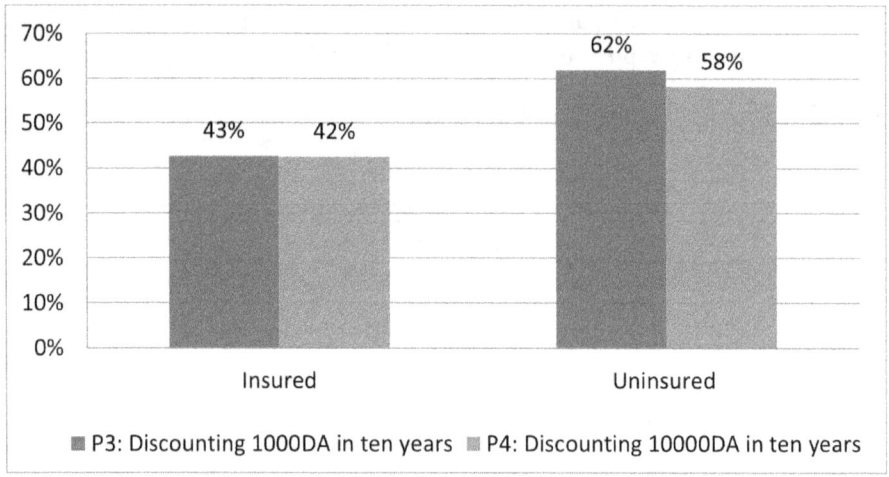

Figure 7.5: Time Discounting and Demand for Social Insurance
Source: Author's data, DDSS survey

Figure 7.5 shows that uninsured respondents discount the future more than the insured do. The time-discounting rate for insured people was 43 per cent (P4=42 per cent) and 62 per cent (P4=58 per cent) for the uninsured. Hyperbolic time discounting confirms this relationship: 28 per cent for the insured and 32 per cent for the uninsured. This again supports our hypothesis about the negative impact of time discounting on the demand for social insurance. In the next section we confirm our theory using direct choice models.

In our survey we asked respondents about their risk aversion. Many methods have been used to measure risk aversion (Merouani et al. 2016; Barsky et al. 1997; Luttmer and Samwick 2012). However, in this article we present a unique method that asks respondents to rank themselves on the Lickert scale, from one (which means 'I always take a risk') to five (which means 'I never take risks in my daily life'). This method is straightforward but the best method according to Dohmen et al. (2011). The relationship between risk aversion and time discounting is presented in Figure 7.6.

Figure 7.6 reveals the negative relationship between risk aversion and time discounting: risk-averse people discount the future less than risk-tolerant people. The relationship between these two variables is interesting but much discussed in the literature. Arrondel et al. (2005) stipulate that risk aversion and forward-looking thinking have a positive relationship. However, other authors have found an opposing relationship when they measure financial risk aversion. Epper (2015) recognised, as we do, that the relationship between time discounting and risk aversion depends on the nature of the latter (Merouani et al. 2016). In the case of pensions, people who are risk-averse to work in the future (for example, for health reasons) are more likely to demand an entitlement to a pension system. In the case of financial risk, individuals may see a pension system as a gamble that offers a gain if they live until retirement but represents a loss if they die before retirement age (Gottlieb 2012). Hence, more risk-averse people will be less likely to demand a pension because of the uncertainty surrounding their future benefit. We test the relationship exposed above using an econometric model in the next section. This model (the logit model) reveals the impact of time discounting and knowing about social policy on the demand for social insurance.

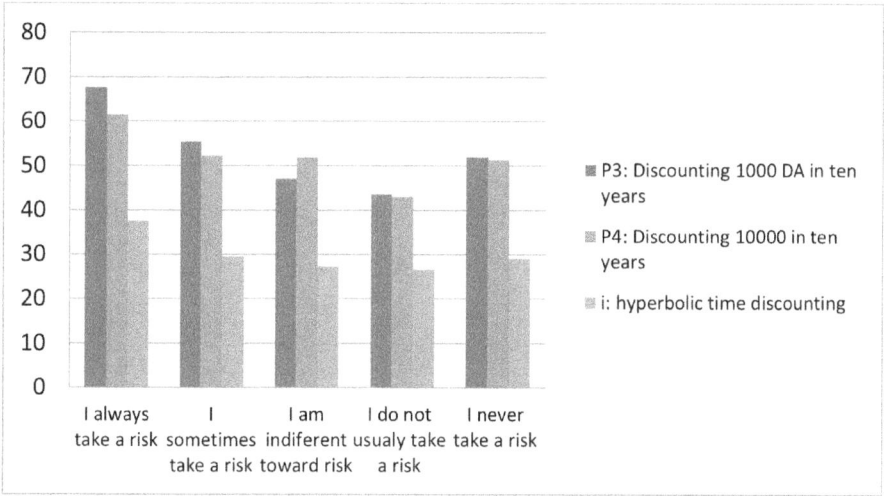

Figure 7.6: Time-discounting Rate and Risk Aversion
Source: Author's data, DDSS survey

Econometric Analysis

In this section, logit models are used to show the effect of time discounting, knowledge about social security and other socioeconomic variables on the demand for social security. The dependent variable in the model is the demand for social security: the value is 1 if the individual demands social security (is enrolled in the social security system) and 0 if not. In order to test collinearity, we calculate VIF (Variation Inflation Factors) (Mansfield and Helms 1981). These factors measure the inflation of the coefficients of the model induced by correlations of the independent variables. In our case, VIFs are listed in Table 7.10, which shows that they are all inferior to 10, which means that there is no problem of collinearity in our three logit models.

Table 7.9: Logit Models

Dependent Variable: Demand for Social Insurance	Model 1	Model 2	Model 3
Low knowledge about social security		0.671**	
		(0.135)	
No knowledge about social security		0.265**	
		(0.149)	
AGE	1.029***	1.028***	1.030***
	(0.0097)	(0.0091)	(0.0091)
Income (Ref Var Income<DZD 18,000)			
Income DZD 18,000–36,000		2.531**	2.588**
		(0.945)	(0.964)
Income DZD 36,000–56,000		5.096***	5.254***
		(1.949)	(2.004)
Income>DZD 56,000		5.342***	5.622***
		(2.206)	(2.319)
Ref Var: I know about social security			
2. I don't know about social security		0.448***	0.429***
		(0.113)	(0.108)
3. I moderately know about social security		0.878	0.860
		(0.212)	(0.208)
P4/ time-discounting rate	0.976***		
	(0.00321)		
Female	0.482***		
	(0.133)		
Ref Var: less than 6 years of education			
2. Between 7–9 years of education	1.170		
	(0.467)		
3. More than 9 years of education	2.957***		
	(1.143)		
Non-permanent salaried workers	0.254***		
	(0.0593)		
Self-employed	0.348***		
	(0.0827)		

Good and medium knowledge of social security			1.544**
			(0.310)
Hyperbolic discount factor	0.403***		
	(0.047)		
Constant	0.473	0.111***	0.0659***
	(0.287)	(0.0589)	(0.0357)
Observations	645	630	630

Source: Author's data. DDSS survey.

* = significant at 10 per cent level;
** = significant at 5 per cent level;
*** = significant at 1 per cent level.
Standard error in brackets.

Table 7.10 displays the results of the three logit models that confirm our hypothesis. It explains the impact of time discounting (forward-looking thinking) and the degree of knowledge about social security on the demand for this. Model 1 shows that an increase of 1 per cent in the exponential time-discounting rate decreases the probability of demand for social insurance by 1.02 times, and a 1 per cent increase in the hyperbolic discounting rate decreases the probability of demand for social insurance 2,5 times. Age increases the willingness to demand insurance. The literature has shown that older people are more forward-looking (Arrondel et al. 2004). Women are 2.08 times less likely to demand social insurance. Previous studies (Brown et al. 2015; Wang et al. 2009) showed that education improves forward-looking thinking. Our model indicates that more educated respondents are more likely to demand social insurance. The respondents who had studied for more than ten years were 2.95 times more likely to demand social insurance than the respondents who had less than six years of education. Non-permanent salaried workers are four times less likely to demand social insurance. Self-employed workers are 2.95 times less likely to demand social insurance. The literature shows that the self-employed are risk tolerant and less likely to cover themselves against risk (Cramer et al. 2002).

Model 2 shows the impact of knowledge about social security on the demand for it. The respondents who have poor knowledge of social security are 1.46 times less likely to demand social insurance. Respondents who have no knowledge about social security are 3.84 times less likely to demand it. The older we are, the higher the probability of demanding insurance (odds ratio = 1.02). The model also reveals that the higher one's income, the higher the probability of demanding insurance. Respondents who earn an income of between DZD 18,000 and 36,000 are 2.53 times more likely to demand insurance than those who earn less than DZD 18,000 (reference variable).

Table 7.10: Collinearity Diagnostics

Variable	Vif	Squared Vif	Tolerance	R-Squared
Model 1				
AGE	1.11	1.05	0.8994	0.1006
P4/ time-discounting rate	1.64	1.28	0.6099	0.3901
Female	1.05	1.02	0.9569	0.0431
Education	1.05	1.02	0.9544	0.0456
Non-permanent salaried workers	1.59	1.26	0.6276	0.3724
Self-employed	1.49	1.22	0.6714	0.3286
Hyperbolic discount factor	1.59	1.26	0.6273	0.3727
Model 2				
Low knowledge about social security	1.36	1.17	0.7334	0.2666
No knowledge about social security	1.44	1.20	0.6952	0.3048
AGE	1.14	1.07	0.8788	0.1212
Income	1.09	1.05	0.9143	0.0857
Existence of social security system	1.02	1.01	0.9827	0.0173
Knowing about social security	1.04	1.02	0.9631	0.0369
Model 3				
AGE	1.08	1.04	0.9235	0.0765
Income	1.12	1.06	0.8941	0.1059
Knowing about social security	1.13	1.06	0.8864	0.1136
Medium knowledge about social security	1.08	1.04	0.9273	0.0727
Good knowledge about social security	1.16	1.08	0.8594	0.1406

Source: Author's data using Stata

The respondents who earn between DZD 36,000 and 56,000 are 5.09 times more likely to demand insurance than those who earn less than DZD 18,000. Respondents who earn more than DZD 56,000 are 5.34 times more likely to demand social insurance. Brown et al. (2015 found that income has a positive relationship with forward-looking thinking. Respondents who declared that they didn't know about social security rules were 2.38 times less likely to demand social insurance than respondents who declared that they did know about social security (reference variable). Model 3 shows that the respondents who have good and medium knowledge of social security are 1.54 times more likely to demand social insurance.

The econometric models confirm our hypothesis. Our result seems to be coherent with and corresponds to the literature. Demand for social insurance is low in Algeria because people do not take the future into consideration. Indeed, they discount it very highly. They also know very little about social security. They don't know how important social security benefits are, or that the replacement ratio for an old age pension can be 80 per cent. On the basis of these results, and considering successful experiences in some developing countries, we suggest some ways to motivate people to demand social security.

Conclusion

This chapter deals with a complicated issue. Extending social security is a topical question that the World Bank and ILO pursue. Our approach is quite different from the many previous studies that suppose that the social security system is not efficient enough to cover everyone. We look at social security from the point of view of agency. We study the behaviour and factors that keep people from seeking social insurance. We have used innovative surveys to measure our variables and to verify the hypothesis.

A high disregard for the future (due to . focus on the present) may be counterbalanced by offering immediate benefits to insured workers and their families, for example, by introducing childcare into the social security system (Jhabvala 1998) or improving family allowances and extending them to the self-employed. Calvo et al. (2010) demonstrated the positive impact on insurance demand of extending the family allowance to self-employed workers in Chile. Unemployment benefits should also be improved and extended to non-permanent salaried workers. Forward-looking thinking can be encouraged by promising people a higher income (in the form of a pension) in the future. It can be also improved by reducing the payroll tax for people who save for retirement with contributions to the social security system.

The results of our survey showed that people in Algeria are not sufficiently informed about social security. This lack of information denies them the incentive to cover themselves against social risks by demanding insurance. The social security system should be more visible. Information about how it functions and its benefits should be readily available. The information that is provided is perhaps too limited or inaccessible. A social security system should spread information using digital technology (via smartphones, the internet, etc). In addition, the social security system must be fitted to the needs of informal workers. And the mechanism for collecting premiums and paying benefits has to be adequate and easily accessible.

Most recent experiences in other countries provide some lessons. Jhabvala (1998) showed that the market could help to improve social coverage. Insurance companies which send their sales representatives door to door could instruct people on the advantages of enrolling in social insurance. Therefore, the insurance market should be developed in Algeria. There is no private company that provides health or pension insurance in Algeria.

Many countries in Latin America have established a monotax system (ILO 2014), which allows informal workers to make just one contribution containing all the usual taxes (social security contribution, taxes on income, etc.). This monotax is fixed according to the total income of the workers, their electricity bill and the area in which they live (Charmes and Remaoun 2014). Monotax systems have increased the rate of social coverage in many countries in Latin America, including Brazil, Argentina, Ecuador and others. Such a reform could prove successful for Algeria.

Acknowledgements

We are thankful to Amirah El Haddad for her constructive remarks on the earlier version of this manuscript. All remaining errors are our own.

Funding

This paper was generously funded by the Centre for Research on Applied Economics for Development (Algeria). It was also sponsored by the Economic Research Forum (ERF) and has benefited from both financial and intellectual support. The contents and recommendations do not necessarily reflect ERF's views. The preliminary results were published in ERF Working Paper Series, no. 1212, 2018. http://erf.org.eg/publications/18311/.

Notes

1. The EITC is the largest cash transfer programme for low-income families in the United States and it generates large marginal subsidies or taxes on the earnings of recipients.
2. For more details about the surveys please see https://www.federalreserve.gov/pubs/feds/1999/199905/199905pap.pdf.
3. For more details about the questionnaire survey see Merouani et al. 2016. This reference is not given in the list. Please provide.
4. The possible answers to this question are Yes, No or Moderately.
5. Some of the risks are not social and they are not covered by social security.
6. The number of widowed and divorced is very small in our sample; this is why we focus only on married and single respondents.

References

Barsky, R., Juster, T., Kimball, M. and Shapiro, M., 1997, Preference Parameters and Behavioral Heterogeneity: An Experimental Approach in the Health and Retirement Study, *The Quarterly Journal of Economics*, Vol. 112, No. 2, pp. 538–579.

Becker, G. S. and Mulligan C. B., 1997, The Endogenous Determination of Time Preference, *The Quarterly Journal of Economics*, Vol. 112, No. 3, pp. 729–758.

Bellache, Y,. 2010, L'Économie Informelle en Algérie, Une Approche par Enquête Auprès Des Ménages: Le Cas de Bejaia, Thèse pour obtention du diplôme de docteur en sciences économiques de l'Université de Bejaia (Algérie) et de l'Université Paris-Est Créteil (France).

Bernheim, B. D., 1987, Dissaving after Retirement: Testing the Pure Life Cycle Hypothesis, in Bodie, Z., Shoven, J. and Wise, D., *Pensions and Retirement in the United States*, Chicago: University of Chicago Press.

Bommier, A., 2006, Uncertain Lifetime and Intertemporal Choice: Risk Aversion as a Rationale for Time Discounting, *International Economic Review*, Vol. 47, No. 4, pp. 1223–1246.

Brown, J. R., Ivkovic, Z. and Weisbenner, S., 2015, Empirical Determinants of Intertemporal Choice, *Journal of Financial Economics*, Vol. 116, Issue 3, pp. 473–486.

Caire, G., 2002, *Économie de la Protection Sociale*, Paris: Bréal.

Calvo, E., Bertranou, F. and Bertranou, E., 2010, Are Old-age Pension System Reforms Moving Away from Individual Retirement Accounts in Latin America?, *Journal of Social Policy*, Vol. 39, No. 2, pp. 223–234.

Chapman, G. and Coups, E., 1999, Time Preferences and Preventive Health Behavior: Acceptance of the Influenza Vaccine, *Medical Decision Making*, Vol. 19, Issue 3, pp. 307–314.

Charmes, J. and Remaoun, M., *L'Économie Informelle en Algérie: Estimations, Tendances, Politiques, Paper presented at International Labour Organization workshop on Improving the Knowledge Base of the Informal Economy in Algeria, 28 September 2014*, Algiers: ILO.

Chetty, R. and Saez. E., 2013, Teaching the Tax Code: Earnings Responses to an Experiment with EITC Recipients, *American Economic Journal: Applied Economics*, Vol. 5, No. 1, pp. 1–31.

Cramer, J., Hartog, J., *Jonker*, N. and Van Praag, C., 2002, Low Risk Aversion Encourages the Choice for Entrepreneurship: An Empirical Test of a Truism, *Journal of Economic Behavior & Organization*, Vol. 48, No. 1, pp. 29–36.

Dohmen, T., Falk, A., Huffman, D., Sunde, U., Schupp, J. and Wagner, G., 2011, Individual Risk Attitudes: Measurement, Determinants, and Behavioral Consequences, *Journal of the European Economic Association*, Vol. 9, No. 3, pp. 522–550.

Epper, T., 2015, Income Expectations, Limited Liquidity and Anomalies in Intertemporal Choice, Economics Working Paper Series 1519, University of St. Gallen, School of Economics and Political Science.

Gottlieb, D., 2012, Prospect Theory, Life Insurance and Annuities, The Wharton School Research Paper No. 44. Available at online at http://ssrn.com/abstract=2119041.

Hausman, J.,1979, Individual Discount Rates and the Purchase and Utilisation of Energy-Using Durables, *The Bell Journal of Economics*, Vol. 10, No. 1, pp. 33–54.

International Labour Organization (ILO), 2010, World Social Security Report 2010/11, Providing Coverage in Times of Crisis and Beyond, Geneva: ILO.

Jhabvala, R., 1998, Social security for unorganised sector, *Economic & Political Weekly*, Vol. 33, No. 22, L7-L11.

Kessler, D., 1986, *Sur les Fondements Économiques de la Sécurité Sociale*, Revue Française des Affaires Sociales, No. 1, pp. 97–113.

Kirby, K. N., 1997, Bidding on the Future: Evidence Against Normative Discounting of Delayed Rewards, *Journal of Experimental Psychology: General*, Vol. 126, No. 1, pp. 54–70.

Kirby, K. N. and Marakovic, N. N., 1995, Modeling Myopic Decisions: Evidence for Hyperbolic Delay-Discounting Within Subjects and Amounts, *Organizational Behavior and Human Decision Processes*, Vol. 64, No. 1, pp. 22–30.

Kirby, K. N., Petry, N. M. and Bickel, W. K., 1999, Heroin Addicts Discount Delayed Rewards at Higher Rates than Non-Drug Using Controls, *Journal of Experimental Psychology: General*, Vol. 128, No. 1, pp. 78–87.

Kling, J. R., Mullainathan, S., Shafir, E., Vermeulen, L. and Wrobel, M., 2011, Comparison Friction: Experimental Evidence from Medicare Drug Plans, Unpublished manuscript, Harvard University.

Laibson, D., 1997, Life-cycle Consumption and Hyperbolic Discount Functions, *European Economic Review*, Vol. 42, pp. 861–871.

Lawrance, E., 1991, Poverty and Rate Time Preference: Evidence from Panel Data, *Journal of Political Economy*, Vol. 99, No. 1, pp. 54–77.

Liebman, J. and Luttmer, E., 2011, Would People Behave Differently If They Better Understood Social Security? Evidence from a Field Experiment, *American Economic Journal: Economic Policy*, Vol. 7, No. 1, pp. 275–299.

Loewenstein, G., 1987, Anticipation and the Valuation of Delayed Consumption, *The Economic Journal*, Vol. 97, No. 387, pp. 666–684.

Loewenstein, G. and Prelec, D., 1991, Decision Making Over Time and Under Uncertainty: A Common Approach, *Management Science*, Vol. 37, No. 7, pp. 770–786.

Loewenstein, G. and Prelec, D., 1992, Anomalies in Intertemporal Choice: Evidence and Interpretation, *The Quarterly Journal of Economics*, Vol. 107, No. 2, pp. 573–597.

Loewenstein, G. and Thaler, H., 1989, Anomalies: Intertemporal Choice, *The Journal of Economic Perspectives*, Vol. 3, No. 4, pp. 181–193.

Luttmer, E. and Samwick, A., 2012, The Welfare Cost of Perceived Policy Uncertainty: Evidence from Social Security, *American Economic Review*, Vol, 108, No. 2, pp. 275–307.

Mangot, M., 2007, *Choix Intertemporels: Un Modèle Comportemental d'Escompte Quasi-Hyperbolique*, PhD thesis, Paris: Université Panthéon-Sorbonne, Economies et Finances.

Mansfield, E. R. and Helms, B. P., 1981, Detecting Multicollinearity, *The American Statistican*, Vol. 36, No. 3a, pp. 158–160.

Merouani, W., 2014, *Modélisation des Dépenses et Recettes du Système Algérien des Retraites*, Saarbrucken: Éditions universitaires européennes.

Merouani, W., Hammouda, N. E. and El Moudden, C., 2014, Le Système Algérien de Protection Sociale entre Bismarckien et Beveridgien, *Les cahiers du CREAD*. Vol. 107-108.

Merouani, W., Hammouda, N. E. and El Moudden, C., 2016, The Microeconomic Determinants of Demand for Social Insurance: Evidence from the Algerian Labor Market, *Institutions and Economies*, Vol. 8, Issue 1, pp. 25–61.

Mitchell, O. S., 1988, Worker Knowledge of Pension Provisions, *Journal of Labor Economics*, Vol. 6, pp. 21–39.

Nyman, J., 2003, *The Theory of Demand for Health Insurance*, Stanford, CA: Stanford University Press.

Office of National Statistics (ONS), 2014, *Enquete Emploi auprès des Ménages* (Employment Survey 2014, Algiers: Government of Algeria.

Peart, J. S., 2000, Irrationality and Intertemporal Choice in Early Neoclassical Thought, *The Canadian Journal of Economics / Revue canadienne d'Économique*, Vol. 33, No.1, pp. 175–189.

Samuelson, P., 1937, A Note on Measurement of Utility, *The Review of economic Studies*, Vol. 4, No. 2, pp. 155–161.

Samwick, A., 1998, Discount Rate Heterogeneity and Social Security Reform, *Journal of Development Economics*, Vol. 57, pp. 117–146.

Starr-McCluer, M. and Sunden, A., 1999, Workers' Knowledge of their Pension Coverage: A Reevaluation, in Haltiwanger, J. C., Lane, J. I., Spletzer, J. R., Theeuwes, J. J. M. and Troske, K .R., eds, *The Creation and Analysis of Employer-Employee Matched Data (Contributions to Economic Analysis, Vol. 241)*, Bingley, UK: Emerald Group Publishing Limited, pp. 469–583.

Wang, M., Rieger, M. and Hens, T., 2009, An International Survey on Time Discounting. *Management Science*, Vol. 37, No. 7, pp. 770–786. Available online at http://www.socialpolitik.ovgu.de.

Warner, J. T. and Pleeter, S., 2001, The Personal Discount Rate: Evidence from Military Downsizing Programs, *American Economic Review*, Vol. 91, No. 1, pp. 33–53.

8

Interests, Resources and Policy Networks: Understanding the Adoption of Social Protection Policies in Kenya

Marion Ouma and Jimi Adesina

Introduction

Social protection policies and programmes have expanded rapidly in low-income countries around the world over the past two decades. In particular, the number of cash transfer programmes targeted at the those living below the poverty line in Africa has grown significantly as a response to poverty and vulnerability (World Bank 2015). The current wave of cash transfers (CT) originated in the late 1990s from Latin America, where their uptake was domestically driven as a response to poverty and a realisation of social and political threats presented by rising inequality. The ensuing 'success', witnessed in a decrease in poverty and inequality levels, drew international attention and the same programmes have been transferred to Africa and other developing countries (Costa Leite, Suyama and Pomeroy 2013).

Viewed as part of global social policy, the adoption of these policies in Africa is a result of pressure from powerful international organisations, notably the World Bank, DFID, ILO and UNICEF, working in collaboration with well-connected epistemic communities (Deacon 2013). As non-veto players, transnational organisations advocating for the adoption of the policies have not acted alone. They have relied on domestic actors, comprising civil society organisations, national bureaucrats and politicians forming a web of interactions and relationships and thereby creating a policy network. Subsequently, the policymaking process in developing countries has opened up to an array of actors, both domestic and international, advocating government adoption of the policies.

Policy change occurs when there is a pursuit of interests, a process in which different actors within a policy domain compete and exercise their preferences over others. In addition, actors bring structural and resource differences into the policy network. Networks therefore comprise different interests and resources (Peters and Zittoun 2016). In explaining the adoption of social protection policies, however, little attention has been given to how actors in the policy space pursue their different interests and manipulate resources to bring about policy change. The aim of this article is to investigate how the convergence of interests and the resource base of actors within the social protection policy network in Kenya led to the adoption of the Cash Transfer for Orphans and Vulnerable Children (CT-OVC) and the Hunger Safety Net Programme (HSNP).

Since 2004, the Government of Kenya in collaboration with international organisations has initiated a number of cash transfer programmes as part of its social protection agenda. Growing child poverty levels resulting from orphanhood, and the burden of care on older people, provided the impetus for the implementation of the CT-OVC and the Older Persons Cash Transfer programmes, respectively. In Northern Kenya, the government adopted the HSNP as a response to perennial hunger and drought. Meanwhile, the Persons with Severe Disability Cash Transfer, as the name suggests, targets people living with disability.

The key question our study sought to examine was how divergent interests shaped the policy adoption process. To answer this question, it was important to determine the nature of relationships among social actors based on the different resources they brought to the social protection policy network.

In this chapter we argue that while there was a convergence of different interests—public and social, political and institutional, individualistic and ideological—the last, which comprised narrow interests, were more powerful in the policy network. The most important factor was that the interests of the promoters were compatible with those of the domestic actors. This could be made possible since the promoters possessed significant knowledge and financial resources, which enabled them to influence interests.

This chapter is divided into the following sections: a review of the theoretical literature on policy networks and policy transfer, a brief description of the method of the study, an exploration of the different interests and their convergence within the policy network, a discussion of the findings, and the conclusion.

Policy Networks in Policy Transfer: A Review of the Literature and Theoretical Framework

The literature on the current adoption of cash transfer programmes points to globalised forces as the significant driver of reforms, with transnational action and epistemic communities at the forefront. With globalisation, policymaking is no longer a national role solely, but now attracts a large number of international actors as well. One significant development in the last two decades is the policymaking process of a social policy instrument in the form of cash transfers in developing countries. Growing interest in the adoption of social protection programmes in Africa has produced a significant amount of research examining the processes and actors within the policy space.

Three significant bodies of literature have emerged to explain the process of policy uptake. First, is the literature that explains the process of adoption as a form of coercion akin to the push and pressure exerted by international financial institutions (IFIs) in imposing structural adjustment programmes (Mkandawire 2010; Adesina 2011). These studies assess the adoption of cash transfer policies as emanating from persistent structural inequalities between international organisations and developing countries as the key driver to the adoption of cash transfer programmes. Here, conditionality attached to aid and global normative practices is considered a driver to the adoption of the policies.

Second, is the literature that focuses on national processes based on political settlements as the explanatory variable to the adoption of social protection policies (Lavers and Hickey 2016). These studies explain the adoption of cash transfers as a political bargain among elites, drawing from discussions on the political settlement approach (Pruce and Hickey 2017; Wanyama and McCord 2017). While national political processes and bargains, and socioeconomic factors, provided a basis for the adoption of cash transfer programmes, their roles were largely mediative and subordinate to transnational agency.

The third strand of literature points to the role of transnational actors as idea purveyors who promote social protection and cash transfer policies through ideational approaches and social learning (Foli 2015). According to this body of literature, countries adopted the policies out of social learning, knowledge transfer and the spread of norms generated by these transnational actors. Though the literature differs in explaining the adoption of the policies, it agrees that transnational actors played a significant role in the transfer and adoption process (Devereux and White 2010; Niño-Zarazúa et al. 2012, 2014).

Beyond the literature discussed above, this chapter suggests the need to focus on interests and resources within the policy network to understand the transfer process. As suggested, policy transfer refers to the '… process by which knowledge about policies, administrative arrangements, institutions and ideas in one political system (past or present) is used in the development of policies, administrative arrangements, institutions and ideas in another political system'. Policy transfer processes can be coercive or voluntary, though in most cases the process is a combination of both. Coercive mechanisms relate to circumstances where transfer agents impose their wishes on the adoption country, often linking adoption to conditionalities. At the other end of coercive mechanisms is 'soft transfer', where policy promoters use social learning and spread norms to influence uptake as a result of paradigmatic change.

Transfer agents often do not act in isolation to bring about policy change. Instead, they seek out others to create relationships with yet other actors to embolden their pursuit through webs of interactions known as policy networks. A policy network describes the patterns of interaction between actors in a policy space in the decision-making process (Henry 2011). It is a social structure comprising actors who interact in the policymaking process. The policy process comprises a plurality of actors acting within policy networks under differentiated interests and who are legitimate in relation to each other. Within networks are power relations that shape policy outcomes as well as the process of transfer (Ingold 2011).

Globally, social protection has been promoted through policy networks that comprise actors with an interest in social protection. Thus, in explaining the speed and the fast-moving adoption of cash transfers in developing countries, Peck (2011) describes the policy networks around social protection as 'flex nets', which prescribe, co-ordinate, implement, promote and justify particular policy prescriptions. Deacon and Stubbs (2013) further note that global policy advocacy coalitions are now to a great deal and extent playing a key role in the reproduction and transfer of global hegemonies, which they are able to do through national networks that they interact with at national and country level. As non-hierarchical social structures, however, most policy networks converge around a 'point of centrality'. This refers to the people or organisation considered most powerful, based on some resource distribution. In the case of the transfer of social protection policies, actors consider international organisations points of centrality because of the financial resources, expertise and knowledge about social protection that they bring to the policy network.

An understanding of policy networks and the interactions within them offers a clear idea of interests within the policy transfer process. Policy networks comprise webs of interaction based on interests, beliefs, resources and power (Dente 2013; Shearer, Abelson, Kouyaté, Lavis and Walt 2016), which actors in the policy space leverage to influence others. Scholars suggest that policy actors are endowed with a variety of resources, which endorses their legitimacy within the policy space. These resources range from 'the formal legal authority for decision-making, public opinion, information supporters, financial resources and skilful leadership with the distribution of these resources having an impact on policy change' (Henry 2011; Ingold 2011). Resource distribution provides different kinds of legitimacy to different actors. The actors depend on their resources to bring about policy change by pulling different resources together (Henry 2011).

As mentioned above, international organisations bring significant resources into the policy network. While they are non-veto players in the policy process,

Béland and Orenstein, citing Barnett and Finnemore, state that legitimacy for the agency and influence of international organisations in domestic policy emanates from four sources:

> the rational-legal authority that comes from their charters, the delegated legitimacy that they derive from states, the moral legitimacy that comes from their important missions, and the expert legitimacy based on their widely accepted expertise in core areas (Béland and Orenstein 2013: 128).

The aim of the actors in policy transfer in the policy network is to transform the interests and preferences of actors within the policy space to bring about the adoption of their preferred policies by governments. Literature sources identify six main categories of actors (elected officials, political parties, bureaucrats/civil servants, pressure groups, policy entrepreneurs/experts and supra-national institutions) involved in policy transfer, who, in the pursuit of their interests, form the policy network (Dolowitz and Marsh 1996). The ability to change government preference in the adoption of programmes is dependent on the network's resources (Ingold 2011). In promoting social protection policies, international organisations reach out to national bureaucrats as their first point of contact, assuming that their 'interests in policy transfer are compatible with the efficiency gains advocated by the policy instrument' (Tambulasi 2013: 82). Bureaucrats advise governments on policy and are critical in the successful implementation of adopted policies, which is why international organisations choose to work closely with them (Adesina 2011; Tambulasi 2013). But within policy transfer processes, the attitude of national bureaucrats is often shaped and influenced by the donor agencies with whom they work.

In addition to international organisations, the literature on global social policy focuses on the significant role of the epistemic community on whom international organisations often rely for the promotion or uptake of the policies. Their power of influence emanates from their ability to frame ideas and to craft persuasive narratives that promote policy adoption. Franzoni and Voorend (2011) describe them as a small, closed group whose expertise, international knowledge and competence in development of new programmes, ideas, policies and institutional structures is often relied upon by governments and organisations.

Method

To address the research question, we conducted a qualitative case study of the policy process. Drawing on the setup of two cash transfer programmes, the Cash Transfer for Orphans and Vulnerable Children (CT-OVC) and the Hunger Safety Net Programme (HSNP), we explored the realities and experiences of actors in the social protection policy arena. Semi-structured interviews comprised the primary source of data—interviews with government officials, members of parliament, social protection advisors of bilateral and multilateral organisations, representatives of international and national non-governmental organisations, independent consultants and representatives from national and independent think tanks. Twenty-nine interviews lasting between one and three hours were carried out during fieldwork in Kenya between January 2016 and September 2016. Additional interviews were conducted after the period with respondents who could not be reached during the fieldwork period. Bearing in mind the nature of the study, interviewees were selected based on their confirmed participation in the policymaking process. The participants in the study included past and present members of various organisations.

To triangulate the data collected from the key informant interviews, we analysed documents that comprised official government documentation, aid documents and agreements, organisation documents and reports. In addition, the first author attended four in-country forums as a participant and observed various aspects and relationships of the ongoing social protection discussion in the country. Our experience, having been part of the process from 2007 to 2015, was valuable in this case and we drew from it. Data collected from the interviews and notes from observations were transcribed before they were entered into ATLAS.ti, and then thematically analysed for results.

Converging Interests in the Policy Network

Public and Social Interests

Governments are always looking for policy solutions to solve domestic problems. Issues shape interests and therefore the long-standing problems of poverty and vulnerability were at the forefront in the quest for policy solutions. Though all the actors within the policy space coalesced around this interest, our findings indicated that the interest was more pronounced among members of parliament and bureaucrats. Government officials sought to enact the policies to address both new and old problems associated with poverty in the country. With a rise in the number of orphans as a result of the HIV/AIDS pandemic, urgent intervention was required to meet their needs (Bosworth, Alviar, Corral, Davis and Musembi 2016). In addition, perennial hunger and food insecurity in Northern Kenya prompted the provision of cash instead of food aid. Public interests therefore influenced actors, especially the bureaucratic and political classes who considered the CT-OVC and HSNP models likely to address the problems (Weyland 2007). Characteristics related to public and social interests were 'for the people', and a broad coverage of aims in national development plans and for collective interests, as described below.

For the Public, for the People

National bureaucrats pursued the adoption of the policies based on their promise to improve the quality of life for the poor and the vulnerable. By virtue of government structure, bureaucrats in the policy process represented the implementation arm of government. Their interests centred around their mandate as civil servants to translate government policies into programmes that could work for the poor and vulnerable, and therefore they considered the adoption of these programmes a step in this direction. Charged with translating policies as set out by the legislature into programmes, these bureaucrats had close working relations and contact with lawmakers. They were therefore key agents in the policy network, a point of centrality for relations with other actors. As epicentres of policy development and implementation of programmes, their interest lay in advancing government policies for the benefit of citizens. A government official explained this thus,

> Policy implementation is one of the greatest tasks for the bureaucrats … and we learn and borrow from other countries to advance the well-being of citizens from other countries. (MFP-03, 29 July 2016)

For politicians, their support and interest in the programme emanated from their role as individuals legally mandated with veto power to formulate policies for their constituents' interests. In articulating their duty as lawmakers, they referred to the programmes as 'for the benefit of all Kenyans and those they represent'. Their interest in the social protection policymaking process was linked to that of their constituents and their participation sought to expand the programmes to them. Likewise, members of civil society described their interest in participating in the policymaking process as representatives of the poor and vulnerable.

Broad Interests with Long-Term Developmental Perspectives

Politicians and bureaucrats situated the cash transfer programmes within long-term national development perspectives. The broad interests here 'considered the intersectional linkages and cross thematic framings' (Adesina 2011) in addressing poverty rather than the narrow view limited to social protection. National bureaucrats and politicians discussed the programmes from the perspective of broader government development plans like Vision 2030. For this reason, their support for the programmes aligned to other existing public policies, like health and education. In addition, domestic actors were interested in long-term programmes rather than short-term ones as promoted by other actors.

Furthermore, actors clustering around public and social interests preferred programmes that would reach a wider group of people rather than just a few. For this reason, they advocated a larger geographical targeting of a greater spread of benefits rather than poverty alone. The political class preferred this diffusion of programmes within a wider geographical area as it boosted their political base. Bureaucrats supported geographically spread programmes to gain the support of the political class for the adoption of the programmes. Moreover, geographically spread programmes, according to interviewed members of parliament, promoted a sense of collectiveness in the ethnically diverse country. As 'representatives of all people, whether children or older persons', politicians resisted pressure from other actors for the allocation of funds to particular categories of the population, arguing that their duty was to all citizens (MP-01, 31 August 2016). This finding confirms arguments that politicians often refrain from single-focus advocacy, and that therefore, in contestations between different international organisations pushing for their preferred categories of recipients, politicians involved in the policy process resisted from taking sides.

Political Interests

Elected political officials' participation in policymaking processes emanates from their role as representatives of the people. As members of parliament, their power lies in their constitutional right as legislators and in the approval of national budgets (Dente 2013). They therefore wield significant power and influence in determining the direction of government policies. Politicians promote programmes reaching a large number of people for political interests. This indicates that politicians do not only pursue cash transfer programmes goals to bring about transformation to their constituents, but also for political expediency (Weyland 2007; Niedzwiecki 2016). Political interests therefore tend to be short-term in relation to election cycles.

The expansion of the cash transfer programmes to more people was considered an avenue through which politicians could garner votes. This view was not only expressed by other informants but by the political elites interviewed. A member of parliament explained it as part of the political game in which perceptions matter; as MPs they have to be seen by their constituents as promoting policies on their behalf (MP-01, 31 August 2016). This was discussed further by a domestic actor who pointed to increased interest in social protection by politicians near election periods (MGCSD-01, 23 March 2016). The finding is not surprising as pro-poor programmes can be used to gain political mileage and used for patronage.

Due to their powerful sway on policy matters, however, politicians were sidelined at various stages of the policymaking process, thus minimising their contribution to the process. Their participation therefore became reactionary in response to other actors' actions. Their exclusion by the coalition of bureaucrats and international organisations stemmed from the fear that their political involvement would scuttle the adoption process before the programmes could be established. As explained by a participant from an international organisation, the deliberate exclusion of politicians from the policymaking process was because they did not want them to bring 'politics into the programmes' (IOS-02, 23 March 2016).

Politicians are often excluded from policy processes under the assertion that the programmes would otherwise fall prey to patrimonial interests, leading to patronage politics (Mkandawire 2015). Apart from compromising national ownership of programmes, this exclusion also signalled the disregard in which other actors held them as elected officials accountable to their constituents. The policy network thus relegated the importance of the political class. As one respondent explained,

> Politicians destroyed and they interfered with the programmes as they insisted that targeting of the programmes has to be done their way. (TT/C-01, 1 April 2016)

The power of politicians in budget approval for the expansion of programmes is critical, especially in the current constitutional dispensation, which makes it difficult to override them or constrain their agency.

Individualistic/Ideological Interests

The third interest driving the adoption of the CT-OVC and the HSNP evolved around organisations seeking to pursue either their self-interest or ideological persuasions aligned to their institutions. Individual and ideological interests are narrow, individualistic and based on material and pecuniary interests. Actors who clustered around this interest group were international organisations described as 'heavyweight agencies and big names in development studies' (Sabates-Wheeler and Devereux 2007: 1) in relation to their powerful influence in policymaking. Besides international organisations, other agencies that promoted individual interests were domestic civil society organisations. Individualistic and ideological interests were characterised by a narrow approach, material appeal and self-interest.

Narrow Approach

The narrowness of the interests was demonstrated in several ways. First, it involved advocacy of a strict targeting mechanism on poverty and the promotion of a single instrument not anchored in broader social policy and national development plans. In addition, international organisations focused on ex-ante remedies instead of giving broader attention to the structural factors that perpetuate inequality and poverty. Also, the focus was on individual wellbeing rather than collective welfare (Adesina 2011), with the idea of social policy narrowed down to a single instrument— cash transfers (Adesina 2015). The narrowing of the instrument and of social policy indicated the ideological persuasions of the different organisations in the policy space. For example, the World Bank promoted safety nets which provided only temporary relief to households in times of distress and shocks.

Besides proposing temporary programmes, the World Bank preferred schemes that strictly targeted poverty. This narrow focus on poverty is inadequate in reducing poverty as it avoids the 'grand narratives' of development and concentrates instead on small-scale microlevel projects (Mkandawire 2010). Interests based on organisational ideology are characterised by short-term perspectives not embedded in the broader social development national narrative. In addition, the financing by international organisations rarely went beyond ten-year cycles, indicating short-term agendas.

Material and Pecuniary Appeals

While the primary focus of civil society organisations lies in the promotion of social welfare, other interests evolved around the material benefits accrued from promoting the cash transfer programmes. Our findings indicated that NGOs were created specifically to promote social protection on the continent. International organisations brought financing to the policy space to which domestic actors had access. With decreased funding over time, however, some of these domestic civil society organisations are no longer functional, and some have moved on to other agendas. Critics of the process of transfer of the policies note that civil society organisations promoting social protection policies were a creation of the international organisations and that their participation therefore did not emanate from national imperatives. Rather, it was in response to supporting an agenda from which they could access funds. This finding was confirmed by a member of civil society who confessed:

> It was the first time we were hearing about social protection. We had no idea what it was but there was money to start a Platform and we figured we would learn along the way. (CSO-01, 6 April 2016)

From the statement, two observations emerge. First, that the promotion of the cash transfer agenda was not part of the civil society agenda in Kenya and that civil society organisation were engaged in the policy network to promote the efforts of the international organisations. Their interest in the social protection network was driven by the funds these organisations offered. The new agenda therefore presented a potential area of financing for domestic organisations. As the CSOs had little knowledge of the agenda, they depended on the international organisations for advocacy direction. It was noted, however, that the international organisations preferred to work with international NGOs who were largely composed of foreigners and considered to have no ties to domestic actors or clientelistic forces and partnerships (Mkandawire 2010).

Second, though acting in the social interest, the impetus for international agencies getting domestic CSOs onto the social protection 'bandwagon' was the need for legitimisation. Through financing, international organisations created and formed strategic networks with the CSOs to give legitimacy to their work and to promote the policy instruments agreed upon by the bilateral agencies (Adesina 2014). CSO alignment with international organisations was based on acquiring resources in exchange for their support for these international organisations. Domestic civil society organisations acted as middlemen between the bureaucrats and the international organisations on one hand and politicians on the other and were therefore instrumental in mediating a number of policy processes.

Other actors within the policy space with individualistic interests were members of the epistemic communities. Comprising consultancy firms, academics and individuals, this group was described as experts in social protection. Their participation and intervention in the policy process derived from their perceived knowledge of the matter and therefore their ability to structure the collective problem and find the most appropriate solutions. Similar to CSOs, members of the epistemic community were linked to international organisations on the basis of financial resources (Adesina 2011). Policy transfer agents contracted them to conduct impact assessments, programme and policy design and, in some cases, implementation of the programmes. It was presumed that due to their knowledge and expertise, they had the ability to define interests and set agendas. As experts, and having the power to strengthen certain positions based on their research and knowledge, they were recruited by international organisations to promote the cash transfer agenda and their clients' interests (Dente 2013).

To be considered 'national', consultancy firms set up offices at national level forming alliances with academics and think tanks within the country. Some former employees of international organisations set up consulting firms, which guaranteed them contracts from their former employers. Another interest pursued within the policy space was academic advancement by conducting research and publishing evidence on the impact and other aspects of the programmes.

Self-Interest Purposes

Although politicians stated that they were advocating the programmes to bring about change to citizens, they did so also out of self-interest. They explained that their enthusiasm for the adoption of the programmes lay in the freedom it offered them from personally having to be 'social protection for their constituents. Members of parliament said that the provision of the cash transfer programmes freed them from obligations to contribute to their constituents' medical fees, burial expenses and school fees, and they therefore expressed support for the cash transfer agenda based on this expectation. Expounding on this viewpoint, a participant explained:

> So, essentially the support mechanisms came from individuals and from politicians. They took on the burden of being the 'cash transfer'. If there was a problem the politician provided the hearse, medical support, school bursaries—the politician was basically everything. And it is these issues that cash transfers are resolving. (CSO-01, 12 February 2016)

Political promotion of cash transfers was therefore justified out of self-interest, for political expediency and for public interest.

Power Resource and Legitimacy

The success of those who promoted the cash transfer programmes depended on several factors. These included their path-dependent involvement in policy formulation in Kenya, their skilful persuasion and lobbying of the government, their adroit manipulation of knowledge, position and financial resources within the policy network, and their recognition of windows of opportunity.

International actors, as policy prescriptors, were aware of their disadvantage as non-veto players within the policy network. To overcome this deficiency, international organisations identified domestic actors to build alliances in the policy network. These actors were chosen based on the resource base they possessed—financial and knowledge. To begin with, contrary to assertions that international organisations find domestic allies to work with (Dolowitz and Marsh 2000), where such allies did not exist these organisations undertook to create them from scratch. A case in point is the creation of the Africa Platform for Social Protection, supported by international organisations to drive continental advocacy efforts for social protection, and charged in turn with creating national coalitions of social protection. International organisations therefore provided funding to domestic civil society organisations and opened up avenues for training and co-operation at the global level. These organisations were supplied with resources—ideas, technical expertise, international recognition and financial and material support—to promote the adoption of cash transfer policies.

On the other hand, domestic civil society organisations who acted as 'mediators' mostly between the political class and international organisations brought to the policy network their mandate to speak on behalf of the public. Funded civil society organisations had a dual role: first, they lobbied the political class; and second, they were expected to drum up support at the grassroots level. The second role aimed to build the demand side of social protection and hence 'make the claims that the reform agenda corresponds to the will of the citizens and the elites' (Delpeuch and Vassileva 2017).

The international organisations provided knowledge of the basics of social protection and cash transfers in the form of reports and information which corresponded with that of think tanks and epistemic communities. CSOs therefore depended on international organisations for capacity-building and knowledge transfer upon which to frame their advocacy. But they also depended on them for legitimacy. Despite the national identity of CSOs and being representatives of the people, their ideas and positions had no weight and did not bear significantly on the policy reform process within the policy network. Even within their advocacy to government and members of parliament, it was important for them to show alignment with international organisations in order to make inroads. Policy advice from local producers of knowledge is rarely taken seriously and to get their policy proposals and preferences considered, domestic civil society organisations needed to associate themselves with international organisations to make their views become 'international recommendations'. In addition to funding and knowledge, international organisations created ties for domestic civil society organisations with international global coalition and networks of social protection.

Bureaucrats on the other hand, formed a point of centrality within the policy network. Based on their legal power as implementers of policy decisions and conveners of the social protection committee, they brought together all the relationships within the network. Their strong relationship with international organisations was based on technical support in the form of knowledge and material support in the form of equipment and finance needed to run the programmes. As conveners and the central point for the promotion of the policies, they formed the core team determining inclusion and invitation into the policy network. Through exercising this power, they decided on who could enter the policy network and at what time. For this reason, they were able to exclude other actors, particularly those they considered did not bring in significant resources, like civil society organisations or those whose participation would derail the policy adoption process, like politicians.

The significant power of politicians in the policy process lay in their role as policymakers. Their involvement was required in passing the Social Protection Bill and Act, and civil society members were mandated to lobby them for support and to increase budgetary allocation for the programmes. In recognition of their power as lawmakers and their allocation of resources for the programmes, through a number of meetings with civil society organisations and government bureaucrats, members of parliament were influenced to support the programmes.

Findings: Convergence of Interests and Resource Base

Successful policy transfer was the result of a compatibility of interests. Though the policy network had different interests—public, political and ideological/individualistic—the match between domestic actors' interests and those of international actors converged to bring about policy uptake.

The discussion above has shown that strong interests—those that were individualistic, narrow, material and short-term—significantly influenced social protection policy uptake. Actors with those interests were able to develop relationships with other actors based on their financial and knowledge resources. International organisations possessed both influential resources and strong interests. In forming relationships with others, their resource base strengthened their position within the policy network. As points of centrality in the policy network, they controlled the policymaking process to a great extent by excluding other actors, manipulating resources and creating new actors to bring into the policy network. In addition, they produced knowledge, offered financial incentives, funded government operations within the national secretariat and provided funding for other organisations like NGOs. These attributes and strategies employed within the policy network enabled international organisations to strongly influence and coerce national actors and convince them that the adoption of the programmes was in their interest (Mkandawire 2010). This resonates with Gramsci's conceptualisation of hegemony, in which legitimacy is achieved by the presentation of sectional interests as popular interests to foster 'popular consent' (Gramsci 1971) where consent is key to the achievement of hegemony. Our research therefore demonstrates the centrality, power and influence that international organisations exercised within the policy network despite the narrow agenda they promoted.

Second, our observations and findings indicate that political interest was significant in promoting policy uptake as it was closely allied to the individualist interests of international organisations. Our observations indicate that the veto power of politicians, while necessary for policy change, is not sufficient and does not play a significant role in policy change and uptake in cases where the policy is promoted by international organisations and where governments are dependent on donor financing. The impact of the political class was limited due to their exclusion in the policy process. Successful policy uptake, however, was the result of the compatibility of political interests with individualistic interests associated with the policy-carriers and prescriptors.

Lastly, international organisations, actors who derived their legitimacy from a resource base of knowledge and finance, were able to influence the interests of others by forming tactical relationships and interactions with local actors. This is in line with Jones (2009), who stated that though there may be different interests in competition, the more adept and better resourced actor wins. The relationships they formed increased their dominance in influencing the preference and desires of other actors especially those bureaucrats with whom they had a close working relationship. Their capacity to influence bureaucrats who are policy implementers derived from their resource base and their international reputation as norm-setters.

Conclusion

Explaining the recent uptake of social protection policies in Kenya requires going beyond the variables of social learning, political settlements and conditionality. A better explanation requires an understanding of the web of interactions that actors form to influence policy change. For this reason, an examination of the policy network as the space of interaction between a plurality of actors with different and varied interests, resource base and legitimacy provides a more nuanced understanding. This is particularly central in situations where policy networks are based on asymmetrical power relations derived from differential resources. Incorporating policy network into policy transfer allows an understanding of the complexity of relationships, interactions and interests within the policy space.

Policy transfer enabled an understanding of the dynamic that connected international organisations with domestic actors in the transfer and adoption of the OVC and the HSNP programmes. By exploring policy networks within policy transfer processes, this study demonstrates how the web of compatible interests and linkages led to policy adoption through the manipulation of resources to influence others. Policy transfer and policymaking in themselves constitute a complex, interactive, uncertain process, making it a challenge to attribute policy transfer success to only one set of interests or a specific policy transfer entrepreneur.

Acknowledgements

The authors would like to acknowledge the National Research Foundation of South Africa, which funded the study through the South African Research Chair in Social Policy. This publication was also made possible by support from the Social Science Research Council's Next Generation Social Sciences in Africa Fellowship, with funds provided by Carnegie Corporation of New York.

References

Adesina, J., 2011, Beyond the Social Protection Paradigm: Social Policy in Africa's Development, *Canadian Journal of Development Studies / Revue Canadienne d'Études du Développement*, Vol. 32, No. 4, pp. 454–470. DOI: 10.1080/02255189.2011.647441.

Adesina, J., 2014, Accounting for Social Policy: Reflections on Recent Developments in Sub-Saharan Africa, Draft paper prepared for the UNRISD Conference, New Directions in Social Policy: Alternatives from and for the Global South, 7–8 April, 2014, Geneva: UNRISD. Available online at: http://www.unrisd.org/80256B3C005BCCF9/(httpAuxPages)/15F0DC9FE0A6AE8FC1257D07005D9C04/$file/Adesina.pdf. Accessed 12 October 2016.

Adesina, J., 2015, Return to a Wider Vision of Social Policy: Re-reading Theory and History, *South African Review of Sociology*, Vol. 46, No. 3, pp. 99–119. DOI: 10.1080/21528586.2015.1077588.

Béland, D. and Orenstein, M. A., 2013, International Organizations as Policy Actors: An Ideational Approach, *Global Social Policy*, Vol. 13, No. 2, pp. 125–143.

Bosworth, J., Alviar, C., Corral, L., Davis, B., Musembi, D., 2016, The Cash Transfer Programme for Orphans and Vulnerable Children: The Catalyst for Cash Transfers in Kenya, in Davis, B., Handa, S., Hypher, N., Rossi, N., Winters, P. and Yablonski, J., eds, *From Evidence to Action: The Story of Cash Transfers and Impact Evaluation in Sub Saharan Africa*, Oxford, Rome, New York: Oxford University Press.

Costa Leite, I., Suyama, B. and Pomeroy, M., 2013, Africa–Brazil Co-Operation in Social Protection: Drivers, Lessons and Shifts in the Engagement of the Brazilian Ministry of Social Development, WIDER Working Paper, Helsinki: UNU-WIDER. Available online at: http://www.econstor.eu/handle/10419/81027. Accessed on 15 July 2015.

Deacon, B., 2013, *Global Social Policy in the Making: The Foundations of the Social Protection Floor*, Bristol, UK: Policy Press.

Deacon, B. and Stubbs, P., 2013, Global Social Policy Studies: Conceptual and Analytical Reflections, *Global Social Policy*, Vol. 13, No. 1, pp. 5–23. DOI: 10.1177/1468018112469798.

Delpeuch, T. and Vassileva, M., 2017, Judicial Reforms as a Political Enterprise: American Transfer Entrepreneurs in post-Communist Bulgaria, in Hadjiisky, M., Pal, L. A. and Walker, C., eds, *Public Policy Transfer: Micro-Dynamics and Macro-effects*, Cheltenham, UK and Northampton, MA: Edward Elgar Publishers.

Dente, B., 2013, *Understanding Policy Decisions*, Bonn: Springer International Publishing AG.

Devereux, S. and White, P., 2010, Social Protection in Africa: Evidence, Politics and Rights, *Poverty & Public Policy*, Vol. 2, No. 3, pp. 516–540. DOI 10.2202/1944-2858.1078.

Dolowitz, D. and Marsh, D., 1996, Who Learns What From Whom: A Review of the Policy Transfer Literature, *Political Studies*, Vol. 44, No. 2, pp. 343–357.

Foli, R., 2015, Transnational Actors and Policymaking in Ghana: The Case of the Livelihood Empowerment Against Poverty, *Global Social Policy*, Vol. 16, No. 3, pp. 268–286.

Franzoni, J. M. and Voorend, K., 2011, Actors and Ideas Behind CCTs in Chile, Costa Rica and El Salvador, *Global Social Policy*, Vol. 11, No. 2–3, pp. 279–298.

Gramsci, A., 1971/1989, *Selections from the Prison Notebooks*, Hoare, Q. and Smith G. N., eds, New York: International Publishers Co.

Henry, A. D., 2011, Ideology, Power, and the Structure of Policy networks, *Policy Studies Journal*, Vol. 39, No. 3, pp. 361–383.

Ingold, K., 2011, Network Structures Within Policy Processes: Coalitions, Power, and Brokerage in Swiss Climate Policy, *Policy Studies Journal*, Vol. 39, No. 3, pp. 435–459.

Jones, H., 2009, Policy-making As Discourse: A Review of Recent Knowledge-To-Policy Literature, ODI-IKM Working Paper No.5, London, UK: Overseas Development Institute.

Lavers, T. and Hickey, S., 2016, Conceptualising the Politics of Social Protection Expansion in Low Income Countries: The Intersection of Transnational Ideas and Domestic Politics, *International Journal of Social Welfare*, Vol. 25, Issue 4, pp. 388–398. DOI 10.1111/ijsw.12210.

Mkandawire, T., 2010, How the New Poverty Agenda Neglected Social and Employment Policies in Africa, *Journal of Human Development and Capabilities*, Vol. 11, No. 1, pp. 37–55. DOI: 10.1080/19452820903481400.

Mkandawire, T., 2015, Neopatrimonialism and the Political Economy of Economic Performance in Africa: Critical Reflections, *World Politics*, Vol. 67, No. 3, pp. 563–612. DOI: 10.1017/S004388711500009X.

Niedzwiecki, S., 2016, Social Policies, Attribution of Responsibility, and Political Alignments: A Subnational Analysis of Argentina and Brazil, *Comparative Political Studies*, Vol. 49, No. 4, pp. 457–498.

Niño-Zarazúa, M., Barrientos, A., Hickey, S. and Hulme D., 2012, Social Protection in Sub-Saharan Africa: Getting the Politics Right, *World Development*, Vol. 40, No. 1, pp. 163–176. DOI: 10.1016/j.worlddev.2011.04.004.

Peck, J., 2011, Global Policy Models, Globalising Poverty Management: International Convergence or Fast-Policy Integration? Global Policy Models, *Geography Compass*, Vol. 5, No. 4, pp. 165–181. DOI: 10.1111/j.1749-8198.2011.00417.x.

Peters, B. G. and Zittoun, P., eds, 2016, *Contemporary Approaches to Public Policy: Theories, Controversies and Perspectives*, London, UK: Palgrave Macmillan.

Pruce, K. and Hickey, S., 2017, The Politics of Promoting Social Protection in Zambia, ESID Working Papers No. 5, Manchester: Effective States and Inclusive Development Centre, pp. 1–75.

Sabates-Wheeler, R. and Devereux, S., 2007, Social Protection for Transformation, *IDS Bulletin*, Vol. 38, No. 3, pp. 23–28.

Shearer, J. C., Abelson, J., Kouyaté, B., Lavis, J. N. and Walt G., 2016, Why Do Policies Change? Institutions, Interests, Ideas and Networks in Three Cases Of Policy Reform, *Health Policy and Planning*, Vol. 3, No. 9, pp. 1200–1211. DOI: 10.1093/heapol/czw052.

Tambulasi, R., 2013, 'Why Can't You Lead a Horse to Water and Make It Drink?' The Learning-Oriented Transfer of Health Sector Decentralisation Reforms and Bureaucratic Interests in Malawi, in Carroll, P. and Common, R., eds, *Policy Transfer and Learning in Public Policy and Management: International Contexts, Content and Development*, Oxford: Routledge, pp. 80–104.

Wanyama, F. O. and McCord, A. G., 2017, The Politics of Scaling Up Social Protection in Kenya, ESID Working Paper, No 87, Manchester: Effective States and Inclusive Development Centre. Available online at: https://papers.ssrn.com/sol3/papers.cfm?abstract_id=2963685. Accessed on 26 May 2017.

Weyland, K., 2007, *Bounded Rationality and Policy Diffusion: Social Sector Reform in Latin America*, Princeton, NJ: Princeton University Press.

World Bank, 2015, *The State of Social Safety Nets 2015*, Washington, DC: The World Bank Group. Available online at http://elibrary.worldbank.org/doi/book/10.1596/978-1-4648-0543-1. Accessed on 8 September 2015.

9

Non-State Actors and Social Policy in Africa: Issues and Perspectives for Agenda 2063

Jonathan Makuwira

Introduction

The involvement of non-state actors (NSAs) in the formulation and implementation of public policies has increased in the last few decades and, as such, has become a major feature of public policy, not only in developed but also in developing countries. In many cases, this practice has become a new form of how citizens engage in a participatory democracy which, by definition, underscores the importance of citizen's voices and a consensual way of making public as well as social policy through dialogue with all key stakeholders.

Over the years, the opening up of the state to non-state actors has created a form of identity among non-state actors to the extent that most of them are increasingly becoming interested in being part of the development process. In Africa, their prominence has been necessitated by the roll-back of the state as a result of the neoliberal prescriptions that have seen the state's role being replaced by the market and the third sector.

The purpose of this chapter is to contribute to the ongoing debate about the role of NSAs in social policy, in the wake of Africa's Agenda 2063. I argue that while Africa has made significant steps in participatory policy formulation, there remains a yawning gap in the academic discourse and in the evidence of where such participation has worked. In other words, the debate on the role of NSAs in social policy formulation in sub-Saharan Africa has not received much attention. There have been numerous claims and counterclaims on both sides, which require thorough examination to unmask the intricacies of their engagement. Using Malawi and other countries in southern and eastern Africa as case studies, this chapter calls for a robust debate on the political economy of NSAs and their contribution to social policy formulation. I argue that NSAs can contribute to development policy if they understand their role within government development agendas whose ultimate goal is to achieve Africa's Agenda 2063.

Besides the introduction, the chapter is divided into five major sections. The first highlights major arguments about development in Africa. In particular, it canvasses the political, social and economic trends that have shaped Africa as we see it today. The second section examines the role of non-state actors which, in this chapter, will interchangeably be referred to as non-governmental organisations (NGOs). The emphasis in this part will be around their political economy and how they interact with the state. By teasing out the tensions and contradictions, the chapter offers a critique on how NSAs have found their way into the mainstream development practice and become a key player in social policy. The third section discusses examples and case studies from Malawi, Tanzania and other countries in sub-Saharan Africa. Section four draws on the cases to identify lessons that may inform the development of a new agenda for Africa's development. The conclusion draws the key debates together to make an argument for the way forward.

Africa's Development Trajectory

The NSA discourse cannot be understood without navigating Africa's development trajectory. As we may appreciate, Africa, more than any other continent in the world, is under constant scrutiny. Despite housing abundant energy and mineral resources, Africa's development trajectory has generally been paradoxical. On the one hand, it has vast underground resources; on the other, it is very poor above ground (Ainger 2007). This contradiction has given impetus to a more critical analysis of the geostrategic and economic interests of donor agencies that finance local and international NSAs.

The financing of their activities does not come without strings attached and should not be seen through a simplistic lens. Rather, it should be viewed as a political economy of international relations and social policy influence. For example, part of Ronald Reagan's inaugural speech in 1981 emphasised that 'government is not the solution to our problems; government is the problem' (Reagan 1981, cited in Nega and Schneider 2014: 486). The essence of this statement cannot be overemphasised in an analysis of the current global social policy and of Africa's historical past. In particular, what ensued soon after Reagan's speech, as was the case after Harry Truman's maiden speech of 1949, was the introduction of Structural Adjustment Programmes (SAPs), which had devastating effects on the African continent that still linger across the African economy (Mkandawire 1988; Makuwira 2014a). SAPs came with a package of policy prescriptions which, inter alia, diminished the role of the state in preference to the role of the private sector and NSAs. Of particular importance was governments' privatisation of the delivery of public services to non-state actors. Because of this, not only did the shrinking role of the state mean that bilateral and multilateral funding to government was to be reduced but it also meant an increase in funding to NSAs which, according to Dietrich (2012: 2) revealed that:

> OECD donors channel significant amounts of bilateral assistance around recipient governments and through non-state development actors: in 2008, OECD donors committed a total of US$ 112 billion and delegated over 30 percent of the aid, approximately US$ 41 billion, for implementation through non-state development actors, which include NGOs, multilaterals, public-private partnerships, and private contractors (OECD 2010), only to name the more prominent bypass channels. These non-state actors are hired for specific project delivery and remain accountable to the donors.

Not only did the introduction of the SAPs simply exacerbate aid dependence and push many African countries into deeper economic crisis but it also meant that development was, and continues to be, dictated by conditionalities that often require aid recipients to adhere to specific rules before aid is provided (Stokke 1995). The mushrooming of NSAs on the continent has now surpassed expectations with the discourse of civil society participation echoing everywhere. In the words of Amfred et al. (2007: 9), today, 'Africa is still the continent where international (mainly western) economic actors reap huge business returns'.

Non-State Actors in the African Context

While there is no agreed definition of non-state actors in the current development discourse, the existing literature seems to suggest that non-state actors are entities which may include private and third-sector organisations (see Kironde 2007; Carbone 2003; Steer, Gustafsson-Wright and Latham 2015). This definition is further expanded when the notion of the 'third sector' is put under microscopic scrutiny. In this, third-sector organisations can include civil society organisations, trade unions, employers' organisations, private business, consumer organisations, academic and research institutions, co-operatives, youth organisations, human rights and advocacy organisations, just to name a few. There is no doubt that defining non-state actors as above can only be described as 'loose and baggy' (Knapp and Kendal 1995). One could easily argue that their diversity could, in turn, be viewed as a coherent whole—an entity with its own distinct social form and practical logic.

In his paper 'Non-state actors in law-making and shaping of policy', Von Bernstorff (2007) elaborates further on the notion of non-state actors, noting that these can be defined as organisations which are independent from the state and have not been established by intergovernmental agreement. Such a definition provides a platform for further analysis linked to development discourses. First, there is an element indicating the integration of non-state actors in the broader development discourse. Second, the definition gives clues to a governance agenda, which calls for an active role in participating, on behalf of the most vulnerable, in the decision-making processes that affect society. Third, is the legitimacy issue. In this, the argument is that the legitimacy of NSAs is contingent on how accepted they are at the governmental, intergovernmental, and supranational levels.

A distinction needs to be made between different categories of NSAs. While there is no agreed classification as such, this chapter adopts the World Bank's categorisation which is on the basis of the kind of activity they engage in. The first category is a cluster of NSAs that are development-oriented which, according to the World Bank, are classified as 'operational NGOs'. According to Fowler (2011) and Makuwira (2014b), these are NGOs that are actively engaged in the design and implementation of development projects. But the World Bank further divides operational NGOs into three other categories, namely: community-based organisations (CBOs), national organisations and international organisations, on the basis of the geographic coverage of their activities.

The second category constitutes what is referred to as 'advocacy NGOs'. Advocacy, as practised and understood by NGOs, is intended to mitigate unequal power relations. Thus, equalising power relations is both the nature and goal of advocacy. I argue that all NSAs' activities can be viewed as having an advocacy aspect, and all are inherent in the contested process of development given that, by inference, development is a political process. Furthermore, the fact that NSAs operate in a political space governed by an elected government, inevitably, advocating for the most vulnerable means taking sides on behalf of the poor and the politically repressed. Like operational NGOs, advocacy NGOs can be community-based, national or international organisations.

The reason these non-state actors have gained visibility over the past seven decades is their presumed comparative advantage (Tvedt 1998). Broadly speaking, there is a belief that NSAs in the form of operational NGOs are closer to the targeted public than bureaucratic state institutions, and that they have grassroots links. Most CBOs, in particular, are believed to be rooted in the community—meaning that they reflect the interests of the community. In reflecting the interests of communities, they are, by inference, thought to have a better understanding of the problems of the communities they purport to support. Another presumed strength of these non-state actors is their supposed expertise in field-based development work. Unlike government institutions that are often located in peri-urban and urban centres, non-state actors work in the field with the affected population, thereby giving them hands-on experience and the expertise that comes with it to better come up with practical solutions to the problems facing their constituencies. Their size is believed to be an advantage. These organisations are small and usually function in specific areas. This gives them a better view of the challenges they encounter and they can use their capacity and flexibility to adapt to changing circumstances. These NSAs are also credited for using participatory development approaches, thereby giving them an edge in providing sustainability to a project even after the organisation that initiated the project is long gone.

These 'articles of faith' (Tendler 1982) are not unproblematic. Over the years, there has been a wave of critiques, some of which question these mega claims. Scholars like Bebbington (2004), Reimann (2005), Nunnenkamp (2008), Makuwira (2014b) and Matthews (2017) have offered different perspectives and views on the efficacy and effectiveness of NSAs' claims and counter-claims. In part, the various criticisms of NSAs have called for attention to the validity, tensions, contradictions and inconsistencies of their many claims. Much of the criticism centres on their failure to advance a progressive agenda, their performance and actual effectiveness, accountability issues, issues of autonomy, commercialisation and ideological and/or political interpretations of their rising influence. This criticism cannot be understood unless we understand, in the context of this chapter, Africa's development trajectory, to which I now turn.

Social Policy in Africa

Africa's development trajectory reflects its social policy which, in part, is heavily influenced by its historical past. In an ideal situation, any social policy is meant to promote social development. But I want to agree with Hall and Midgley (2004), who acknowledge the difficulty in defining social policy which, they argue, is full of ambiguities and confusion. However, several attempts have been made to come up with a reasonable understanding. Three sets of scholarly thinking on the topic are summed up in Table 9.1.

Table 9.1: Different Viewpoints about Social Policy

Name of Scholar	Views on Social Policy	Emphasis
Adesina, J. O. (2009)	Collective public efforts aimed at effecting and protecting social wellbeing of people in given territory.	Social protection
Mkandawire, T. (2004)	Instrument for a sense of citizenship. Collective interventions affecting transformation in social welfare, social institutions and social relations. Access to adequate and secure livelihoods.	Production of human capital; redistribution of resources; and protecting the vulnerable.
Addison, T., Niño-Zarazúa, M. and Tarp, F. (2015)	Actions and principles that, through the provision of healthcare, education, water and sanitation, as well as social protection, enhance human welfare.	Enhanced human welfare

The emphasis on social protection and enhancement of social welfare underscores the fundamental issues of social justice, which are highlighted in the case studies below.

Case Studies
Case Study 1: Malawi
Malawi—Federation of Disability Organisations in Malawi (FEDOMA)

Formed in 1999, the Federation of Disability Organisations in Malawi (FEDOMA) is an umbrella organisation for all disability-specific, representative organisations in Malawi. Formed to provide a unified voice for all persons with disabilities through lobbying and advocacy activities towards an inclusive Malawi, FEDOMA's members include Malawi Union of the Blind (MUB), Malawi National Association of the Deaf (MANAD), Malawi Disability Sports Association (MADISA), Association of the Physically Disabled in Malawi (APDM), Parents of Disabled Children Association in Malawi (PODCAM), The Albino Association of Malawi (TAAM), Disabled Women in Development (DIWODE), Disabled Widows Orphans of Malawi (DWOOM) and Visual and Hearing Association of Malawi (VIHEMA).

Since the advent of Malawi's second independence—Âthe move from one-party political system to multi-party politics—the mushrooming of the non-governmental sector signalled a new era of associations. The reconfiguration of the NGO sector also meant a significant awareness of the role of government on its citizenry. It was due to this wind of change that most NGOs began to engage in lobbying and advocacy on a number of policy fronts, many of which were to do with social policy. While FEDOMA belongs to the national NGO umbrella organisation—The Council for Non-Governmental Organisations in Malawi (CONGOMA)—both CONGOMA and FEDOMA, using their membership networks, began to lobby government to shift the way in which people with disabilities were to be treated. This resulted in the development of the National Policy on the Equalisation of Person with Disabilities.

National Policy on the Equalisation of Opportunities for Persons with Disabilities

The National Policy on the Equalisation of Opportunities for Persons with Disabilities, an initiative that was precipitated by FEDOMA, was launched in 2006 with a commitment to be reviewed every five years. In an era of political pluralism, the purpose of the policy was to respond to one of the major social policy gaps—the inclusion of people with disabilities in the mainstream development narrative, active participation in the decision-making processes. Therefore the policy was meant to promote the rights of people with disabilities and ensure that concrete steps were taken for people with disabilities to access the same fundamental rights and responsibilities as any other Malawian citizen. This meant that there had to be a deliberate effort to integrate disability issues into all government development strategies, planning and programmes. Since the inception of this policy, there has been a significant change on the social policy front. For example, the Malawi Disabilities Act of 2012, Malawi Inclusive Education Policy and International Convention on the Rights of Persons with Disabilities (ICRPD), ratified in August 2009, are three major policy achievements. Currently, through FEDOMA, some academic institutions have now developed specific 'inclusion policies', to allow people with disabilities to be selected to universities, for example—which had not been done before. In some cases, libraries are now busy transcribing reading materials into braille. In Malawi, mainstreaming disability is a very high priority in every sector of the economy.

Case Study 2: Ethiopia
Adult and Non-Formal Education Association in Ethiopia (ANFEAE)

Education remains one of the most critical human rights issues across Africa and numerous non-state actors are actively engaged in providing it as a basic social service across sub-Saharan Africa. In Ethiopia, for example, one of the NSAs engaged in advancing social policy is the Adult and Non-Formal Education Association in Ethiopia (ANFEAE) (UNESCO 2008). Established in 1996 to help economic and social development of the country through promoting Life-Long Learning and facilitating high-quality and life-enhancing education and training for adults, the youth and children in rural and urban areas of Ethiopia, ANFEAE works with community-based institutions to help implement and manage educational projects, transformative advocacy, educational training, material development and networking and research. Since its inception, ANFEAE has trained 1,200 civil servants and published seventeen training manuals into four national languages.

For example, in the Gambela, Oromiya, Gumuz and Amhara regions, attempts to increase literacy rates across all sectors of society form part of the effort. As education is, perhaps, a major social policy area, it is not surprising that ANFEAE is focusing on it. Besides, linked to basic education are increased activities in small and medium enterprise (SME) activities, which augment livelihoods through promoting functional and life-related basic education and skills training, with special emphasis on girls and women.

Case Study 3: South Africa
Treatment Action Campaign (TAC)

The global HIV/AIDS pandemic has had its effect on social policy in sub-Saharan Africa. One of the most contentious issues over the years has been, and continues to be, access to antiretroviral drugs for people affected with the disease. Many NSAs have been vocal in advocating access to free treatment. The Treatment Action Campaign (TAC), a South African NGO established in 1998 to campaign for access to AIDS treatment, is widely acknowledged as one of the most important civil society organisations active on AIDS in the developing world. Its major vision is premised on equity and social justice through a unified, high-quality healthcare system which provides equal access to HIV prevention and treatment services for all people. This essentially means that TAC ensures that every person living with HIV has access to comprehensive prevention and treatment services, in order to live a healthy life and contribute to the development of South Africa and, indeed, the region and ultimately sustainable development.

While the TAC may have performed remarkably well in advancing an effective global campaign to radically reduce the prices of key AIDS treatments, the wider war for access to medicines still lingers not only in South Africa but in Africa in general. As a non-state actor engaging in seemingly political issues, TAC's achievements so far have provided a platform for further advocacy. For example, issues of funding are critical to the success of its work, yet the government of South Africa is loath to support it. This is why achieving strong social policy is not a sole effort. It relies on strategic coalition-building to effect strong advocacy. In other words, a complex set of TAC strategies drew on a sophisticated analysis of the governance and social context as well as the internal strengths of the organisation, to contribute to its success.

These case studies, though few due to the space available for the chapter, provide insights into some of the intricacies of social policy in Africa. For sub-Saharan Africa in particular, the need to engage in active advocacy and lobbying for the millions of people who find themselves on the fringes of society cannot be overemphasised. But the question that needs more attention is, what lessons do these cases provide in advancing Africa's ambitious project over the next forty-four years? In the next section, I try to elaborate on and link these cases to Africa's Agenda 2063.

Africa's Agenda 2063 and how it Should be Achieved

In commemorating the 50th anniversary of the establishment of the Organisation of African Unity (OAU), now the African Union, heads of states and governments in Africa in 2013 agreed on a fifty-year plan to accelerate development and technological progress. The emphasis was to 'build an integrated, prosperous and peaceful Africa driven and managed by its own citizens and representing a dynamic force in international Arena' (African Union 2015: 4), given its long history of colonisation, conflicts and perpetual poverty. Agenda 2063 opens up an opportunity not only to reflect on the past successes and failures but also to build on existing opportunities that can help Africa embark on an ambitious development agenda for the next forty-four years and, more importantly, build policy frameworks that can enhance social policy across the continent.

As is the case with other international development instruments, like the Sustainable Development Goals, Agenda 2063's operational framework is key to its success. For now, it is envisaged that the agenda be set as a long-, medium- and short-term plan to be implemented in phases of ten-year plans but also further broken into a five-year implementation plan, depending on country-specific targeted initiatives. This operational framing allows windows of opportunities to monitor, reflect on and evaluate the development initiatives, feedback that could then be used to improve the next phases in the implementation process. Agenda 2063 is driven by seven aspirations, which highlight its central ambitions:

1. A prosperous Africa based on inclusive growth and sustainable development;
2. An integrated continent, politically united and based on the ideals of Pan Africanism and the vision of Africa's Renaissance;
3. An Africa of good governance, democracy, respect for human rights, justice and the rule of law;
4. A peaceful and secure Africa;
5. An Africa with a strong cultural identity, common heritage, values and ethics;
6. An Africa where development is people-driven, unleashing the potential of its women and youth; and
7. Africa as a strong, united and influential global player and partner (African Union 2015).

While these aspirations represent a noble agenda of making Africa realise its long-term dream of a united continent free of poverty and conflict, there is yet to be a critical analysis of how some of the aspirations will be achieved. Besides, while the documentation claims there was a widely engineered consultation process to put the background document together, the majority of millions of Africans across the continent, those whose lives are affected by the ravages of poverty, may have no idea about this ambitious plan. Furthermore, the success of this continental programme depends not only on how good it is on paper but how it becomes a shared dream communicated through education and responsive social policy. And, from a social policy front, the seven aspirations have to be seen from a wider perspective, that achieving them means achieving social development on the continent. I want to pick one fundamental silence in the social policy narrative—the role of regimes in enhancing the contribution of NSAs and, ultimately, social policy in Africa.

The Role of Regimes in Shaping NSAs' Contribution to Social Policy in Africa

Regimes, no matter how we define them, have a critical role in enhancing the contribution of NSAs in shaping social policy in Africa. Africa's dependency on foreign aid over the past seven decades has, in part, created a yawning gap which, over the years, has been filled by these NSAs (Moyo 2009; Makuwira, 2013, 2014b). However, these organisations have not had an easy ride. The nature of regimes has contributed to their success and/or failure. While this chapter is not about regime change, I attempt to look at different types of regimes and examine them in light of the potential contribution a type of regime can make in enhancing social policy in Africa. My argument is informed by Hofisi and Hofisi (2013). Their framework sets out four different types of regimes. Although these are oriented in theory, the authors provide insights on which type of regime can offer space for the active contribution of NSAs and, subsequently, map out ways in which they can work collaboratively to achieve Agenda 2063. In Table 9.2, I outline four types of regimes and their perceived characteristics.

Table 9.2: Type of Regimes and their Characteristics

Type of Regime	Characteristics	Examples
Liberal	• Low government expenditure • Well-developed NGO sector • Strong middle class • Social development spearheaded by NGOs	Very hard to identify any regime in Africa that fits this type of regime
Social democratic	• Strong government expenditure • Weak NGO sector • Strong middle class with political power to foster social development	South Africa (although even this is not precise)
Corporatist	• State and NGOs work collaboratively • Elites accommodate NGOs	Rwanda (equally hard to fit into this type)
Statist	• Low government expenditure • Low participation of the NGO sector due to capacity constraints • Authoritarian state	Ethiopia, Kenya, Uganda, Zimbabwe, Malawi, Tanzania (my suggestions only)

Source: Adapted from Hofisi and Hofisi (2013, pp. 293–294)

A closer scrutiny of these types of regimes highlights one fundamental issue, that is, that the nature of the regime is very important to the development of responsive social policy in Africa. While these regimes may be classified in the moment, they are not static and have to be viewed as regimes in transition due to the dynamics in the social, political and economic environment prevailing in the country. A good example is Zimbabwe, which, at the time of writing the chapter, was undergoing a regime change from Robert Mugabe to Emmerson Mnangagwa. This change has obvious implications on how the new regime relates to NSAs as it tries to fix the collapsed economy and, at the same time, respond to the needs of the majority of Zimbabweans. Crucially, the change in regime entails a reconfiguration of social policy in respect to Zimbabwe's affiliation with the African Union.

Another dimension worth noting is that regimes may mimic the characteristics of more than one kind of regime. This is especially the case where most of the NSAs are active in shaping social policy and the nature of politics (Ware 2014). For example, where a government spends more on social development (social democratic regime), it is highly likely that there will be an influx of NSAs. But similarly, where the government is characterised by low expenditure (a liberal regime), the need to fill the gaps left by government is strong, hence a strong presence of NSAs. However, in this case (the liberal regime), both the state and NSAs have to manage the relationship (taking on the features of a corporatist regime) in order to achieve positive results. By inference, it is through the management of these kinds of partnerships that we also see the engagement of the elites whose interests cannot be overlooked. They provide support to NSAs as it is in their interest to maintain the status quo. It is this kind of scenario that invites a critical look on how Africa's Agenda 2063 needs to unfold.

What African Governments Can Do

For Africa to transform its social policy, the participation of NSAs is inevitable. This means creating an enabling environment in which both the emerging and established NSAs can thrive and offer alternative thinking in a non-confrontational manner. More importantly, governments in Africa need to acknowledge that NSAs are here to stay, and both governments and NSAs need to acknowledge the existence of each other through a clear regulatory framework. For African governments to achieve their country-specific sustainable development goals and, indeed, Agenda 2063, they need to tread very carefully around regulating NSAs. The potential that exists in both local and international NSAs needs to be nurtured through mutuality and understanding that there is a common agenda for both entities — to reduce inequality and, ultimately, poverty. There is need to engage even in what Scott (2002) calls 'fierce conversations', as long as these provide a basis for understanding and offer leadership avenues. Not only do African governments need to be transparent and accountable in formulating their social policies, they also need to support NSAs by building their capacity rather than co-opting them into a status quo that does not breed transformation.

What NSAs Need to Do

NSAs need to understand that they will never replace a state but can only make a contribution through a state apparatus. As already argued, both the state and NSAs need each other. While there seems to be a tension between neoliberalism and socialism in the current global political order of development, governments still hold the ultimate prerogative over the 'political space' in which they can command the activities of NSAs. That said, NSAs can only be effective if they respond to national development agendas for which critical social policies are supposedly and aptly articulated. Not only will this command respect on part of the government but also bring respect to governments who try to accommodate differing views on different social policy debates. This requires a better understanding on the part of NSAs with regard to the different types of leadership needed to spur a type of relationship that commands such a respect.

Conclusion

In this chapter, I have tried to argue for a closer scrutiny and understanding of the role of NSAs in contributing to social policy in Africa. These arguments come amid the realisation that governments in Africa are experiencing constant resource constraints. Coupled with dwindling aid provision, the gaps left by governments are being filled by NSAs whose legitimacy differs from that of governments. However, I have argued that both NSAs and governments can work collaboratively if they acknowledge each other's potential and contribution. For this to happen, the NSA approach to activism to support better informed social policies in Africa has to be dictated by a kind of activism that demands a degree of political power but which should not be viewed as threatening by the government.

More critical to the success of NSAs in Africa and of African governments is structural transformation. UNAIDS (2016) documents that while Africa has made significant progress towards social policy outcomes, with poverty levels dropping in the various countries of sub-Saharan Africa, further structural transformation and capacity reinforcement are needed in order to achieve Agenda 2063 and the Sustainable Development Goals. This applies to NSAs. Given that most NSAs are resource-dependent, the need to develop sustainable approaches to engaging government cannot be overemphasised. The process to transformation for both parties has to be evidence-based. The manner in which social policy processes are informed by research and better monitoring and evaluation will dictate the kind of contribution both NSAs and governments can make to each other.

References

Adesina, J. O., 2009, Social Policy in Sub-Saharan Africa: A Glance in the Rear-View Mirror, *International Journal of Social Welfare*, Vol. 18, No. 1, pp. 37–51.

African Union, 2015, Agenda 2063. Available online at http://www.un.org/en/africa/osaa/pdf/au/agenda2063-framework.pdf.

Ainger, K., 2004, The Scramble for Africa, in *New Internationalist Magazine*, 2 May 2004. Available online at https://newint.org/features/2004/05/01/keynote.

Arnfred, S. and Utas, M., eds, Re-thinking Africa: A Contribution to the Swedish Government White Paper on Africa, Uppsala: Nordic Africa Institute. Available online at https://www.diva-portal.org/smash/get/diva2:304784/FULLTEXT01.pdf.

Bebbington, A., 2004, NGOs and Uneven Development: Geographies of Development Intervention, *Progress in Human Geography*, Vol. 28, No. 6, pp. 725–745. DOI: https://doi.org/10.1191/0309132504ph516oa

Carbone, M., 2003, The Role of Non-State Actors in Development Policy: Perceptions and Changing Practices, *The Courier ACP-EU*, No. 199, pp. 14–15. Available online at http://ec.europa.eu/development/body/publications/courier/courier199/en/en_014.pdf.

Dietrich, S., 2012, Bypass or Engage? Explaining Donor Delivery Tactics in Foreign Aid Allocation, *International Studies Quarterly*, Vol. 57, No. 4, pp. 1–15.

Fowler, A., 2011, Development NGOs, in Edwards, M., ed., *The Oxford Handbook of Civil Society*, Oxford, UK: Oxford University Press, pp. 42–54.

Gumede, V., 2017, Social Policy for Inclusive Development in Africa, *Third World Quarterly*, Vol. 39, No. 1, pp. 122–139. DOI: 10.1080/01436597.2017.1374834.

Hall, A. and Midgley, J., 2004, *Social Policy for Development*. London: SAGE Publications.

Kendall, J. and Knapp, M.,1995, *Voluntary Means, Social Ends*, Canterbury: PSSRU, University of Kent.

Kironde, J. M. L., 2007, The Role of Non-State Actors in Enhancing Participatory Governance and Local Development, Paper presented at the African Local Government Action Forum Phase VII: Enhancing Participatory Governance and Local Development, 1 June 2007.

Kpessa, M. W. and Béland, D., 2013, Mapping Social Policy Development in Sub-Saharan Africa, *Policy Studies*, Vol. 34, No. 3, pp. 326–341.

Makuwira, J. J., 2013, Balancing the Act in Foreign Development Assistance: A Radical Approach. Paper presented at the 1st International Conference on Development Finance and Economic Transformation, University of Limpopo, Polokwane, South Africa, 27–29 October 2013.

Makuwira, J. J., 2014a, Zimbabwe: Issues and Perspectives on Fragility and Failure, in: Ware, A., ed., *Development in Difficult Socio-political Contexts*, Basingstoke: Palgrave Macmillan, pp. 224–247.

Makuwira, J. J., 2014b, *Non-Governmental Development Organisations and the Poverty Reduction Agenda: The Moral Crusaders*, London: Routledge.

Matthews, S., 2017, The Role of NGOs in Africa: Are They a Force For Good?, in *The Conversation*, 25 April 2017. Available online at https://theconversation.com/the-role-of-ngos-in-africa-are-they-a-force-for-good-76227.

Mkandawire, T., 2001, Thinking About the Developmental States in Africa, *Cambridge Journal of Economics*, Vol. 25, No. 3, pp. 289–313.

Mkandawire, T., 2004, Social Policy in a Development Context: Introduction, in Mkandawire, T., ed., *Social Policy in a Development Context*, Basingstoke: Palgrave Macmillan, pp. 1–33.

Moyo, D., 2009, *Dead Aid: Why Aid Is Not Working and How There Is a Better Way for Africa*, New York: Farrar, Straus and Giroux.

Nunnenkamp, P., 2008, Aid Effectiveness: The Myth of NGO Superiority, in *Global Policy Forum*, April 2008. Available online at https://www.globalpolicy.org/component/content/article/177-un/31624.html.

Steer, L., Gillard, J., Gustafsson-Wright, E. and Latham, M., 2015, Non-State Actors in Education in Developing Countries: A Framing Paper for Discussion, Center for Universal Education at Brookings. Available online at https://www.brookings.edu/wp-content/uploads/2016/06/102215-Non-State-Actors-in-Education-Framing-paper-Final.pdf. Accessed 10 January 2018

Stokke, O., 1995, Aid and Political Conditionality: Core Issues and the State of the Art, in Stokke, O., ed., *Aid and Political Conditionality*, London: Frank Cass.

Reagan, R., 1981, First Inaugural Address, 20 January, 1981. Available online at http://www.presidency.ucsb.edu/ws/?pid¼43130. Accessed March 23, 2013.

Reimann, K. D., 2005, Up to No Good? Recent Critics and Critiques of NGOs, Political Science Faculty Publications, 5, Georgia State University. Available online at http://scholarworks.gsu.edu/political_science_facpub/5.

Tendler, J., 1982, Turning Private Voluntary Organisations into Development Agencies: Questions for Evaluation, AID Program Evaluation Discussion Paper No. 12, Washington, DC: USAID.

Tvedt, T.,1998, *Angels of Mercy or Development Diplomats? NGOs and Foreign Aid*, Trenton, NJ and Oxford, UK: James Currey and Africa World Press.

UNESCO, 2008, The winners of the UNESCO International Literacy Prize 2008. http://unesdoc.unesco.org/images/0016/001626/162601e.pdf.

Von Bernstorff, J., 2007, Non-State Actors in Law-Making and in the Shaping of Policy: On the Legality and Legitimacy of NGO Participation in International Law, Study for the Konrad Adenauer Foundation's Conference on International Law 2007. Available online at http://www.kas.de/wf/doc/kas_12358-544-2-30.pdf?071119171748.

Ware, A., ed., 2014, *Development in Difficult Socio-political Contexts*. Basingstoke: Palgrave Macmillan.

10

Excavating Communal Mutual Support Praxis in two Townships in South Africa: Preliminary Notes for Social Policy Learning

Kolawole Omomowo and Jimi Adesina

Introduction

Rethinking social policy, especially in the African context, hinges on three broad ideas—social policy is not the exclusive preserve of the state and formal private sector in a political economy (Adesina 2009); mutual aid in co-operation for survival and security, and not survival of the fittest, better defines human societies (Kropotkin 1972, cited in Katz and Bender 1976); and socioeconomic reproduction is fundamental to social policy, rather than the treatment of market failure, which hinges on the embeddedness of the economy within the society (Mkandawire 2004; Polanyi 2001). These ideas revolve around the concept that social wellbeing should be fundamental to socioeconomic policies. Hence, how it is achieved becomes imperative. The structure of the political economy of a society, in a way, could reflect how a society seeks to achieve social wellbeing.

The satisfaction of productive, individual and collective consumptions, in a capitalist society, is fundamental to social reproduction (Dickinson and Russell 1986). This fosters the interaction between the economic, family/household and state institutions for extraction/production, distribution and consumption (Picchio 1992; Dickinson and Russell 1986). Therefore, productive consumption in the economy and collective consumption (formal and non-formal) should centre on individual consumption in the family/household to facilitate social wellbeing. These are expressed in the capital–labour nexus, through wage funds in production (Heinrich 2012) and collective consumption, often co-ordinated or led by the state, but which also happens in daily social (familial and communal) praxis in mutual support mechanisms. This chapter discusses the non-formal social praxis, which focuses on the improvement of social wellbeing.

Social Wellbeing

The improvement of social wellbeing is at the heart of Amartya Sen's 'Idea of Justice' (Sen 2009). This suggests that any institutional structure, agent or praxis that facilitates or undermines social wellbeing is important for social analysis. 'Wellbeing achievement' or functioning is also at the crux of Sen's (2008) capability conception of poverty. The achievement of social wellbeing is the motivation for different economic and social policies, conceptually suggesting different trajectories to the same goal. Beyond the residual idea of social policy, which suggests the mutual exclusiveness of social and economic policies, a comprehensive approach suggests the mutual embeddedness of socioeconomic policies (Adesina 2009; Kangas and Palme 2009; Mkandawire 2004) — a wider view, that social policy encompasses different social practices to foster social wellbeing.

It is this wider approach to social policy, as an undertone to 'wellbeing achievement', that informs our focus on the study of non-formal mutual support and social provisioning in two townships in Pretoria, South Africa. It was important for our purpose to understand the underlying driving values of mutual support, as well as the values these practices promoted. Beyond mutual support and social provisioning within the associational context, this chapter takes into consideration the mutual-support praxis that happens within familial and communal contexts. We posit that these seemingly organic, non-formal, mutual-support practices within and outside of associations could be a rich knowledge bank for the crafting of formal social policy to foster social wellbeing.

Theoretical Framework and Literature — Mutual Aid

The theoretical underpinning of mutual-aid or self-help groups and practices could be broadly viewed through economic and social explanations (Peterlechner 2009). The social explanation draws on Polanyi's ([1944] 2001) argument of the social embeddedness of economic activities. For Polanyi ([1944] 2001) there is no free self-regulating market, because economic relations are embedded within the broader society. The state management of fictitious commodities (land, money and labour) is an indication of market embeddedness. The social concept of a self-help group sees it as founded on the principle of reciprocity, which is an important determinant of economic behaviour in Polanyi's view (Peterlechner 2009).

The other broad theoretical explanation for the persistence of self-help groups is economic rationality, such as low transactional cost compared to formal financial institutions, savings, reduced waiting period to acquire durable indivisible goods, and protection of savings from immediate household consumption, by women (Peterlechner 2009). Drawing on these two theoretical foundations, Peterlechner argues that 'economic rationality and social value' account for the enduring nature of mutual-aid groups. For her, economic and social factors are mutually dependent and reinforcing. The combination of economic rationality and social value facilitates the institutionalisation of mutual-aid groups for social wellbeing. Economic rationality and social values are important for the nature of social policy in any context. While economic rationality is easily perceptible, the impact of social values on policy is not easily discernible.

This broad conceptual position could be immediately connected to the 'transformative social policy' theoretical framework, which was developed as a product of the United Nations Research Institute for Social Development (UNRISD) research project on Social Policy in Development Context (UNRISD 2006). This theme was subsequently elaborated by Mkandawire (2007) and Adesina (2011). 'Transformative social policy' emphasises the wider view of social policy as being capable of serving multiple developmental functions through diverse policy instruments, applicable to the peculiarity of different contexts. The ensuing argument is that social policy could be used to drive development through the multiple functions of production, social reproduction, redistribution, social protection and social cohesion, delivered through multiple instruments as informed by the context (Adesina 2011).

This wider view hinges on the prevailing norms and values of a society, such as solidarity and equality. It gives room for the consideration of social policy beyond the state and private formal sector, to include community-driven social provisioning (Adesina 2009). This thinking informs our focus on mutual-aid organisations and activities beyond the state and formal private sector. A comprehensive conception of social policy includes a range of issues, such as the socioeconomic effects of any policy (Norwegian Agency for Development Cooperation 2008), investment in human capability, protection through diverse instruments (Elqura 2012), basic sevices, social inclusion, inequality and human rights (Hall and Midgley 2004).

Mutual-Aid Associations/Activities

The study of self-help groups (such as *stokvels* in South Africa) and activities could be located within the mutual-aid discourse. The early expression of mutual aid could be found in friendly societies (Katz and Bender 1976; Weinbren and James 2005). The ground-breaking work of Peter Kropotkin on mutual aid contrasts with the idea of Social Darwinism. He contends that co-operation better describes the survival of different animal species, as with humans, and not the survival of the strong at the expense of the weak (Kropotkin 1972, cited in Katz and Bender 1976). Folk societies thrived on social justice and co-operation, informed by social mores, norms and laws. For Kropotkin, civilisation developed out of human co-operation for security and food, a precursor to the village community as a form of social organisation.

Mutual-benefit societies broadly encompass financial and social co-operation to deal with the challenges of unemployment, low wages, old age and death of breadwinners. This co-operation is built on mutualism, thrift, individual responsibility and human care (Glenn 2001). For Kropotkin, mutualism goes beyond insurance against risk, but emphasises moral uplifting and the dignity that comes with helping each other when needed.

> O'Hearn and Grubačić (2016) see mutual aid as imperative for survival at the margins (exilic spaces) of capitalist and state markets and formal structures respectively. 'Exilic spaces' are social relations that are exclusive, but complementary, to capitalist market competition. Mutual aid is directly opposed to the 'possessive individualism' that defines capitalism. Therefore, mutual aid (in a subsistence economy) includes practices that are excess to the market (formal) economy (O'Hearn and Grubačić 2016). O'Hearn and Grubačić appropriate Polanyi's ([1944] 2001) idea of 'double movement' and Kropotkin's (1972, cited in Katz and Bender 1976) mutual aid to facilitate freedom and social wellbeing beyond capitalist and state structures.

The concept of mutual aid broadens the intellectual space of the different types of organisations and activities that might be considered as self-help. It goes beyond the *stokvel* in our consideration of mutual support in the South African context. It enables the treatment of *stokvels* as a sub-set of mutual-aid associations and practices. We contend that mutual-aid praxis should not be limited to informally constituted associations but includes activities and practices that happen outside associations, such as communal support for bereavement and celebration. This includes mutual-support activities that may span familial, community and work contexts. The use of self-help here does not suggest the rolling back of state intervention in the economy, but rather sees it as a reservoir of organic praxis that could inform the broad planning of collective consumption to foster social wellbeing.

Enabling Social Values and Norms of Self-Help Groups

For our purpose, we equate self-help groups with all forms of mutual-aid association. Rotating Savings and Credit Associations (ROSCAs) are prominent in the international literature as a type of self-help group, though there are diverse shapes of self-help association. Why people join self-help groups and functions are informed by contextual needs (Low 1995) and existing social values and norms. They often exist outside the legal structure because they are non-formal, hence, they are regulated by social control to adhere to organisational rules, norms and customary law (Bisrat, Kostas and Feng 2012; Bouman 1995a). Erring members may lose respect and trust within the community.

The enabling values and norms of self-help groups can be viewed as 'antecedent and consequent', non-exclusive categories. Antecedent norms and values inform the practice of self-help groups or activities in a particular context, whereas consequent norms and values result from the practices of self-help groups and activities. According to the literature, prominent norms and values that facilitate the practice of self-help groups and activities include trust, balanced reciprocity, honesty, social solidarity, mutual obligation, self-discipline, hope, social collateral, self-esteem, democracy and social capital (Benda 2012; Bisrat et al. 2012; Etang, Fielding and Knowles 2011; Peterlechner 2009; Anderson and Baland 2002; Verhoef 2001; Aliber 2001; Buijs 1998; Smets 1996; Low 1995; Moodley 1995; Bouman 1977, 1995a, 1995b).

Trust is at the heart of all the values because self-help groups and activities are often not legally binding because of their non-formality. The imperative of trust was emphasised by Etang et al. (2011), who make the distinction between 'trust, trustworthiness and trusting' and the appropriation of trust to sustain social relations among self-help group members. While only trustworthy people are accepted as members, more trusting people are driven to join, and successful participation increases members' trusting and trustworthiness (Etang et al. 2011).

It can be argued that all other values serve to deepen social solidary and social collateral among group members. Social solidarity is important for collective action, such as self-help groups and activities, to foster social wellbeing primarily among members and their family, and by implication the broader society. Therefore, we argue, self-help groups and activities are forms of collective consumption, which may be complementary to, or inform formal social-policy architecture. In order to make sense of this we view social policy as collective investment, production and consumption to promote social wellbeing. It allows the consideration of self-help groups and activities. Mkandawire (2011, cited in Adesina 2011: 455) broadly defines social policy as:

> a 'collective intervention to directly affect social welfare, social institutions and social relations. It is concerned with the redistributive effects of economic policy, the protection of people from the vagaries of the market and the changing circumstances of age, the enhancement of the productive potential of members of society, and the reconciliation of the burden of reproduction with that of other social tasks. Successful societies have given social policies all these tasks, although the weighting of tasks has varied among countries and, within each country, from period to period'.

Methodology

Our project was a small-scale qualitative study of self-help groups and activities in two townships in Pretoria, South Africa. Mamelodi and Atteridgeville townships were selected as the sites to study the social wellbeing impacts of self-help groups and activities in these two communities. Qualitative research reveals the social reality through the experiences and perception of the research subjects. It takes social context and processes seriously and seeks to understand the social world through the lived experiences and interpretations of the people studied (Bryman and Teevan 2005).

Case study research design was used for this study, as informed by the research questions and the objective of the study (Yin 2009). Case study takes the historical and social contexts of the study seriously (Chadderton and Torrance 2011). The selection of study sites (cases) was informed by access and the opportunity they provided to learn about the study phenomenon. The selection of two study sites was not informed by the need to compare, but to excavate the different dynamics that self-help organisations and practices take.

Sampling Methods and Data Collection

The participants were selected using purposive and snowball sampling methods. These are non-probability sampling methods; every member of the study group or population does not have an equal chance of being selected for the study. The criteria for selection were determined by the researcher based on the purpose of the study (Burgess 1984). Snowball sampling was used to get more participants who suited the study criteria, informed by the purpose of the study. This involved drawing on the network of the initial participants to recruit subsequent participants (Kumar 2005).

Data was collected through one-on-one in-depth interviews and focus group discussions (FGDs). These methods are suitable for a study of this nature because they transcend the limitation of the ontological divide between objectivism and constructionism in social research (Miller and Glassner 2011). These methods allow for a deep probing of the interviewees' experience and the contextual prevailing views about the phenomenon of the study. A total of twenty-nine in-depth interviews (including five interviews with *stokvel* organisers) and four FGDs were conducted in Atteridgeville. A total of eighteen in-depth interviews (including two interviews with *stokvel* organisers) and five FGDs (including two FGDs with *stokvel* organisers) were conducted in Mamelodi. The data was transcribed into text and analysed thematically.

Mutual Support in South Africa

This study recognises mutual support in the form of self-help groups, as well as activities that occur in the study communities without groups. Familial and neighbourhood communal activities were taken into consideration. Self-help groups are often referred to as *stokvels* or societies in South Africa, among several other local names given by the predominant contextual cultures (Verhoef 2001; Buijs 1998). *Stokvels* have been extensively researched in South Africa. However, this study contributes to the literature by looking beyond the *stokvel* to include other forms of mutual-support activities that are not defined by *stokvel*-type associations. Particularly, we interrogate the 'antecedent and consequent' values that enable self-help groups and communal practices to see how they can inform the crafting of a formal social-policy framework.

The savings function of *stokvels* is overtly emphasised, though it is organised in diverse ways (Aliber 2001; Verhoef 2001; Moodley 1995). Verhoef identifies four major types of *stokvels* in South Africa: savings clubs, burial societies, investment groups and high-budget *stokvels*. Moodley categorises *stokvels* into rotating savings associations, fixed-fund savings associations and fixed-fund savings and credit associations. Economic and social reasons are adduced for joining *stokvels* in the South African literature. Saving, profit and the bringing of people together in trust, solidary and mutual aid are prominent aims of *stokvels*. Pooled resources are often spent on expensive household indivisible goods, such as shelter, food, bride price and school fees (Bophela and Khumalo 2019; Verhoef 2001; Buijs 1998; Smets 1996; Moodley 1995).

Verhoef (2001: 263) defines *stokvels* as 'a type of credit union in which a group of people, by voluntary and mutual agreement, regularly contribute money to a common pool and circulate the pool among the group'. The diversity of the practices of *stokvels*, with regards to purpose, structure and dynamics, are unambiguous. A close reading of the textual data shows that 'mutual support', rather than 'self-help' better describes the groupings and praxis in the South African context. Also, drawing on the interviewees' voices and the literature, the term 'societies' better captures the diverse dynamics, structure and activities of mutual-support groups and practices in this context. Therefore, 'mutual-support societies' or 'societies' are used interchangeably in the data analysis section.

There are accounts that *stokvels* emerged among the black population during apartheid, as a result of their exclusion from the formal financial system (Aliber 2001; Verhoef, 2001). A further connection, it seems, could be made with indigenous cultural practices of social support, such as cattle-lending among the Xhosa ethnic group of South Africa (Peires 1981). The expanding activities and the recognition of the activities of *stokvels* led to the formation of the National Stokvel Association of South Africa (NASASA) in 1988, which was formalised by Government Notice 404 of 25 May 2012. The national association claims to have more than one million persons distributed over 800,000 groups across the nine provinces, with an estimated value of ZAR 49 billion (www.nasasa.co.za). However, the suspect nature of these statistics (number of groups, membership and economic value) is evident in the contrasting estimates given by African Response surveys (2011, 2014). While the 2011 survey estimates the number of *stokvel* groups at approximately 812,000, with a total membership of 11.4 million persons and a value of ZAR 44 billion, the 2014 survey puts it at 421,000 groups with a total of 8.6 million members and an economic value of ZAR 25 billion respectively. The imprecise nature of this data suggests caution (African Response 2014).

While the available national data regarding mutual-support groups should be treated circumspectly, the proliferation of the practice in the study sites was unambiguous during the fieldwork. The experience of the snowball sampling process supports this view. We can confirm that mutual-support practices within and beyond groups are a significant part of the way of life of the people in the two study townships. The data, as discussed below, shows that mutual-support praxis is fast becoming a significant component of the social reproduction process in these communities. Both employed and unemployed interviewees were of the view that it enables them to achieve things that are vital to their functioning, which they would not have done without mutual support.

Data Analysis

The data analysis converged around six major themes: why people organise and join mutual-support societies; the practice and experiences of mutual-support societies and activities; the enabling norms and values of mutual-support societies and activities; the social reproduction function of mutual-support societies and practices; communal co-operation and mutual support; and mutual-support societies and formal financial institutions. These themes collectively suggest the importance of this form of collective consumption, in our view, for the quality of social reproduction of concerned family/households.

While the interviewees' experiences of their participation in mutual-support societies and activities suggested positive change or improvement in their quality of social reproduction, there were also negative consequences. There are accounts of instances of people who borrowed money from the societies but could not repay their loans, which caused financial loss for all members. The non-formality of these associations means they are not legally registered and have no legally enforceable registered constitution, which, at times, causes difficulty in the enforcement of rules and the resolution of conflict.

The Reasons why People Organise and Join Mutual-Support Societies

It was revealed that people joined self-help groups in order to achieve what they would not have been able to alone. The co-operation or solidarity in the association directly led to the improvement of wellbeing of members because of the improved quality of consumption. Alfred, who is the only income-earner in a family of seven (a wife, four children and two grandchildren), said that joining a society enabled him to acquire expensive indivisible goods, while Alice (a house maid and single mother of one, who lives with her sister) said it allowed her to buy grocery in bulk to support her family. Beauty, who is self-employed (and lives with her husband and four children), recounted that the association gave her the discipline to save and that saving this way was cheaper than doing it through the banks. Peter (who earns income only from piece jobs) joined a self-help group (society) in order to raise money for his junior brother's university registration fee.

> Mmm, you know it is difficult to pop out from the pocket if one wants to buy straight from the shop, but eh, if we collect something each and every month it seems to be very much better. (A1_24062017_Alfred)

> Mmm … the reason is that, eh, society because of grocery, it helps us neh. Because I have children and when I am here I just send money and they put that money in the society and help my children with grocers at the end of the six month, eh. In terms of the reasons that are not met, there is nothing that is not met by members in this society. (A2_03062017_Alice)

> The reasons why I joined this societies is because if I save alone the money will be less than when I do it with other women and I will not be able to cover all my plans. With the money that I save with women I can do bigger things … if I save using bank there are bank charges but in societies I can just communicate with other members if I don't have money for that month and they will not charge me … if I am not a member in this societies I wouldn't have reached my goals, there was no way I could do it alone or it was going to take me a very long time. (A3_04062017_Beauty)

> I joined so that my little brother can register at Unisa … I am fulfilled because the money we split in January can help register for my little brother's university fees and also buy grocery … I am a breadwinner at home, so these societies are really helping me because January I can register for my little brother and buy groceries and everything that is needed. (M10_19082017_Peter)

Some of the self-help groups provide members with access to credit. Beauty said that her grocery self-help group gave her the opportunity to borrow money at every contribution, especially when there was an emergency to attend to. Constance, whose monthly income combined with that of her husband is about ZAR 8,500 for a family of six, also alluded to the opportunity they had to borrow money from the group in order to satisfy important needs.

> We only borrow money from the grocery self-help group, we contribute R300 each member when we meet each month and before we can bank the money we ask if there is any member who needs the money. If you want the money it must come back with 20 per cent interest… when you are in an emergency you can borrow money from grocery society as I said it is the only self-help group that I am involved in that borrows member's money. Some members take money mostly when they want to fulfil other household's conflicts. (A3_04062017_Beauty)

> Yah, we take money, just like me this year my child went for initiation school and I did not have money, the society gave me money to pay for him and now he is back with me. After a particular period I have to bring this money back, however, I agree with them on how I will bring the money back, either per month or at once. (A14_15072017_Constance)

The Practice and Experiences of Mutual-Support Societies and Activities

The experience of the participants in self-help groups and practices highlights the benefit of co-operation as a form of collective consumption and the positive impacts it could have on social wellbeing. Dikeledi, a self-employed mother of two who lives with her boyfriend, was of the view that the collective consumption enabled by the self-help group helped her to achieve what she could not have done alone, and that these societies respond to emergencies, such as death.

> To me I think it has made a significant impact. Because as I see, if you do things alone you won't go far, for you to do things sometimes in a successful way you need to bring yourself close to others and then share advices with others like contributing and taking the money to the bank and other things you gain something and if you do it alone you won't benefit that much. You have to work with other. (A4_04062017_Dikeledi)

> Let's say it's society and we just buried someone not so long and we experience some couple of funerals per month maybe one, two or three funerals per month, and it happens that maybe other month we have funerals fast and when we check and realise that we cannot afford to help them anymore, we then agree as women that we come together and see how best can we help them. And then if money is very low in the bank and we are afraid that we may have funerals that will need to be catered for, we make an agreement to raise the contribution monthly fee for two to three months and if we were paying R100 we can then start paying R150 for the next three months so that we can increase the money in the bank. The emergency that I remember was that there was an instant death and the money that was there was not enough and we had to contribute quickly so that we can help the person. (A4_04062017_Dikeledi)

Ayanda, who gets a monthly old age pension of only ZAR 1,600 and lives with her son and grandson, talked about how fast self-help groups respond to their members' need for money. She mentioned how the community came together at times of burial and marriage ceremonies.

> Banks give you time, you need seven days' notice, but with societies they are always here when you need them, you get tents, chairs, coffin, and community come to assist in times of ceremonies like funerals, weddings and parties … Yes we do benefit, I remember when I was burying my husband and my son, the society helped me very fast, and they provided me with the things that I need in time, they don't waste time. (M1_17122016_Ayanda)

Enabling Norms and Values of Mutual-Support Societies and Activities

The norm of mutual support was evident. The interviewees simply stated that they help each other because they have differing socioeconomic statuses. Social solidarity is reflected in the value of helping each other, especially the less privileged among them. Beyond helping each other, self-help groups also support non-members and their families in times of need and emergency. This kind of activity is informed by the sense of community and the duty of care. Constance recounts how the self-help group she belongs to helps non-members of her community.

> Sometimes there may be a problem at home and you don't have money to buy things, let's say for instance, you have a sudden death and the deceased did not have any society, we are able to take from the grocers and assist the person. We are also able to assist neighbours because in December other children don't have food and we try to get some from our package and share with them so that they can have something too. There are also other parents who are sick and you find out that they are taking care of young kids; we also try to get something's for them to eat. (A14_15072017_Constance)

Tello, an unemployed woman who lives with her husband who sells vegetables, also stressed the norms of mutual support, peace and trust as important for the perpetuation of self-help groups (societies).

> They promote the norm of helping each other, so that one knows where to run to in times of trouble … they help because when you are working, you cannot save money for yourself that when you are in trouble you can just use that money, joining societies is a way of saving money … living in peace makes it possible for us to do things together, and trust and helping one another helps community to do things together, people work together so that they can conquer all. (M8_26052017_Tello)

Alfred stated that they have to help one another because of inequality:

> What are the norms, the values? Mmm … what can I say, you know just to help each other. We help each other because one cannot have anything anytime, we just doing this to help one another. People are not the same, some are rich, some are poor we just help one another … ok this is to help one another in fact, it is to help one another like I said before that we are not the same I have got two teeth and I have twenty teeth it's like I have R20 and you have R5 but when the family came together is a sort of helping one another, helping those who are unable to do something, so we help one another. Yes, we do have some meetings; we have to talk this and this just to help one another there. (A1_24062017_Alfred)

The value of self-discipline is reflected in the savings culture of self-help groups (societies). It is self-deprivation in order to take care of needs or emergency situations that occur at a later stage, such as death. Munyai, who sells chickens informally, tells how saving through self-help groups (societies) enabled her to save up money to start her small-scale trading. This is what Rutherford (2000, cited in Vonderlack and Schreiner 2002; Bisrat et al. 2012) described as 'saving up', as distinct from 'saving down' and 'saving forward'. Saving small amounts for later accumulates a fund outflow, an accumulated cash outflow (credit) that precedes savings of small amounts, and accumulates funds that are accessible at intervals, respectively.

> The reason why I joined this *stokvel* is that I want to save money because when you save money it comes handy at the end of the year and you are able to do many things with it. This is the reason why I am talking about selling chickens, this money is the one that gave me a start in this business … I can see this *stokvel* paying dividends because it is the reason why I am able to work and sell the chickens. (A9_03062017_Munyai)

The Social Reproduction Function of Mutual-Support Societies and Practices

Self-help groups and activities ensure that families/households improve the quality of their social reproduction. Constance was clear about how the association enabled members to take better care of their needs. Dikeledi spoke about women's empowerment and the leverage the self-help group gave her to take care of her children and plan for their future. Mapula and Lucky, a married woman with three children and a pensioner respectively, spoke of the financial stability to raise their children that the societies provided, despite their low income.

> We give the community wisdom and that they must see the light through our work that the social club is here please join so that you can be able to help your families. This mostly assists many families to be able to continue with life without stress and we are able to pay school fees in January because we don't buy food. Also that we are able to buy fridge because in January we don't buy food, we already have enough to sustain us for the next six to seven months. Because food is expensive and you wouldn't want to starve, like in January your life becomes easier. (A14_15072017_Constance)

> … first, I am a parent of two children and now there are no employment opportunities. Even though I can look at my partner, you will never trust someone because everyone is looking up for his or her things. This makes me as a woman to stand up on my feet and work as a woman you see, so that I can then be able to raise my children so that one day they can be something in life. Eh, at this one of social I am looking sideways because my firstborn child is fifteen years and some years to come he will be looking to go to universities and I can then be able to budget money for him so that he can go to school. (A4_04062017_Dikeledi)

> For burial is to get financial support when it happens I lose one of my family members because death is unpredictable, for grocery one its purpose of joining was me not spending lot of money in December. I can say my most important reason was to get financial stability as we don't have enough income in the household … so far I don't have financial depression anymore, in that way I can say my purposes and expectations are fulfilled. (A7_04062017_Mapula)

> This was because I was already married by then and I have children and I then realise that the money was going to help me if something happen you see. Because you know that old generation like us, white people played games with us because they were not giving us money that much; we were working because we had to raise our kids you see. There is no one person in my age who will tell you lie about what I am saying, it is not a secret because we were just working from hand to mouth. (A10_17062017_Lucky)

Communal Co-operation and Mutual Support

Beyond the mutual support that happens within the self-help context, the communal praxis is evident. Ayanda said that the community met when there was a need, such as when there was a robbery in the community. She alluded to the role of love, respect and getting along in informing co-operation and fostering understanding among people in the community at large. Ntombi and Melissa, who were both unemployed, were of the same view about the imperative of co-operation within the community. Similarly, Katy, who was also unemployed, and Munyai, emphasised the coming together of the community for service delivery and in response to a stand against crime:

> Every month end, family meet, it's a family gathering and we change households monthly. In the community people meet when there is something wrong like during robberies ... family gathering, funerals, parties, weddings and tombstone ceremony ... Love, respect and getting along... We learn to understand of each other and things around the community. (M1_17122016_Ayanda)

> Community comes together in times of robberies, we use a whistle to let people know what happened and in the family, we meet in parties, weddings and family reunions ... We meet in times of funerals in our street and the next street only, some do contribute money but I don't, I just attend to show support only ... we learn to get to know other people, we learn to get along with people and love each other. (M2_17122016_Ntombi)

> In my family mostly we meet in family gatherings, parties, wedding and funerals, and in the community mostly we meet when there are things to discuss like talking about robbers and we also meet talking about political things. We also meet when one of our society members has passed on, as a society we meet. (M4_19052017_Melissa)

> In my family we meet during funerals and during family society, parties and weddings. In the community we meet during strikes maybe complaining for service delivery. We also blow a whistle in times like during robberies, when one is raped or when someone is missing. (M5_20052017_Katy)

> Ooh, community do call us sometimes as a block and they have meetings with us, they share much about roads, houses, criminality and garbage collections and also

when a person is being attacked on the street and cry out for help they do the same and come help. Sometimes they buy the whistles to alert others on the problem and they come running to help. (A9_03062017_Munyai)

Mutual-Support Societies and Formal Financial Institutions

In their comparison of self-help groups (societies) with formal banking institutions, the interviewees were of the view that societies responded to needs and emergencies any time their support was required (there was no official time, no waiting period) and people did not have to be formally employed to be involved. Ntombi, Kofo and Melissa, who were all unemployed, stated that a person needs to be employed in order to access formal banking services. Constance, to a large extent, emphasised the cost savings that societies afford:

> Banks give you notice if you have saved money with them and you need to be working if you want to borrow money there … in terms of loans, banks give you money only when you are working, because they need pay slips, but with societies you can ask for money any time, they don't need to check if you are working like banks do. (M12_17122016_Ntombi)

> The bank can give me loan, and societies gives me a coffin, a bus for people to travel, and banks need a pay slip, with societies you can join even if you are not working … societies help very fast unlike banks that still need to investigate if the person is really dead. And I remember when I was getting married, these society of buying drinks really helped me because I did not have to buy alcohol from my own pocket. (M3_19052017_Kofo)

> They differ because these formal institutions need a death certificate, and with societies they help very fast and formal institutions have a long process before they can offer you their services. (M4_19052017_Melissa)

> Mmm… eish, I have never put money in the bank because banks want interest and when we take our money we get half of it. The money that we contribute in a year it's equivalent to what we want to buy but if we take it to the bank, they are going to deduct some money and you will find that we can no longer afford to buy what we wanted to buy. You may find that if we want to buy for instance three bags of sugar, in the bank you will only be able to buy two, this means that they have taken out their interest. (A14_15072017_Constance)

Making Sense of the Themes

The themes discussed above hinge on the following phrases that are taken from the textual data, which, we contend, could inform the crafting of formal social policy: 'working together'; 'caring for each other'; 'we need to help each other', 'comforting each other'; 'uplifting each other in the family and community', 'working together in peace'; and 'love and support'. These phrases, in turn, point to values of social solidarity (emphasised in the transformative social-policy framework), mutual support, collective action, uplifting of human dignity and improving social wellbeing, which is at the centre of social policy. The mixture of 'economic rationality and social value' (Peterlechner 2009) speaks to the social practice of mutual-support societies and praxis in this context. This is an indication that economic choices cannot be divorced from the social context in which they occur, and that economic and social policies are mutually embedded and reinforcing (Mkandawire 2004).

It was demonstrated that non-formal collective consumption (even for remote things, such as dealing with security challenges in the community) is important for the improvement of social wellbeing, even when it is marginal to the formal market economy. The values and norms that enable these praxes and the values and norms they promote could be important for the development of organic formal social policy. It is our view here that a social policy that is structured around the inherent values and norms of a society is likely to get the most buy-in and least resistance from the broad spectrum of a society. Therefore, paying due attention to non-formal mutual support and social provisioning could be viewed as developing social policy bottom-up, as against top-down.

Concluding Thoughts

The self-help groups and practices within these communities are clear demonstrations of collective consumption and how it has a direct impact on social wellbeing and improves the quality of social reproduction of the community at large. It was revealed that mutual support transcends associational relationships to include an organic, non-formal social praxis through which the community takes care of each other. This could inform the crafting of a broadly inclusive social policy architecture

The organic development of social institutions and communal praxis shows how formal policy could benefit from non-formal mutual-support practices as a form of collective consumption to foster social wellbeing. The rethinking of social policy in the African context, it is argued, requires drawing on existing embedded social praxis in African societies or communities. This will provide a solid value and normative foundation for formal social policy.

References

Adesina, J., 2009, Social Policy in Sub-Saharan Africa: A Glance in the Rear-View Mirror, *International Journal of Social Welfare*, Vol 18, No. 1: pp. 37–51.

Adesina, J., 2011, Beyond the Social Protection Paradigm: Social Policy in Africa's Development, *Canadian Journal of Development Studies / Revue Canadienne d'Études du Developpement*, Vol. 32, No. 4, pp. 454–470.

African Response, 2014, Latest Stats on Stokvel Released, in *African Response*, www.africanresponse.co.za. Accessed on August 29, 2015.

Aliber, M., 2001, Rotating Savings and Credit Associations and the Pursuit of Self-Discipline: A Case Study in South Africa, *African Review of Money Finance and Banking*, pp. 51–73.

Anderson, S. and Baland, J-M., 2002, The Economics of RoSCAS and Intrahousehold Resource Allocation, *The Quarterly Journal of Economics*, Vol. 7, Issue 3, pp. 963–995.

Benda, C., 2012, Community Rotating Savings and Credit Associations as an Agent of Wellbeing: A Case Study from Northern Rwanda, *Community Development Journal*, Vol. 48, No. 2, pp. 232–247.

Bisrat, A., Kostas, K. and Feng, L., 2012, Are There Financial Benefits to Join RoSCAs? Empirical Evidence from Equb in Ethiopia, *Procedia Economics and Finance*, Vol. 1, pp. 229–238.

Bophela, M. J. K. and Khumalo, N., 2019, The roles of stokvels in South Africa: A Case of Economic Transformation of a Municipality, *Problems and Perspectives in Management*, Vol. 17, No. 4, pp. 26–37.

Bouman, F. J. A., 1977, Indigenous Savings and Credit Societies in the Third World. A Message, *Savings and Development*, Vol. 1, No. 4, pp. 181–219.

Bouman, F. J. A., 1995a, ROSCA: On the ORigin of the Species, *Savings and Development*, Vol. 19, No. 2, pp. 117–149.

Bouman, F. J. A., 1995b, Rotating and Accumulating Savings and Credit Associations: A Development Perspective, *World Development*, Vol. 23, No. 3, pp. 371–384.

Bryman, A. and Teevan, J. J., 2005, *Social Research Methods*, Toronto: Oxford University Press.

Buijs, G., 1998. Savings and Loan Clubs: Risky Venture or Good Business Practice? A Study of the Importance of Rotating Savings and Credit Associations for Poor Women, *Development Southern Africa*, Vol. 15, No. 1, pp. 55–65.

Burgess, R., 1984, *In the Field: An Introduction to Field Research*, London: Routledge.

Chadderton, C. and Torrance, H., 2011. Case Study, in Somekh, B. and Lewin, K., eds, 2011, *Theory and Methods in Social Research* (2nd ed), Los Angeles: SAGE, pp. 53–60.

Dickinson, J. and Russell, B., 1986, Introduction: The Structure of Reproduction in Capitalist Society, in Dickinson, J. and Russell, B., eds., 1986, *Family, Economy and State: The Social Reproduction Process Under Capitalism*, London: Croom Helm Ltd.

Elqura, L., 2012, Towards Comprehensive Social Policy for Equality and Millennium Development Goals, Working Paper No. 5, Social Development Division, United Nation Economic and Social Commission for Western Asia (ESCWA).

Etang, A., Fielding, D. and Knowles, S., 2011, Trust and ROSCA Membership in Rural Cameroon, *Journal of International Development*, Vol. 23, Issue 4, pp. 461–475.

Glenn, B. J., 2001, Understanding Mutual Benefit Societies at the Turn of the Twentieth Century, Division II Faculty Publications, Paper 77. Available online at http://wesscholar.wesleyan.edu/div2facpubs/77.

Hall, A. and Midgley, J., 2004, *Social Policy for Development*, London: SAGE.

Heinrich, M., 2012, *An Introduction to the Three Volumes of Karl Marx's Capital*, New York: Monthly Review Press.

Kangas, O. and Palme, J., 2009. Making Social Policy Work for Economic Development: The Nordic Experience, *International Journal of Social Welfare*, Vol. 18, Issue S1, S62–S72.

Katz, A. H. and Bender, E. I., 1976, Self-Help Groups in Western Society: History and Prospects, *The Journal of Applied Behavioral Science*, Vol. 12, No. 3, pp. 265–282.

Kumar, R., 2005, *Research Methodology: A Step-by-step Guide for Beginners*, London: SAGE.

Low, A., 1995, *A Bibliographical Survey of Rotating Savings and Credit Associations*. Oxford: Oxfam.

Miller, J. and Glassner, B., 2011, The 'Inside and the 'Outside': Finding Realities in Interviews, in Silverman, D. ed., 2011. *Qualitative Research: Issues of Theory, Method and Practice* (3rd ed.), London: SAGE, pp. 131–148.

Mkandawire, T., 2004, Social Policy in a Development Context: Introduction, in Mkandawire, T., ed., *Social Policy in a Development Context*, Basingstoke: UNRISD/Palgrave Macmillan, pp. 1–33.

Mkandawire, T., 2007, Transformative Social Policy and Innovation in Developing Countries, *The European Journal of Development Research,* Vol. 19, No. 1, pp. 13–29.

Moodley, L., 1995, Three Stokvel Clubs in the Urban Black Township of KwaNdangezi, Natal, *Development Southern Africa*, Vol. 12, No. 3, pp. 361–366.

Norwegian Agency for Development Cooperation (Norad), 2008, Comprehensive Social Policy: Fighting Poverty Through Investing in Social Protection, *Norad Report 9/2008* discussion.

O'Hearn, D. and Grubačić, A., 2016, Capitalism, Mutual Aid, and Material Life: Understanding Exilic Spaces, *Capital and Class,* Vol. 40, No. 1, pp. 147–165.

Peires, J. B., 1981, *The House of Phalo: A History of the Xhosa People in the Days of their Independence*, Johannesburg: Ravan Press.

Peterlechner, L., 2009, ROSCAS in Uganda—Beyond Economic Rationality?, *African Review of Money Finance and Banking,* pp. 109–140.

Picchio, A., 1992, *Social Reproduction: The Political Economy of the Labour Market*, Cambridge, UK: Cambridge University Press.

Polanyi, K., [1944] 2001, *The Great Transformation: The Political and Economic Origin of Our Time* (2nd paperback ed.), Boston, MA: Beacon Press.

Sen, A., 2008, Capability and Wellbeing, in Hausman, D. M., ed., 2008, *The Philosophy of Economics: An Anthology* (3rd ed.), Cambridge, UK: Cambridge University Press.

Sen, A., 2009, *The Idea of Justice*, Cambridge, MA: The Belknap Press of Harvard University Press.

Smets, P., 1996, Community-Based Finance Systems and their Potential for Urban Self-Help in a New South Africa, *Development Southern Africa,* Vol. 13, No. 2, pp. 173–187.

United Nations Research Institute for Social Development (UNRISD), 2006, Tranformative Social Policy: Lesson from UNRISD Research, UNRISD Research and Policy Brief 5, Geneva: UNRISD.

Verhoef, G., 2001, Informal Financial Institutions for Survival: African Women and Stokvels in Urban South Africa, *Enterprise and Society,* Vol. 2, No. 2, pp. 259–296.

Vonderlack, R. M. and Schreiner, M., 2002, Women, Microfinance, and Savings: Lessons and Proposals, *Development in Practice*, Vol. 12, No. 5, pp. 602–612.

Weinbren, D. and James, B., 2005, Getting a Grip: The Role of Friendly Societies in Australia and Britain Reappraised, *Labour History*, No. 88, pp. 87–103.

Yin, R. K., 2009, *Case Study Research: Design and Methods* (4th ed.), Los Angeles: SAGE.

11

The Nigerian Social Health Insurance System: Reconceptualising the Approach to Meeting Universal Coverage

Augustine I. Omoruan

Introduction

A great deal of attention in social policy research and health financing circle in recent decades has focused on Social Health Insurance (SHI), not only as a substitute to out-of-pocket (OOP) payments for healthcare, but also to protect households from catastrophic health expenditure and improve their access to healthcare (Okpani and Abimbola 2015; Hsiao and Shaw 2007; Carrin and James 2004). SHI became an alternative option for most low- and middle-income countries (LMICs) due to continued rise in healthcare expenditure and difficulty in funding healthcare (WHO 2010). As a result, SHI has been explored as a strategy that could provide more revenue and ensure a flow of funds into the health sector by a combination of risk-pooling and mutual support (Talampas 2014; Bärnighausen and Sauerborn 2002).

The Nigerian model of SHI, the National Health Insurance Scheme (NHIS), is lagging in its mandate to ensure access, protect Nigerians from financial hardship and establish successful universal coverage. Why is the NHIS failing in its mandate? This question is increasingly crucial not only because the NHIS is waning, but also because many LMICs are facing similar challenges (Talampas 2014; Ayepong and Adjei 2008; Bärnighausen and Sauerborn 2002). This paper therefore attempts to fill this gap by exploring the design and performance of the NHIS vis-à-vis three selected countries, namely Germany, Thailand and Rwanda, based on their different institutional arrangements for funding, delivering and meeting universal healthcare coverage. The chapter is organised as follows: a brief overview of the historical development of the NHIS, strategies adopted to achieve universal coverage, the challenges that stem from the strategies, and lessons learned from the studied countries.

The Historical Development of Nigeria's National Health Insurance Scheme

Healthcare in Nigeria in the pre-1980s was financed by general taxation, which guaranteed universal access to healthcare at no direct cost to the citizenry. Thus, healthcare was readily available at public hospitals and clinics at no charge. In this regard, financial barriers to healthcare access were avoided, as social spending on health was seen as social investment to enhance economic growth and development (Adesina 2007, 2008). Adesina further argues that similar to education, 'social spending on health was part of the wider objectives of defeating the triad of ignorance, poverty and disease' in the immediate post-independence era of most African states (Adesina 2008: 6).

In addition, the nationalist ideology was driven by a socialist approach to development, in which all aspects of development were primarily government-driven without external interference. The result of this was a positive correlation between health-related indicators and economic growth in the first decade of post-independence Nigeria (Adesina 2009). For instance, Nigeria witnessed tremendous growth in Gross Domestic Product (GDP), from 3.1 per cent in 1960 to 7.5 per cent in 1970, with agriculture and manufacturing largely responsible for the astronomical growth of the economy. In addition, the total population per medical doctor declined drastically, from 73,710 to 15,740 between 1960 and 1975. Infant and under-five mortality per 1,000 live births declined from fifty in 1970 to twenty-two in 1979 (World Bank 1980).

The post-1980 period, however, was characterised by slow economic growth as a result of poor agricultural output, the decline in international petroleum prices, a balance-of-payment deficit and fiscal crisis, and an increase in government budgetary obligations (World Bank 1987; Helleiner 1983), which in turn resulted in social spending cuts (Adesina 2009). The health sector and other basic social services then began to receive less allocation from the Federation account, starting from the early 1980s. For instance, public health expenditure as a percentage of GDP between 1981 and 1989 was as follows: 2.0 per cent in 1981; 1.6 per cent in 1982; 2.0 per cent in 1983; 1.1 per cent in 1984; 1.99 per cent in 1985; 1.82 per cent in 1988 and 1.50 per cent in 1989 (CBN 1983, 1990). In addition, health spending as a proportion of government expenditures dwindled from an average of 3.5 per cent in the 1970s (World Bank 1980), to less than 2 per cent in the 1980s and 1990s (Obono 2007; Ogunbekun, Ogunbekun and Orobaton 1999).

Given the low economic growth rate and limited fiscal space of the 1980s, the international financial institutions, led by the World Bank and International Monetary Fund (IMF), introduced Structural Adjustment Programmes (SAPs) as the prerequisite for structural adjustment loans for sub-Saharan countries (Obasan 2013; Adesina 2007; Obono 2007). The conditions of the loans included minimal government intervention in the economy, private participation and the introduction of user fees for government facilities, with the proposition that there would be more funds in the system through private participation which would subsequently be used to improve the quality of and increase access to healthcare (World Bank 1987, 1993).

On the contrary, these neoliberal policies reversed healthcare financing from the government to individuals and households. For instance, private health expenditure in Nigeria between the years 2000 and 2006 accounted for 66.5 per cent and 70.3 per cent, while government expenditure accounted for 33.5 per cent and 29.7 per cent respectively. In the same period, further analysis of private health expenditure shows that OOP payments accounted for 92.7 per cent and 90.4 per cent respectively (WHO 2009). The abrupt changes in Nigerian healthcare financing from the government to the individual denied the vast majority of the population access to basic healthcare services. For example, evidence reveals that in 1999 the Maternal Mortality Ratio (MMR) and Infant Mortality Ratio (IMR) were 1,200 deaths per 100,000 live births and 114.70 deaths per 1,000 live births respectively. Based on the devastating effect of user fees and minimal government intervention in healthcare, SHI was then considered as an alternative model for healthcare financing, having more flexibility and government intervention (WHO 2000).

Due to the generally poor state of healthcare services in the country, dwindling funding of healthcare in the face of rising costs coupled with the devastating effect of user fees, among other reasons, the NHIS was instituted in 1999 (NHIS Act 2004). However, the scheme became operational only in 2005, with the Formal Sector Programme. By 2008, the Community Based Insurance Programme was introduced to expand cover to informal sector workers and the rural population, in order to increase population coverage and ensure universal access. The NHIS Act states:

> There is hereby established a scheme to be known as the National Health Insurance Scheme (in this Act referred to as 'the Scheme') for the purpose of providing health insurance which shall entitle insured persons and their dependants the benefit of prescribed good quality and cost effective health services as set out in this Act. (NHIS Act, 2004)

With the aim to:
> facilitate fair-financing of healthcare costs through pooling and judicious utilisation of financial resources to provide financial risk protections and cost-burden sharing for people against high cost of healthcare through various prepayment programmes prior to their failing ill. (NHIS, 2012)

As mentioned earlier, in order to achieve financial risk protection and cost-burden sharing among the Nigerian people, different programmes/plans were developed for different segments of the population. The following section presents the NHIS programmes.

Nigeria's National Health Insurance Scheme Programmes/Plans

The NHIS has a wide range of programmes/plans. These include:

1. The Formal Sector Social Health Insurance Programme (FSSHIP), which covers people employed in the public sector, organised private sector, armed forces and allied services. The FSSHIP provides healthcare benefits for an insured member, a spouse and four children under eighteen years.
2. The Voluntary Individual Social Health Insurance programme (VISSP), which covers organisations with less than ten employees, interested individuals, families, political office-holders, retirees, foreigners and every other person not covered in any other programmes.
3. The Informal Sector Social Health Insurance Programme (ISSHIP), which covers low-income earners and rural community dwellers. The programme under this sector includes the Community Based Health Insurance Programme (CBHIP).
4. The Tertiary Social Health Insurance Programme (TSHIP), for students at higher institutions.
5. The Vulnerable Group Social Insurance Programme (VGSIP), which provides healthcare services to people who, because of a disability, cannot engage in any productive activity. These include physically challenged persons, prison inmates, pregnant women, children under five, refugees, victims of human trafficking, internally displaced persons, etc. (NHIS 2012).

Approaches to Achieving Universal Health Coverage

Achieving universal health coverage is currently in the spotlight and is an aim widely promoted by the international agencies, notably the World Health Organisation (WHO 2005) and the United Nations (UN 2012). The General Assembly of the UN in 1948 adopted and proclaimed the Universal Declaration of Human Rights. Article 25 of the declaration states, inter alia, that 'everyone has the right to a standard of living adequate for the health and wellbeing of himself and his family including medical care' (UN 1948). Besides this, the

Alma-Ata Declaration of 1978, among others, states that governments have a responsibility for the health of their people, which could be fulfilled basically by the provision of primary healthcare services to achieve the set goal of universal healthcare (Alma-Ata Declaration 1978).

In 2012, the United Nation General Assembly reiterated that all its member states should pursue the transition of their health systems towards universal coverage (UN 2012). Universal coverage was also debated as a possible goal for the United Nation's post-2015 global development agenda, so that all people would have access to services and would not suffer financial hardship in paying for them (Global Health Strategies 2015). In the light of the several international calls and declarations, several countries committed to achieving the goal of universal coverage (Gustafsson-Wright and Schellekens 2013; Hsiao and Shaw 2007).

There are two main options for universal coverage via SHI: full population coverage at the onset, and targeting a limited group(s) at the beginning, with the aim of expanding coverage gradually to the rest of the population. The latter is sub-divided into two methods: first, starting with the coverage of formal-sector workers, such as public and organised private employees, and expanding inclusion gradually to informal-sector workers; second, initial coverage of small- and informal-sector workers, then gradually including employees in the formal sector. Literature has shown that countries such as Germany, Japan and Austria, which adopted the second option, that is, the 'bottom-up' approach, moved faster in achieving universal coverage than countries such as Nigeria, Ghana and Vietnam, which started with the first option, that is, the 'top-down' approach (Nicholas et al. 2015; Hsiao and Shaw 2004; Bärnighausen and Sauerborn 2002).

In Nigeria, the formal sector programme was launched in 2005 to cover government and organised private-sector employees. However, because the population covered by the formal-sector programme was insignificant, the informal-sector programme for informal workers and rural populations was instituted in 2008 to fast-track population coverage. Despite this, the informal-sector programme has made no meaningful contribution to the expansion of health coverage, and the population coverage is stuck at about 3 per cent of the Nigerian population (Uzochukwu et al. 2016; Okpani and Abimbola 2015; Odeyemi and Nixon 2013; Odeyemi, 2014).

Challenges to Achieving Universal Coverage in Nigeria

A number of challenges that hinder the achievement of universal coverage in Nigeria have been identified. First, there is the difficulty in expanding coverage to informal-sector workers and the rural populations that make up 70 per cent of the Nigerian population (Obasan 2013). Obasan further opines that because of the large number of Nigerians in the rural areas, who are engaged in the rural economy, the implementation of the NHIS has continued to be a challenge.

Second, a lack of mutual and social solidarity among the beneficiaries of health insurance programmes has been identified as undermining the principles of social insurance (Bärnighausen and Sauerborn 2002). The German social health insurance system, for example, started with small, informal and voluntary insurance schemes with attributes of self-help, social justice and solidarity, and then evolved into more formal or statutory social health insurance. In Nigeria, however, the beneficiaries of NHIS programmes lacked these attributes because they were of differing occupations, social economic status and ideological understanding. Thus, the attributes of social justice and self-help might not be taken seriously in the NHIS programmes.

Third, there is inadequate resource mobilisation. (Odeyemi 2014; Odeyemi and Nixon 2013; Hsiao and Shaw 2004). Starting coverage with formal-sector employees was premised on the fact that they were economically viable and collection of their contributions would be easily accessible, which in turn would enhance their access to healthcare services (Odeyemi and Nixon 2013). This proposition has not yielded the desired result, however, not only because many employees in this group have yet to register but also because revenue generated from the group remains abysmally low.

Fourth, the proliferation of fund pools (Dutta and Hongoro 2013), and especially small ones, suggests that the 'top-down' approach has resulted in a fragmentation of the scheme, with inequitable benefit packages for different segments of the population. This has negatively affected the scheme's capacity to ensure efficient and equitable distribution of financial protection and benefits among its beneficiaries.

A number of benefit packages within the scheme provide access to preventive and curative care. However, while some packages cover three levels of care (primary, secondary and tertiary care), others are limited to primary and secondary care only (Omoruan 2019). Besides, access to benefit packages depends on the robustness of individual programmes. In addition to the limited-benefit package, there is no transfer or cross-subsidisation among the existing programmes. In other words, every programme takes care of its members only. As a result, the well-resourced programmes have access to more benefits and financial protection than the less-resourced programmes do. The existence of multiple programmes/plans has led to a tiered health insurance system with inequitable benefit packages for different segments of the population and thus has further fragmented the scheme (Omoruan 2019).

Lessons from Selected Countries

Germany, Thailand and Rwanda are among many countries with a high level of universal coverage. These countries were chosen as case studies because they are categorised as high-, middle- and low-income countries respectively. Besides, the three countries have made substantial progress in achieving universal coverage, based on different institutional arrangements for funding, delivering and meeting healthcare needs. This section briefly discusses the processes employed by these countries to attain their high level of universal coverage.

Germany

Germany is globally considered to be the source of the SHI model of health insurance. Since the end of the seventeenth century, a number of relief funds were developed in different regions of Germany, including relief funds for journeymen, artisans, factory workers, traders/workers and other people who could not fit into the other existing funds. Statutory sickness funds evolved out of the relief funds, animated by the principles of solidarity, community self-help and social justice (Carrin and James 2004; Bärnighausen and Sauerborn 2002).

The German healthcare system developed incrementally. For instance, in the pre-Bismarckian statutory health insurance system, laws were made based on the tenets of community-based funds, from general principles to more concrete rules. First, rules and regulations detailed how sickness funds could be organised, including provisions for contributions, benefit packages, entry conditions and the management of the funds. Second, the character of the laws gradually changed from liberal to obligatory. In 1843, the Common Law of Trade allowed municipal authorities to recognise existing voluntary funds and make contributions to these funds compulsory. By 1849, local governments were permitted to make insurance compulsory for certain groups of employees, and in 1854 all uninsured people were compelled to create insurance funds for mutual support. Third, compulsory insurance moved from regional to supraregional in 1854, and for the first time one professional group in the entire region of Germany—the miners—was required to join one of the numerous miners' regional funds (Bärnighausen and Sauerborn 2002; Sigerist 1999).

The three incremental phases in the development of Germany's health insurance system paved the way for the introduction in 1883 of social health insurance for a larger number of professional groups. Thus the approach adopted in Germany led to the achievement of universal coverage.

By some estimates, sickness insurance coverage among workers doubled from 5 per cent to 10 per cent of the population. Subsequently, the coverage of statutory health insurance grew steadily from 11 per cent in 1885 to 37 per cent in 1910. By 1930 and 1950, population coverage reached 50 per cent and 70 per cent respectively. In 1981, other professional groups, such as artists and publicists, were covered and by 2000, 88 per cent of the German population had enrolled in the SHI. Although universal coverage via SHI in Germany was not 100 per cent, the remaining 12 per cent are largely covered under private health insurance; above a certain income level one can opt out of the SHI for other health insurance schemes (Busse et al. 2005; Busse and Riesberg 2004; Bärnighausen and Sauerborn 2002; European Observatory of Health Systems 2000).

Thailand

Before universal coverage was rolled out in Thailand, in 2001, a wide range of schemes existed, including universal coverage for the poor, workmen's compensation funds, and low-income schemes, among others (Talampas 2014). However, by 2001, the existing funds were merged into four schemes for the entire Thai population. These included:

1. The Medical Welfare Scheme (MWS), which provided coverage for the poor and vulnerable, including the elderly, children, secondary school students, the disabled and war veterans, among others;
2. The Health Card Scheme (HCS), for non-poor households who were not eligible for the MWS;
3. The Civil Servants Medical Benefits Scheme (CSMBS) for retired civil servants and their dependants; and
4. The Social Security Scheme (SSS) for employees of organisations with more than ten workers but not for their dependants.

Later, the MWS and HCS were further merged to form the Universal Coverage Scheme (UCS) (Talampas 2014; Dutta and Hongoro 2013).

The consolidation of the existing funds into three major funds was a major reform in Thailand; it has been estimated that 85 per cent of Thai population was covered by 2002 as a result (Dutta and Hongoro, 2013). Table 11.1 presents the three health insurance funds in Thailand with reference to population coverage, funding, legal framework, benefit packages, etc.

Table 11.1: Health Insurance Plans in Thailand

Description	Civil Service Medical Benefit Scheme (CSMBS)	Social Security Scheme (SSS)	Universal Coverage Scheme (UCS)
Beneficiary population	Government employees as well as pensioners and their dependents (parents, spouses and up to three children under 20 years old)	Private-sector employees, excluding dependents	The portion of the population not covered by SSS or CSMBS

Legal framework and governance	1982: Decree of Civil Service Medical Benefit Scheme	1990: Social Security Act; managed by the Social Security Organisation under the supervision of the Ministry of Labour	2002: National Health Security Act; the National Health Security Office designs benefit packages and payment arrangements
Sources of funding	General tax; non-contributory	Payroll tax; tripartite contribution of 1.5% of salary from employee, employer and government	General tax; non-contributory
Approximate number of beneficiaries (2012)	6 million people or 9% of the population; beneficiaries live mainly in urban areas	10.7 million people or 16% of the population; beneficiaries live mainly in urban areas	50.3 million people or 75% of the population; beneficiaries primarily live in rural areas and rely on district health services
Benefit packages	Comprehensive package, considered slightly better than SSS or UCS; excludes special nurses	Comprehensive package; covers inpatient / outpatient care for non-work-related illnesses, injuries, maternity, disability and old age; excludes special nurses and private beds	Comprehensive package similar to SSS; covers inpatient / outpatient care at registered primary care and referral to secondary facilities; excludes special nurses, private beds and certain services
Accessibility	Free choice of public providers without registration	Contracted public or private hospitals and the network of referral facilities; requires registration of member in advance	Access to contracted CUP hospital and its referral network (mainly public); requires registration of member in advance
Income group	Middle or high income	Middle or high income	Low income
Purchasing mechanism	Reimbursement model: fee for service with direct disbursement to providers for outpatient care; use of DRGs for inpatients	Contract model: capitation payment for outpatient and inpatient services, with additional payment schedules for accident, emergency, and high-cost care	Contract model: capitation payments cover outpatient care; a global budget with case-based payments using DRGs covers inpatient care
Expenditure per capita (2010)	US$367	US$71 (government: US$24)	US$79

Source: Adapted from Dutta and Hongoro, 2013

Rwanda

Rwanda was recognised as one of the nine countries in Africa and Asia that made significant progress in achieving universal healthcare system after 2012. According to Nyandekwe et al. (2013), five basic factors underscored Rwanda's commitment to the attainment of universal healthcare. These included:

1. A long-term strategy, Vision 2020, with strategic social protection through universal access to healthcare promulgated in the year 2000;
2. Rwanda's *Politique Nationale de Développement des Mutuelles*, promulgated in 2004;
3. Law No: 62/2007 of 30 December 2007 declared in March 2008, which states categorically that all Rwandan residents must be affiliated to a health insurance scheme that provides quality healthcare;
4. The Rwanda Community Based Health Insurance Policy declared in 2010; and
5. The Rwanda National Health Insurance Policy promulgated in 2010 (Rwanda Ministry of Health 2010).

The country began a dramatic reform of its healthcare system in 1999, and by 2000 the country was committed to universal coverage. *Mutuelles de Santé (Mutuelles)* is a community-based health insurance programme established by the Government of Rwanda (GoR) as the main component of the national strategic plan to providing universal health coverage (Rwanda Ministry of Health 2010). Although other social health insurance programmes, such as the Military Medical Scheme and the *Rwandaise d'Assurance Maladie* were available, they cover an insignificant proportion of Rwanda's population. The Community Based Health Insurance scheme (CBHIS) took the central stage of Rwanda's strategic health plan in achieving universal coverage, with the majority of the population (90 per cent) enrolling in it (Nyandekwe et al. 2014). Figure 11.1 shows Rwanda's population distribution by health insurance coverage.

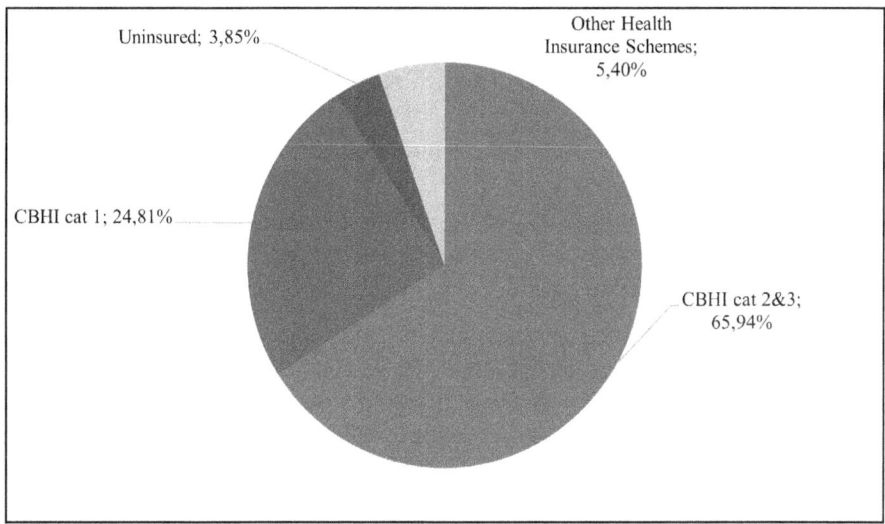

Figure 11.1: Population Distribution by Health Insurance Plans
Source: Ministry of Health, Health financing unit/CTAMS, Annual report 2011–2012

Further, the laudable achievement of high universal coverage through CBHIS in Rwanda was contingent on receiving 45 per cent of its revenue from other sources, such as tax revenue, external funding, other insurance plans, etc. and 55 per cent from contributions as depicted in Figure 11.2.

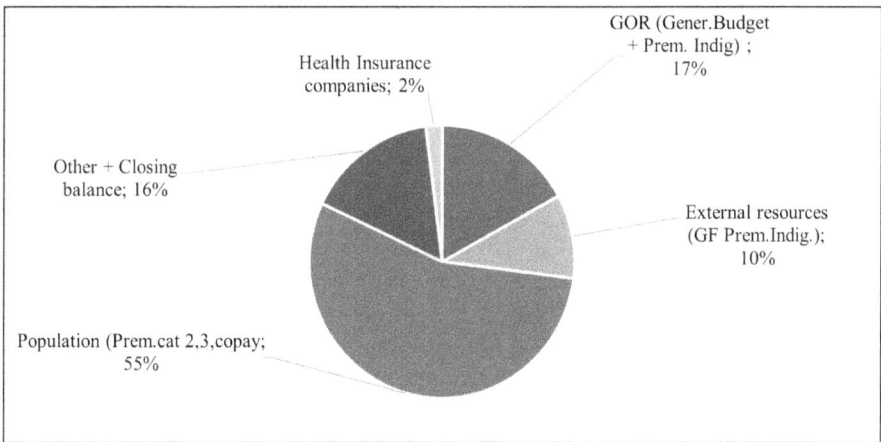

Figure 11.2: Community-based Health Insurance Sources of Financing
Source: Ministry of Health, Health financing unit/CTAMS, Annual report 2011–2012

Lessons Learned

A number of lessons were learned from the three countries. These included the amalgamation of existing health insurance plans into smaller and manageable numbers. For example, in Thailand, a considerable number of existing schemes were merged into three, which cover different population segments of the country, yielding a population coverage of 85 per cent. In the same way, in Rwanda, a large number of CBHIS were harmonised into category 1 and 2 for different segments of the population, and thus, the two categories cover about 90 per cent of the entire population.

Second, in both of the cases above there was strong government commitment. For example, a range of legal frameworks were passed to support the universal coverage agenda, including mandatory health insurance, and strong financial commitment to the universal access through tax revenue. For instance, in Thailand, certain categories of the population were exempted from contributions and received healthcare free of charge because their medical bills were paid for through tax revenue.

Third, all three adopted the 'bottom-up' approach, establishing insurance first for low-income informal workers and rural dwellers and then graduating to high-income formal workers. This method increased the pace of achieving universal coverage.

Conclusion

The 'top-down' approach of Nigeria's NHIS to effectively expand population coverage to the preponderance of the Nigerian population has been fraught with pitfalls. More successful was the 'bottom-up' strategy with gradual process that was used to scale up population coverage in Germany, Thailand and Rwanda, with more emphasis on comprehensive coverage. In addition, evidence from the selected countries explored shows strong government commitment, by making health insurance mandatory and supporting the scheme with tax revenue especially for the poor who cannot pay contributions. The lessons from the three studied countries could contribute to the debate of expanding coverage in Nigeria. By adopting mandatory coverage for the entire population, coalescing existing programmes/plans, equalising risk between the programmes/plans and allocating tax revenue, Nigeria could provide basic healthcare for all.

References

Adesina, J. O., 2007, In Search of Inclusive Development: Introduction, in Adesina, J., ed., *Social Policy in Sub-Saharan African Context: In Search of Inclusive Development*, Basingstoke: Palgrave Macmillan.

Adesina, J. O., 2008, *Transformative Social Policy in a Post-Neoliberal African Context: Enhancing Social Citizenship*, Paper prepared for the RC 19 Stockholm 2008 Annual Conference, The Future of Social Citizenship: Politics, Institution and Outcomes, 4–6 September 2008.

Adesina, J. O., 2009, Social Policy in Sub-Saharan Africa: A Glance in the Rear-View Mirror, *International Journal of Social Welfare* Vol.18: S37–S51.

Adesina, J. O., 2015, Return to a Wider Vision of Social Policy: Re-reading Theory and History, *South African Review of Sociology*, Vol. 46, No. 3, pp. 99–119. DOI: 10.1080/21528586.2015.1077588.

Alma-Ata Declaration, 1978, International Conference on Primary Health Care, Alma-Ata, USSR, 6–12 September 1978. Available online at http://www.who.int/publications/almaata_declaration_en.pdf. Accessed 4 April 2019.

Ayepong, I. R. and Adjei, S., 2008, Public Social Policy Development and Implementation: A Case Study of the Ghana National Health Insurance, *Health Policy and Planning*, Vol. 23, pp. 150–160.

Bärnighausen, T. and Sauerborn, R., 2002, One Hundred and Eighteen Years of the German Health Insurance System: Are There Any Lessons for Middle- and Low-Income Countries?, *Journal of Social Science Medicine*, Vol. 54, pp. 1559–1587.

Busse, R. and Riesberg, A., 2004, Health Care Systems in Transition: Germany, Copenhagen: WHO Regional Office for Europe on behalf of the European Observatory on Health Systems and Policies.

Busse, R., Stargardt T. and Schreyögg, J., 2005, Determining the 'Health Benefit Basket' of the Statutory Health Insurance Scheme in Germany Methodologies and Criteria, *European Journal of Health Economics*, Vol. 1, No. 6, pp. 30–36.

Carrin, G. and James, C., 2004, Reaching Universal Coverage via Social Health Insurance: Key Design Features in the Transition Period, FER/EIP Discussion Paper No. 2, 2004, Geneva: World Health Organization.

Central Bank of Nigeria (CBN), 1983, Annual Report and Statement of Accounts for the Year Ended 31 December 1982, Abuja: Central Bank of Nigeria.

Central Bank of Nigeria (CBN), 1985, Annual Report and Statement of Accounts for the Year Ended 31 December 1984, Abuja: Central Bank of Nigeria.

Central Bank of Nigeria (CBN), 1990, Annual Report and Statement of Accounts for the Year Ended 31 December 1989, Abuja: Central Bank of Nigeria.

Central Bank of Nigeria, 2002, Monetary Credit, Foreign Trade and Exchange Policy of Guidelines for Fiscal 2002/2003, Monetary Circular. No.36, Abuja: Central Bank of Nigeria. Available online at https://www.cbn.gov.ng/documents/cbnannualreports.as. *Accessed on 16 May 2010.*

Dutta, A. and Hongoro, C., 2013, *Scaling Up National Health Insurance in Nigeria: Learning from Case Studies of India, Colombia, and Thailand*, Washington, DC: Futures Group, Health Policy Project.

European Observatory of Health Systems, 2000, Available online at: http://www.euro.who.int/__data/assets/pdf_file/0006/98403/E87923.pdf. Accessed on 10 April 2016.

Global Health Strategies, 2015, Health for all: Universal health coverage day. Available online at *http://universalhealthcoverageday.org/welcome/*. Accessed on 21 January 2019.

Gustafsson-Wright, E. and Schellekens, O., 2013, Achieving Universal Health Coverage in Nigeria One State at a Time: A Public-Private Partnership Community-Based Health Insurance Model, Brooke Shearer Working Paper Series, 2. Available online at http://www.brookings.edu/~/media/research/files/papers/2013/06/achieving-universal-health-coverage-nigeria-gustafsson-wright/achieving-universal-health-coverage-in-nigeria.pdf. Accessed on 12 April 2019.

Helleiner, C. K., 1983, The IMF and Africa in the 1980s, Essays in International Finance, No. 152, July 1983. Available online at: https://www.princeton.edu/~ies/IES_Essays/E152.pdf. Accessed on 12/05/17.

Hsiao, W. and Shaw, R. P., 2007, *Social Health Insurance for Developing Nations*, WBI Development Studies, Washington, DC: The World Bank Group. Available online at https://openknowledge.worldbank.org/handle/10986/6860.

National Health Insurance Scheme (NHIS), 2012, Operational guidelines: Revised Version, Federal Government of Nigeria. Available online at http://www.nhis.gov.ng/index.php?option=com_contentandview=articleandid=92andItemid=77. Accessed 1 September 2013.

National Health Insurance Scheme (NHIS), Act 2004, Available online at http://www.nhis.gov.ng Accessed 12 August 2016.

Nicholas, D., Yates, R., Warburton, W. and Fontana, G., 2015, Delivering Universal Health Coverage: A Guide for Policy Makers, Report of the WISH Universal Health Coverage Forum 2015. Available online at http://www.multivu.com/players/English/7449051-world-innovation-summit-health-2015/links/7449051-WISH_UHC_Forum_Report_08.01.15.pdf. Accessed on 29 January 2021.

Nyandekwe, M., Nzayirambaho, M. and Kakoma, J., 2014, Universal Health Coverage in Rwanda: Dream or Reality, *Pan African Medical Journal*, Vol. 17, Article 232. Available online at: http://www.panafrican-med-journal.com/content/article/17/232/full/#.Vm8za7_23IU. Accessed on 10 October 2019.

Obasan, S. J., 2013, Healthcare Financing in Nigeria: Prospects and Challenges, *Mediterranean Journal of Social Sciences*, Vol. 4, No. 1, pp. 221–236.

Obono, O., 2007, Social Policy in the Development Context: Water, Health and Sanitation in Ghana and Nigeria, in Adesina, J., ed., *Social Policy in Sub-Saharan African Context: In Search of Inclusive Development*, Basingstoke: Palgrave Macmillan.

Odeyemi, A. O., 2014, Community-Based Health Insurance Programmes and the National Health Insurance Scheme of Nigeria: Challenges to Uptake and Integration, *International Journal for Equity in Health*, Vol. 13, Article 20. Available online at http://www.equityhealthj.com/content/. Accessed on 18 July 2019.

Odeyemi, A. O. and Nixon, J., 2013, Assessing Equity in Healthcare Through the National Health Insurance Schemes of Nigeria and Ghana: A Review-Based Comparative Analysis, *Journal for Equity in Health*, Vol. 12, No. 9, pp. 1–18.

Ogunbekun, I., Ogunbekun, A. and Orobaton, N., 1999, Private Healthcare in Nigeria: Walking the Tightrope, *Health Policy and Planning*, Vol. 14, No. 2, pp. 174–181.

Okpani, A. and Abimbola, S., 2015, Operationalising Universal Health Coverage in Nigeria Through Social Health Insurance, *Nigeria Medical Journal*, Vol. 56, pp. 305–310.

Omoruan, A. I., 2019, The Design and Implementation Policy of National Health Insurance Scheme in Oyo State, Nigeria, Unpublished PhD thesis.

Republic of Rwanda, Ministry of Health, 2010, Rwanda National Health Insurance Policy, Kigali: Republic of Rwanda.

Sigerist, H. E., 1999, From Bismarck to Beveridge: Developments and Trends in Social Security Legislation, *Journal of Public Health Policy*, Vol. 20, No. 4., pp. 476–496.

Talampas, R. G., 2014, Review of Experience of Social Health Insurance in Three Asian Countries: China, Thailand, and Vietnam, Discussion paper series No. 2014–46, Philippine Institute of Development Studies. Available online at *dirp3.pids.gov.ph/webportal/CDN/PUBLICATIONS/pidsdps1446.pdf. Accessed on 10 March 2016.*

United Nations (UN), 1948, Universal Declaration of Human Rights. Available online at www.un.org/en/universal-declaration-human-rights. Accessed on 10 May 2018.

United Nations (UN), 2012, Global Health and Foreign Policy: Resolution Adopted by the General Assembly, 2012. Available online at www.un.org/press/en/2012/ga11326.doc.htm. Accessed on 19 December 2018.

Uzochukwu, B. S. C., Ughasoro, M. D., Etiaba, S., Okwuosa, C., Envuladu, O. E. and Onwujekwe, O. E., 2016, Healthcare Financing in Nigeria: Implications for Achieving Universal Health Coverage, *Nigerian Journal of Clinical Practice*, Vol. 18, pp. 437–444. Available online at: www.njcponline.com/article.asp?issn=1119-3077;year=2015;volume=18. Accessed on 2 March 2016.

World Bank, 1980, World Development Report 1980, New York: Oxford University Press. Available online at: https://openknowledge.worldbank.org/handle/10986/5963. Accessed on 10 June 2017.

World Bank, 1987, *Financing Health Services in Developing Countries: An Agenda for Reform*, a World Bank Policy Study, Washington, DC: World Bank Group. Available online at http://documents1.worldbank.org/curated/en/468091468137379607/pdf/multi-page.pdf.

World Bank, 1989, *Sub-Saharan Africa: From crisis to sustainable growth—A long-term perspective study*, Washington, DC: World Bank Group. Available online at http://documents1.worldbank.org/curated/en/498241468742846138/pdf/multi0page.pdf.

World Bank, 1993, *World Development Report 1993: Investing in Health*, New York: Oxford University Press. Available online at https://openknowledge.worldbank.org/handle/10986/5976.

World Bank, 2010, *Accelerated Development in Sub-Saharan Africa: An Agenda for Action*, Washington, DC: World Bank Group. Available online at http://documents.worldbank.org/curated/en/702471468768312009/Accelerated-development-in-sub-Saharan-Africa-an-agenda-for-action.

World Health Organization (WHO), 2000, *The World Health Report 2000—Health Systems: Improving Performance,* Geneva: WHO.

World Health Organization (WHO), 2005, *Sustainable Health Financing, Universal Coverage and Social Health Insurance*, Geneva: WHO.

World Health Organization (WHO), 2009. World Health Statistics 2009, Geneva: WHO. Available online at *http://www.who.int/gho/publications/world_health_statistics/2015/en/*. Accessed on 1 February 2016.

World Health Organization (WHO), 2010, The World Health Report 2010, Health Systems Financing—The Path to Universal Coverage, Geneva: WHO.

12

Land Reform as Social Policy: Exploring the Redistribution and Social Protection Outcomes in Goromonzi District, Zimbabwe

Clement Chipenda

Introduction

This chapter explores the redistribution and social protection outcomes of the fast-track land reform programme (FTLRP) undertaken in Zimbabwe from July 2000, using the transformative social policy framework as a conceptual and evaluative tool. This is in a backdrop of where two decades after the official launch of the programme, the story of the FTLRP is still incomplete.

The FTLRP became one of the largest land transfers in recent history. It managed to reverse a racially skewed agrarian structure, which Zimbabwe had inherited at independence in 1980. At that time, Zimbabwe's agrarian structure was made up of 6,000 white, large-scale commercial farms on 17.5 million hectares of land and 700,000 African households on 15.5 million hectares (Moyo 2013; Scoones 2015). In just over a decade, the FTLRP managed to resettle 180,000 families on 13 million hectares (Scoones et al. 2015; Hanlon et al. 2013). This was a vast improvement on earlier post-independence land reform initiatives, which had seen only 70,000 families resettled on 3.4 million hectares, a number that fell far short of the 162,000 families who were initially targeted for resettlement in the 1980s (Moyo 1995, 2013; GoZ 1981).

The immediate impact of the FTLRP was the emergence of a tri-modal agrarian structure, which replaced the largely colonial bi-modal agrarian structure comprising large-scale commercial farms and the communal farming areas. The tri-modal agrarian model organised rural Zimbabwe into the peasantry, the middle to large capitalist farms, and the agro-estates (Moyo 2004; Moyo and Yeros

2005; Binswanger-Mkhize and Moyo 2012). It changed the agrarian landscape in the country, giving rise to an increased number of differentiated landholdings, production patterns, markets and livelihood trajectories (Moyo 2011, 2013).

Using empirical evidence from the Goromonzi District in Mashonaland East Province, this chapter explores the social policy outcomes of the FTLRP. This is in a context where there have been polemical debates on the FTLRP that narrowly focused on processes and implementation. The focus of the debate has now changed and is now on the impact of the FTLRP on peasant households.

This chapter is divided into three sections. Firstly, it looks at the debates about the FTLRP that have formed a foundation for understanding the programme. Secondly, it discusses social policy, land reform and transformative social policy, and lastly it presents empirical evidence on the outcomes of the FTLRP in Goromonzi, focusing on redistribution and social protection.

Debates on the FTLRP

Due to the scale and unprecedented nature of the FTLRP, it has for the past decade and a half been a subject of polemical debates which have polarised academia. The programme was criticised as being a political tool of the ruling Zimbabwe National African Union–Patriotic Front (ZANU–PF) to boost its waning political fortunes. ZANU–PF was accused of using cronyism and political patronage to control the programme and to reward its supporters (Rutherford 2007; Zamchiya 2011; Hammar et al. 2003; Sachikonye 2003). The FTLRP was seen as contributing to agricultural decline, food insecurity and the displacement of farmworkers. The subsistence farmers who benefitted from it were viewed as not having the expertise or experience to engage in commercial agriculture (Bond 2008). The tenure system was perceived as insecure, and the FTLRP was accused of leading to human rights abuses and the violation of property rights (resulting in the death of forty people), and of stimulating the unprecedented economic collapse in Zimbabwe after 2000 (Richardson 2005; Worby 2003; Sacco 2008).

This narrative has been countered by other scholars who have argued that a more nuanced and empirically grounded analysis on the impact of the FTLRP is needed. For example, on the issue of the FTLRP being politically driven by ZANU–PF, Moyo (2011), Scoones et al. (2010) and Sadomba (2013) have asserted that the programme was in fact a 'bottom up' political initiative which was a result of peasant mobilisation. They state that it cannot be seen as a monolithic neopatrimonial project, which has been the view of its critics. On decreased agricultural production, Scoones (2017a, 2017b), James (2015) and Binswanger-Mkhize and Moyo (2012) have proposed that other factors need to be taken into consideration. These include climate change, the effects of El Niño, recurrent droughts and the diversion of inputs from food crop production to cash crops. In addition, the impact of HIV/AIDS, lack of financial support for agriculture and the challenging socio-economic conditions in the country have all contributed to a reduction and fluctuations in agricultural production. The programme is seen as having benefitted different population sectors. While some political and business elites did benefit from it, other people from different social classes also benefitted (Moyo et al. 2009; Scoones et al. 2010).

It is important to note that the debates on the FTLRP are quite numerous and cannot all be covered in this chapter. They are based on various analytical, ideological and epistemological approaches by different scholars. Every criticism of the FTLRP has been countered, making readings on the FTLRP not only interesting but also academically engaging. In the past few years, the debates have gradually shifted, with less attention paid to the shortcomings of the programme and its processes and more to its outcomes. This shift is aptly captured by Cliffe, Cousins and Gaidzanwa (2011: 907), who state:

> The emergence of a range of studies into what has transpired over a lengthy period provides a 'reality check' and an opportunity to extend debates beyond policy prescriptions and their initial implementation to an assessment of what has actually been happening on the ground as a result of the land redistribution that occurred in the early 2000s.

The changed focus of the debates, onto outcomes, is quite progressive and is evident in several studies undertaken across Zimbabwe. Work by Moyo et al. (2009), Scoones et al. (2010), Dekker and Kinsey (2011), Mkodzongi (2013), Murisa (2009), Matondi (2012) and Mutopo (2011), among others, are just a few of these. This chapter is a further contribution to the literature on the outcomes of the FTLRP. Using the transformative social policy framework, it argues that although the work by the scholars highlighted above covers the social-policy dimensions of the programme these are not presented as such. It argues, and presents the evidence, that land reform in Zimbabwe has discernible redistribution and social protection outcomes which have impacted on the lives of beneficiaries. Most of the literature on the FTLRP, while acknowledging these outcomes, does not present them from a social-policy perspective.

Social Policy and Land Reform

Social policy has been defined by Marshall (1950) in his book *Citizenship and Social Class*,

> ... not as a technical term with an exact meaning but as referring to policies by the government with regards to having a direct impact on the welfare of the citizens, by providing them with services or income. The central core consists therefore of social insurance, public (or national) assistance, the health and welfare services (Marshall 1950, cited in Titmus 1974: 30).

This definition is corroborated by Hagenbach (1958: 205, cited by Titmus 1974: 31), who states that the '… meaning of social policy may be said to be the desire to ensure every member of the community certain minimum standards and opportunities.' This minimum standard of living for citizens is ensured through social policy, which includes social welfare, social security, pensions, labour market interventions, land reform, progressive taxation and other redistributive policies (UNRISD 2006). In this context, social policy has to be understood as '… collective public efforts aimed at affecting and protecting the social well-being of people within a given territory' (Adesina 2007: 1). Social policy is aimed at guaranteeing that every citizen is able to live a life of dignity regardless of status, ethnicity, gender or age. It therefore encapsulates collective efforts which are put in place by social welfare, social institutions and social relations (UNRISD 2006; Mkandawire 2007).

While land reform is acknowledged as one of many social policy tools, the existing body of literature does not examine land reform as a social policy tool. One possible explanation for this is given by Mkandawire (2007), who argues that the literature on social policy is dominated by scholars from the Organisation for Economic Co-operation and Development (OECD), creating what he calls an 'OECD bias' that reduces social policy to mono-tasking with an emphasis on social protection and welfare provision. Mkandawire (2005, 2007, 2011) and Holzman and Kozel (2007) argue that this form of social policy focuses primarily on social safety nets or social assistance and social protection. The challenge this presents is that it limits the transformative role of social policy in terms of redistribution and social protection. Land reform as a social-policy tool (just like taxation, social welfare and other redistributive policies) is rarely acknowledged and excessive focus is on the global North at the expense of the global South.

Thus, social policy in developing countries (in this case sub-Saharan Africa), according to Yi and Kim (2015), Yi (2015) and Adesina (2014, 2015), has been constituted by a neoliberal, residual approach. It is residual in the sense that the policy design and implementation are designed to serve the neoliberal agenda. It is detached from the economy and serves as an anti-poverty policy which fails to address the broader structural causes of poverty and underdevelopment. This approach has tended to be palliative, proposing remedial action to address the adverse effects of economic policies that have been aimed at stabilisation and adjustment in a context of market-led growth. In developing countries it has failed to solve social problems, problems of inequality and inequity, and has failed to inspire and strategise effective development initiatives. The residual approach has thus had limited capacity to guarantee all citizens decent living standards. Residual social policy has continued to exist because of the preponderance of donor-driven, multilateral and bilateral efforts aimed at shaping the social-policy landscape in the global South (Adesina 2014). These efforts are based on highly restrictive and conditional cash transfer programmes. Vulnerability is viewed ex-post and the focus is on extreme poverty, vulnerability and precarity. This is a major challenge when it comes to development in sub-Saharan Africa.

Recognition of the challenges of mainstream social policy has given rise to a new way of thinking around the subject, resulting in the transformative social policy concept. The concept can be traced to the United Nations Institute for Social Development (UNRISD), which set up a flagship project titled 'Social Policy in a Development Context' which was aimed at examining the neglected dimensions of social policy in the context of development (UNRISD 2006) and develop another perspective on social policy. Transformative social policy can be understood best as social policy that is multifaceted, goes beyond addressing economic challenges and market failures, and provides welfare through initiatives that drive development. Transformative social policy has multiple functions, which are redistributive, protective, reproductive, productive and ensure social cohesion. These functions play a transformative and developmental role in societies and the economy (Mkandawire 2001; Adesina 2008, 2011; UNRISD 2006). Adesina (2010) argues that transformative social policy can be understood best from the point of view of 'visionary agenda setting', which is the basis of building a socially inclusive developmental agenda. For Adesina, social policy must be viewed as having multiple functions and, when addressing developmental challenges like poverty, there is need for:

> A return to holistic development thinking, with emphasis on inter-sectoral linkages among policy instruments, rather than the fragmentary thinking and single-issue policy merchandising that currently suffuse the international debate; it requires a return to the wider vision of development and social policy. It is this wider vision that is encapsulated in the idea of transformative social policy. (Adesina 2010: 16)

Transformative social policy is built on the recognition that social policy has lost its developmental orientation (Myrdal 1960). It is embedded in the idea that the social and the economic are inseparable. Its imperative is a holistic approach to economic, political and social relations and policy linkages. If social policy interventions are comprehensive they have the potential to transform existing unequal and unjust social, economic and political relationships (Yi and Kim 2015). This point of view is supported by Adesina (2010: 19) who sees transformative social policy as offering:

> … conceptual tools and the policy parameters for such a return to a wider vision of how we may enhance human capabilities and economic development. Rather than social policy being defined almost exclusively in terms of social protection, transformative social policy calls the objectives of social policy to our attention. Central to the new agendas is girding the economy with the same norms of equality and solidarity.

There are several examples of transformative social policy. Chung (2014) points out examples in the history of industrialised nations, not only in Europe, in countries such as Germany, but also in East Asia, such as Japan, South Korea and Taiwan. These countries have made great strides in development and some of this success has been attributed to their social policies. In the case of South Korea, Chung argues that transformative social policy was important in the shift from the conventional approach, which was aimed at protection and distribution functions. It was significant in directly ameliorating social problems arising from capitalist economic growth. Transformative social policies were seen to enhance social capability, which in turn influenced broad areas and development, transforming the economy as well as the society. A representation of the transformative conceptual framework is shown in Figure 12.1:

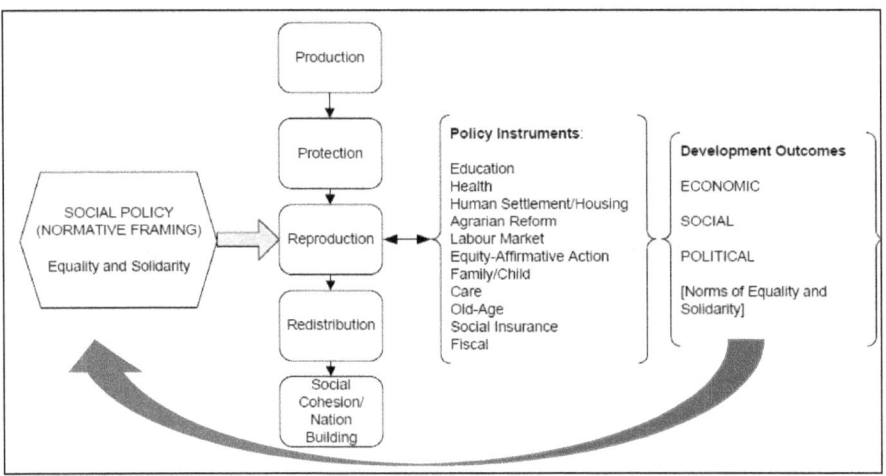

Figure 12.1: Transformative Social Policy: Norms, Functions, Instruments and Outcomes
Source: Adesina 2011

Using the transformative social policy framework, this chapter focuses on two functions of the framework, namely the redistribution and protection outcomes. In social policy, the concept of redistribution refers to the redistribution of wealth and assets to reduce poverty and vulnerability. According to Esping-Andersen (1990), in his writings on the welfare state; the state, the family and markets have a role to play in ensuring the equitable distribution of welfare provision. There is what he sees as collective and institutionalised social risk and political compromise between the three parties, which stimulates redistribution. For there to be growth and reduction of poverty, the redistribution of assets is important. On redistribution, Mkandawire (2011) has argued that the proceeds from economic development should be redistributed in society. This would ensure that there was the equitable sharing of the benefits of development, and is the responsibility of the state. Redistribution is achieved through progressive taxation, social transfers, adequate occupational welfare for everyone, decent jobs and wages.

The concept of social protection used in this chapter is the transformative social protection concept (see Devereux and Sabates-Wheeler 2004). The thrust of this approach is to transfer assets and income to the poor and to protect the vulnerable against livelihood risks. It also seeks to enhance the social status and rights of those who are marginalised, to extend the benefits of economic growth to the poor while reducing vulnerability. Devereux and Sabates-Wheeler argue that this approach is useful in addressing vulnerability and the power imbalances that create and sustain economic inequality and social exclusion. The approach is an alternative to the World Bank-inspired Social Risk Management (SRM) framework. According to Holzman and Kozel. (2007), this framework is used to reduce vulnerability and poverty. It targets countries that are seen as not having the instruments and space to manage risks, and unable to deal with natural and manmade risks such as earthquakes, war, inflation, flooding, etc.

Methodology

This chapter is based on an empirical study of small-scale A1 farmers[1] in Goromonzi District. Data-gathering took place over a fourteen-month period from January 2015 to March 2016, when I was attached to the Sam Moyo African Institute for Agrarian Studies (SMAIAS) in Harare and doing ethnographic fieldwork using multiple instruments. These instruments included in-depth interviews, focus-group discussions (FGDs) and observations. The study targeted 150 A1 farmers who had been allocated plots on twenty-five former large-scale commercial farms (LSCF). An additional forty-eight informants and sixty-six FGD participants also gave their input on the study. Respondents and plots targeted in the study were selected using multiple sampling methods and the intention was to have as much coverage and diversity as possible. The research was based on the interpretive research paradigm and it used a mixed-methods research design combining qualitative and quantitative research approaches. This framework was considered useful as it enabled an integrative and complementary approach that would maximise strengths and minimise weaknesses in the research process (Creswell and Plano-Clark 2011; Creswell 2003; Tashakkori and Teddlie 2010). The primary data collected during the fieldwork was complemented by secondary data sources, mainly from the SMAIAS Household Survey (2013–2014)[2] and statistical data from government agencies.

The Emergent Agrarian Structure and the Land Redistribution Outcomes of the FTLRP

From a social policy perspective, land reform—just like policies on progressive taxation, social transfers, decent jobs and wages—has an important societal role. It ensures that the proceeds of economic development are redistributed to society

(Mkandawire 2011). Land reform can be used to redistribute wealth, equalise opportunities, improve economic growth and address poverty (Prasad, Hypher and Gerecke 2013; Deininger and Squire 1998). The issue of the redistributive nature of the FTLRP has been at the centre of the debates around the programme. As noted in the introductory section, questions have arisen around who benefitted from the FTLRP and the extent of its redistribution. In this section, we will briefly look at the redistributive nature of the FTLRP in the context of the emergent tri-modal agrarian structure.

One indisputable outcome of the FTLRP from a national perspective was the redistribution of land. The land tenure system was transformed with a change in ownership of land, from private to predominantly state ownership. The second outcome was the emergence of a new agrarian structure—a tri-modal agrarian structure which replaced the bi-modal agrarian structure, according to Binswanger-Mkhize and Moyo (2012). There emerged three modes of social organisation of labour (Moyo 2011) which are: a differentiated peasantry,[3] who are the A1 and communal farmers; small- to medium-scale farmers; and private and public agro-industrial estates and conservancies. The new structure led to an expansion in the numbers of small- and middle-scale agricultural producers.

At a national level, the FTLRP saw the resettlement of 180,000 families: 150,000 families were resettled on A1 farms while 30,000 families were resettled on A2 farms. The amount of land acquired for resettlement was estimated to be at 13 million hectares (Scoones 2015; Moyo 2013; Hanlon et al. 2013). In Goromonzi the agrarian structure mentioned above is evident. There are the A1 and communal farmers who comprise the differentiated peasantry, the small- to medium-scale capitalist farmers (who are the A2 farmers) and the old small-scale commercial farmers, and the large-scale agro-estates. According to the Lands Officer (Interview, 12 October 2015) and the SMAIAS Household Survey (2013–14), in Goromonzi there are 2,822 A1 beneficiaries (on 32,628 hectares previously owned by seventy-five LSCF), 846 A2 beneficiaries (on 84,455.72 hectares previously owned by fifty-one LSCF) and 16 agro-estates. The FTLRP has enlarged the number of farm households in the district from 20,253 to 23,733. Prior to 2000, there were 19,976 households in the communal areas and eighty-nine small-scale farms or the former Native Purchase Areas.

Farmers in the A1 sector own an average of 19.39 hectares each, which includes grazing and arable land. This contrasts with the 3.72 hectares owned by the old peasantry in the communal areas. The small- to medium-scale capitalist farmers own an average of 493.8 hectares, which is 20 per cent less than those in this category in 1980. The agro-estates have more than 1,400 hectares of land. The FTLRP reduced the area of land controlled by the LSCFs from 68 per cent to 29 per cent. During the same period, the peasantry increased their share of land from 32 per cent to 45 per cent. As a peri-urban district, there is high demand for land in the district, which meant the peasantry got a smaller share of the land and larger land allocations were made for the A2 farms when compared with the rest of the country. When asked whether the FTLRP had been redistributive, the Lands Officer for Goromonzi said:

> In this district, we currently have 2,822 A1 farmers and these subdivisions came from 75 farms before the year 2000. We also have 846 A2 farmers and these A2 farms were subdivided from 51 farms which were owned by single individuals. So, you can judge for yourself on how much the FTLRP has redistributed the land in this district. The programme was not a joke or a political gimmick as some people portrayed it, it has really resulted in a lot of people owning farms and these are 3 000 plus people in one district imagine the numbers at provincial level and national levels. (Interview, 12 October 2015)

This was corroborated by one of the farmers who was allocated a plot at Dunstan farm.

> The land reform programme has resulted in the resettlement of many people from different areas. Goromonzi has rich soils so there was a high demand for land here. Previously, this farm was an estate, together with many other farms like Banana Grove, Xanadu, Fordyce and others. It was owned by the Calinan family and Mike Guysford a grandson of the family took it over in the 1990s. But now with the FTLRP, there are over 116 families which were allocated A1 plots. The same applies with other farms in this area at some you will find 80 farmers on others 50 farmers and these were farms which had only one owner before. (Interview, 13 April 2015)

As indicated earlier, at the centre of the debates on the FTLRP has been the accusation that it benefitted the political and business elite only, through patronage, clientism, cronyism and capture. In order to get insights on who the beneficiaries of the FTLRP were and where they originated from, the study looked at the areas of origin of the beneficiaries. The findings are summarised in Table 12.1, which shows that most of the A1 beneficiaries in the study sample originated from the rural areas, giving credence to the findings in other studies that some of the beneficiaries were from the land poor, unproductive and congested communal areas (see Moyo et al. 2009; Scoones et al. 2010; Mkodzongi 2013). They also confirm observations by some scholars that some beneficiaries, who came from urban areas, were either unemployed or held precarious and insecure jobs, which made them opt for resettlement (see Scoones 2017b). Table 12:1 summarises the areas of origin of the beneficiaries in the study.

Table 12.1: Areas of Origin of A1 Beneficiaries (N=150)

Area of Origin	Province	Rural/Urban/Peri-urban	No. of Farmers	Percentage (%)
Goromonzi	Mashonaland East	Rural	42	28
Epworth	Harare	Peri-urban	26	17.3
Harare	Harare	Urban	21	14
Murehwa	Mashonaland East	Rural	12	8
Mutoko	Mashonaland East	Rural	10	7
Chitungwiza	Harare	Urban	7	5
Seke	Mashonaland East	Rural	5	3.3
Uzumba Marimba Pfungwe	Mashonaland East	Rural	4	3
Ruwa	Harare	Urban	3	2
Marondera	Mashonaland East	Urban	3	2
Marange	Manicaland	Rural	2	1.3
Domboshava	Mashonaland East	Peri-urban	2	1.3
Juru	Mashonaland East	Rural	1	0.6
Chihota	Mashonaland East	Rural	1	0.6
Hwedza	Mashonaland East	Rural	1	0.6
Guruve	Mashonaland Central	Rural	1	0.6
Shamva	Mashonaland Central	Rural	1	0.6
Bindura	Mashonaland Central	Urban	1	0.6
Kadoma	Midlands	Urban	1	0.6
Shurugwi	Midlands	Rural	1	0.6
Gokwe	Midlands	Rural	1	0.6
Buhera	Manicaland	Rural	1	0.6
Nyanga	Manicaland	Rural	1	0.6
Headlands	Manicaland	Rural	1	0.6
Honde Valley	Manicaland	Rural	1	0.6
Total			150	100

Source: Author's own fieldwork (2015–16).

Thus, the evidence from a national perspective as well as in Goromonzi shows that there has there been land redistribution and a change in the country's agrarian structure. All the farmers in the study had legal documentation granting them usufruct rights over the land (evidence that the land was given to them legally to use): 137 (91 per cent) had offer letters while thirteen (9 per cent) had A1 permits. The FTLRP has thus been effective in reversing the racialised agrarian structure inherited in 1980, which post-independence programmes failed to resolve. By 2013 (Moyo 2013), more than 200,000 families had benefitted from post-independence land reform programmes. From a social-policy perspective, it can be argued that by addressing historical injustices in land tenure, the FTLRP managed to deal with unjust social and economic relations that existed in the agrarian sector. Through having a broadened agrarian structure it has set the necessary conditions for empowerment and availed beneficiaries and communities with economic opportunities. According to Yi and Kim (2015), this is one of the objectives of transformative social policy—to enhance the productive capacities of beneficiaries.

Farm Residency

As we discuss the redistributive outcomes of the FTLRP it is important to briefly look at farm residency, to ascertain the extent to which farmers are living on the farms, engaging in productive activities there, and showing some level of commitment to the programme. This is in the context of criticism that the FTLRP gave land to non-resident 'cell-phone farmers' and that this has negatively impacted their ability to be productive.

The SMAIAS Household Survey (2013–2014) showed that 87.1 per cent of A1 farmers and 61.1 per cent of A2 beneficiaries reside permanently on the farms. For A1 farmers, it showed that 0.8 per cent live in the communal areas, forty-nine (10.4 per cent) in urban areas and four (0.8 per cent) live in the diaspora. The findings suggest that a large number of A1 farmers use the farms as their place of residence. This implies (to some extent) that they have either relocated permanently or did not have land prior to benefitting from the FTLRP and have now established their homes on the farms. It dispels the notion that the beneficiaries of the FTLRP are 'cell-phone farmers' not residing on the land.

But if one looks at the A2 farms, there is a worrying indication that some farmers do not permanently reside on the farms, and, for some observers, this places doubt on their full commitment to commercial farming. This is against a background of LSCF owners who permanently resided on the farms and ran them as a business (interview with Lands Officer). The statistics are important in showing that the majority of A1 farmers live on the farms and that their presence translates into improved productivity and enhanced livelihoods. It also shows that some of the beneficiaries have alternative places of residency in urban areas (which they own or rent) and communal areas. In addition, some of the beneficiaries have alternative sources of income, like employment, which cause them to live away from the farms. This is the reason there are some beneficiaries living in urban areas. The findings on farm residency by SMAIS Household Survey are shown in Table 12.2.

Table 12.2: Farm Residency

Residency of Plot Owner	Settlement Type					
	A1		A2		Total	
	No.	%	No.	%	No.	%
On Farm	412	87.1	179	61.1	591	77.2
Communal Area	4	0.8	6	2.0	10	1.3
Urban Area	49	10.4	95	32.4	144	18.8
Diaspora	4	0.8	6	2.0	10	1.3
Other	4	0.8	7	2.4	11	1.4
Total	473	100	293	100	766	100

Source: SMAIAS Household Survey (2013–2014)

The study in Goromonzi corroborated the findings by the SMAIAS Household Survey that a large number of A1 beneficiaries reside on the farms. Table 12.3 shows that, from my study sample of 150 A1 beneficiaries, 139 (92 per cent) reside on the farms, with the second highest number residing in the urban areas (4 per cent). The findings show interesting dynamics in the residency status of the beneficiaries of the FTLRP in the A1 sector.

Table 12.3: Residency of Owner (A1 Farms—Goromonzi)

Residency of Plot Owner of A1 Farm	No.	%
On Farm	139	92
Communal Area	3	2
Urban Area	6	4
Diaspora	2	1
Other	1	1
Total	150	100

Source: Author's own fieldwork (2015)

Women and Land Redistribution

Gender is an important matter when it comes to land and livelihoods in Africa. Many scholarly works on gender roles in Africa agree that gender relations have not been favourable for women in Africa (O'Laughlin 1998; Jacobs 2010; Whitehead and Tsikata 2003; Mutopo 2011, 2014; Gaidzanwa 1994, 2011). Patriarchy and the colonial dispensation are seen as having subjugated women and worsened their plight compared to men. This study looked at the gender dynamics of the FTLRP and how women benefitted from the programme.

According to the Presidential Land Review Committee (PLRC 2003) (Manjengwa and Mazhawidza 2009), during and after the FTLRP process there had been demands especially by advocates of gender equality that at least 20 per cent of the land should be redistributed to women. As a result, 18 per cent of women benefitted under the A1 model while 12 per cent benefitted under the A2 model. This fell far short of expectations. Women were seen as accessing land through husbands or male relatives and not owning land in their own right.

Data from the Agriculture and Livestock Survey (ALS) (ZIMSTAT 2012, 2015) and the Understanding Gender Equality in Zimbabwe: Women and Men Report (ZIMSTAT 2016), provides insights into the redistributive and gender dimensions of the FTLRP. The ALS was undertaken across all the provinces in Zimbabwe. Across all the categories there are fewer women landowners than men. The result of the survey is summarised in Table 12.4.

Table 12.4: Ownership of Agricultural Land by Gender of Landowner (ZIMSTAT 2015)

Agricultural Category	Gender of Landowner		Total	Percentage of Female Landowners (%)
	Male	Female		
Large scale	638	118	756	15.6
Small scale	16,431	2,722	19,153	14.2
A1	104,247	27,650	131,897	21
A2	16,380	1,874	18,254	10.2
Communal	593,907	435,025	1,028,932	42.2
Old resettlement farms	67,070	31,839	98,909	32
Total	798,673	499,228	1,297,901	38.5

Source: Understanding Gender Equality in Zimbabwe: Women and Men Report (2016)

The study in Goromonzi corroborated the findings in the survey above that fewer women benefitted from the FTLRP than men. Results from the study sample indicated that 117 men and thirty-three women had benefitted from the FTLRP. This translated to 78 per cent of men benefitting compared with 22 per cent of women. However, while only some women have access to land in their own right, they often have secondary access to land. This secondary access to land is evident in Goromonzi as in other study sites (see Mutopo 2011; Mutopo et al. 2014; Chiweshe et al. 2015; Matondi 2012). A respondent (Interview 22 November 2015), provided insights on how women have secondary access to land.

> My husband has two other wives. He married me when he had already been given this farm in 2002 and he married me in 2007. I have never seen the title deeds *(I took this to mean the offer letter)* of this farm and he keeps them at his other

> home in Marondera. I understand that they are in his name only. He is in charge here and has built houses for each of us and given us fields where we practice our agriculture. We have the freedom to plant what we want there and to sell or eat the produce and no one interferes with the activities of others. *Baba* has his own fields and we assist there as well as this is where food to eat and money for our upkeep comes from. We used to work together but this created problems as some of these women and their children do not want to work and they are lazy. When the money comes in or the produce they quarrel a lot. So, this is the reason we were given our own portions but we also help *Baba*. In my fields I plant what I want and last year my brother even helped me, and we shared the produce equally.

The response by the participant raised two important insights on the redistributive nature of the FTLRP. Firstly, women have secondary access to the land without necessarily being officially recognised as beneficiaries of the FTLRP. Secondly it confirmed what has been noted by Bourdillon (1992), that in Shona culture marriage grants a woman access to resources and carries with it symbolic social, cultural, political and economic significance. So, for families, it does not matter whose name the farm is in. By virtue of being a member of the family, a woman (in this case if there is marriage) has access to land. It confirmed the observation by Mutopo (2011; Mutopo et al. 2014) that women access land through marriage bonds. Mutopo observed that after a certain period of time women are given a field to in appreciation of their reproductive roles. Among the Karanga people whom Mutopo studied, the field is called a *tsewu*, and is understood as a means of allowing women to have access to productive resource while opening up other opportunities, for example, access to natural resources that had previously been enclosed in the LSCF and were therefore inaccessible. A pattern of accumulation has emerged involving women as well as men who benefitted from the FTLRP (after Neocosmos 1993; Cousins 2010). Women are now part of a new class of petty commodity-producers who are in a continuous process of selling and investing. Scoones (2015) calls this group 'farm-based entrepreneurs', and my findings in Goromonzi corroborate their observations in Masvingo Province. Lastly, women now have land and there are statutory enactments and initiatives to ensure tenure security for them. Some of the women are able to use tenure documents as capital, dispelling the notion of some critics of the FTLRP, who cite De Soto (2000), that land tenure in Zimbabwe has been turned into 'dead capital'.

Social Protection Outcomes of the FTLRP

The transformative social protection framework described by Devereux and Sabates-Wheeler (2004) and the transformative social policy approach emphasise the importance of social protection in responding to social and economic risks in developing countries (Yi 2015). Devereux and Sabates-Wheeler (2004) argue that social-protection programmes need to be holistic and comprehensive.

They must include concepts like participation, empowerment and rights-based improvements. This holistic approach also has to include protection, prevention, promotion and transformation (Yi and Kim 2015). This approach differs from the social protection or social safety net approach widely used in developing countries, including those in sub-Saharan Africa.

The argument presented by the transformative social protection approach is also reflected in the transformative social policy approach. This foregrounds social protection as one of the multiple functions of social policy, which contributes in varying degrees to the transformation of societies (Yi 2013, 2015). In the context of the FTLRP, the study looked at the extent to which the programme is an ex-ante social protection tool that has been used to manage risks, disparities, challenges and inequalities in the farming areas. In the sections below I explore some of the social protection outcomes of the FTLRP. Note that most of them are not 'conventional approaches' to social protection as dominant in the literature.

Shelter

Shelter and adequate housing are recognised as rights enshrined in human rights law. Shelter should ensure that people have sufficient space as well as protection from the cold, damp, heat, rain, wind and other adverse weather conditions which are a threat to human health. Shelter needs to be affordable, accessible and culturally appropriate. Adequate shelter has to ensure that citizens have dignity, that it is sustainable for the family and human life and that it is necessary for personal safety, security and protection from disease. The concept of shelter as a right fits into Marshall's (1950) concept of social rights and citizenship. When it comes to land reform in Zimbabwe, Sacco (2008) argues that land reform through the FTLRP was a means through which economic, social and cultural rights were achieved. It can be argued that shelter is one of the tangible gains of the beneficiaries of the FTLRP. In addition to accessing land for agricultural purposes, beneficiaries managed to access land on which they have built their houses. In this context, it serves a social protection function.

In Goromonzi, results from the study sample showed that 149 (99.3 per cent) beneficiaries had managed to build a house for themselves on the farms. These consisted of either improved thatch huts or brick houses, or both. The total number of houses that the farmers built was 300. The study showed that since farmers have built houses for themselves, 92.6 per cent of them now reside permanently on their farms. These findings were corroborated by the SMAIAS Household Survey, which showed that in six districts, 87.1 per cent of A1 farmers and 61.1 per cent of A2 farmers now permanently reside on their plots. When it comes to investing in housing, the survey showed that 156 A1 farmers (32.7 per cent) did so in 2011, 133 (27.9 per cent) in 2012 and 87 (18.2 per cent) in 2013. For A2 farmers it was 20.2 per cent in 2011, 17.5 per cent in 2012 and 18.2 per cent in 2013. This shows that beneficiaries do not only have access to shelter but they are also making investments in building and improving it. According to the Lands Officer in Goromonzi, the confidence that farmers now have in investing in farm infrastructure and housing can be traced to the Statutory Instrument 53 of 2014. Through this legislation, the government of Zimbabwe committed itself to pay for all improvements made on the land. This addressed issues of tenure insecurity and uncertainty which previously had discouraged beneficiaries from making investments on the land. The investment by beneficiaries in shelter is reflected at the national level: between 2009 and 2014, A1 farmers increased their investment in housing from USD 10,418,820 to USD 19,145,449, a rise of USD 8,726,629, or 84 per cent (ALS 2015).

The FTLRP has thus provided beneficiaries with an opportunity to own houses. This has protected them from the vulnerabilities that come with lack of shelter. In the study sample, seventy-two (51.3 per cent) of the beneficiaries prior to being allocated land did not have houses and they were renting, staying at family-owned houses or houses owned by their employers, or had other living arrangements. Beneficiaries who participated in FGDs said they found it easier to build houses through the FTLRP. They did not have to buy land (which is quite expensive in Zimbabwe) and most of the materials used to build the houses were locally available. In this context, by availing shelter to beneficiaries, the FTLRP could be seen has having served an ex-ante social protection function.

The Musha/Ekhaya

Closely associated with shelter is the phenomenon of the *musha/ekhaya*. In Shona culture, the *musha* refers to the home of the family or kinship group. Mkodzongi (2013) highlighted the *musha* in his study in Mhondori-Ngezi District and the same factors he noted are discernible in Goromonzi. According to Soroka (1997), the *musha* does not represent individual proprietorship but belongs to the family and kinship group, and can be mobile. The FTLRP has given beneficiaries the opportunity to establish a *musha*. Some beneficiaries now consider their plots to be their *musha*, which has become a home for both the nuclear and extended family. It plays the same role that the *musha* used to play in the communal areas. The mobility of the *musha* as described by Soroka is evident in the fact that, for some beneficiaries, the *musha* has moved from the communal areas to the farming areas.

The farms have thus become places of residence, they are places where members of a clan congregate on occasion, they provide burial grounds for family members and they are a safety net that members of the family can fall back on if they face challenges in life. Former farm workers living on a farm compound were not allowed to have a *musha* of their own. They were labelled as *vanhu vasina musha* (people without a home). This has changed now that they are landowners.

Respondents in FGDs in the study indicated that the *musha* gives them dignity and is an asset that they will pass on to their descendants. From the study sample, it was noted that 149 of the 150 (99.3 per cent) respondents have built houses on their farms and the farms have become a *musha* for most of them. The FTLRP has enabled the concept of the *musha*, which formerly was found only in the communal areas, to be established in the farming areas as well. From a social-policy perspective, the *musha* is a safety net against vulnerability and a productive resource that can be used to reduce poverty. It is available to all members of the family and can be used as an instrument to empower the weak and vulnerable.

The Bindu

The *bindu* (family garden) is another social structure that households use as an instrument to cope with minor shocks. *Bindu*s have always existed in the communal areas but, through the FTLRP, they are now found on the farms. They are not part of the arable land or fields, but are cultivated as a family garden, usually where the ground has a high moisture content (near a stream, for example). Locally, in Goromonzi, a *bindu* is also known as *jeke*. It is used to grow crops like leaf vegetables, tomatoes, chillies, onions, bananas, sugarcane, etc. The *bindu* is usually but not exclusively cultivated by women. During the study in Goromonzi, across the farming sectors, we found that seventy-two households (53.1 per cent) had *bindu*s that were being actively cultivated, while thirty-seven farms (25 per cent) indicated that while they were not cultivating the *bindu* at the time of the fieldwork, they had one, and had not been tending to it due to various reasons, including the time of the year (season), commitment elsewhere, water challenges, etc. The Agricultural Extension Officer (Interview 13 October 2015) indicated that farmers use it to supplement household income and nutrition. Traditionally, the *bindu* was cultivated just after the harvesting season (from April). Now, however, beneficiaries of the FTLRP cultivate it all year round. This is due to the availability of water pumps, wells, boreholes and streams that cut across the district.

The notion of the *bindu* correlates in some ways to the *tsewu* (women's fields) in the study by Mutopo (2011). In Goromonzi, for some respondents, the term *tsewu* refers to fields where women cultivate groundnuts. For Mutopo, the *tsewu* are fields given to women in appreciation of their reproductive roles. There, they cultivate crops of their choice for sale or to be consumed by the household. In Goromonzi, however, the *bindu* is a family garden and is not exclusively tended by women.

In Goromonzi, vegetables grown in the *bindu* are sold at source to individuals, or at local vegetable markets, in urban areas or along the major highways. Leaf vegetables, for example, sell for USD 1 each. The money raised is used to cover minor household expenses, although for some households it covers major expenses. The *bindu* can be quite profitable. One respondent indicated that she was making a profit of between USD 200 and USD 250 a month from it, depending on the market and the season. This amount was considered quite reasonable, and the respondent joked that it amounted to half the salary of a teacher, which was quite true. Herbs and other vegetables which supplement household nutrition are also grown in the *bindu*. The *bindu* thus has a social protection function for the family and is a social safety net. In some instances, neighbours and kin also get assistance from the *bindu* and can access food that otherwise they may be unable to afford. Conditions set by neighbours and kin to access the *bindu* differ, but usually it is in exchange for labour.

The Dura

Most of the A1 beneficiaries produce crops, particularly maize and small-grain cereals. They do not sell all their produce but reserve some for household consumption. Dekker and Kinsey (2011) noted that the output from 0.4 hectares can be more than 1,000 kilograms which can feed a family of five for a year. There is thus a need for storage for the output, where pesticides can be applied without affecting human health. The *dura* (granary) has emerged as an important facility on A1 farms. Not only is it a place to keep produce like maize, groundnuts, small grains, beans, etc., but it is a facility that ensures food security and crop protection for the household as well as the surrounding community and kin. Even though LSCFs had storage facilities (which were modern in most instances), in Goromonzi it was noted that the concept of the *dura* was brought to the A1 farms by farmers from the communal areas, in design and function. The *dura* is not only found in Zimbabwe. Yawitch (1981) and Tapela (2008) claim that the African grain storage system has always existed in traditional societies. They see it as a symbol of indigenous rural livelihood sustenance, useful for post-harvest storage.

The *dura*, just like livestock, is the bedrock of rural livelihoods and community food security and wealth. Devereux (2009) argues that when the *dura* is full, there may not be any need to buy food. Depending on its size, it will store enough food to feed the family until the next harvest. When the *dura* is depleted in an area, due to poor rains or poor harvests, Devereux observes that food prices usually rise, hence the importance of the *dura*.

In the study sample, 139 (93 per cent) of the beneficiaries had a structure on their farms that they designated as the *dura*. The structure and material used to make the *dura* differed, which informants indicated was usually determined by the cultural background of the owner. Some call it *hozi* and others *chipembwe* or *gombana*. The function is mostly the same, to store grain and to protect it from dampness as well as insects and pests. Some of the farmers in the study were observed using traditional preservation methods to protect their crops in the *dura*.

The Agricultural Extension Officer indicated that the *dura* is important for household food security. This has seen efforts being made by the government to train farmers in best practices in the post-harvest management of crops. This facility, which is now in the farming areas, has emerged to become an important and vital social protection tool for food security.

Livestock as Social Insurance

> When things are tough and we do not have any money in the house we always have the option of selling livestock. My husband is a truck driver so at times he goes for long periods to the Congo even up to two months. So, money for food and household supplies which the money he leaves for food can run out before he returns. So, we sell chickens and goats so that we get money to buy basic necessities and we do this even when we have poor harvests. The other option which we have is to sell vegetables but the returns are small and there are so many vegetable producers in this area. (Mai Chenai, Interview 12 February 2016)

This was said by a respondent from Chibvuti farm in Goromonzi, in relation to the importance of livestock at the farms. Her sentiments were echoed by a respondent at Lot 3 Buena Vista farm (Interview, 10 October 2015), who said:

> I keep livestock because it helps me in case of emergencies. Keeping livestock is good because it is money that you invest which keeps on reproducing and growing. So, it's better than putting your money in the bank. But if your animals are attacked by diseases and they die or they are stolen, it's a big loss. If you have livestock, and things are tough or you have health or school fees or food issues which need cash you can always sell your livestock. But when I talk of selling livestock, I mean chickens, sheep and goats. Cattle are not just sold because of small problems; those ones are the last to go and they only go if there is a major problem.

The statements captured above show the importance of livestock as a form of accumulation and insurance in instances of urgent need. Devereux (2009) has noted that smallholders adopt various coping strategies in the face of production failures. Selling livestock and assets is one of these strategies. Other strategies identified by Devereux include rationing food, which can include skipping meals, diversifying diets and reducing household expenses by cutting spending on non-food items. The importance of livestock for a rural community's social protection and social reproduction is captured by Dorward et al. (2016: 17):

> Livestock are very important to the livelihoods of some rural people, sometimes in production and income, and sometimes as assets for use in accumulation, buffering and insurance. There has been a tendency for livestock development services to focus on the income generating role of livestock at the expense of attention to low cost, low risk livestock keeping to fulfil more 'social protection' functions of accumulation, buffering and insurance.

The Livestock Production Extension Officer (Interview 30 September 2015) indicated that livestock are an important asset for households. They sell them to meet household needs or keep them for investment in productive activities, to acquire other assets and to manage risk. He said that farmers integrate crop and livestock production so as to maximise on production and diversify household income. Cattle are kept for draught power, which helps the farmers in their crop production.

The Officer indicated that the livestock market for A1 farmers in the district is dominated by smaller livestock, such as goats and chickens. Cattle are kept in the district but smallholder farmers do not easily sell them. In Goromonzi he said that farmers own an average of four cattle, but the range is between one and twenty-five. Cattle are not readily sold because they provide draught power, milk, manure and meat. They are also a store of wealth for the farmers and serve multiple purposes, which include payment of dowry, income generation, use during cultural practices and as insurance during a drought or for emergency use during funerals. From the study sample, the animals sold in the highest number were chickens: 58 per cent of the beneficiaries indicated that they had sold chickens in the 2014–2015 season, and most of the chickens they sold were broilers;[4] 32 per cent sold goats; 24 per cent had sold cattle. Only 2 per cent of the beneficiaries had sold a donkey. Livestock products like milk and eggs were sold by less than 10 per cent of the farmers.

As Goromonzi lies in a favourable agro-ecological region, beneficiaries are rarely pressed to sell their livestock in response to shocks and deprivation. The study noted that the sale of vegetables from the *bindu* is the immediate response of families to vulnerability and it is only when this option is not viable that they resort to selling livestock. In this way, livestock in the district has become a welfare instrument that beneficiaries use for temporary relief. It assists them to recover from emergencies. It is one of the production and social-protection outcomes of the FTLRP.

The FTLRP and Input Transfers

Social protection is seen by Devereux et al. (n.d.) as an essential public service that encompasses a broad range of functions. It provides direct support to help people deal with risk, vulnerability, exclusion, hunger and poverty. One major element of social protection is social transfers. The other elements are social legislation and social insurance, but it must be noted that these typologies are contested in the literature. Devereux et al. (n.d.: 1–2) define social transfers as:

> Non-contributory (in the sense that the recipient is not required to pay for them through premiums or specific taxes) social assistance provided by public and civic bodies to those living in poverty or in danger of falling into poverty.

Social transfers benefit the individual or household, they can be means-tested, community-targeted and geographically, categorically or self-targeted. They include cash, food or agricultural inputs (such as seeds or fertiliser, assets, tools or livestock). In Goromonzi, it was noted that the FTLRP has opened up channels through which social transfers in the form of agricultural inputs are being provided to A1 farmers. From a social policy perspective, Yi (2013) has argued that social transfers strengthen individual and social resilience as well as capabilities. They empower the weak and vulnerable and are a basis for equitable, democratic and sustainable growth. While social transfers exist in Goromonzi in the form of the Harmonised Social Cash Transfer (HSCT) scheme, they have excluded the beneficiaries of the FTLRP. According to the District Social Services Officer (Interview, 19 August 2015), beneficiaries of the FTLRP do not qualify under the HSCT as they have a productive resource (through land ownership), the household is usually not labour-constrained and in normal circumstances they do not qualify under the means test.

Although A1 beneficiaries are excluded from the HSCT scheme, they benefit from another social transfer programme, mainly the Presidential Input Scheme (although there are other initiatives by the government and NGOs which provide free or subsidised inputs). In the 2013 2014 season, the scheme managed to mobilise USD 252.3 million for A1, old resettlement, communal and small-scale farmers (Bankers Association of Zimbabwe, 2014). The programme has had its challenges, with the late disbursement of inputs being the major one. In Goromonzi, the Agricultural Extension Officer (Goromonzi South) indicated that all of the A1 farmers under his jurisdiction were registered under the input support scheme and were receiving 50 kilograms of fertiliser (compound D and ammonium nitrate) and seed maize, every season. He said the inputs were enough to cultivate at least 0.4 hectares of maize and, depending on farming methods, the weather and their dedication, they can harvest up to one tonne of maize. While the programme has its challenges, it can be argued that the provision of inputs and subsidies is aimed at building resilience, enhancing incomes and capabilities of the beneficiaries of the FTLRP. This view was corroborated by most of the responses from participants in all four FGDs with A1 beneficiaries, who said that the input scheme was particularly helpful for the poor peasants, even though inputs sometimes came late. They said that the inputs are always put to use either in that season or in the following one. In Moyo's (2011) tri-modal agrarian structure, the poor peasantry are the ones hardest hit by droughts and economic crisis. They are the farmers who benefit most from the protection function of the input programmes provided under the FTLRP.

Conclusion

This chapter has explored some of the social-policy outcomes of the FTLRP using the transformative social policy framework. It has focused on the redistribution and protection functions. Due to space constraints, it has not exhausted all aspects but has reported on the major outcomes, explored against the backdrop of the debates about the FTLRP. The chapter has shown that when we look at the emergent tri-modal agrarian structure that now exists in Zimbabwe, there are discernible reproduction and social protection outcomes. Land has been redistributed to people of diverse social classes and backgrounds, some of whom were previously landless, poor peasants. The FTLRP is shown as having impacted on residency and women's access to land, and this has presented new and unique dimensions to its redistributive nature. From a social-protection perspective, the FTLRP has impacted on shelter, with most of the beneficiaries now owning houses. Some practices that were found mostly in the communal areas are now seen in the farming areas too. This is exemplified by the *bindu* and the *dura* which serve important household protection functions. The use of livestock as social insurance and agricultural inputs can also be seen as a social transfer.

The issues discussed show the importance of the FTLRP as an alternative approach when dealing with development issues. It is an alternative to the largely residual and reductionist social policy approaches that have been dominant in the global South. It demonstrates that land reform as a social policy can be transformative and can be used to provide ex-ante social protection from vulnerability and be a stimulant for development.

Acknowledgements

This paper was made possible by funding from the SARChI Chair in Social Policy at the University of South Africa. Appreciation goes to Professor J. Adesina who has supervised this work which is part of my PhD thesis and he provided important insights, which have been included.

Notes

1. This is a model created by the FTLRP. It comprises a villagised settlement scheme in which the household is allocated 5–6 hectares of land. This type of settlement has a common grazing area just like villages in the communal areas. Alternatively, the A1 model is a self-contained variant in which farmers are allocated pieces of land on which they decide where to place the homestead and which areas will be for grazing and agriculture.
2. The SMAIAS Household Survey (2013–2014) is still to be published. It is a survey which was undertaken in six districts in Zimbabwe, namely: Goromonzi, Kwekwe, Chiredzi, Mangwe, Zvimba and Chipinge. It collected quantitative data on the new agrarian structure, characteristics of land beneficiaries, production

and land-use patterns, social institutions and organisation, legal documents in the farmers' possession, and other changes brought about by the emergent tri-modal agrarian structure.
3. Peasants are '… smallholders that work their land, individual plots of land as their principal source of income' Boltivinik (2010: 4). Differences of peasants are based on the labour they hire, sources of income and access to markets. Most peasants sell their labour to supplement income (Moyo and Yeros 2005; Bryceson 2000).
4. These are chickens which are domesticated and bred specifically for meat.

References

Adesina, J., 2004, In Search of Inclusive Development: Introduction, in Adesina, J., ed., *Social Policy in Sub-Saharan African Context: In Search of Inclusive Development*, Basingstoke: UNRISD/Palgrave Macmillan, pp. 1–53.

Adesina, J. O., 2009, Social Policy in Sub-Saharan Africa: A Glance in the Rear-View Mirror, *International Journal of Social Welfare,* Vol. 18, S37–S51.

Adesina, J. O., 2010, Return to a Wider Vision of Development: Social Policy in Reframing a New Agenda, Keynote address delivered at the 48th Session of the UN Commission for Social Development, 3 February, New York: United Nations.

Adesina, J., 2011, Beyond the Social Protection Paradigm: Social Policy in Africa's Development, *Canadian Journal of Development Studies / Revue Canadienne d'Études du Developpement*, Vol. 32, No. 4, pp. 454–470.

Adesina, J. O., 2014, Accounting for Social Policy: Reflections on Recent Developments in Sub-Saharan Africa, Paper prepared for the UNRISD Conference, New Directions in Social Policy: Alternatives From and For the Global South, 7–8 April 2014, Geneva: UNRISD. Available online at: http://www.unrisd.org/80256B3C005BCCF9/(httpAuxPages)/15F0DC9FE0A6AE8FC1257D07005D9C04/$file/Adesina.pdf. Accessed 12 October 2016.

Adesina, J. O., 2015, Return to a Wider Vision of Social Policy: Re-reading Theory and History, *South African Review of Sociology*, Vol. 46, No. 3, pp. 99–119. DOI: 10.1080/21528586.2015.1077588.

Alexander, J., 2006, *The Unsettled Land: State-Making and the Politics of Land in Zimbabwe, 1893-2003*, Harare: Weaver Press.

Amin, S., 1972, *Neocolonialism in West Africa*, Harmondsworth: Penguin.

Arrighi, G., 1973, The Political Economy of Rhodesia, in Arrighi G. and Saul, J. S., eds, *Essays on the Political Economy of Africa* New York: Monthly Review Press, pp. 336–77.

Bankers Association of Zimbabwe (BAZ), 2014, *Bankers Association of Zimbabwe Newsletter 2014*, Harare: BAZ.

Binswanger-Mkhize, H. and Moyo, S., 2012, *Zimbabwe: From Economic Rebound to Sustained Growth: Note II: Recovery and growth of Zimbabwe Agriculture*, Harare: World Bank Group.

Bond, P., 2008, Response to Lessons of Zimbabwe: An Exchange Between Patrick Bond and Mahmood Mamdani. Available online at: http://links.org.au/node/815/9693. Accessed 27 September 2017.

Bourdillon, M. F. C., 1992, *The Shona Peoples: An Ethnography of the Contemporary Shona*, Gweru: Mambo Press.

Bryceson, D., 2009, Sub-Saharan Africa's Vanishing Peasantries and the Specter of a Global Food Crisis, *Monthly Review*, Vol. 61, No. 3.

Chambati, W., 2013, *Agrarian Labour Relations in Zimbabwe After Over A Decade of Land and Agrarian Reform*, Brighton: Future Agriculture Consortium.

Chiweshe, M. K., 2011, Farm Level Institutions In Emergent Communities In Post Fast Track Zimbabwe: Case of Mazowe District, Unpublished PhD thesis, Rhodes University.

Chiweshe, M. K., Chakona, L. and Hellicker, K., 2015, Patriarchy, Women, Land and Livelihoods on A1 Farms in Zimbabwe, *Journal of Asian and African Studies*, Vol. 50, No. 6, pp. 716–731.

Chung, M. K., 2014, The Development of Transformative Social Policy in South Korea: Lessons from the Korean Experience, in Yi, I. and Mkandawire, T., eds, *Learning from the South Korean Developmental Success. Effective Developmental Cooperation and Synergistic Institutions and Policies*, New York: Palgrave MacMillan, pp. 108–135.

Cliffe, L., 1988, Zimbabwe's Agricultural 'Success' and Food Security in Southern Africa, *Review of African Political Economy*, Vol. 43, No. 2, pp. 4–25.

Cliffe, L., Alexander, J., Cousins, B. and Gaidzanwa, R., 2011, An Overview of the Fast Track Land Reform in Zimbabwe: Editorial Introduction, *Journal of Peasant Studies*, Vol. 38, No. 5, pp. 907–938.

Cousins, B., 2010, What is a 'Smallholder'? Class Analytical Perspectives on Small Scale Farming and Agrarian Reform in South Africa, PLAAS Working Paper No. 16, Cape Town: Institute for Poverty, Land and Agrarian Studies (PLAAS), University of Western Cape.

Creswell, J. W., 2003, *Research Design: Qualitative, Quantitative and Mixed Methods*, 2nd ed., London: Sage Publications.

Creswell, J. W. and Plano-Clark, V. L., 2011, *Designing and Conducting Mixed Methods Research*, 2nd ed., Thousand Oaks, CA: Sage.

De Soto, H., 2000, *The Mystery of Capital: Why Capitalism Triumphs in the West and Fails Everywhere Else*, New York: Basic Books.

Deininger, K. and Squire, L., 1998, New Ways of Looking at Old Issues: Inequality and Growth, *Journal of Development Economics*, Vol. 57, No. 2, pp. 259–287.

Dekker, M. and Kinsey, B., 2011, Contextualising Zimbabwe's Land Reform:Long Term Observations from the First Generation, Journal of Peasant Studies, Vol. 38, No. 5, pp. 995–1020.

Devereux, S., 2009, Seasonality and Social Protection in Africa, FAC Working Paper 11, Brighton: University of Sussex.

Devereux, S. et al., n.d., What are Social Transfers? Available online at https://europa.eu/capacity4dev/file/12912/download?token=McPvGtEc. Accessed 4 September 2017.

Devereux, S. and Sabates-Wheeler, R., 2004, Transformative Social Protection, IDS Working Paper 232, Brighton: IDS.

Dorward, A., Sabates-Wheeler, R., MacAuslan, I., Buckley, C. P., Kydd, J. and Chirwa, E., 2006, Promoting Agriculture for Social Protection or Social Protection for Agriculture: Strategic Policy and Research Issues, Food, Agriculture and

Natural Resources Policy Analysis Network Discussion Paper 004, Brighton: University of Sussex. Available online at https://citeseerx.ist.psu.edu/viewdoc/download?doi=10.1.1.359.5958&rep=rep1&type=pdf.

Esping-Andersen, G., 1990, *The Three Worlds of Welfare Capitalism*, Cambridge: Polity Press.

Gaidzanwa, R., 1994, Women's Land Rights in Zimbabwe, *Issue: A Journal of Opinion*, Vol. 22, No. 2, pp. 12–16.

Gaidzanwa, R., 2011. Women and Land in Zimbabwe, Paper presented at the conference: Why Women Matter in Agriculture, Stockholm, Sweden, 4–8 April 2011.

GoZ, 1981, *Intensive Resettlement Policies and Procedures*, Harare: Ministry of Lands and Rural Resettlement.

Hagenbuch, W., 1958, *Social Economics*, Welwyn: James Nisbet and Company, Ltd.

Hammar, A., Raftopolous, B. and Jensen, S., 2003, Introduction, in Hammar, A., Raftopolous, B. and Jensen, S., eds, *Zimbabwe's Unfinished Business: Rethinking State and Nation in the Context of Crises*, Harare: Weaver Press.

Hanlon, J., Manjengwa, J. and Smart, T., 2013, *Zimbabwe Takes Back Its Land*, Sterling, VA: Kumarian Press.

Holzman, R. and Kozel, V., 2007, The Role of Social Risk Management in Development: A World Bank View, *IDS Bulletin*, Vol. 38, No. 2, pp. 8–13.

James, G. D., 2015, Transforming Rural Livelihoods in Zimbabwe: Experiences of Fast Track Land Reform, 2000-2012, Unpublished PhD thesis, Edinburgh: University of Edinburgh.

Jacobs, S., 2010, *Gender and Agrarian Reforms*, New York and London: Routledge.

Manjengwa, P. and Mazhawidza, P., 2009, Gender Implications of Decentralised Land Reform: A Case of Zimbabwe, PLAAS Policy Brief 30, Cape Town: Institute for Poverty, Land and Agrarian Studies (PLAAS), University of Western Cape.

Marshall, T. H., 1950, *Citizenship and Social Class*, Cambridge, UK: Cambridge University Press.

Matondi, P., 2012, *Zimbabwe's Fast Track Land Reform*, London: Zed Books.

Mkandawire, T., 2001, Social Policy in a Development Context, Social Policy and Development Paper No. 25, Geneva: UNRISD.

Mkandawire, T., 2005, Maladjusted African Economies and Globalisation, *Africa Development*, Vol. 30, No. 1–2, pp. 1–33.

Mkandawire, T., 2007, Transformative Social Policy and Innovation in Developing Countries, *The European Journal of Development Research*, Vol. 19, No. 1, pp. 13–29.

Mkandawire, T., 2011, Welfare Regime and Economic Development: Bridging the Conceptual Gap, in: Fitzegerald, V., Heyer, J. and Thorp, R., eds, *Overcoming the Persistence of Poverty and Inequality*, Basingstoke: Palgrave MacMillan.

Mkodzongi, G., 2013, Fast Tracking Land Reform and Rural Livelihoods in Mashonaland West Province of Zimbabwe: Opportunities and Constraints 2000-2013, Unpublished PhD thesis, University of Edinburgh.

Moyo, S., 1995, *The Land Question in Zimbabwe*, Harare: Sapes Books.

Moyo, S., 2004, *The Overall Impacts of the Fast Track Land Reform Programme*, Harare: African Institute for Agrarian Studies.

Moyo, S., 2011, Land Concentration and Accumulation After Redistributive Reform in Post Settler Zimbabwe, *Review of African Political Economy*, Vol. 38, No. 128, pp. 257–276.

Moyo, S., 2013, Land Reform and Redistribution in Zimbabwe Since 1980, in Moyo S. and Chambati, W., eds, *Land and Agrarian Reform in Zimbabwe: Beyond White-settler Capitalism*, Dakar: CODESRIA, pp. 29–77.

Moyo, S., Chambati, W., Murisa, T., Siziba, D., Dangwa, C., Mujeyi, K. and Nyoni, N., 2009, *Fast Track Land Reform Baseline Survey in Zimbabwe: Trends and Tendencies 2005/06*, Harare: African Institute for Agrarian Studies.

Moyo, S. and Yeros, P., 2005, Land Occupations and Land Reform in Zimbabwe: Towards the National Democratic Revolution, in Moyo, S. and Yeros, P., eds, *Reclaiming the Land: The Resurgence of Rural Movements in Africa, Asia and Latin America*, London and Cape Town: Zed Books, pp. 165–208.

Murisa, T., 2009, An Analysis of Emerging Forms of Social Organisation and Agency in the Aftermath of 'Fast Track' Land Reform in Zimbabwe, Unpublished PhD thesis, Rhodes University.

Mutopo, P., 2011, Women's Struggles to Access and Control Land and Livelihoods after Fast Track Land Reform in Mwenezi District, Zimbabwe, *Journal of Peasant Studies*, Vol. 38, No. 5, pp. 1021–46.

Mutopo, P., Manjengwa, J. and Chiweshe, M. K., 2014, Shifting Gender Dimensions and Rural Livelihoods after Zimbabwe's Fast-Track Land Reform Programme, *Agrarian South: Journal of Political Economy*, Vol. 3, No. 1, pp. 45–61.

Myrdal, G., 1960, *Beyond the Welfare State: Economic Planning and its International Implications*, New Haven: Yale University Press.

Neocosmos, M., 1993, *The Agrarian Question in Southern Africa and 'Accumulation from Below'*, Uppsala: Nordic Africa Institute.

O'Laughlin, B., 1998, Missing men? The Debate Over Rural Poverty and Women-headed Households in Southern Africa, *The Journal of Peasant Studies*, Vol. 25, No. 2, pp. 1–48.

PLRC, 2003, Presidential Land Review Committee under the Chairmanship of Dr C. M. B. Utete, Vol. 1 Main Report and Vol. 2 Special Studies, Harare: Government Printers.

Prasad, N., Hypher, N. and Gerecke, M., 2013, *Seeing Big: Transformative Social Policies in Small States*, Geneva: UNRISD.

Raftopolous, B., 2003, Authoritarian Nationalism, Selective Citizenship and Distortions of Democracy in Zimbabwe, in Hammer, A., Raftopolous, B. and Jensen, S., eds, *Zimbabwe's Unfinished Business: Rethinking Land, State and Nation in the Context of Crises*, Harare: Weaver Press.

Richardson, C., 2005, Loss of Property Rights and the Collapse of Zimbabwe, *CATO Journal*, Vol. 25, No. 3, pp. 541–565.

Rutherford, B., 2003, Belonging to the Farm(er): Farm Workers, Farmers and the Shifting Politics of Citizenship, in Hammer, A., Raftopolous, B. and Jensen, S., eds, *Zimbabwe's Unfinished Business: Rethinking Land, State and Nation in the Context of Crises*, Harare: Weaver Press, pp. 191–216.

Rutherford, B., 2007, Shifting grounds in Zimbabwe: Citizenship and Farm Workers in the New Politics of Land, in Nugent, P., Hammett D. and Dorman, S., eds, *Making Nations, Creating Strangers: States and Citizenship in Africa*, Leiden: Brill Publishers, pp. 105–122.

Sacco, S., 2008, Human Rights and Land Reform: The Place of the Individual, in Moyo, S., Helliker, K. and Murisa, T., eds, *Contested Terrain—Land Reform and Civil Society in Contemporary Zimbabwe*, Pietermaritzburg and Harare: S &S Publishers and African Institute for Agrarian Studies, pp. 340-376.

Sachikonye, L. M., 2003, From Growth With Equity to Fast Track Reform: Zimbabwe's Land Question, *Review of African Political Economy*, Vol. 30, No. 96, pp. 227–240.

Sachikonye, L. M., 2004, The Promised Land: From Expropriation to Reconciliation and Jambanja, in Raftopolous, B. and Savage, T., eds, *Zimbabwe: Injustice and Political Reconciliation*, Cape Town: Institute for Justice and Reconciliation, pp. 1–18.

Sachikonye, L. M., 2005, The Land is the Economy: Revisiting the Land Question, *Africa Security Review*, Vol. 14, No. 3, pp. 31–44.

Sadomba, Z. W., 2008, War Veterans in Zimbabwe: Complexities of a Liberation Movement in an African Post-colonial Settler Society, Unpublished PhD thesis, Wagenigen University.

Sadomba, Z. W., 2013, A Decade of Zimbabwe's Land Revolution: The Politics of the War Veteran Vanguard, in Moyo, S. and Chambati, W., eds, *Land and Agrarian Reform in Zimbabwe: Beyond White Settler Capitalism*, Dakar and Harare: CODESRIA and African Institute for Agrarian Studies, pp. 79–122.

Scoones, I., 2015, Zimbabwe's Land Reform: New Political Dynamics in the Countryside, *Review of African Political Economy*, Vol. 42, No. 144, pp. 190–205.

Scoones, I., 2017a, Livelihoods, Land and Political Economy: Reflections on Sam Moyo's Research Methodology, *Agrarian South: Journal of Political Economy*, Vol. 5, No. 2–3, pp. 1–19.

Scoones, I., 2017b, How Persistent Myths Distort Policy Debate on Land in Zimbabwe, *zimbabweland*, 9 January 2017. Available online at https://zimbabweland.wordpress.com/2017/01/09/1892/. Accessed 8 August 2017.

Scoones, I., Marongwe, N., Mavedzenge, B. and Murambinda, F., 2010, *Zimbabwe's Land Reform: Myths and Realities*, Oxford: James Currey Press.

Scoones, I. et al., 2011, Zimbabwe's land reform: Myths and Realities, *Africa Today*, book review, Vol. 57, No. 4, pp. 125–129.

Soroka, E., 1997, The Politics of Preternatural Space at the Great Zimbabwe, Paper given at ACSA European Conference, Berlin, s.n.

Tapela, N., 2008, The African Granary as a Dying Symbol of Sustainable Rural Settlement: Food Security, Livelihood Sustainability and Environmental Adaptability, *Paradigms*, Issue 15, pp. 24–38.

Tashakkori, A. and Teddlie, C., 2010, *Mixed Methodology*, London: SAGE.

Titmus, R., 1974, *What is Social Policy?*, London: Allen and Unwin.

United Nations Research Institute for Social Development (UNRISD), 2001, *Social Policy in a Development Context*, Geneva: UNRISD.

United Nations Research Institute for Social Development (UNRISD), 2006. *Transformative Social Policy: Lessons from UNRISD Research*, Research and Policy Brief 5, Geneva: UNRISD.

Whitehead., A and Tsikata., D., 2003, Policy Discourses on Women's Land Rights in Sub-Saharan Africa: The Implications of the Re-turn to the Customary, *Journal of Agrarian Change*, Vol. 3, No. 1–2, pp. 67–112.

Worby, E., 2003, The End of Modernity in Zimbabwe? Passages from Development to Sovereignty, in Hammar, A., Raftopolous, B. and Jensen, S., eds, *Zimbabwe's Unfinished Business: Rethinking Land, State and Nation in the Context of Crisis*, Harare: Weaver Press, pp. 49–81.

Yawitch, J., 1981, *Betterment: The Myth of Homeland Agriculture*, Johannesburg: South African Institute of Race Relations.

Yi, I., 2013, Lessons of good social policy, *The Broker*, 4 March 2013. Available online at https://www.thebrokeronline.eu/lessons-of-good-social-policy-d34/. Accessed 5 September 2017.

Yi, I., 2015, New Challenges For and New Directions In Social Policy, Paper presented at Expert Group Meeting on the priority theme of the 53rd and 54th sessions of the Commission for Social Development, 19–20 May 2015, Geneva: UNRISD.

Yi, I. and Kim, T., 2015, Post 2015 Development Goals (SDGs) and Transformative Social Policy, *OUGHTOPIA: The Journal of Social Paradigm Studies*, Vol. 30, No. 1, pp. 307–335.

Zamchiya, P., 2011, A Synopsis of Land and Agrarian Change in Chipinge District, Zimbabwe, *The Journal of Peasant Studies*, Vol. 38, No. 5, pp. 1093–1122.

Zimbabwe National Statistics Agency (ZIMSTAT), 2012, Agriculture and Livestock Survey in A1 Farms 2012, Harare: Government of Zimbabwe.

Zimbabwe National Statistics Agency (ZIMSTAT), 2015, Agriculture and Livestock Survey in A1 Farms 2015, Harare: Government of Zimbabwe.

Zimbabwe National Statistics Agency (ZIMSTAT), 2016, Understanding Equality in Zimbabwe: Women and Men Report 2016, Harare: Government of Zimbabwe.

13

The Male Breadwinner Myth: The South African Case

Marlize Rabe

Introduction

Social policy is a broad term that covers a number of sectors and plays out differently in various localities. The different forms of social policy suggest that there is no singular mechanism, or proverbial silver bullet, that can address the wide variety of vulnerabilities and wishes of people. In response to the inequalities and poverty witnessed globally since the late 1980s, there has been a tendency for social-policy initiatives to focus on social protection in the form of cash transfers or safety nets. This social-policy approach originated in Western countries with specific entrenched cultural and social dynamics, but it also spread to developing countries (Kangas 2012). Holmes and Lwanga-Ntale (2012: 18–19) observed that different social-protection programmes are notable in different regions of Africa. For example, in Anglophone African countries, grants are the preferred option for dealing with disabled people, whereas in Francophone African countries, people with disabilities are integrated into special institutions that are subsidised. Other mechanisms are also discernible in dealing with poverty in North African countries where Islam is a dominant religion. Factors such as the colonial history and dominant religions may thus influence the type of social-protection systems the specific state in question undertakes.

In reaction to this narrow social-protection focus, the concept of transformative social policy was put forward to indicate that a far more extensive and collective approach is required to address the needs of people and develop a conducive environment for wellbeing. Thus, transformative social policy goes beyond 'destitution, vulnerability, and short-term risk analysis' but takes a more holistic approach (Adesina 2011). A transformative social policy has a wide range of focus areas, including production, protection, redistribution, reproduction and even social cohesion (Mkandawire 2007; Adesina 2010; Adesina 2011).

In line with this latter thinking on social policy, this chapter aims to explore some of the gendered implications of a transformative social policy at a collective level, especially as it applies to young and unemployed men. The gendered approach, rather than a family approach, is the focus here since gendered relations beyond (but not excluding) kin structures are of concern. In this way a restrictive discussion on an imagined 'caring traditional African extended family' that 'shaped the whole discussion of social security' in the mid-twentieth century (Ferguson 2015: 69) is avoided, since other insititutions are also under scrutiny here.

In South Africa, a country of soaring unemployment figures, men are still expected to be the primary breadwinners and are often blamed or ignored if they are not able to fulfil this role adequately. This perspective follows the narrow Western ideology of a heterosexual nuclear family, which portrays the mother as the primary caregiver and the father as the primary economic provider (Rabe 2017). It will be argued below that this emphasis on men as the breadwinner, an expectation that many men cannot meet, has serious implications for their gender identity (even their mental health) and undermines their potential role as active caretakers.

The first subsidiary aim of this chapter is to briefly assess the most visible South African social-policy interventions by the state to address inequality, namely social assistance grants (a form of redistribution and protection) and additional employment opportunities (trying to boost production). Although the South African government seems to to follow a gender-neutral approach in these policies, a consideration of the practices reveals a heavily gendered picture. It is important to further note that not only 'the state' and 'the individual' are involved in social policy, but a range of other 'non-state actors' (Holmes and Lwanga-Ntale 2012; Kangas 2012) and therefore a second subsidiary aim is to explore the contributing role of non-profit organisations (NPOs)[1] in the transformative social policy context. NPOs can play a positive role in the development and implementation of social policy, especially if they do not duplicate state services but rather augment them. The NPO sector is explored in this chapter by focusing on the work of one example, Sonke Gender Justice, concerned with, among other things, gendered caregiving. Issues related to social cohesion and reproduction are at stake here, but they are not disengaged from production or paid labour as is shown below in the discussion on socially constructed masculinities.

Unemployment and State Interventions in South Africa

Unemployment figures are alarmingly high in South Africa, with the overall official unemployment rate being 29.1 per cent in the fourth quarter of 2019 (StatsSA 2019: 2). The expanded unemployment rate, which includes people who have given up on seeking employment, is far more grim and was reported as 38.7 per cent in the fourth quarter of 2019[2] (StatsSA 2019: 7). An overview of the unemployment rate by sex in South Africa from 2011 to 2019 shows that a higher number of women were unemployed compared to men, and that there was a growing overall unemployment trend (StatsSA 2019: 11). Employment opportunities are thus increasingly hard to come by. Youth unemployment levels are of particular concern and the consequent high levels of frustration and impatience among the youth have been described as a ticking bomb (Steyn 2015; Graham and De Lannoy 2016; Naidoo and Hoque 2017). The unemployment figures from the fourth quarter of 2019 for South Africa reveal that 32 per cent of people between the ages of fifteen and twenty-four were not in employment, education or training (the so-called NEET category) (StatsSA 2019: 8). Similar figures were analysed according to race in the NEET category in 2017, which found that 9.9 per cent of white, 22.7 per cent of Indian/Asian, 35 per cent of coloured and 33.6 per cent of black young people were unemployed and not actively engaged in any form of formal training or education (StatsSA 2017: 10), indicating that racial inequalities were still at play.

In earlier research on the reasons why young people are not engaged in further education, family commitments and pregnancies were frequently cited as barriers by South African women, whereas men were more likely than women to indicate that they were working and therefore unable to continue their education (StatsSA 2013: 54). The fact that young men indicated work commitments as preventing them from further education or training opportunities is probably related to the informal sector, which 'refers to production and employment in unregistered enterprises' (Meagher 2013: 2). In South Africa this sector increased in numbers in 2017 (StatsSA 2017: 1) although there was a decline in the third quarter of 2019 (StatsSA 2019: 11). A robust informal sector has been observed in developing countries in general (Meagher 2013: 3). Both age and gender differences in employment, unemployment and education are thus discernible.

The main general responses in addressing the needs of the population by the South African state (specifically the ANC-led elected government in power since 1994) include giving more households access to piped water, sanitation and electricity; building houses; free basic schooling for children whose caregivers cannot afford to pay school fees (including no-fee schools in certain areas); and free health services to pregnant women and children under the age of six.

A more direct approach to addressing poverty is the targeted social assistance project and certain employment schemes. The former is far-reaching while the success of the employment schemes is in dispute (see also Patel 2014: 249). Although the targeted social assistance approach ensures tangible benefits in the short and medium term (for instance, in measurable improved child health) (Patel et al. 2017), it does not automatically lead to sustainable poverty reduction and may create a widening gap between wealthy and poorer residents—the opposite of social cohesion (Adesina 2007: 40). Clearly this approach has to be revisited as it is not sustainable in the long run.

The Scope of Social Assistance Grant Systems

South Africa has one of the most extensive state-supported social assistance grant systems in the world, with children (defined as people younger than eighteen years), the elderly (defined as people sixty years and older) as well as disabled people being the main individual recipients. In 2016–2017 it was reported that there were 16.5 million recipients of a social assistance grant in South Africa (Knijn and Patel 2017). Since the total population was calculated to be 51.77 million at the last census in 2011 (StatsSA 2012: 18), it means that roughly a third of individuals received a state-supported grant. Ferguson (2015: 10) regards this as part of 'a new politics of distribution', which acknowledges that large numbers of people simply do not have (and may never have) access to wage labour and hence there is a willingness to 'just give money to the poor'.

In some African countries, citizens who were previously employed in the formal sector can apply for short-term unemployment insurance from the state. Apart from the state, there is also formal financial assistance from the market (or private sector) to people who were formally employed for a number of years (see Kangas 2012 for an analysis of assistance from the state and the market in various African countries). Although financial assistance is always given to a specific individual, financial resources are shared with family members in a formal manner (for example, through private medical aid coverage) or an informal one (such as sharing the money from an old age pension).

Given this logic, Seekings and Moore (2013) analyse economic support in South Africa in more detail. They assert that if the South African population consists of roughly fifty million people, about twenty million are dependent children under the age of eighteen and three million are people over the age of sixty years without an income. Added to this are one million people between the ages of eighteen and sixty years who are either disabled or sick (including those affected by AIDS-related illnesses), and a further twelve million people are not employed (either voluntarily or involuntarily) and thus financially dependent on others. According to this calculation by the authors, only fourteen million people in South Africa are formally employed. Perhaps in recognising the scope of this dilemma and the exclusion of grants to able-bodied adults, other work-related initiatives were also introduced by the South African state.

Economic Initiatives

In order to address unemployment, from 2003 the South African government introduced initiatives such as the Expanded Public Works Programme (EPWP). Although the EPWP in South Africa was rolled out on a smaller scale than the grant system, it was envisaged that two million employment opportunities would be created annually in South Africa in order to redress inequality (National Planning Commission 2013: 154).

Hlatshwayo (2017) argues that the EPWP was implemented to address poverty in line with the Reconstruction and Development Programme (RDP) that was developed by the ANC-led government (later replaced by the Growth Employment and Redistribution Strategy). Bryce (2017) explains that the EPWP includes various sub-programmes, such as the Community Work Programme, which employs people for two days per week to do community-related work that is prioritised by the community. People can only work in the areas where they live and one of the aims is to make people feel like worthy members of their communities because they provide services to co-residents. More lofty expectations of these programmes are that they will contribute to violence prevention since they can potentially provide 'structure, meaning and dignity' to especially chronically unemployed people. Yet, research by the Centre for the Study of Violence and Reconciliation suggests that especially young men are not keen to take up these opportunities since they are not on par with their expectations. Even if they have no other options available, there are still reluctant to join these programmes (Bryce 2017).

Similar trends have been seen in developed countries (such as Japan and Germany) and developing countries (such as Nigeria and India), where young people were not interested in 'blue-collar artisanal trades' (Naidoo and Hoque 2017). Yet, according to South Africa's National Development Plan, 'EPWP has an important role to play but it cannot be the only instrument to address unemployment' and '[s]ocial protection is at the heart of reducing poverty and inequality' (National Planning Commission 2013: 382).

A more specific response to the high unemployment figures of young people is the Youth Wage Subsidy, or Employment Incentive Bill. This Bill offers a tax incentive to employers to employ young people with limited work experience (Naidoo and Hoque 2017). Although it was estimated that 423,000 new jobs would be created for young and less skilled people from 2011 to 2014 through this incentive, the net job creation was believed to be closer to 178,000 because young people would have been newly employed in this period regardless of the incentive (Steyn 2015). Steyn (2015) refers to different analyses of the youth wage subsidy, one of which found that the employment absorption rate for people between the ages of eighteen and twenty-four stayed at more or less 30 per cent in 2014. Another revealed that 183,000 jobs were created through this scheme since its inception, but most of these were in the agriculture and mining sectors and not did not necessarily meet the minimum requirements of employment. Another perspective is that workers in this age category lose jobs at the same rate as which jobs are found. Companies have thus become wary of spending time training young people who may resign before the companies can capitalise on their training. Mentoring is one factor that may play a role since adequate mentoring can be successful in training and retaining young employees, but in an insecure economic environment, older workers may be fearful of losing their own jobs and therefore reluctant to provide adequate mentoring (Naidoo and Hoque 2017).

Since these state-led opportunities mainly target people with low skill levels, they may not be sustainable since the current labour market in South Africa is geared towards highly skilled employees. Advanced technological skills are required while labour-intensive agriculture is on the decline (Graham and De Lannoy 2016). It is thus not surprising that South Africans without a matric certificate (successful completion of Grade 12) have by far the highest unemployment levels (34.6 per cent), especially when compared with graduates (7.6 per cent) (StatsSA 2019: 12).

Graham and De Lannoy (2016) suggest practical steps to address unemployment among the youth, such as employers revisiting their employment criteria (for example, a cashier does not really require a matric certificate), addressing spatial barriers for job-seeking by providing a transport subsidy for job-seekers, assisting with information and not assuming that all young people are lazy and feel entitled. Although these suggestions seem practical, there is a persistent belief that social grants create an entitlement mentality among young people. Yet, research on young people undergoing artisan training at a particular company showed that those who gain full-time employment shared certain characteristics, such as self-motivation, taking on difficult tasks and accepting responsibility for mistakes. In other words, the work ethic of the individual is also crucial (Naidoo and Hoque 2017).

Despite all the above efforts, there is a general belief that the high unemployment rates in South Africa (and elsewhere) will continue for some time to come. In fact, there is a more pessimistic (or realistic) view that the idea of continuous economic growth cannot be attained (Ferguson 2015) and should not even be strived for since it is built on the illusion that the growth economy is desirable. In reality, the neoliberal economic growth we have become accustomed to has a negative impact on environmental resources by slowly obliterating the natural resources many Africans depend on, and hence, it ultimately affects people's wellbeing negatively (Fioramonti 2017). Given these realities, a gendered analysis of accessing and using limited resources follows.

Masculinities

The high incidence of gender-based violence with men as perpetrators (Van den Berg et al. 2013), the high incarceration rates of men (Department of Correctional Services 2019: 47) and their poorer performance in education compared to women (among other factors) are often linked to the shrinking roles of men and suggest an urgent revisit of the 'African masculinities in crisis' discourse. Masculinity studies (including a specific focus on African men) have grown exponentially in the last three decades (see, for example, Everitt-Penhale and Ratele 2015; Langa 2020; Van den Berg and Makusha 2018) and the power hierarchies between men have been well documented (see, for example, Morrell, Jewkes and Lindegger 2012). But social policy documents focusing on poor and vulnerable groups of men (including perpetrators of violence) and their coping mechanisms have been more elusive. However, it is clear that whether men are employed, unemployed or underemployed, they have fewer relational responsibilities than women. In other words, men do less care work and if they do care work, they struggle to reconcile it with their masculine identity (Reddy, Meyer, Shefer and Meyiwa 2014; Dworzanowski-Venter 2017).

Employment

As stated above, there has been general pessimism about the notion of economic growth in recent times and the precariousness of waged work has long been a point of discussion. There is general consensus that especially unskilled and semi-skilled employment are at risk as increasing technological development ensures growing mechanisation. Processes such as privatisation, restructuring and downsizing are intensified by globalisation, and all employment sectors, but especially manufacturing, agriculture and mining, are affected by them (Rabe 2006: 73–74; Ferguson 2015: 4; Graham and De Lannoy 2016). Young people, and men with low skill levels, are therefore commonly excluded from secure employment.

Concomitantly, adults (especially men) are expected to have paid employment or some form of stable income. The targeted approach to poverty by the South African government, which excludes healthy able-bodied men and women between the ages of eighteen and sixty from social assistance grants, clearly illustrates this notion. If such adults do not have (or recently had) paid employment and they live in households where children or the elderly are recipients of the grants, they inadvertently become dependent on those who receive the grants. Since grant money is shared in poor households, dependents—as defined by the state—become 'income earners' and able-bodied adults become their financial dependents.

A few qualitative studies in poor regions show that families or other household members expect adult women to earn money in some way (Wright, Noble and Ntshongwana 2014) and that women also want this for themselves (Hochfeld and Plagerson 2011). However, the male breadwinner ideology has been found to be particularly pervasive (see Rabe 2016). Although a large number of men are unable to fulfil the breadwinner role satisfactorily, they face:

> a value system associated with industrial capitalism in which it is socially demeaning for adult men to be dependent on anyone but themselves while it is socially acceptable for women, children, and the aged to be dependent on male kinsmen or on state benefits. This value system perpetuates both gender inequality and the criminalization of the long-term employed. (Ferguson 2015)

Ferguson (2015: 43) expands that if men were to be given a grant 'they might be in this way rendered "dependent" [which] is threatening to a certain imagination of masculinity within which "independence" and "autonomy" are the very ground and guarantor of male power'.

Although certain men ostentatiously have disproportionate amounts of wealth in South Africa, this wealth is by no means the norm. Given the discussed high unemployment rate in South Africa, the difficulties experienced in the informal sector and the restricted access to arable land, it can be said that both the market and the state have failed many men.

Care Work

Care work, regardless of the nature or type, is dominated by women the world over (Reddy et al. 2014: 3) and has even been described as a 'woman-specific concept' (Daly and Lewis 2000: 283), and South Africa is no exception (Rabe 2017). Despite the development of masculinity studies, male care work has still not received much attention.

Prior to the colonial period, older African men passed on collective understandings of masculine identities to younger men, especially during the teenage years. Due to the huge impact of the mining sector in southern Africa, much of this learning of masculinity was relocated to the mining premises where men lived for increasingly longer periods (Harries 1994: 157–158). Consequently, young men became detached from their fathers but also from other adult male members of the family and eventually also from other male role models, such as teachers, due to poor educational environments with very few male teachers (Delius and Glaser 2002). In southern Africa, the eroding relationships between men and their families meant that older men increasingly could no longer play a guiding and caring role, and if they could not be financial providers either, they had almost nothing left to tie them to their families (Rabe 2006). It is therefore not surprising that if women are the recipients of individual grants (such as the old age grant), they are more likely to reduce household poverty (Burns, Keswell and Leibbrandt 2005). What is then expected of men?

MenCare, a global fatherhood initiative co-ordinated by Promundo and Sonke Gender Justice, reports a particularly insightful research finding from the Democratic Republic of Congo (2015: 20). It was found that women's caregiving roles help them to 'endure the negative effects of war' while men resort to destructive behaviour such as drinking instead of seeking help. In the State of Africa's Fathers report (which included a multi-site survey and qualitative interviews), it was found that involved fathers are more likely than other men to cope with adverse circumstances and influence those around them positively. In certain cases, men's lack of intimate social ties (which grow from caring for others) leads to self-harming, but it may also be negative for those with whom they interact. Self-harm can range from active practices, such as alcohol and substance abuse, to passive practices, such as neglecting one's health (Slegh, Barker and Levtov 2014).

In the Africa's Fathers report, three main reasons are cited for why fathers do not share care work in the home:

1. Gender socialisation that perpetuates the notion of caregiving being 'women's work';
2. The realities in the economic sphere which assumes a 'traditional' division of labour; and,
3. Policies that reiterate the unequal distribution of caregiving (MenCare 2015: 20).

The above aspects point to restrictive masculine constructions that inhibit men from forming close social ties with family members and engaging in care work for kin members. When men are employed as caregivers, many of them regard such work as more ideal for women and some want to move on to more 'important' positions or careers (Dworzanowski-Venter 2017; Morrell and Jewkes 2014). Yet, if masculine roles become more equitable, expressive and respectful, the lives of men, women and children improve (Van den Berg et al. 2013). In sum, many men are denied economic opportunities, and through narrow gender socialisation practices they are also prevented from embracing caregiving and hence seldom see it as part of their core identity.

Non-Profit Organisational Interventions

In essence, social policy should enhance the wellbeing or quality of life of individuals and communities. Of course, such aspects always have objective and subjective criteria. If we focus on a specific aspect of social policy, such as care, it becomes clear that the term is complicated in theory and in practice since the state, the family, the market and communities (or non-profit organisations) are all involved in providing forms of social and economic assistance. Razavi (2014: 40) explains the interconnectedness between these four sectors as a 'care diamond'. In certain countries the state may provide free care for different categories of people (for example, state-funded early childhood centres and institutional care for severely disabled people), but in other countries citizens have to either pay for care (the market) or provide it themselves (usually through kin structures). Ochiai (2009), for example, compares six East Asian countries in terms of caregiving for children and older people as provided by the four sectors in the care diamond. The author reports notable variations between the countries, such as state support, which predominates in Japan and China, and market caregiving, which is prevalent in Taiwan and South Korea. In South Africa, the relationship between the family, the state and the market has received a lot of attention in relation to care work (see, for example, Seekings and Moore 2013; Reddy et al. 2014; Button, Moore and Seekings 2018). However, the role of the NPO sector has been much less studied (Patel 2014),[3] and this sector is also neglected in the policy sector in general.

There are hundreds of non-profit organisations registered in South Africa, the majority of them involved in social services, culture and recreation, development and housing projects (Patel 2014: 250). Patel (2014: 252–253) identifies four different types of NPOs, namely:

1. Formal public service contractors who provide services on behalf of the state;
2. Donor-funded NPOs who may have greater autonomy than the former to determine their activities;
3. Faith-based organisations who are mainly funded by religious bodies; and,
4. Community-based organisations who are usually informally organised and not registered, and hence rely on unpaid volunteers to execute their activities.

The NPO type that is of interest here is the donor-funded type, since they have little or no direct control from the state and are fairly structured. Meagher (2013: 25–26) cautions, in relation to the linkages between the formal and informal economic sectors, that NGOs (or NPOs) can be 'agents of the state or of international economic interests'. Indeed, similar to the state, donors may also dictate to NPOs, but many NPOs may have a number of donors who usually wish to support their aims. In addition, these NPOs are usually registered and have some degree of formalisation. South Africa also has an active civil society in which the NPO sector often plays a substantial role, such as the well-known and historically entrenched Black Sash (founded in 1955), which fought against apartheid and then continued the struggle against poverty and inequality after the first democratic election in 1994 (Black Sash 2017). Other examples include the Treatment Action Campaign (founded in 1998), which focuses on access to public healthcare in South Africa, especially for HIV and tuberculosis (Treatment

Action Campaign 2017) and the faith-based NPO, Gift of the Givers Foundation (founded in 1992) which is best known for the disaster relief they provide.[4] These and other NPOs are engaged in practical strategies to improve the quality of life for others. Occasionally, their activist work challenges the state, but in addition, their practical support to individuals and communities supplements the care work of the state and kin networks. Such NPOs thus fulfil a unique task in society.

I want to highlight the NPO Sonke Gender Justice here, since they focus much of their work on the gendered lives of men. Their aims include advocacy activities (to influence specific social policy aspects) as well as doing the groundwork to change perceptions and gendered practices through face-to-face interventions. Sonke Gender Justice, founded in 2006, is an NPO with five regional offices in South Africa (Cape Town, Johannesburg, Bushbuckridge, Diepsloot and Gugulethu), whose activities and programmes reach twenty African countries. The organisation's self-description is:

> Sonke works to create the change necessary for men, women, young people and children to enjoy equitable, healthy and happy relationships that contribute to the development of just and democratic societies. Sonke pursues this goal across Southern Africa by using a human rights framework to build the capacity of government, civil-society organisations and citizens to achieve gender equality, prevent gender-based violence (GBV) and reduce the spread of HIV and the impact of AIDS. (Sonke Gender Justice 2016: 5)

Their day-to-day activities include:

> a broad mix of social change strategies, reaching nearly 25,000 men each year through workshops and community dialogues, nearly ten million listeners a week via community radio shows, and millions more as a result of media coverage of high-profile advocacy work to effect change in government policies and practice (Van den Berg et al. 2013).

One of their aims is to promote gender equitable relations and engage men in positive parenting. Initiatives such as One Man Can (Van den Berg et al. 2013) and the Men Engage Alliance (Sonke Gender Justice 2016) are aimed at encouraging men to speak up against violence against women, and being activists in preventing the spread of HIV. The organisation casts itself as a feminist movement with almost 50 per cent female employees at all levels and seeking out and working with women-led women's rights organisations (Van den Berg et al. 2013).

Sonke Gender Justice's electronic communications include a website with a number of summaries, pamphlets, videos and links to social media platforms (Sonke Gender Justice 2020).[5] They also engage in activist and legal work with various civil society groups, for example the Silicosis Class Action settlement agreement, which focused on mineworkers who contracted silicosis and were sent home without compensation for them or their families. They have also lobbied for paternal leave in South Africa, which was finally promulgated in November 2017 under the Labour Relations Amendment Bill, 2017.

One of the prominent aims of Sonke Gender Justice is a focus on positive parenting. Fathering practices, improved communication with children, different discipline strategies (especially alternatives to corporal punishment) and socialising children to share household responsibilities in an equitable manner are changes that the One Man Can workshops aim for. These aims are not easily attained, as men find it difficult to act differently in front of other men since their view of being a provider rather than caregiver is very narrow and difficult to overcome. It is noteworthy that older men are more likely to make changes compared to younger men (Van den Berg et al. 2013).

Highlighting how a NPO can change the way in which men engage with others in their daily lives shows how difficult it is to change entrenched norms and practices. However, if NPOs are not contributing to such changes, gender equity may never be reached, since, in countries with high inequality (such as South Africa), the state has the capacity to intervene only in extreme cases. Gendered socialisation is entrenched in family rituals and hence alternative gender roles change slowly within kin structures. NPOs are thus important organisations to initiate alternative gender practices.

Conclusion

In this chapter, I indicated the huge unemployment reality in South Africa, which is not going to change in the near future. Young people and unskilled people are especially affected. Despite specific state efforts to employ unskilled and inexperienced people, the uptake by young men in particular is slow since unskilled work does not meet the expectations all young men have of their future. However, it cannot be concluded that all young men have notions of entitlement, since many young people are willing to take up lowly paid employment if structural barriers are removed.

Simultaneous to persistent unemployment, there is an entrenched norm in society that men should be the breadwinners. Although there are also indications that it is increasingly expected from women to be providers, men's identity is often closely associated with their ability to earn an income, an expectation which is shared by men, women and children. Since the economic landscape makes financial contributions from many men impossible, it has a negative effect on their self-esteem. Compared to women, men are not nearly as involved or focused on taking care of family members or doing paid care work. If they do care work, they often see it as 'beneath' their status.

The majority of men do not qualify for any kind of social assistance grant in South Africa and in very poor households where nobody earns wages, they inadvertently become dependent on others who do qualify for grants. Even in cases where men and women qualify for grants, as in the case of people over the age of sixty years, women are better able or likely than men to share their grants with others in such a way as to alleviate poverty more effectively. On the other end of the spectrum, men who are high-income earners are held in high regard and are not necessarily expected to contribute any further support to the household.

Within this social realm, the NPO Sonke Gender Justice does groundwork in changing attitudes. Their work includes targeting social policies to, for example, qualify men for paternity leave. Even more challenging is changing the views of men about physical and emotional care work on a daily basis. The benefits of getting men involved in caring include greater gender equality. Just as importantly, providing care helps men to have fulfilled and satisfying relationships. This type of groundwork in changing perceptions and actions is essential if we want societies in which men can feel proud of themselves regardless of the size of their income. A transformative social policy must include more equitable gender relationships. An NPO such as Sonke Gender Justice is one of the few bodies actively working towards such greater gender equality in Africa by focusing on changing the behaviour of men and hence this sector requires more recognition in the transformative social policy discourse.

Notes

1. In South Africa the Non-profit Organisations Act (No. 71 of 1997) implies certain advantages when registering as an NPO (Patel 2014: 250) and hence the term Non-government Organisation (NGO) is rarely used. Also, since NPOs can and often do apply for government funding, NPO is a more suitable term since there is a relationship between the government and certain NPOs in terms of funding and legislation that is obscured by the term NGO.
2. Due to the lockdown regulations following the Covid-19 pandemic, it has been difficult to compare unemployment figures from 2020 with previous trends (StatsSA, 2020), hence the latest 2019 figures were used.
3. In the care diamond literature, communities and NPOs are sometimes used interchangeably and in certain countries the one term is preferred above the other. Clearly, there is a difference in that NPOs are usually, but not necessarily, more structured and specific in their aims. Communities are far more general in nature and community-based approaches may be seen as more 'traditional' (see for example Holmes and Lwanga-Ntale, 2012: 5). In countries where there is not a large NPO sector, communities may fulfil the role of NPOs, especially in smaller rural areas. The overlap and possible tensions between NPOs and communities require more systematic analysis than is possible here.
4. See https://giftofthegivers.org.
5. See https://genderjustice.org.za/.

References

Adesina, J. O., 2007, In Search of Inclusive Development: Introduction, in Adesina J. O., ed., *Social Policy in sub-Saharan Context*, Basingstoke: UNRISD/Palgrave Macmillan, pp. 1–53).

Adesina, J. O., 2010, Rethinking the Social Protection Paradigm: Social Policy in Africa's Development, Paper prepared for the conference Promoting Resilience through Social Protection in Sub-Saharan Africa, European Report on Development, Dakar, Senegal, 28–30 June 2010. Available online at http://erd.eui.eu/media/BackgroundPapers/Adesina.pdf.

Adesina, J. O., 2011, Beyond the Social Protection Paradigm: Social Policy in Africa's Development, *Canadian Journal of Development Studies / Revue Canadienne d'Études du Developpement*, Vol. 32, No. 4, pp. 454–470.

Black Sash, 2017, Black Sash. Making Human Rights Real. Retrieved from https://www.blacksash.org.za/.

Bryce, D., 2017, Structural Youth Unemployment Solutions Require New Thinking and New Institutions, *Mail & Guardian*, 26 June. Available online at https://mg.co.za/article/2017-06-26-00-structural-youth-unemployment-solutions-require-new-thinking-and-new-institutions.

Burns, J., Keswell, M. and Leibbrandt, M., 2005, Social Assistance, Gender and the Aged in South Africa, *Feminist Economics*, Vol. 11, No. 2, pp. 103–115.

Button, K., Moore, E. and Seekings, J., 2018, South Africa's Hybrid Care Regime: The Changing and Contested Roles of Individuals, Families and The State After Apartheid, *Current Sociology*, Vol. 66, No. 4, pp. 602–616. DOI:10.1177/0011392118765243.

Connell, R., 1995, *Masculinities,* Cambridge, UK: Polity Press.

Daly, M. and Lewis, J., 2000, The Concept of Social Care and the Analysis of Contemporary Welfare States, *British Journal of Sociology*, Vol. 51, No. 2, pp. 281–298.

Delius, P. and Glaser, C., 2002, Sexual Socialisation in South Africa: A Historical Perspective, *African Studies*, Vol. 61, No. 1, pp. 27–54.

Department of Correctional Services, 2019, Annual Report 2018/2019. Available online at http://www.dcs.gov.za/wp-content/uploads/2019/12/DCS-Annual-Report-_web-version.pdf.

Dworzanowski-Venter, B., 2017, An Intersectional Analysis of Male Caregiving in South African Palliative Care, *Agenda: Empowering Women for Gender Equity*, Vol. 31, No.1, pp. 78–90.

Everitt-Penhale, B. and Ratele, K., 2015, Rethinking 'Traditional Masculinity' as Constructed, Multiple, and ≠ Hegemonic Masculinity, *South African Review of Sociology*, Vol. 46, No. 2, pp. 4–22.

Ferguson, J., 2015, *Give a Man a Fish: Reflections on the New Politics of Distribution*, The Lewis Henry Morgan Lectures, Durham, NC: Duke University Press.

Fioramonti, L., 2017, *Wellbeing Economy—Success in a World Without Growth*, Johannesburg: Pan Macmillan.

Goldblatt, B., 2005, Gender and Social Assistance in the First Decade of Democracy: A Case Study of South Africa's Child Support Grant, *Politikon: South African Journal of Political Studies*, Vol. 32, No. 2, pp. 239–257.

Graham, L. and De Lannoy, A., 2016, Youth Unemployment: What Can We Do in the Short Run?, *Polity.Org* 13 December 2016. Available online at. https://www.polity.org.za/article/youth-unemployment-what-can-we-do-in-the-short-run-2016-12-13.

Harries, P., 1994, *Work, Culture and Identity. Migrant Laborers in Mozambique and South Africa, 1860-1910*, Portsmouth, NH: Heinemann.

Hlatshwayo, H., 2017, The Expanded Public Works Programme: Perspectives of Direct Beneficiaries, *The Journal for Transdisciplinary Research in Southern Africa*, Vol. 13, No. 1. DOI: https://doi.org/10.4102/td.v13i1.439.

Hochfeld, T. and Plagerson, S., 2011, Dignity and Stigma Among South African Female Cash Transfer Recipients, *IDS Bulletin*, Vol. 42, No. 6, pp. 53–59.

Holmes, R. and Lwanga-Ntale, C., 2012, *Social Protection in Africa: A Review of Social Protection Issues in Research*, Nairobi: Partnership for African Social and Governance Research.

Kangas, O., 2012, Testing Old Theories in New Surroundings: The Timing of First Social Security Laws in Africa, *International Social Security Review*, Vol. 65, No.1, pp. 73–97.

Knijn, T. and Patel, L., 2017, Family Life and Family Policy in South Africa: Responding to Past Legacies, New Opportunities and Challenges, in Rostgaard, T. and Eydal, G. B., eds, *Family Life and Family Policy in South Africa: Dealing with the Legacy of Apartheid and Responding to New Opportunities and Challenges*, Cheltenham: Edward Elgar Publishing.

Langa, M., 2020, *Becoming Men: Black Masculinities in a South African Township*, Johannesburg: Wits University Press.

Manderson, L. and Block, E., 2016, Relatedness and Care in South Africa and Beyond, *Social Dynamics*, Vol. 42, No. 2, pp. 205–217.

Meagher, K., 2013, *Unlocking the Informal Economy: A Literature Review on Linkages Between Formal And Informal Economies in Developing Countries*, WIEGO Working Paper No 27, Cambridge, MA and Manchester: WIEGO.

MenCare, 2015, *The State of Africa's Fathers: A MenCare Advocacy Publication*. Available online at https://bettercarenetwork.org/sites/default/files/State%20of%20Africa's%20Fathers%202015.pdf

Mkandawire, T., 2007, Transformative Social Policy and Innovation in Developing Countries, *The European Journal of Development Research*, Vol. 19, No. 1, pp. 13–29.

Morrell, R. and Jewkes, R., 2014, 'I Am a Male, Although I Am a Little Bit Soft': Men, Gender and Care Work in South Africa, in Reddy, V., Meyer, S., Shefer, T. and Meyiwa, T., eds, *Care in Context: Transnational Gender Perspectives*, Cape Town: HSRC Press, pp. 326–341.

Morrell, R., Jewkes, R. and Lindegger, G., 2012, Hegemonic Masculinity/Masculinities in South Africa: Culture, Power and Gender Politics, *Men and Masculinities*, Vol. 15, No. 1, pp. 11–30.

Naidoo, M. and Hoque, M. E., 2017, Reducing Youth Unemployment Beyond the Youth Wage Subsidy: A Study of Simtech Apprentices, *SA Journal of Human Resource Management*, Vol. 1, pp. 1–10.

National Planning Commission, 2013, *National Development Plan 2030. Our Future—Make It Work*, Pretoria: The Presidency, Republic of South Africa.

Ochiai, E., 2009, Care Diamonds and Welfare Regimes in East and South-East Asian Societies: Bridging Family and Welfare Sociology, *International Journal of Japanese Sociology*, Vol. 18, No. 1, pp. 60–78.

Patel, L., 2014, Gender and Care in the Non-Profit Sector in South Africa: Implications for Welfare Policy, in Reddy, V., Meyer, S., Shefer, T. and Meyiwa, T., eds, *Care in Context: Transnational Gender Perspectives*, Cape Town: HSRC Press, pp. 246–264.

Patel, L., Knijn, T., Gorman-Smith, D., Hochfeld, T., Isserow, M., Garthe, R., ... Kgaphola, I., 2017, *Family Contexts, Child Support Grants and Child Well-Being in South Africa*, Programme to Support Pro-Poor Policy Development, Centre for Social Development in Africa, University of Johannesburg.

Rabe, M., 2006, Black Mineworkers' Conceptualisations of Fatherhood. A Sociological Exploration in the South African Goldmine Industry, PhD Thesis, University of South Africa, Pretoria.

Rabe, M., 2016, Revisiting the Gendered Discourse on Parenting in South Africa, in Makiwane, M., Nduna, M. and Khalema, N. E., *Children in South African Families. Lives and Times*, Newcastle upon Tyne: Cambridge Scholars Publishing, pp. 116–138.

Rabe, M., 2017, Family Policy for All South African Families, *International Social Work*, Vol. 60, No. 5, 1189–1200.

Razavi, S., 2014, Revisiting the UNRISD Research on the Political and Social Economy of Care: Implications for Future Research and Policy, in Reddy, V., Meyer, S., Shefer, T. and Meyiwa, T., eds, *Care in Context: Transnational Gender Perspectives*, Cape Town: HSRC Press, pp. 32–51.

Reddy, V., Meyer, S., Shefer, T. and Meyiwa, T., 2014, Towards a Critical Theory of Care, in Reddy, V., Meyer, S., Shefer, T. and Meyiwa, T., eds, *Care in Context: Transnational Gender Perspectives*, Cape Town: HSRC Press, pp. 1–27.

Seekings, J. and Moore, E., 2013, *Kin, Market and State in the Provision of Care in South Africa*, Working Paper for Centre for Social Science Research, University of Cape Town.

Slegh, H., Barker, G. and Levtov, R., 2014, Gender Relations, Sexual and Gender-Based Violence and the Effects of Conflict on Women and Men in North Kivu, Eastern Democratic Republic of the Congo, Results from the International Men and Gender Equality Survey, Final Report, Washington, DC: Promondo and Sonke Gender Justice.

Sonke Gender Justice, 2016, Sonke Annual Report, March 2015–February 2016, Celebrating 10 Years of Advancing Gender Justice. Available online at https://genderjustice.org.za/publication/sonke-annual-report-2015-2016/.

Sonke Gender Justice, 2020, Retrieved from http://www.genderjustice.org.za/.

StatsSA, 2012, Census 2011, Census in Brief, Report No. 03-01-41, Pretoria: Statistics South Africa.

StatsSA, 2013, *Gender Report,* Pretoria: Statistics South Africa.

StatsSA, 2019, Quarterly Labour Force Survey, Quarter 4: 2019 P0211, Pretoria: Statistics South Africa.

StatsSA, 2020, Quarterly Labour Force Survey Quarter 2: 2020 P0211, Pretoria: Statistics South Africa.

Steyn, L., 2015, Analysts Split over Wage Subsidy, *Mail & Guardian* 27 November. Available online at https://mg.co.za/article/2015-11-27-00-analysts-split-over-wage-subsidy.

Surender, R., Noble, M., Wright, G. and Ntshongwana, P., 2010, Social Assistance and Dependency in South Africa: An Analysis of Attitudes to Paid Work and Social Grants, *Journal of Social Policy*, Vol. 39, No. 2, 203–221.

Treatment Action Campaign, 2017, *TAC. Working for Access to Quality Public Healthcare in South Africa*. Available online at https://tac.org.za/.

Van den Berg, W., Hendricks, L., Hatcher, A., Peacock, D., Godana, P. and Dworkin, S., 2013, 'One Man Can': Shifts in Fatherhood Beliefs and Parenting Practices Following a Gender-Transformative Programme in Eastern Cape, South Africa, *Gender and Development*, Vol. 21, No. 1, pp. 111–125.

Van den Berg, W. and Makusha, T., 2018, *State of South Africa's Fathers 2018*, Cape Town: Sonke Gender Justice and Human Sciences Research Council.

Wright, G., Noble, M. and Ntshongwana, P., 2014, The Impact of Poverty and Inequality on the Dignity of Lone Mothers in South Africa, Department of International Development Working Paper, DFID/ESRC. Available online at https://opendocs.ids.ac.uk/opendocs/handle/20.500.12413/11978.

14

Does How We Measure and Explain Income Inequality Make a Difference for Social Policy? A Case Study of Kenya

Boaz Munga

Introduction
Background of the Study

As part of informing various aspects of social policy, there has been increasing interest in measuring and examining inequality at global, regional and national levels. With respect to the measurement of the level of inequality in Africa, there are several studies that have estimated inequality levels at a point in time or across time. Most of them have generally focused on the Gini index as a measure of inequality. Among those that have studied inequality in Kenya are Bigsten (1986), World Bank (2009) and Bigsten, Manda, Mwabu and Wambugu (2014).

The analysis of inequality is predicated on its possible negative impacts on development objectives, such as the attainment of high economic growth rates. With respect to its direct impacts, an increase in the Gini index has been found to reduce the growth rate in poor countries but is good for growth in richer countries (Birdsall 2007; Barro 2008).[1] The negative association between disparities and growth is thought to emerge at high levels of inequality. Among its indirect impacts, high inequality may undermine economic growth through stifling human capital investments (Galor and Zeira 1993; Romer 1994; Aghion, Caroli and Garcia-Peñalosa 1999). High income inequality may also fuel a propensity for populist redistributive policies, a greater volatility of policies, and a greater likelihood of sociopolitical unrest and instability—all of which may undermine physical investment and economic growth (Alesina and Perotti 1996; Benhabib and Rustichini 1996; Odedokun and Round 2004).

These findings, among others, suggest that reducing income inequality may lead to better socioeconomic performance.

Besides the Gini index, examples of other measures of inequality include the Atkinson index, the Generalised Entropy (GE) indices, and decile ratios.[2] The Gini index, which varies from 0 (no inequality) to 1 (perfect inequality), is perhaps the most popular measure. The Atkinson index is an attempt to improve on the weaknesses of the Gini; it too varies between 0 (no inequality) and 1. Unlike the Gini index, the Atkinson index allows for varying sensitivity by introducing a sensitivity parameter or income aversion parameter, commonly denoted by epsilon (ε) (Xu 2003; Araar 2006). The GE indices also incorporate sensitivity parameters, denoted by theta (θ), which typically vary from 1 to 2 in most studies. When the sensitivity parameter (theta) is equal to 1, the measure is equally sensitive to changes across the distribution, and when theta is close to 0, these measures are sensitive to changes at the lower tail of the distribution. Higher values of the parameter are associated with more sensitivity of the index at the top of the income distribution (Litchfield 1999; Xu 2003).

Using Kenya as a case study, this chapter seeks to demonstrate that the use of one measure of inequality may fail to adequately inform social-policy prescriptions on inequality. The study also assesses the potential value of a concomitant examination of the determinants of inequality on social-policy recommendations.

Objectives of the Study

The overall objective of this study is to trace how income inequality has evolved in Kenya in the recent past to compare what is known vis-à-vis what emerges using various measures. The specific objectives are to:

1. Estimate the levels of income inequality among Kenyan households over time using various inequality measures;
2. Decompose the total income inequality by population subgroups; these include region and education;
3. Assess how the results may alter or extend social policy prescriptions.

Significance of the Study

Although the Gini index is commonly used as a measure of inequality, its use may present some limitations. One of these is that it does not distinguish between dissimilar kinds of inequality. As an example, Lorenz curves may intersect, reflecting diverse patterns of income distribution but resulting in similar Gini coefficient values (De Maio 2007). The Gini is also more responsive to changes in the middle of the income distribution. The Gini may thus fail to unearth the inequality dynamics at the top and bottom ends of the income distribution. Recommendations emanating from trend analyses of inequality solely based on the Gini indices may thus fail to guide the design of optimal social policies.

Besides the complexity of using the Gini at a point in time, an examination of the evolution of income inequality relying on separate distinct studies may be misleading and/or complex. This is because separate studies often use dissimilar definitions or formulations for computing measures of income inequality (Xu 2003). An additional source of complexity in comparing separate studies across time is that studies may examine inequality at different levels, for example at the individual or household levels. These complexities may make trend assessments of inequality based on separate studies inaccurate or misleading.

To demonstrate the extent of these challenges, this study, besides estimating the Gini index, also measures income inequality using the Atkinson index, the Theil index and the coefficient of variation. Deciles of income and decile ratios including the Palma index are also reported. The value of this study's approach is that the use of several inequality measures allows for a deeper assessment of inequalities on different parts of the income spectrum (Jenkins 1999). This study also examines whether changes in inequality were statistically significant—a feature that is lacking in most of the previous studies. Although Kenya is used as a case study, the findings are applicable to other countries.

Besides measuring inequality, this study also decomposes total income inequality by population subgroups, including locality (rural versus urban), region and education level. Decomposing inequality enables the main determinants of inequality to be identified by isolating how various components (such as subgroups) contribute to total inequality (Araar 2006). This addresses a key gap in previous studies on inequality and its evolution in Kenya.

What is Known about the Evolution of Inequality in Kenya?

This subsection discusses the evolution of Kenya's inequality as documented by various studies. The decomposition of inequality is also discussed, albeit briefly. A brief global picture is presented before focusing on the Kenyan context.

Global inequality in the mid-2000s, by some accounts, was about the same as it was in the late 1980s (Ferreira, Lopez-Calva, Mulligan, Olinto and Saavedra 2012). Until the late 1990s, it was assumed that inequality in sub-Saharan Africa (SSA) was relatively lower than that of other regions. Much of the focus was on inequality in Latin America. Nevertheless, inequality in Africa was found to be one of the highest in the world by many studies, including that by Deininger and Squire (1998). As summarised in Table 14.1, based on the Gini, in 2005 Kenya's inequality was relatively higher than most of her East African neighbours, as well as other countries across the world. Other African countries, including South Africa and Rwanda, have some of the highest levels of inequality in the world. More recent developments indicate that Kenya is among a few countries for which inequality declined substantially in the mid-2010s relative to the immediate earlier measure of inequality (in the mid-2000s and early 2010s).

Table 14.1: Income Inequality in Selected Countries

Country	Gini (Reference Year)	Gini (Reference Year)
Brazil	52.9 (2013)	53.9 (2018)
Burundi	33.4 (2006)	38.6 (2013)
Egypt	30.8 (2008)	31.5 (2017)
Ghana	42.8 (2005)	43.5 (2016)
Ethiopia	33.2 (2010)	35.0 (2015)
Rwanda	51.3 (2010)	43.7 (2016)
South Africa	63.4 (2011)	63.0 (2014)
Tanzania	37.8 (2011)	40.5 (2017)
Uganda	42.4 (2012)	42.8 (2016)
Kenya	48.5 (2005)	40.8 (2015)

Source: World Development Indicators, 2015 and 2020[3]

Comparisons of the Gini indices across time as measured by Bigsten (1986) suggest that income inequality in Kenya was high in the 1960s, 1970s and 1980s—with the Gini index exceeding 0.63; estimates based on later household surveys (1992, 1994, 1997 and 2005) suggest relatively lower but still substantial income inequality. As an example, the World Bank estimated a Gini index of 0.431 (World Bank 2019) and 0.450 (World Bank 2019) using survey data for 1994 and 1997 respectively.[4]

Table 14.2 summarises estimates of inequality in Kenya from various studies. Some of the earliest evidence is provided by Vandemoortele (1982) and Bigsten (1986). Income inequality measures suggest inequality was quite high (even in relative terms) in the 1960s and 1970s. Vandemoortele (1982) in his paper addresses the relationship between income distribution, regional and sectoral income disparities, and poverty in Kenya. Using the Social Accounting Matrix (SAM) of 1976, the Gini for income (proxied by consumption) is estimated at about 0.59. In his estimations three different household groups were distinguished: urban households, smallholders and other rural families. The intragroup Gini ratios of these clusters were estimated to be 0.45, 0.35 and 0.62 respectively. Vandemoortele concludes that there is a disparity between urban and rural regions, and that there is a marked dualism within rural Kenya (that is, between smallholders and other rural families). This dualism suggests that the separation of households by income groups in studying inequality offers a more comprehensive analysis of the changes in inequality. The estimates in the 1990s suggest a decline even though the measured inequality is still substantial relative to the performance of other countries.

Table 14.2: Trends in Income Inequality Estimates for Kenya and Economic Growth, 1964–2005/06

Author	Reference Year	Data Source	Gini Coefficient	Economic Growth (%)
Bigsten 1986	1964	Research study	0.630	5.0
Lecaillon et al.	1969	Research study	0.604	8.0
Bigsten 1986	1974	Research study	0.690	4.1
ILO 1984	1976	Based on National Accounts	0.520	2.2
Vandemoortele 1982	1976	1976 (SAM and population census)	0.590	2.2
Van Ginneken and Park 1984	1977	Social Accounting Matrix (synthetic data)	0.590	9.5
Milanovic 1994	1982	Research study – Chen, Datt and Ravallion, 1993	0.573	2.1
Deininger and Squire, World Bank 2004	1992	Welfare Monitoring Survey I	0.599	0.5
World Bank 2019	1992	PovcalNet	0.575	0.5
World Bank 2019	1994	PovcalNet	0.431	3.0
World Bank 2019	1997	PovcalNet	0.450	2.4
Society for International Development 2004	1999	Research study – Integrated Labour Force Survey	0.570	1.4
National statistical Authority	2006	Kenya Integrated Household Budget Survey (KIHBS) 2005–2006	0.459	6.1
World Bank 2019	2006	PovcalNet	0.465	6.1
World Bank 2019	2016	PovcalNet	0.408	5.7

Source: UNU-WIDER, World Income Inequality Database (WIID). Growth figures are from KNBS (various) Economic Survey

Bigsten (1986) offered some explanations on the changes observed for inequality in Kenya. In his study, he presents estimates of per capita income, income distribution and poverty in Kenya for the period 1914 to 1976. Table 14.3 reproduces some of these results. In the period between 1914 and 1950, inequality increased. In the earlier period, 1914 to 1921, the rise in inequality was attributed to the increasing economic differentiation between the white settlers and the local population—whereas in the latter period, 1946 to 1950, the rise in inequality was attributed mainly to the restraints or neglect imposed on the 'traditional sector' by the colonial government. Thereafter, inequality stayed below the 1950 level through to 1971. The fall in inequality in the 1950s was attributed to a booming economy (resulting from rising demand in the agricultural sector, including traditional agriculture) as a result of the Korean War. The government also introduced favourable policies for smallholders (such as growing cash crops) following the Mau Mau struggle from 1950 to 1955 (Bigsten 1986).

Table 14.3: Trends in Income/Expenditure Inequality Estimates for Kenya, 1914–1976

Year	1914	1921	1927	1936	1946	1950	1955	1960	1964	1967	1969	1971	1974	1976
Per capita income	296	214	402	609	629	862	1177	1165	1365	1451	1568	1636	1665	1618
Inequality (Gini)	0.50	0.57	0.58	0.63	0.64	0.70	0.63	0.68	0.63	0.66	0.68	0.70	0.69	0.68
Poverty (Sen's index)	0.57	0.75	0.56	0.46	0.48	0.43	0.23	0.31	0.21	0.23	0.24	0.25	0.25	0.25

Source: Bigsten (1986)

Bigsten (1986) also notes that inequality and poverty rose between 1964 and 1971—the period just after Kenya attained its independence. Among the expanding African labour force, per capita incomes rose especially within the public sector following a rise in demand for skilled labour. However, there was also a large group of Africans who did not benefit, including those with little or poor land, the landless and the pastoralists. Rapid expansion of the economy in the 1970s explains the fall in inequality in this period. Bigsten (1986) found that there was a strong correlation between a change in the Gini coefficient and a change in the urban–rural income gap. He concluded that measures that decrease the urban–rural income gap promote equity. The potential impact of these measures shall be assessed in our decompositions.

Income Inequality in the 1990s to the Present

Based on the computations of the Gini index, income inequality in Kenya has risen only slightly by some accounts. World Bank (2019) measures based on the Welfare Monitoring Survey (WMS) of 1994 and 1997 and the Kenya Integrated Household Budget Survey (KIHBS) 2005/06 (GoK 2006) indicate a larger Gini of 0.452 in 2005/06 relative to the estimates of 0.431 and 0.450 in 1994 and 1997 respectively (Table 14.2). It should be noted that the 2005/06 Gini estimate is lower than that provided by the Society for International Development (SID 2004), which was 0.556—perhaps resulting from differing definitions (say, of income measure) and/or methodologies.

The World Bank (2009), besides other objectives, attempted to address what happened to poverty and inequality over time in Kenya. With respect to inequality, the study centres on comparing 1997 to 2005/06, years for which national survey data were available. Their findings indicated that 'inequality is large and growing' in Kenya. The study also found that that the 'national consumption decile ratio rose from 13 to 19 between 1997 and 2005/06'. This is interpreted as suggesting a large and growing inequality (World Bank 2009: 11, 15).

Bigsten et al. (2014) examined incomes, inequality and poverty in Kenya over a 100-year period. Their study compared inequality in 1994 and 2005 using per adult equivalent expenditures. Their findings on inequality suggest that overall inequality increased between 1994 and 2005/06, with reported Gini coefficients of 0.428 and 0.516 respectively. A dichotomy between rural and urban inequality finds that overall inequality is higher in urban areas and the gap in inequality between rural and urban areas widened in 2005 relative to its 1994 measure.

In a more recent study on inequality trends in Kenya, Manda et al. (forthcoming) assessed various data between 1994 and 2015/16. They note that inequality in real per capita consumption expenditure in Kenya was still high but declined in 2015/16 relative to 2005/06. The recent decrease in inequality was larger for urban than in rural areas thus narrowing the inequality gap. Even so, the decline was not observed for all regions (counties) suggesting diversity in the evolution of inequality. Their study avers that the decline was as a result of increase in the share of expenditure going to the middle 50 per cent and the lower 40 per cent of the population.

Besides measuring inequality, this study also seeks to analyse the determinants of inequality. This is partly achieved by decomposing inequality measures. One of the main reasons for doing this is to understand the main determinants of inequality by isolating how each component (of, say, income) contributes to total inequality (Araar 2006). Income inequality can be studied by separating total income as the sum of several components. Earlier studies on the decomposition of income inequality were mainly based on the analysis of the mathematical properties of inequality indices. Examples of these studies include Shorrocks (1982).

Although inequality decomposition may shed some light on key patterns of inequality or its determinants, there appear to be only a few studies on Kenya on the decomposition of income inequality. Ndirangu and Mathenge (2010), in one of the few studies for Kenya, note that 'there is little analytical work in patterns of inequality in Kenya'. In their study they attempt to determine the contribution of different income sources to overall income inequality. Their work is however restricted to a rural sample.

In yet another Kenyan study, Nafula, Ndirangu and Onsomu (2013) aimed to determine the contribution of growth and inequality components in poverty reduction. The study decomposed inequality by expenditure components. A key finding was that a rise in non-food expenditure was associated with an increase in inequality. A rise in food expenditure was associated with a decrease in inequality.

Analytical Methods and Data

As is now evident, there are potential limitations in using separate studies across time to identify a trend in income inequality. To begin with, the results of any given study are sensitive to the definition of income and income units as well as the method of estimation used. As an example, some of the estimations of inequality for Kenya reviewed above relied on national accounts data and population census data, for example, Vandemoortele (1982). Bigsten (1986), World Bank (2009) and Bigsten et al. (2014) remain quite useful studies in analysing inequality trends in Kenya. Part of the limitation of these studies is their focus on computing only the Gini index and/or the decile ratios.

Estimation Procedures/Methods

In order to achieve the first objective, the Gini coefficient, the Theil index, the Atkinson index and the coefficient of variation as well as decile ratios were estimated. The estimation of the inequality indices was performed using the Distributive Analysis for Stata Package (DASP) (Araar and Duclos 2013).[5]

For the second objective, that is decomposing the inequality measures, we decomposed the Generalised Entropy index by population subgroups. Following Araar and Duclos (2013) and Litchfield (1999) the GE indices of inequality can be expressed as a sum within group inequality and between group inequalities.

Data

This study used several sources of data. The Kenya Integrated Household Budget Survey (KIHBS) 2005/2006 (GoK 2006) was used to provide more recent measures of income inequality among households. The Welfare Monitoring Survey (WMS) of 1994 was used to provide past measures of inequality in Kenya. There were a number of data manipulation procedures that merit discussion. This is because inequality assessments are typically clouded by conceptual and methodological uncertainties. These are related to a number of factors, which include the choice of wellbeing indicator, the control for differences in the cost of living, and the treatment of household size and composition. The data manipulations were effected in close collaboration with the Kenya National Bureau of Statistics, which is Kenya's national statistical agency.

The Choice of Wellbeing Indicator

The choice of wellbeing indicator used in the estimations was guided by the availability of data on the indicator. All the data sets had expenditure data and so expenditure was chosen as a convenient wellbeing indicator in the estimations. It is recognised that income typically varies more than expenditure from one period to another and is thus less preferable than expenditure. This is even more the case in economies dominated by self-employment in agriculture (Deaton 1997). In the data sets used, expenditure was defined to include food and non-food consumption; the purchase of durable goods, assets, repayment of loans, rents paid and imputed rent for accommodation.

The Control for Differences in Cost of Living

To compare distributions across different regions, such as rural versus urban, spatial consumer price indices (CPI) should be applied to regional distributions prior to any distributional analyses. In our analyses, the data for 2005/06 was deflated using regional CPIs computed by the Kenya National Bureau of Statistics (KNBS). The CPIs were used to adjust expenditure in these regions for the cost-of-living differences.

The Treatment of Household Size and Composition

Households differ in size and composition, which may mean adjustments are required to improve the assessment of distributions. In related studies, it is recognised that there may be economies of scale in a household, implying for instance that a household with three members may not necessarily consume thrice as much as a household of one (Deaton 1997). In addition, individuals within a household have different needs depending on a number of variables, such as age and gender. A common practice to improve these household characteristics is to divide total income by the number of equivalent adults living in the household. This is usually given by some equivalence scale in which each member of the household counts as some fraction of a reference person. The expenditure data used was adjusted using the number of equivalent adults in a household. The head of the household received a weight of 1 while other adults were given a weight of 0.7. Children (defined as those aged fourteen or less) received a weight of 0.5.

Results and Discussions

Appendix Tables 1A and 1B represent the summary statistics for the WMS 1994 data and the KIHBS 2005/06 data. The WMS 1994 data set had about 10,700 households. The mean household size is 5.4 and the mean number of adults (those aged above fourteen years) and children (those aged fourteen years or less) was 4.1 and 1.3 respectively. The mean of total annual household expenditure was about KES 52,000. Food expenditure is the highest expenditure item accounting for about 66 per cent of the mean annual expenditure. As presented in Appendix Table 1B, the mean household size for the KIHBS 2005/06 data was 5.1.

Measures of Income Inequality

Table 14.4 summarises various measures of inequality in 1994 and 2005/06. Per adult equivalent expenditures are used as income proxies. The total Gini coefficient for 1994 was about 0.47 while that of 2005/06 was about 0.46. The difference between the two overall Gini inequality indices was tested for significance and the results indicate that the null hypothesis 'that the difference between the two measures is zero' cannot be rejected (p-value of 0.4929) (see Appendix Table 1C). Thus, based on the Gini measure, total inequality may not have changed significantly between the two periods.

For both periods, urban inequality is higher than rural inequality. Urban inequality (using per adult equivalent monthly expenditure in regionally deflated prices) worsened while rural inequality eased. Both differences were statistically significant.

Table 14.4: Measures of Income Inequality in Kenya 1994 and 2005/06

	1994			2005/06		
	Total	Rural	Urban	Total	Rural	Urban
Gini Index	0.4693 (0.0085)	0.3995 (0.0044)	0.4525 (0.0198)	0.4637 (0.0059)	0.3893 (0.0045)	0.4725 (0.0112)
Atkinson Measure ($\varepsilon = 0.5$)	0.1905 (0.0082)	0.1360 (0.0033)	0.1797 (0.0168)	0.1822 (0.0052)	0.1244 (0.0028)	0.1885 (0.0091)
Atkinson Measure ($\varepsilon = 1.0$)	0.3352 (0.0100)	0.2609 (0.0057)	0.3081 (0.0222)	0.3141 (0.0068)	0.2335 (0.0046)	0.3211 (0.0125)
Atkinson Measure ($\varepsilon = 2.0$)	0.7616 (0.0457)	0.7260 (0.0547)	0.6287 (0.0689)	0.5257 (0.0112)	0.4433 (0.0130)	0.5173 (0.0155)
Generalised Entropy index ($\phi = 0$)	0.4042 (0.0097)	0.3023 (0.0031)	0.3683 (0.0225)	0.4052 (0.0103)	0.2871 (0.0068)	0.3887 (0.0177)
Theil Index – Generalised Entropy index ($\phi = 1$)	0.4417 (0.0241)	0.2725 (0.0036)	0.4274 (0.0465)	0.4426 (0.0175)	0.2692 (0.0073)	0.4580 (0.0270)
Generalised Entropy index ($\phi = 2$)	1.1163 (0.2328)	0.3644 (0.0128)	0.9955 (0.2572)	1.0310 (0.0869)	0.3813 (0.0185)	0.9546 (0.0890)
Coefficient of variation	1.4942 (0.1757)	0.8536 (0.0256)	1.4110 (0.2033)	1.4360 (0.0605)	0.8733 (0.0212)	1.3818 (0.0644)

Source: Computed from the WMS 1994; KIHBS 2005/06
Note: Numbers in parentheses are standard errors.

The Atkinson index was computed for the income aversion parameter values ranging from 0.5 to 2 as is standard. Higher values of epsilon are associated with more sensitivity of the Atkinson index to inequalities at the bottom of the distribution of income.[6] Based on the Atkinson index (for epsilon values of 1 and 2), total inequality declined in 2005/06 relative to 1994. The differences in the

Atkinson indices for the two periods, that is, 1994 and 2005/06 for epsilon=1 and epsilon=2 are both different from 0, whereas that for epsilon=0.5 is not statistically significant (Appendix Tables 1C). Total inequality changed significantly if more weight was placed at the bottom of the income distribution. The index values suggest a clear dichotomy between changes in rural versus urban inequality over the two periods (Tables 14.5 and 14.6). For epsilon values of 0.5 and 1.0, urban inequality worsened whereas rural inequality declined. An increase of the sensitivity of the measure to inequalities at the bottom (epsilon=2) suggests that, overall, inequality—rural and urban—worsened in 2005/06 relative to the mid-1990s. A corresponding interpretation of the Atkinson index (for epsilon=1) of 0.3352 in 1994 and 0.3141 in 2005/06 is that in 1994 society could have achieved the same level of social welfare with only 66 per cent of total income if the incomes were perfectly distributed (and this rises to nearly 69 per cent in 2005/06).

The measures of the General Entropy (GE) class are computed for theta values of 1 and 2. For theta=1, that is, when equal weights are applied across the income distribution, the index is slightly higher in 2005/06 and suggests a worsening distribution of per capita expenditure for the total population. Even so, the difference in this overall measure is not statistically significant. The measure supports the earlier observation of declining rural inequalities and worsening urban inequalities.

If more weight is given to the bottom of the distribution (theta=0), total inequality increased slightly from about 0.404 to 0.405 and the difference was found to be statistically significant. Rural inequalities declined (from about 0.30 to 0.29) whereas urban inequality increased (from about 0.37 to 0.39). If more weight is given to high incomes (theta=2) total inequality seems to have declined slightly and the difference in total inequality is not different from 0. Rural inequalities actually worsened while urban inequalities improved. Finally, even though the coefficient of variation measure suggests an improvement in the total inequality, the difference was not statistically significant.

The results indicate that there is no correspondence in the changes in inequality over time between urban and rural regions. Relying on the Gini alone may fail to unearth the peculiar differences in the changes that occur if more weight is attributed to the bottom and top ends of the income distribution. To firm up these discussions, the next subsection summarises inequality measures using the decile and/or decile ratios.

Deciles of Income and Decile Ratios

To characterise inequality further, Tables 14.5 and 14.6 show the percentage of total per adult equivalent household expenditure by deciles of the population in 1994 and 2005/06. For the total population in 1994, the top 10 per cent of households controlled about 28 per cent of total expenditure, while the bottom 10 per cent controlled 1.5 per cent of total expenditure, The share of expenditure of the top 10 per cent of households was larger in 2005/06 at about 45 per cent, reflecting a less egalitarian or less equal society.

Table 14.5: Household per Adult Equivalent Expenditure Shares by Deciles, 1994

Decile	Total Population (N = 10,710)		Rural (N = 9,031)		Urban (N = 1,679)	
	Expenditure Share (%)	Cumulative Share	Expenditure Share (%)	Cumulative Share	Expenditure Share (%)	Cumulative Share
1	1.52	1.52	1.58	1.58	2.45	2.45
2	3.18	4.71	3.30	4.88	4.96	7.41
3	4.35	9.05	4.60	9.49	5.99	13.40
4	5.69	14.74	5.46	14.95	6.71	20.11
5	7.26	22.00	7.22	22.17	8.13	28.24
6	8.48	30.48	8.60	30.77	9.77	38.00
7	10.63	41.11	10.09	40.86	9.75	47.75
8	13.37	54.48	12.53	53.39	13.28	61.04
9	17.14	71.63	16.84	70.24	15.65	76.68
10	28.37	100.00	29.76	100.00	23.32	100.00

Source: Computed from the Welfare Monitoring Survey 1994 data

In 1994, the top 10 per cent of rural households controlled about 30 per cent of income, and in 2005/06 this was 26 per cent. On the other hand, in 1994 the top 10 per cent of urban households controlled 23 per cent of total income, rising to nearly 42 per cent in 2005/06. This indicates that the distribution of income among urban households worsened, with the richest decile gaining a larger proportion of total income at the expense of the other income groups in 2005/06 relative to 1994.

Table 14.6: Household per Adult Equivalent Expenditure Shares by Decile, 2005/2006

Decile	Total Population (N = 13,155)		Rural (N = 8,475)		Urban (N = 4,683)	
	Expenditure Share (%)	Cumulative Share	Expenditure Share (%)	Cumulative Share	Expenditure Share (%)	Cumulative Share
1	1.70	1.70	2.99	2.99	2.41	2.41
2	2.70	4.39	4.66	7.65	3.56	5.97
3	3.33	7.72	5.74	13.39	4.08	10.05
4	4.11	11.84	6.42	19.82	5.59	15.64
5	5.06	16.90	7.76	27.58	6.12	21.76
6	6.22	23.12	8.73	36.31	5.73	27.49
7	7.79	30.91	10.71	47.02	7.52	35.01
8	10.50	41.41	12.02	59.04	8.97	43.98
9	13.73	55.14	15.36	74.40	14.08	58.06
10	44.86	100.00	25.60	100.00	41.94	100.00

Source: Computed from the KIHBS 2005/06 data

The Palma ratio is also becoming a popular measure of inequality. Palma proposed that changes in inequality are largely the result of variations in the share of the richest 10 per cent and poorest 40 per cent of the population. This is attributed to stability of incomes for the middle groups. Estimates of this ratio for the Kenyan data indicate that the ratio increased in 2005/06, to 3.79 from 1.81 in 1994 (Table 14.7). This is interpreted to suggest that the richest 10 per cent of society earned nearly four times the income share of the poorest 40 per cent in 2005/06. The ratios suggests that the adverse change mainly took place in the urban areas.

Table 14.7: Palma Ratio, 1994 and 2005/06

Total		Rural		Urban	
1994	2005	1994	2005	1994	2005
1.81	3.79	1.99	1.29	1.16	2.68

Source: Computed from the Welfare Monitoring Survey 1994 data and the KIHBS 2005/06 data

Even so, the decile ratios or measures are often likely to be underestimated. This is attributed to several limitations which can be ascribed to survey data, including under-sampling of high-income households, and the related under-reporting of incomes by richer households.[7]

Decomposition of Inequality by Population Subgroups

Our decomposition examines the contribution of locality (rural versus urban), region (both county and former provinces) and education in overall per adult equivalent expenditure to inequality in Kenya. The Generalised Entropy index is decomposed with theta set to 1 and 2 respectively. The result of the decomposition of per capita expenditure by locality (rural or urban) is summarised in Table 14.8. The per capita total consumption expenditure, in regionally deflated prices, for urban areas is about 2.5 times greater than that in rural areas in 2005/06. This compares to nearly three times for the 1994 distribution (Appendix Table 2).

The results of the Theil index decomposition (for theta=1) show that about 22 per cent of inequality in 2005/06 could be attributed to differences between rural and urban areas. Most of the inequality (about 78 per cent) could be attributed to inequality within these localities. The 1994 distribution had approximately similar decomposition results (Appendix Table 2). The contribution of urban areas to total inequality rose with the increase in the weighting parameter from 1 to 2, or as more weight was given to incomes at the top end. The results suggest that measures to reduce the rural–urban income gap would have had relatively limited impact in promoting equity, since most of the inequality is explained by the within-group component.

Table 14.8: Measurement and Decomposition of Inequality by Locality, Kenya 2005/06

	Population Share	Per Capita Expenditure of the Group	Gini Index	Atkinson Index (2)	Theil Index (1)	Theil Index (2)
Locality						
Rural	0.7930	22,693.43	0.3893	0.4433	0.2692 (0.3640)	0.3813 (0.1670)
Urban	0.2070	57,282.72	0.4724	0.5173	0.4580 (0.4155)	0.9546 (0.7212)
Total	1.0000	31,510.90	0.4637	0.5257	0.4426	1.0310
Within-group component of inequality					0.7795	0.8882
Between-group component of inequality					0.2205	0.1118

Note: the figures in parentheses are percentage contributions of inequality within each locality to aggregate inequality.

Table 14.9 provides measures and decomposition of inequality by education level of the household head. Two groups are isolated: individuals with at least twelve years of education and those with less than twelve years of education. The more educated group form a smaller proportion of the overall population (about 23 per cent). The distribution of income for the more educated group is more unequal (Gini index of 0.47) and this group (despite their lower population proportion) contributed about 44 per cent to overall inequality (for theta=1) and about 74 per cent (for theta=2) or when more weight was attached to higher incomes. Most of the inequality (about 69 per cent to 86 per cent) is explained by the within-group component of inequality.

Table 14.9: Measurement and Decomposition of Inequality by Education Level, Kenya 2005/06

	Population Share	Gini Index	Atkinson Index (2)	Theil Index (1)	Theil Index (2)
Education level (years)					
Less than twelve years*	0.5351	0.3778	0.3750	0.2519 (0.2454)	0.3541 (0.1194)
Twelve years or more	0.2351	0.4707	0.4970	0.4555 (0.4452)	0.9607 (0.7418)
Total	1.0000	0.4637	0.5257	0.4426	1.0310
Within-group component of inequality				0.6907	0.8612
Between-group component of inequality				0.2248	0.1088

Note: the figures in parentheses are percentage contributions of inequality within each education level to aggregate inequality. *includes those with no education.

In analogous results, Table 14.10 provides measures and decomposition of inequality across major regions in Kenya using the 2005/06 data. These regions correspond to the former eight provinces of the country, including Nairobi.

Table 14.10: Measurement and Decomposition of Inequality across Regions, 2005/06

Population Share (%)	Per Capita Expenditure of the Group	Gini Index	Atkinson Index (2)	Theil Index (1) (Relative Contribution)	Theil Index (2) (Relative Contribution)
8.19	70,374.41	0.4860	0.5297	0.4735 (0.2259)	0.9113 (0.4817)
12.84	33,681.45	0.3917	0.4128	0.2711 (0.0887)	0.4084 (0.0647)
9.19	29,844.50	0.4364	0.4524	0.3457 (0.0606)	0.5374 (0.0342)
16.50	24,566.57	0.4011	0.4253	0.3017 (0.0896)	0.6266 (0.0637)
2.92	14,488.30	0.3707	0.4067	0.2325 (0.0075)	0.2887 (0.0020)
14.13	24,269.92	0.3914	0.4047	0.2814 (0.0758)	0.4353 (0.0426)
24.30	28,956.24	0.4445	0.5751	0.4076 (0.1991)	0.9203 (0.1717)
11.93	21,375.11	0.3724	0.3650	0.2540 (0.0487)	0.3978 (0.0233)
				0.7962	0.8839
				0.2038	0.1161
100.00	31510.90	0.4637	0.5257	0.4426 (1.0000)	1.0310 (1.0000)

Note: the figures in parentheses are percentage contributions of inequality within each region to aggregate inequality

Based on the Gini estimates, a measure which is responsive to transfers in the middle of the distribution, inequality is highest in the most urbanised region in Kenya, Nairobi. Inequality is also relatively higher in the Coast region—a region with the second-largest urban centre, Mombasa. These estimates are largely consistent with earlier findings that associate urban regions with higher levels of inequality (for example, World Bank 2009). Inequality is lowest in Western and North-Eastern regions with Gini indices of about 0.37. There is a relatively clear positive relationship between inequality (as measured by the Gini) and per capita regional consumption expenditure. Inequality is observably higher in the regions with higher per capita total consumption expenditure.

If more weight is given to inequalities at the bottom of the distribution (based on the Atkinson index) the overall results change slightly. The Rift Valley region emerges as the most unequal region, moving from its former rank of second under the Gini measure. The regions with the lowest inequalities for the Atkinson indices are Western, Nyanza and North-Eastern regions.

The decomposition of the Theil index (theta=1) indicates that within-region inequality contributes about 80 per cent to aggregate inequality. This implies that the contribution of between-region inequality to total inequality is only about 20 per cent. When more weight is given to the incomes at the higher end of the distribution (theta=2), the within-region contribution increases to about 88 per cent.

When the inequality measure is equally sensitive to incomes across the distribution (theta=1), the figures suggest that Nairobi, with a 'population share' of about 8 per cent, contributes about 23 per cent to aggregate inequality. The Rift Valley region, with a population share that is nearly three times larger than that of Nairobi, contributes about 19 per cent to aggregate inequality. When more weight is given to incomes at the higher end of the distribution (theta=2), the contribution of Nairobi region to overall inequality rises to about 48 per cent, whereas that of Rift Valley falls slightly to about 17 per cent. The contribution of each of the other regions to overall inequality is less than 9 per cent for theta values of 1 and 2 (that is, when more weight is given to higher incomes or otherwise).

Table 14.11 provides measures and decomposition of inequality across counties.[8] The table indicates the counties with the largest and lowest inequality measures. With respect to the level of inequality, Turkana, Uasin Gishu and Marsabit counties exhibit the highest Gini measures of 0.58, 0.57 and 0.49 respectively. The top rankings (of the most unequal) do not change much when more weight is given to higher incomes (using the Atkinson index with theta=2). Nairobi and other relatively more urbanised counties are also observed to have relatively high rankings. Based on the Gini measure, the least unequal counties are Garissa, Wajir and Bomet, with Gini indices of 0.32, 0.29 and 0.28 respectively.

Table 14.11: Measurement and Decomposition of Inequality across Counties, 2005/06

	Population Share (%)	Gini Index	Atkinson Index (2)	Theil Index (1) (Relative Contribution)	Theil Index (2) (Relative Contribution)
County					
Turkana	1.47	0.5761	0.6978	0.7329 (0.0058)	1.9784 (0.0016)
Uasin Gishu	2.19	0.5681	0.5685	0.7580 (0.0558)	1.9800 (0.0930)
Marsabit	0.58	0.4907	0.6352	0.4515 (0.0028)	0.7236 (0.0009)
Nairobi	8.19	0.486	0.5297	0.4735 (0.2259)	0.9113 (0.4817)
Machakos	3.41	0.4436	0.4539	0.4138 (0.0257)	1.4618 (0.0313)
Laikipia	1.22	0.4311	0.5316	0.3338 (0.0096)	0.4852 (0.0063)
Kisumu	2.84	0.4267	0.4342	0.3416 (0.0257)	0.5458 (0.0206)
Kilifi	2.74	0.4199	0.4131	0.3354 (0.0133)	0.5672 (0.0062)
West Pokot	1.02	0.4186	0.4400	0.3077 (0.0043)	0.4149 (0.0015)
Taita Taveta	0.9	0.4165	0.3909	0.3465 (0.0060)	0.5959 (0.0038)
Siaya	2.27	0.3466	0.3531	0.2061 (0.0093)	0.2599 (0.0045)
Mombasa	2.59	0.3459	0.2994	0.2202 (0.0175)	0.3228 (0.0149)
Elgeyo Marakwet	1.04	0.3456	0.3070	0.2382 (0.0038)	0.4200 (0.0019)

Vihiga	1.74	0.3445	0.3241	0.2261 (0.0072)	0.3668 (0.0041)
Kitui	2.82	0.3418	0.3116	0.2091 (0.0079)	0.3084 (0.0029)
Homa Bay	2.4	0.3392	0.3640	0.2068 (0.0084)	0.2864 (0.0037)
Lamu	0.22	0.3307	0.2706	0.2094 (0.0010)	0.3271 (0.00067)
Kirinyaga	1.61	0.3305	0.2916	0.1923 (0.0077)	0.2534 (0.0048)
Garissa	1.06	0.3223	0.2987	0.1691 (0.0028)	0.1917 (0.0009)
Wajir	1.04	0.29	0.2144	0.1555 (0.0014)	0.2159 (0.0003)
Bomet	1.27	0.2816	0.2634	0.1492 (0.0026)	0.2033 (0.0009)
Within-county component of inequality				0.7314	0.8598
Between-county component of inequality				0.2686	0.1402
Kenya	100.00	0.4637	0.5257	0.4426 (1.0000)	1.0310 (1.0000)

Note: the figures in parentheses are percentage contributions of inequality within each locality to aggregate inequality

Decomposition results indicate that the within-county component of inequality accounts for 73 per cent of total inequality when theta is fixed at 1. The within-county component increases to nearly 86 per cent when more weight is given to higher incomes. When incomes are equally weighted, Nairobi County contributes by far the largest share (nearly 23 per cent) to overall inequality among the counties. It is followed by Uasin Gishu with 5.6 per cent, Kiambu County with about 4.4 per cent, Kisumu and Machakos 2.6 per cent each, and Meru 2.4 per cent. The relative contributions of the other counties are below 2 per cent with relatively higher values observable for the more urbanised counties, such as Nakuru and Mombasa.

Findings, Conclusion and Policy Implications

Findings

Like most parts of Africa, inequality has remained relatively high in Kenya since the pre-independence period. The analyses in this study measured and decomposed inequality, using per adult equivalent expenditures (and using various indices) for 1994 and 2005/06. Varying weights were applied to the income distribution data. The key results that emerge from the analyses are:

1. Based on the Gini index and General Entropy index for epsilon=0.5, that is, applying equal weights across the income distribution, per adult equivalent

expenditure inequality may not have increased to any significant degree in 2005/06 relative to the mid-1990s.
2. The evolution of inequality varies by locality, and analyses of total inequality ought to be firmed up by careful examination of not only rural versus urban inequality but also the income distribution weightings. As a demonstration of this finding, using the Atkinson measure, if more weight is given to the bottom of the distribution, total per adult equivalent expenditure inequality (urban plus rural) improved to a significant degree and whereas urban inequality worsened rural inequality improved. In corresponding results, if more weight is given to high incomes (theta=2) rural inequalities worsened, urban inequalities improved, while total inequality did not change to a significant degree.
3. Even though more urbanised regions (including counties) have higher incomes, they also exhibit relatively higher levels of income inequality.

The key results emerging from the decomposition of inequality by locality, education and region are:

1. Decomposition of inequality by locality (urban versus rural) indicates that most of the inequality (about 78 per cent) can be attributed to inequality within urban and within rural areas.
2. Decomposition by level of education of the head of the household suggests that the more educated group have a more unequal income distribution. Despite their lower population proportion this group contributed between about 44 per cent to 74 per cent to overall inequality if more weight is attached to low and high incomes respectively.
3. Decomposition results indicate that when incomes are equally weighted, Nairobi County contributes by far the largest share (nearly 23 per cent) to overall inequality among the counties. Other more urbanised counties, such as Uasin Gishu, Kiambu, Kisumu and Machakos, also have large contributions.

Conclusion and Policy Implications

The results indicate that there is no correspondence in the changes in inequality over time between urban and rural regions of Kenya. This suggests that knowing what happens to total inequality is certainly not good enough. This result may suggest that different localities within the same country may require diverse interventions to stem inequality.

In a related vein, evidence points to a lack of correspondence between changes at the upper and lower tails of the income distribution between the two periods examined. Under these circumstances, a single measure of inequality, such as the Gini index, may fail to unearth the peculiar differences in the changes that occur if more weight is attributed to the bottom and top ends of the income distribution. It is recommended that studies of the evolution of inequality should perhaps use diverse measures, which may provide varying trends of inequality at different parts of the income distribution.

Even in cases where rural and urban inequality are measured, care should be taken to examine the factors driving disparity through inequality decomposition as a precursor to informing social-policy prescriptions. As a demonstration, many previous studies indicate that reducing rural–urban inequality would be an effective intervention in reducing overall inequality. The decomposition results discussed here (urban and rural) indicate that most of the inequality (about 78 per cent) can be attributed to inequality within urban and within rural areas. These results suggest that measures to reduce the rural–urban income gap would have relatively limited impact in reducing total inequality, since most of the inequality is explained by the within-group component. The contribution of urban inequality to overall inequality is large and the implication is that the reduction of within-urban inequalities would be significant in the reduction of overall inequality.

The results may also allow an inference to urbanisation versus inequality link. The most urbanised regions in Kenya, including Nairobi County, contributed by far the largest share to overall inequality among the counties. This is partly interpreted to suggest that urbanisation in Kenya is associated with growing inequalities and underpins the need to stem the urbanising effect on inequalities. This would require well thought-out social interventions.

The results of the decomposition by level of education are interpreted to suggest that whereas higher levels of education move households to higher income levels, education does not in itself have an inbuilt mechanism to reduce inequality within the relatively more educated. Interventions to enhance access to education would require other contemporaneous interventions to reduce inequality. Improvements in education (literacy or human capital development) in themselves may not be sufficient to reduce income inequality. The role of contemporaneous social policy interventions would be vital in making education/literacy/human capital interventions more potent.

In all likelihood, the need to employ diverse measures of inequality and to carefully analyse its determinants would be a sine qua non for studies that intend to provide effective evidence-based social-policy prescriptions. This requirement would hold even in the face of the newer and innovative measures of inequality, such as the Palma ratio.

As an area of further research, it should be noted that there is marked dualism between urban and rural areas. An examination of possible dualism within rural areas of Kenya (for example, between smallholders and other rural families) as suggested by Vandemoortele (1982) could form an interesting area for further research.

Notes

1. Poor countries are those below about USD 3,200 per capita.
2. Includes the Theil Index.
3. http://wdi.worldbank.org/table/2.9 and http://datatopics.worldbank.org/world-development-indicators/themes/poverty-and-inequality.html. Accessed October 2020.
4. A UN-ECA (1999) study estimated an African average Gini coefficient of 0.44 for the 1990s. Kenya's Gini coefficient of 0.45 in 1994 was just about equal to this average.
5. The empirical processes of estimating the Gini index as well as the Atkinson and Theil indices in DASP are available at http://dasp.ecn.ulaval.ca/modules/DASP_V2.3/DASP_MANUAL_V2.3.pdf.
6. Atkinson values can be used to calculate the proportion of total income that would be required to achieve an equal level of social welfare as at present if incomes were perfectly distributed (De Maio 2007).
7. The preceding analyses were supplemented by graphical analyses. For the Lorenz curves, the rural Lorenz curve dominates the urban and the overall population Lorenz curves. The distribution for the urban population is more unequal than the total population at parts of the higher income levels in 1994.
8. Kenya has 47 counties which were created by the Constitution in 2010.

References

Aghion, P., Caroli, E. and Garcia-Peñalosa, C., 1999, Inequality and Economic Growth: The Perspective of the New Growth Theories, *Journal of Economic Literature*, Vol. 37, No. 4, pp. 1615–1660.

Alesina, A. and Perotti R., 1996, Income Distribution, Political Instability, and Investment, *European Economic Review*, Vol. 40, No. 6, pp. 1203–1228.

Araar, A., 2006, On the Decomposition of the Gini Coefficient: An Exact Approach, with an Illustration Using Cameroonian Data, Working paper 02-06, CIRPÉE.

Araar, A. and Duclos, J-Y., 2013, User Manual DASP version 2.3 for Stata Package DASP, Montreal: PEP, CIRPÉE and World Bank Université Laval.

Barro J. R., 2008, Inequality and Growth Revisited, Working Paper Series on Regional Economic Integration No. 11, Asian Development Bank (ADB). Available online at https://www.adb.org/sites/default/files/publication/28468/wp11-inequality-growth-revisited.pdf.

Benhabib, J. and Rustichini A., 1996, Social Conflict and Growth, *Journal of Economic Growth*, Vol. 1, pp. 125–142.

Bigsten, A., 1986, Welfare and Economic Growth in Kenya, 1914–76, *World Development*, Vol. 14, No. 9, pp. 1151–60.

Bigsten, A., Manda D. K., Mwabu, G. and Wambugu, A., 2014, Incomes, Inequality and Poverty in Kenya: A Long-Term Perspective, WIDER Working Paper 2014/126, Helsinki: UNU-WIDER.

Birdsall, N., 2007, Income Distribution: Effects on Growth and Development, Centre for Global Development Working Paper Number 118.

De Maio F. G., 2007, Income Inequality Measures. *Journal of Epidemiology and Community Health*, Vol. 61, No. 10, pp. 849–852. DOI: https://doi.org/10.1136/jech.2006.052969.

Deaton, A., 1997, *The Analysis of Household Surveys: A Microeconomic Approach to Development Policy*, Washington, DC: World Bank Group.

Deininger, K. and Squire, L., 1998, New Ways of Looking at Old Issues: Inequality and Growth, *Journal of Development Economics*, Vol. 57, No. 2, pp. 259–87.

Ferreira, F. H. G., Lopez-Calva, L. F., Mulligan, M., Olinto, P. and Saavedra C. J., 2012, *Inequality in Focus*, Vol. 1, No. 1, Washington, DC: World Bank Group. Available online at http://documents.worldbank.org/curated/en/445221468163745476/Inequality-in-focus-vol-1-no-1.

Galor, O. and Zeira, J., 1993, Income Distribution and Macroeconomics, *Review of Economic Studies,* Vol. 60, No. 1, pp. 35–52.

Government of Kenya (GoK), 2006, Kenya Integrated Household Budget Survey, 2005/06, Nairobi: Kenya National Bureau of Statistics. Available online at http://www.kpda.or.ke/documents/Industry-Reports/KIHBS%202005%20Basic%20Report.pdf.

Government of Kenya (GoK), 2007, Basic Report on Well-being in Kenya, based on Kenya Integrated Household Budget Survey, 2005/06, Nairobi: Kenya National Bureau of Statistics.

Jenkins, S. P., 1999, Analysis of Income Distributions, *Stata Technical Bulletin* 484-18.18. Available online at https://www.stata.com/manuals15/rinequality.pdf.

Kenya National Bureau of Statics, 1994, Welfare Monitoring Survey 2, Second Round. Accessible at http://54.213.151.253/nada/index.php/catalog/WMS.

Litchfield, J. A., 1999, Inequality: Methods and Tools. Available online at https://www.researchgate.net/publication/253853150_Inequality_Methods_and_Tools.

Manda, D. K., Kipruto, S., Murithi, M., Mutegi, R., Samoei, P., Mbuthia, A., Oleche, M,, Wambugu, A. and Mwabu, G., (forthcoming), *Inequality Trends and Diagnostics in Kenya*, AFD, France.

Montero, M., 2007, Inequity Aversion May Increase Inequity, *Economic Journal*, Vol. 117, Issue 519, C192–C204. DOI::10.1111/j.1468-0297.2007.02041.x.

Nafula, N., Ndirangu, L. and Onsomu, E., 2013, Poverty Growth and Inequality Decomposition: A Household Survey Analysis, KIPPRA Discussion Paper No. 159, Nairobi, Kenya Institute for Public Policy Research and Analysis.

Ndirangu, L. and Mathenge, M., 2010, Paper presented at the Centre for Studies on Africa Economies (CSAE) Conference on Economic Development in Africa.

Odedokun, M. and Round, J., 2004, Determinants of Income inequality and Its Effects on Economic Growth: Evidence from African Countries, *African Development Review*, Vol. 16, No. 2, pp. 287–327.

Romer, P. M., 1994, The Origins of Endogenous Growth, *Journal of Economic Perspectives*, Vol. 8, No.1, pp. 3–22.

Shorrocks, A. F., 1982, Inequality Decomposition by Factor Components, *Econometrica*, Vol. 50, No. 1, pp. 193–211.

Society for International Development (SID), 2004, *Pulling Apart: Facts and Figures on Inequality in Kenya*, Nairobi: SID.

United Nations, Economic Commission for Africa (UN-ECA), 1999, Economic Report on Africa: The Challenge of Poverty Reduction and Sustainability, Addis Ababa: ECA.

UNU-WIDER, World Income Inequality Database (WIID). Available online at https://www.wider.unu.edu/database/wiid.

Vandemoortele J., 1982, Income Distribution and Poverty in Kenya: A Statistical Analysis, Discussion Paper 275, Nairobi: Institute for Development Studies, University of Nairobi. Available online at https://opendocs.ids.ac.uk/opendocs/handle/20.500.12413/753.

Welfare Monitoring Survey (WMS), 1992, 1994 and 1997, Kenya National Bureau of Statistics, Ministry of finance and planning, Nairobi: Government printer. Available online at http://54.213.151.253/nada/index.php/catalog/WMS.

World Bank, 2008, Kenya Poverty and Inequality Assessment: Vol. I, Synthesis Report, Poverty Reduction and Economic Management Unit, Washington, DC: World Bank.

World Bank, 2009, Kenya — Poverty and Inequality Assessment, Report No. 44190-KE, Washington DC: World Bank Group. Available online at https://openknowledge.worldbank.org/handle/10986/3081.

World Bank, 2019, PovcalNet. Available online at http://iresearch.worldbank.org/PovcalNet/povOnDemand.aspx

Xu, K., 2003, How Has the Literature on Gini's Index Evolved in the Past 80 Years? Dalhousie University Economics Working Paper. DOI: http://dx.doi.org/10.2139/ssrn.423200.

Appendix

Table 1A: Summary Statistics for the WMS 1994 Data

Variable	Mean	Std. Dev.	Minimum	Maximum
Household size	5.4	2.80	1	27
Number of children (those aged less than 15)	1.30	1.46	0	10
Number of adults (aged 15 and above)	4.05	2.08	1	22
Adult equivalent	3.79	1.77	1	18.2
Total household expenditure per annum	51,955.56	48,883.99	0	1,283,336
Urban rural dummy (1 = urban)	0.21	0.41	0	1
Sex of household head (1 = female)	0.24	0.43	0	1
Per capita expenditure per annum (welfare)	19,209.31	36,109.38	0	1,047,830

Number of observations = 10,866

Table 1B: Summary Statistics for the KIHBS 2005/06 Data

Variable	Mean	Std. Dev.	Minimum	Maximum	Observations
Household size	5.1	2.8	1	29	13,155
Education of household head (years)	8.4	3.7	0	21	13,155
Monthly per adult equivalent total household expenditure	3,839.276	6,661.6	499.2*	191,733.5	12,708

Number of observations = 13,155
*A number of outliers removed from the original data
The null is that the estimated difference is not equal to zero.

Table 2: Measurement and Decomposition of Inequality by Locality, Kenya 1994

	Population Share	Mean Expenditure of the Group	Gini Index	Atkinson Index (2)	Theil Index (1)	Theil Index (2)
Locality						
Rural	0.8443	11,487.08	0.3995	0.7260	0.2725 (0.4002)	0.3643 (0.1627)
Urban	0.1557	33,745.07	0.4525	0.6287	0.4274 (0.3402)	0.9955 (0.7069)
Within-group component of inequality					0.7404	0.8696
Between-group component of inequality					0.2603	0.1304
Kenya	1.0000	14,950.19	0.4693	0.7616	0.4417 (1.0000)	1.1163 (1.0000)

Note: The figures in parentheses are percentage contributions of inequality within each locality to aggregate inequality.

Index

A
Abate, 92, 112
Abebrese, 50, 61
Abel-Smith, 43
Abuja, 61, 209
Accelerating Gender Equality, 28
acceleration, 109
access, 25, 50, 66, 73-77, 80-82, 84-85, 87, 89, 91, 93-94, 107-8, 169-72, 197, 201-2, 225-26
Action Campaign, 251
actions, 62, 124, 154, 161, 169, 211, 253
ADB (Asian Development Bank), 278
Addressing Gender Gaps, 116
address structure, 15
address unemployment, 245-46
Africa conference, 10, 28, 161, 237
Africa Institute for Agrarian Studies (AIAS), 90
Africa International Conference, 3, 40
African, x, xi, xii, 1, 4, 7, 12, 13, 14, 18, 19, 20, 21, 22, 23, 24, 26, 27, 28, 33, 34, 35, 40, 42, 45, 46, 54, 55, 61, 62, 65, 69, 78, 83, 84, 85, 87, 88, 89, 113-14, 117, 119, 166, 172, 173, 175-76, 185, 193, 194, 195, 198, 213, 214, 230, 236, 237-39, 246, 247, 254, 255, 264, 280
African countries, 14, 21, 25, 46, 52, 65, 167, 244, 251, 261, 279
    southern, 7
Consortium (AERC), 87
African Local Government Action Forum Phase VII, 177

Africans, 23, 45-46, 54, 173, 246, 264
African Union, 20, 24, 26, 172-74, 176
    ruling Zimbabwe National, 214
African Women and Stokvels, 195
Africa's Development, 2, 3, 12-13, 26, 41, 61, 86, 161, 166, 169, 193, 235, 254
    navigating, 166
Africa's Renaissance, 173
Africa World Press, 178
Afro-euphoria, 14
Agricultural and Resource Economics, 12
AID Program Evaluation Discussion Paper, 178
aid recipients, 167
Atkinson, 9, 268, 269, 273, 276, 278
Attafuah, 48, 60-61
Atteridgeville, 183, 184
Attilo, 115
attributes, 91, 160, 202
attributing, 17
Attribution, 162
Authoritarian Nationalism, 238

B
background, 47, 86, 96, 223, 234, 259
Bangura, 34, 36, 41
    Yusuf, 34
bank charges, 187
Bankers Association of Zimbabwe (BAZ), 233, 235
Banking, 194-95
banks, 124, 187-88, 192, 231
benefits and contributions, 123
benefits for farmers, 107

benefits of development, 218
benefits of economic growth, 219
Benhabib, 259, 278
bereavement, 182
Bismarck, 210
Bismarckian, 122
Bismarckian strategy, 121
Bismarckien, 144
Bismarck Model, 121
Bouman, 182-83, 194
Butegwa, 66, 87
Button, 250, 254
Bwalya, 49, 62

C

Cambridge, 41, 62, 86, 113, 116, 177, 195, 237, 254-55, 256,
Cameroon, 89
Cameroonian Data, 278
Canada's Educational System, 114
Canadian Journal, 12, 86, 113-14, 145, 161, 193, 235, 254
capacity, xi, 14, 24-25, 35, 40, 50, 71, 160, 169, 175, 251-52
    administrative, 34
Carnegie Corporation of New York (CCNY), 161
cases, 19-20, 59, 61, 112, 115, 118-19, 157-58, 160, 162-63, 165-66, 171-72, 236-37, 249
case studies, 46, 165-66, 170, 172, 202, 209
Case Study, 51, 54, 115, 170-71, 184, 194, 209, 259-81
    qualitative, 151
cash transfer policies, 149, 158
cash transfer programme, largest, 142
Cash Transfer Programme for Orphans and Vulnerable Children, 161
cash transfer programmes, 27, 147-49, 151, 153-54, 156-58
    conditional, 217
cash transfers, conditional, 32
cash transfers (CT), x, 7, 16, 60, 93, 147-51, 155, 157-58, 161, 241
Cass, Frank, 177

Catalyst, 161
Centre for Applied Social Sciences, 87
Centre for Social Science Research (CSSR), 62, 256
Centre for Studies on Africa Economies (CSAE), 279
Centre for the Study of Globalisation and Regionalisation (CSGR), 89
century, mid-twentieth, 242
Cheltenham, 89, 118-19, 162, 255
children, 50, 53, 59, 71, 79, 82, 186-87, 189-91, 200, 204, 243-44, 247-52, 256, 267
Children in South African Families, 256
child support, 100
Child Well-Being, 256
Child Well-Being in South Africa, 256
Chile, 141, 162
citizenry, 170, 198
citizenry entitlements, 45
citizens, 1-2, 7, 15-17, 45, 47, 59-60, 91, 93-94, 100, 153-54, 157-58, 165, 215-16
    diseased, 46
    older, 53
    ordinary, 35, 50
    second-class, 45
citizens accessing, 50
citizens decent, 216
citizenship, 14, 18, 20-21, 45, 61, 89, 100, 108, 113, 227, 237-39
Civil Society and Associational Life in Africa, 113
Civil Society Organizations in Ethiopia, 117
civil society participation, 167
CODESRIA, x, xii, 3-4, 10, 12-13, 25-26, 42, 61, 238
CODESRIA and African Institute for Agrarian Studies, 239
    conceptual position, 181
conclusion, 10, 61, 67, 84, 94, 141, 148, 160, 166, 176, 275-76
conference, x, 3, 13-14, 25, 40, 237
Conference on Economic Development in Africa, 279

Index 285

conference on social policy, 13
conference on Social Policy in Africa, 13
CONGOMA (Council for Non-Governmental Organisations in Malawi), 170
CONGOMA and FEDOMA, 170
Consumer Finances, 124
consumer price indices (CPIs), 267
Consumer Research, 88
consumers, 123
Consumers association, 102, 106
Contemporary Approaches, 163
Contemporary Approaches to Public Policy, 163
Contemporary Ethiopian Political Life, 118
contemporary pan-African documents, important, 20
Contemporary Shona, 236
Contemporary Sociology, 86
Contemporary Welfare States, 254
Contemporary World, 90
Contemporary Zimbabwe, 239
contend, 59, 182, 192
Contending Visions, 1
contentandview, 210
contestations, 11, 17, 34, 38, 154
contested notion, 19
Contested Power in Ethiopia, 118
Contested Roles of Individuals, 254
Contested Terrain, 239
Continuities, 115
contracted silicosis, 251
contraction, 24
contracts, 65, 157
Contracts on Rural Income and Production, 12
Convention People's Party (CPP), 51
conventions, 68
  new, 24
convergence, 148
convergence of interests, 148
Convergence of Interests and Resource Base, 159
Converging Interests, 152
Conversation, 177
Conway, 117

Cooperatives and Contracts on Rural Income and Production, 12
co-operatives in Ethiopia, 93
Cooperative Societies Proclamation, 110
Copenhagen, 32, 209
Copenhagen Social Summit, 37
Copenhagen summit, 32
Copenhagen World Summit, 4
coping mechanisms, traditional, 109
Coping Strategies and Social Change, 41
copper, 54-56
copper mining, 57-58
copper revenues, 56
Core Issues, 177
co-residents, 245
cornerstone, 75
Cornwall, 100, 113
Corporate Social Responsibility (CSR), 34, 40
corporations, 38, 40
Corporatist, 174
Corral, 152, 161
Correctional Services, 247, 254
correlation
correlations, 75, 78, 137
Correlations of Household Cultivable Land Size and Selected Social Reproductive Variables, 76
Costa, 88
Costa Leite, 147, 162
Costa Rica, 162
cost-burden, 200
cost of increased surveillance and local politicisation, 110
cost-of-living differences, 267
costs and benefits, 124
costs and benefits of actions, 124
Council, 3, 13, 110
Courier ACP-EU, 176
Cousins, 215, 226, 236
Covariate shocks, 101
Covid-19, 65, 101, 115
Covid-19 pandemic, 65, 253
CPIs, regional, 267
CPIs (consumer price indices), 267

CPP (Convention People's Party), 51
Cramer, 139, 143
CREAD, 144
creation, 18-19, 53-54, 60, 113, 145,
    156, 158
credit, 6, 66, 74, 92, 100, 102, 104-7,
    110, 113, 187, 190
    distribute, 92
Credit Associations, 104, 185, 194
credit groups, 97-99, 111
credit schemes, 7
Credit Societies, 194
credit union, 185
Creswell, 219, 236
crimes, 49, 191
criminal gangs, 24
criminalise, 48
criminality, 191
criminalization, 248
crises, 27, 34, 37, 84, 100-101, 108, 111,
    143, 211, 237-38, 240
    environmental, 14
    financial, 31
    first oil, 57
    fiscal, 30, 198
    generalised institutional, 34
    global debt, 33
    recurrent, 34
    social reproductive, 83
    world oil, 57
Critical, 28
critical component for social
    reproduction, 80
Critical Dimensions of Women's Access to
    Land and Relations, 90
Critical Issues, 26
Critical Reflections, 162
Critical Theory, 41
Critical Theory of Care, 256
critics, 156, 214, 226
critiques, 40, 166, 169, 178
Croatian retirees, 124
cronyism, 214, 221
cronyism and political patronage to
    control, 214

Croom Helm Ltd, 194
Croppenstedt, 101, 113, 116
crop production, 232
    plot-level, 97
crops, 66, 110, 229-32
Crop/seed producer and marketing
    group/co-ops, 97
Crop/seed producer/marketing co-op,
    102, 104-5
Cross-Country Investigation, 115
cross-subsidisation, 202
cross-tabulations, 75
Crummey, 100, 113
crystallising, 46
CSA (Central Statistical Agency), 95, 113
CSAE (Centre for Studies on Africa
    Economies), 279
CSGR (Centre for the Study of Globalisation
    and Regionalisation), 89
CSMBS (Civil Servants Medical Benefits
    Scheme), 204
CSO-01, 156-57
CSO alignment, 157
CSOs, domestic, 156
CSOs (civil-society organisations), 23,
    156-58, 251
CSR (Corporate Social Responsibility),
    34, 40
CSSR (Centre for Social Science Re-
    search), 62, 256
CSSR Working Paper, 62
CT. *See* cash transfers
CT-OVC, 7, 148, 151-52, 155
cultivable land size, 74-75, 78, 80-83
cultural background, 230
Cultural Change, 116
cultural projection, 48
culture, 18-19, 90, 100, 250, 255
    democratic, 11
Culture of Power in Contemporary
    Ethiopian Political Life, 118
CUP hospital, 205
Current Agricultural Extension Program
    in Ethiopia, 115
Current Extension System of Ethiopia, 115

Current Sociology, 254
Currey, James, 116, 178
cycles, 156
  election, 154

D
dabare, 100, 112
Dagmawit Giref Sahile, 91
Dairy Supply Chains, 12
Dakar, 3, 12-13, 26, 41-42, 61, 117, 238-39, 254
Dalhousie University Economics Working
  Paper, 280
Daly, 248, 254
Damtew, 108, 113
Dangwa, 238
Dani, 15-17, 27
Dar-es Salaam, 27-28
dar ber, 42
Dasgupta, 99, 113, 115, 118
Decentralised Land Reform, 237
decile ratios, 9, 260-61, 266, 269, 271
deciles, 269-70
  richest, 270
Deciles of income and decile ratios, 261, 269
Decision Making, 144
Deckers, 117
declarations, 201
declarative question, first, 128
declarative questions, 126
declining numbers, 109
Declining Social Capital, 117
decolonisation, 20
Decolonization, 62
decomposing, 266
Decomposition of Inequality by Development
  Agencies, 178
development agendas, 24, 31, 66
  ambitious, 172
  economic, 52
  national, 175
  transformational, 15
developmental period, 30
developmental role in societies, 217
developmental states, 46, 62, 177
development and nation-building, 47

development and politics, 19
development community, 4
Development Contex, 42
Development Context, 27, 29, 62, 70, 88-89,
  177, 181, 195, 210, 217, 237, 239
Development Cooperation, 181, 195
Development Diplomats, 178
development discourses, 167-68
  international, 4, 31
Development Economics, 1, 62, 145,
  236, 279
Development Economics Research, 26
development efforts, 4, 48
  early post-independence Africa's, 3
  national, 48
development facilities, 49
Development Finance, 177
development goals, 20, 240
  achieving, 37
development groups, 95, 98, 107
development groups in Ethiopia, 107
development industry, 22
  global, 24
development initiatives, 56, 173
  effective, 216
development in sub-Saharan Africa, 217
Development Intervention, 176
development issues, 26, 234
development literature, 29
development models, 33
Development NGOs, 177
development objectives, 50, 259
  wider, 47
development of Germany's health
  insurance system, 203
development of organic formal social
  policy, 193
development of South Africa, 172
Development of Transformative Social
  Policy in South Korea, 236
development organisations, 98
development outcomes, 32
Development Paper, 12, 237
development perspective, 3, 194
development planning, 16

development plans, 52, 57
Development Policy, 166, 176, 279
Development Policy and Economic Change in Zambia, 63
Development Policy Management Forum, 26
Development Policy Review, 112
development process, 14, 16, 31, 165
development processes unfolding, 45
development projects, 17, 101, 107, 109, 168
  small local, 95
Development Research, 27, 116, 118, 195, 237, 255
Development Southern Africa, 194-95
Development Studies, 12, 26-27, 42, 90, 115-16, 155, 161, 193, 211, 235, 254
Development Studies Studies, 86
development teams, 95
development teams/groups, 95
development trajectories, 95
Developpement, 12, 86, 193, 235, 254
DÈveloppement, 161, 206
Difficult Socio-political Contexts, 177-78
digital technology, 141
dignity, 182, 216, 227, 229, 245, 255, 257
  human, 193
Dikeledi, 188, 190
Dilemmas Facing Non-Government Organisations, 115
Dimensionen, 42
Diminished Access, 87
Dinars, 127, 130
Dinkelman, 82, 87
Dinki, 113
Direct Beneficiaries, 255
direct government provision of social welfare, 59
direction, 6, 20, 153-54
disabilities, 30, 50, 53, 122, 126, 148, 170-71, 200, 205, 241
  Discussion, 75, 86, 107, 177, 211
Discussion Paper, 280
disease, 3, 13, 46, 60, 122, 171, 198, 227, 231
Disempowering New Democracies, 42
dismantling, 31, 34, 40

disparities, 227, 259, 262, 277
  sectoral income, 262
  socio-economic, 52
  stark, 47
displaced persons, 200
displacement, 214
disproportionate amounts, 248
disproportionate amounts of wealth in South Africa, 248
disproportionate burden of social reproduction, 71
disproportionate share, 69
disruptions, massive, 22
Dissaving, 143
dissemination, 24
distances, 77, 80
Distortions of Democracy in Zimbabwe, 238
distress, 18, 155
distribution, 60, 72, 108, 150, 254, 260, 267, 269, 271, 273-74, 276-78
  District Social Services Officer, 233
diswelfares, 1-2
diversification, 39
diversifying diets, 231
diversity, 19, 167, 185, 219, 265
Diverted Exclusion, 87
divide-and-rule tactics, 48
division, 68-69
  better gender, 85
  gendered, 69
  traditional, 249
Division II Faculty Publications, 194
divorced/separated/single, 74
DIWODE (Disabled Women in Development), 170
Djeddah, 119
Dlamini, 111, 113
documents, x, 12, 176, 211
documents.worldbank.org, 63
Dohmen, 136, 143
DOI, 62, 89, 112, 115-17, 161-63, 176-77, 209, 235, 237, 254-55, 279-80
Dolowitz, 151, 158, 162
domains, 8
  economic, 56

Index

Domboshava, 222
Domestic Politics, 12, 162
domestic resource mobilisation, 38, 41-42
DWOOM (Disabled Widows Orphans of Malawi), 170
Dworkin, 257
Dworzanowski-Venter, 247, 249, 254
Dying Symbol, 239
Dynamic Risk Management, 119
dynamics, 6-7, 11, 26, 174, 184-85, 224
　changing group membership, 107
　cross-cutting, 24
　global, 15
DZD, 127, 130, 132-33, 138-40

E

early expression of mutual aid, 181
early nationalist experiments in countries, 15
Early Neoclassical Thought, 145
Early Twenty-First Century, 89
Earned Income Tax Credit (EITC), 123, 142
earning decisions, 123
earnings, 2, 66, 69, 85, 142
　male, 69
Earnings Responses, 143
earthquakes, 219
Earthscan Books, 25-26
East Africa, 90
East African, 261
East Asia, 218
East Asian, 250
Eastern Cape, 257
Eastern Democratic Republic, 256
East Province, 214
ECA, 280
Econometrica, 279
econometric analysis, 6, 137
Economic & Political Weekly, 143
economic actors reap, 167
economic analysis, 70, 145
Economic and Social Commission for Western Asia (ESCWA), 194
Economic and social policies, 36
Economic Behavior & Organization, 143

economic behaviour, 180
Economic Change in Zambia, 63
Economic Changes, 118
economic choices, 193
　better, 123
economic policy of Ghana, 58
economic rationality, 180-81, 193, 195
Economic rationality and social values, 181
Economic Rebound, 235
Economic Rebound to Sustained Growth, 235
Economic Report on Africa, 280
Economic Research Forum (ERF), 142
Economic Restructuring, 41
economic risks in developing countries, 226
Economics, 22, 62, 86, 115, 118, 142-45, 177, 185, 194-95, 263
　mainstream, 67
economic significance, 226
Economics of RoSCAS, 194
economic stagnation, 32
economic strategies, important, 20
economic structure, 18
Economic Studies, 145, 279
economic support in South Africa, 244
Economic Survey, 263
Economics Working Paper Series, 143
economic systems in sub-Saharan Africa, 46
Economic Transformation, 20, 27, 177, 194
economic trends, 166
economies and social relations, 60
economies in crisis, 37
economies of scale, 267
…conomique, 145
economists, 29, 66
　monetarist, 30
economy, 1-3, 14, 16-17, 37, 39, 49, 52, 56-58, 60-61, 144, 179, 182, 198-99, 216-18, 267
Economy and State, 194
economy to influence access, 49, 70
Ecuador, 142
Edgerton, 100, 114
Edinburgh, 237

Edir, 92-93, 97, 99-107, 111
Editorial, 90
Editorial Introduction, 236
EDP (Emergency Development Plan), 55
Edward Elgar Publishers, 162
Edward Elgar Publishing, 89, 255
Edwards, 99, 114, 177
e-ferguson-and-david-mcnally, 88
effecting, 49, 169
effecting and protecting social wellbeing of people, 169
Effective Developmental Cooperation, 236
effective nation-building processes in Ghana and Zambia, 61
effectiveness, xi, 169
  concomitant state, 23
Effective States, 163
effect on social policy in sub-Saharan Africa, 171
Effects of Conflict on Women, 256
Effects on Economic Growth, 279
EI (extractive industries), 39
EIAR (Ethiopian Institute of Agricultural Research), 96-97, 102, 104-6
Eighty, 94
EITC (Earned Income Tax Credit), 123, 142
EITC Recipients, 143
EITC rules, 123
elaboration, x
Elson, 68, 88
emancipation, 16, 20-21, 26
emancipation element, 20
emancipatory, 15, 18, 47
emancipatory and transformational development agenda in Africa, 15
embeddedness, 179
  mutual, 180
embittered parochial, 51
Emerald Group Publishing Limited, 145
emergence, 22-24, 213, 215, 220
emergencies, 35, 58, 187-89, 192, 205, 231-32
Emergency Development Plan (EDP), 55
emergency situations, 189

Emergent Agrarian Structure, 219
Emergent Communities, 236
emergent nationhood, 60
Emerging Forms, 238
emerging issues, 15, 24
Emerging Issues in Transformative Social Policy and Inclusive Development, 24
Emmanuel Boon, 45
emphasise, 4, 29, 37, 68
Empirical Assessment, 116
Empirical Determinants of Intertemporal Choice, 143
empirical evidence, 66, 74, 118, 194, 214
Employer-Employee Matched Data, 145
employment generation, 32
Employment Incentive Bill, 245
Enabling Norms, 188
enabling norms and values, 186
enabling norms and values of mutual-support societies, 186
Enabling Norms and Values of Mutual-Support Societies and Activities, 188
encapsulates, 216
encountering, 124
endogenous claims, 7
Endogenous Determination of Time, 142
Endogenous Growth, 279
enduring nature, 181
enemy of the state, 58
energy, 58, 71, 79, 82, 166
  energy demands on women, 80
energy for women, 79, 82
Energy-Using Durables, 143
enforcement, 7, 186
enfranchisement, 45
Engage Alliance, 251
engagement, 2, 162, 165, 175
engines, 66
  multiple, 18
Entrepreneurship, 143
entry conditions, 203
entry point, 72
enumerators, 98
environment, 7, 33-34, 175
  conducive, 241

international, 22
   poor educational, 248
   prevailing capitalist, 8
   violent, 54
Environmental Adaptability, 239
environmental challenges and inequality, 4
environmental challenges and inequality in framing, 4
Environmental Problems, 39
Envuladu, 211
Epidemiology, 279
ERF (Economic Research Forum), 142
ERF Working Paper Series, 142
Erkundungen, 42
erosion, 22
erratic rainfall patterns, 73
Erring members, 182
Escompte Quasi-Hyperbolique, 144
ESCWA (Economic and Social Commission for Western Asia), 194
ESID Working Papers, 163
Ethiopia and Tanzania, 114
Ethiopia Country Strategy Paper, 112
Ethiopia Internship, 115
Ethiopia Mini Demographic and Health Survey, 113
Ethiopian Agricultural Cooperatives, 114
Ethiopian Agriculture, 114
Ethiopian Coffee Cooperatives, 117
Ethiopian Culture, 116
Ethiopian Economic Association/Ethiopian Economic Policy Research Institute, 115
Ethiopian Institute of Agricultural Research. *See* EIAR
Ethiopian Journal, 117
Ethiopian life, 92
Ethiopian People's Revolutionary Democratic Front. *See* EPRDF
Ethiopian person's life, 107
Ethiopian society, 99
Ethiopian women, 99
Ethiopia Poverty Assessment, 119
Ethiopia's Derg, 92
Ethiopia's Growth and Transformation Plan II, 95
Ethiopia's poverty reduction, 94
Ethnic, 62
ethnic background, 59, 111
ethnic balkanisation, 5
ethnic communities, 20
Ethnic Diversity, Democratisation, 61
ethnic factionalism, 5
ethnic factionalism and enhancing nation-building in Zambia, 5
ethnic group of South Africa, 185
ethnicity, 4, 36, 79, 216
ethnic prejudice, 48
ethnic rivalries, 46
Ethnocentrism, 48
ethnographic field study, 73
Ethnography, 236
Etiaba, 211
…tudes, 12, 86, 161, 193, 235, 254
Eurocentric, 51
Europe, 209, 218
European Economic Association, 143
European Economic Review, 144, 278
European experience, 40
European Journal, 27, 117-18, 195, 237, 255
European Journal of Health Economics, 209
European Observatory, 204, 209
European Report, 26, 41, 61, 117, 254
Experimental Approach, 142
Experimental Evidence, 144
Experimental Psychology, 143-44
experiments, 13, 16, 143
   early nationalist, 15
   socioeconomic, 4
Expert Group Meeting, 90, 240
expertise, 150-51, 157, 168, 214
   supposed, 168
   technical, 158
expertise and knowledge, 150
Expert Meeting on Social Inclusion Programmes, 88
experts, 157
Explain Income Inequality Make, 259
Explaining Donor Delivery Tactics, 177

exploitation, 36, 45, 68
exploration, 148
export sales, 55
expost, viewed, 217
Expounding, 157
expression, 16, 115
expression and definition, 16
Expropriation, 239
extended family, 100, 228
    traditional African, 242
Extending Insurance, 114
Extending Social Protection, 117
extension, 3, 38, 116
    agricultural, 96
Extension Directorate, 116
extension information, 110
    sharing agricultural, 95
    transferring agriculture, 110
Extension Service, 22, 114, 116
    agricultural, 112
extraction/production, 179
extractive industries (EI), 39
Extreme Poor, 62
Eydal, 255

F
Faber Books, 27
facet, 50, 59
Facilitator, 114
facilities, 72, 76, 230-31
    expanded educational, 55
    referral, 205
    secondary, 205
    storage, 230
Farrar, 177
fast-paced programme, 55
Fast-Policy Integration, 163
Fast Tracking Land Reform, 237
Fast Track Land Reform, 237-38
Fast-Track Land Reform, 89
Fast Track Land Reform Baseline Survey, 238
Fast Track Land Reform Baseline Survey in Zimbabwe, 238

Fast Track Land Reform in Mwenezi District, 89, 238
Fast Track Land Reform in Zimbabwe, 236
Fast Track Land Reform Programme, 73, 237
Fast-Track Land Reform Programme. See FTLRP
Fast-track policymakers, 85
Fast Track Reform, 239
Fatherhood, 256
Fatherhood Beliefs, 257
Fathering practices, 252
fathers, 85, 242, 248-49, 255
Federation of Disability Organisations in Malawi. See FEDOMA
FEDOMA (Federation of Disability Organisations in Malawi), 170-71
FEDOMA's members, 170
fee, 205
    junior brother's university registration, 187
    monthly, 188
female, 77-78, 91, 97, 115, 125, 138, 140, 225
female employees, 251
Female-headed Household Group Membership, 102-3
Feminist Visions, 115
Feng, 182, 194
Fentale District, 112
FER/EIP Discussion Paper, 209
Ferguson, 67-68, 71, 242, 244, 246-48, 254
    Susan, 67
Fergusson, 88
Ferrant, 79-80, 82, 87
Ferreira, 261, 279
fertilisers, 57, 92, 107, 110, 233
FGD participants, 219
FGDs (focus group discussions), 73-74, 83, 184, 219, 228-29, 233
FHHs (female-headed households), 6, 74, 78-79, 82-83, 98, 102-3, 109
field activities, 75-76
field-based development work, 168
Field Experiment, 144
Fielding, 183, 194

Field Research, 194
Household Survey, 223
First Social Security Laws, 255
First Year Anniversary Lecture, 61
fiscal bases, 22
fiscal devolution, 25
Fischer, 12
Fish, 254
Fishery association, 105
Fitzegerald, 237
Fitzgerald, 12, 88
flagship report, 31
flat rates and value, 38
flex nets, 150
Flint, 49, 61
Flow of Benefits, 115
fluctuations, 215
FNDP (First National Development Plan), 56
focus, x-xi, 9, 11, 14, 29, 31, 141-42, 180-81, 214, 217, 241-42, 247, 249, 251-52
Food and Agriculture Organization. *See* FAO
food crop production, 214
food expenditure, 265, 267
food insecurity, 95, 152, 214
food issues, 231
Food Policy, 113
food preparation, 69
food prices, 230
food production, 65
food security, 49, 112, 115, 230-31, 236, 239
   longer-term, 101
   relative, 8
food security and crop protection, 230
Foreign Trade, 209
Formal, 97, 117-18, 255
formal administrative unit, lowest, 110
formal financial institutions, 180, 186, 192
formalisation, 250
formal legal authority, 150
formal market economy, 193
Formal public service contractors, 250
formal sector, 201, 244

private, 181
formal sector programme, 199, 201
Formal Sector Social Health Insurance Programme (FSSHIP), 200
Formal Social Protection in Ethiopia, 118
Formal Social Protection in Sub-Saharan Africa, 114
Formal Social Protection Systems, 118
Formal Social Protection Systems in Sub-Saharan Africa, 27, 112, 114, 118
forward-lookers, 125
forward looking, 6
forward-looking behaviour and knowledge, 121, 128
Forward-Looking Choices, 132
foundations, 23, 162, 214
Foundations of Social Theory, 113
founders, 19
founding president of Ghana, 46, 51
Fountain Publishers, 27, 112, 114, 118
Fourth Republic, 62
Fowler, 168, 177
Framing Paper, 177
France, 143, 279
Francesconi, 93, 114
Francophone African, 241
Frankfurt, 41
Frankfurt/Madrid, 42
Franzoni, 151, 162
Fraser, 41, 55, 58, 85, 87
Frazer, 61
Frederick, 1
free basic schooling for children, 243
freedom, 14, 16, 20, 27-28, 45, 66, 87, 157, 182, 226
freedom and independence, 20
FTLRP (Fast-Track Land Reform Programme), 5, 73-75, 81-82, 84-85, 213-15, 219-21, 223-29, 232-34, 238
FTLRP and Input Transfers, 232
FTLRP in Goromonzi, 214
FTLRP in Zimbabwe, 81, 84
FTLRP on peasant households, 214
FTLRP process, 225
fuel, 71, 259

G

Gaidzanwa, 215, 224, 236-37
Galor, 259, 279
Gamal Nasser, 21
Gambari, 60
Gambela, 171
game changer, 29
games, played, 191
gap in inequality, 265
gaps, 57, 93, 100-101, 109, 122, 175-76, 197, 265
   a, 102
   analytical, 67
   gendered output, 69
   major social policy, 170
   rural income, 264
   urban income, 271, 277
   widening, 244
   yawning, 165, 173
garbage collections, 191
Garcia, 50, 62
garden, 82-83
Garissa, 274-75
garner votes, 154
Garthe, 256
Gasper, 66, 69, 87
gathered data on ownership, 74
GBV (gender-based violence), 247, 251, 256
GCB, 88
GDP (Gross Domestic Product), 65, 94, 198
GDP growth, 94
GDPs, highest, 55
GE. *See* Generalised Entropy
Gebremedhin, 92, 96, 114
GE indices, 260
GE indices of inequality, 266
Geld, 42
gender, 16, 18, 36, 39, 65-90, 96, 99, 114, 116, 224-25, 251, 254, 256-57
   ignoring, 68
   linking, 67
Gender Analysis, 115
Gender Analysis and Policy, 115
Gender and Agrarian Reforms, 88, 237
Gender and Care, 256
Gender and Care Work in South Africa, 255
Gender and Governance in Rural Services, 119
Gender and Land Reforms, 88
Gender and Social Capital for Agricultural Development, 116
Gendered Politics of Farm Household Production, 86
gendered poverty and inequality, 75, 80-81, 85
gendered processes of poverty and inequality, 66
Gendered socialisation, 252
gender equality, 38, 72, 80, 85, 89, 95, 225, 251, 253
   achieving, 84
Gender Equality Survey, 256
gender equity, 87, 252, 254
gender experts, 29
Gender Gaps, 87, 89
gender identity, 242
gender ideology, 68
Gender Ideology and Social Reproduction, 68
gender ideology in social reproduction, 68
Gender-Impact Analysis of Economic Policy, 88
Gender Implications of Decentralised Land Reform, 237
generating role of livestock, 231
generations, 35, 39-40, 71, 75
   new, 23
   old, 191
Geneva, 3, 12, 27, 41-43, 62, 86, 88-90, 209, 211, 235, 237-40
geographic position, 56
Geographies, 176
Geography Compass, 88, 163
Georgia State University, 178
geostrategic, 166
Gerecke, 71, 89, 220, 238
German healthcare system, 203
German Health Insurance System, 209

Index 295

German population, 203
German social health insurance system, 202
German translation, 43
Germany, 110, 197, 201-3, 208-9, 218, 245
    post-war, 31
Germany Methodologies, 209
Germany's health insurance system, 203
Getnet, 93, 114
Getu, 16, 27, 93, 112, 114, 118
Ghana, 5, 15, 46, 48, 51-54, 58-59, 61-63, 119, 162, 201, 210
    post-independent, 52
Ghana and Vietnam, 201
Ghana and Zambia, 5, 45-48, 59-61
Ghana and Zambia in contemporary times, 47
Ghana Education Trust, 53
Ghanaian government, 54
Ghanaians, 54
Ghana National Health Insurance, 209
Ghana's independence, 53
Ghana's population, 51
Ghana to Zambia, 46
Gift, 251
gift exchange arrangements, 100
giftofthegivers.org, 253
GII (Gender Inequality Index), 95
Gillard, 177
Gimenez, Martha, 67
Gini, 260-62, 264, 269, 272-73, 281
Gini coefficients, 263-66, 278
    total, 268
Gini coefficient values, 260
Gini estimates, 264, 273
Gini for income, 262
Gini index, 9, 259-62, 264, 266, 268, 272, 274, 276, 278
Gini index and General Entropy, 275
Gini Index Atkinson Index, 272
Gini indices, 260, 262, 273-74
Gini inequality indices, 268
Gini measure, 268, 273-74
Gini's Index Evolved, 280
girls, 80, 171

elderly, 83
girls and women, 171
Giroux, 177
Givers Foundation, 251
Glaser, 248, 254
Glassner, 184, 195
Glenn, 182, 194
global architectures, 24
global budget, 205
global campaign, 31
    effective, 172
global climate change programmes, 24
global commitments, xi
Global Commodity Exchange, 114
global context, changing, 34
Global Crisis, 28
Global Development Agendas, 12, 201
Global Development Working Paper Number, 278
GNP (Gross National Product), 54
goal of universal coverage, 201
goals for society, 16
goats, 231-32
    sold, 232
Godana, 257
Godwin R, xii
GoK (Government of Kenya), 148, 264, 266, 279
Gokwe, 222
Gold, 116
Goldblatt, 254
Gold Coast, 53
Goldstein, 52, 61
Golooba-Mutebi, 108, 115
gombana, 230
Gonah, 73, 89
Gonese, 81, 85, 87
good and medium knowledge of social security, 140
Good Business Practice, 194
goods, 68, 72, 124, 129
    durable, 267
    producing, 52
    time-saving household, 81
good social policy, 240

Governance and Performance of
    Ethiopian Coffee Cooperatives, 117
Governance and Social Development
    Resource Centre, 113
governance challenges, 38
Governance in Rural Services, 119
Governance Research, 255
government activities, 95
government agencies, 219

H
Haan, 15-17, 21, 26-27
Habtu, 111, 115
Hadjiisky, 162
Hagberg, 117
Hagenbach, 216
Hagenbuch, 237
Haile, 117
Haki Elimu, 27-28
Hall, 169, 177, 181, 194
HDI, 14
head, male, 98
Headlands, 222
Head W/barrow, 77
health, 22, 25, 32, 34, 56, 58, 71-72, 141-42,
    198, 200-201, 206-7, 209-11, 215
Healthcare in Nigeria, 198
healthcare services, 199-200, 202
    basic, 199
    primary, 201
healthcare system, 206
    achieving universal, 206
    high-quality, 172
Health Care Systems in Transition, 209
Health Economics, 209
health insurance and land reform, 8
health insurance coverage, 206
health insurance funds, 204
health insurance funds in Thailand, 204
Health Insurance Plans, 207
Health Insurance Plans in Thailand, 204
health insurance programmes, 202
health insurance schemes, 204, 206
    individual, 8
Heinrich, 179, 194

Heinrich B^ll Foundation, 28
Heintz, 37, 41, 69, 87
Helleiner, 198, 210
Hellicker, 236
Helliker, 239
Helliwell, 99, 115
Helms, 137, 144
help, 81-83, 96, 111-12, 141, 171, 187-92,
    226, 249
    hired, 5
    in-kind, 93
    women's caregiving roles, 249
help Africa embark, 172
help members start, 112
help register, 187
Helsinki, 12, 27-28, 114, 162, 278
Hendricks, 257
Henry, 66, 88, 150, 162
Hens, 145
Heras, 93, 117
Herbs, 230
Heritage, 28
heritage, common, 173
Heroin Addicts Discount Delayed
    Rewards, 144
    post-colonial, 54
HIV, 172, 250-51
HIV/AIDS, 214
HIV/AIDS pandemic, 152
    global, 171
HIV prevention, 172
hizb aderjajet, 110
Hlatshwayo, 245, 255
Hoare, 162
Hochfeld, 248, 255-56
Hoekstra, 114
Hofisi, 174
holistic, x, 4, 15-17, 226, 241
holistic development thinking, 217
holistic strategies, 16
Holmes, 93, 118, 241-42, 255
Holzman, 216, 219, 237
Homa Bay, 275
HSCT (Harmonised Social Cash Transfer),
    233

HSCT scheme, 233
Hsiao, 197, 201-2, 210
HSNP (Hunger Safety Net Programme), 7, 148, 151, 155
HSNP models, 152
HSNP programmes, 161
HSRC Press, 255-56
Huffman, 143
Hujo frames, 4
Hujo highlights, 4
Hulme, 42, 163
human beings, 18
Human capacities, 72
Human Decision Processes, 144
human development, 14, 16-17, 118, 162
Human Development and International Cooperation, 119
Human Development Indicators, 14
Human Development in Zambia, 63
Human Development Report, 95, 118
human flourishing, 2
Human Geography, 176
Human Insecurity, 86
Humanism, 46, 57
Humanist, 62
Humanities, 117
Human Resource Management, 255
human rights, 20, 37-38, 41-42, 45-46, 110, 167, 173, 181, 200, 211
abused, 94
human rights abuses, 214
Human Rights and Land Reform, 239
Human Rights-Based Approaches, 41
human rights framework, 251
human rights issues, critical, 171
human rights law, 227
human rights standards, 38
human right to social security, 41-42
humans, 8, 181
Human Sciences Research Council, 257
human wretchedness, 45
Hundred, 209
Hunger Insurance, 117
Hunger Safety Net Programme. *See* HSNP

Hyperbolic Delay-Discounting, 144
hyperbolic discount factor, 139-40
Hyperbolic Discount Functions, 144
Hyper-Temporal Imagery, 89
Hypher, 71, 89, 161, 220, 238
hypothesis, 131, 134-36, 139-41, 268

I

IDRC (International Development Research Centre), 25-26, 61, 90
IDRC Scoping Study, 90
IDS Bulletin, 163, 237, 255
IDS Working Paper, 90, 236
IFIs (international financial
IKS (Indigenous Knowledge Systems), 46
illuminating, 70
illustrious, x
ILO (International Labour Organisation), 50, 62, 121, 141-43, 147, 263
ILO Social Protection Floor Recommendation No, 32
ILRI (International Livestock Research Institute), 114, 116
Images of women, 83
imagination, 248
collective, 61
IMF (International Monetary Fund), 58-59, 199, 210
important technique to measure, 80
Inclusive Development Centre, 163
inclusive development in Africa, 25
inclusive growth, 17, 27, 173
Indigenous Knowledge Systems (IKS),
inequality accounts, 275
Inequality and Economic Growth, 278
Inequality and Growth, 236, 279
Inequality and Growth Revisited, 278
inequality in sub-Saharan Africa, 261
inequality is large and growing, 265
inequality levels, 147
Informal Economies, 255
Informal Economies in Developing Countries, 255
informal economy, 33, 36, 255
Informal Economy in Algeria, 143

Informal Employment Globalizing, 37
Informal farmer group, 104
Informal Financial Institutions for Survival, 195
informal groups in Ethiopia, 97
informal groups matter, 94
informal groups matter to farmers, 94
informal institution/group, 97
Informal Institutions, 118
Informal Institutions in Social Accountability, 113
Informal Labor-sharing Arrangements, 116
Informal protections in sub-Saharan Africa, 117
informal sector, 243, 248
  robust, 243
Informal Sector Social Health Insurance Programme (ISSHIP), 200
informal social protection, 91-119
informal social protection in Ethiopia, 93
Informal Social Protection in Sub-Saharan Africa, 118
informal social protection matter, 108
informal social protection mechanisms, 101-2
informal system of social protection, 52
informal system of social protection in Ghana, 52
INGOs, 23
Innovation in Ethiopian Culture, 116
innovative measures of inequality, 277
inpatient, 205
input of agriculture extension knowledge, 107
inputs, 72, 81, 91-92, 94-95, 107, 214, 219, 233
  agricultural, 74, 107, 233-34
  government-supported, 110
  produced, 68
  subsidised, 233
integration of non-state actors, 168
integration of transformative social policy, 14

intellectual career, x
intellectual rationalisations, new, 22
intelligence, 58
  artificial, 23
INTEMPOWERMENT/Resources/Ethiopia, 113
Intensification, 24
Intensive Resettlement Policies, 237
intention, 56, 219
intentionality, 18
interactions, 118, 128, 150, 160-61, 179
interactions and interests, 161
inter-class, 1
interconnectedness, 250
Inter-connected World, 115
interconnections, 68
Interdependent Relationship, 117
interest and resource deployment, 7
interest groups, 40, 155
interest in social protection, 150
interest in social protection by politicians, 154
interest rate, 124
interests in policy transfer, 151
interests of communities, 168
interethnic marriages, 57
interference, external, 198
interferences, 35
intergovernmental, 168
international Arena, 172
international array, 17
International Centre, 117
international commodity boom, 35
International Conference, 26-27, 177
International Conference on Primary Health Care, 209
International Contexts, 38, 163
International Convention, 171
International Convention on the Rights of Persons with Disabilities (ICRPD), 171
International Convergence, 163
International Cooperation, 119
International Development, 88, 117, 194, 263

Index 299

International Development Research Centre. *See* IDRC
International Development Working Paper, 257
international donor community, 32
International Economic Review, 143
International Finance, 210
international financial institutions. *See* IFIs
international funding baskets, 24
international global coalition and networks of social protection, 159
International Household Survey Network, 113
International Implications, 238
internationalisation, 24
International Journal, 12, 26, 86, 162, 176, 193-94, 209-10, 235, 256
International Journal of African Historical Studies, 61
International Journal on Human Development and International Cooperation, 119
international knowledge and competence in development, 151
international knowledge and competence in development of new
International Labour Office, 88
International Labour Organisation. *See* ILO
International Labour Organization, 62, 88, 143
International Law, 178
International Livestock Research Institute (ILRI), 114, 116
International Maize and Wheat Improvement Center, 96
International Monetary Fund. *See* IMF
International opposition, 4
international organisations, 148-51, 154-60, 168
International Publishers Co, 162
international remittances in Africa, 25
International Social Security Review, 41-42, 255

International Social Work, 256
International Studies, 89
International Studies Quarterly, 177
International Women's Studies, 88, 90
Intrahousehold Resource Allocation, 194
ISSHIP (Informal Sector Social Health Insurance Programme), 200
Issue Brief, 43
Issue Paper Series, 115
issues, 24-26, 29, 86-87, 90, 112, 114, 143-44, 162, 165, 169, 172, 194-95, 234, 237, 239
Issue S1, 194
issues of autonomy, 169
Issues Paper, 89
Italian occupation, 94
Italy, 115
Ivkovic, 122, 143
Ivoire, 22, 86

J

Jackson, 115
Jacobs, 67, 79, 88, 224, 237
Jalan, 74, 88
Jaleta, 114
Jambanja, 239
James, 181, 195, 197, 203, 209, 214, 237
James Currey Limited, 62
James Currey Press, 239
Japan, 31, 201, 218, 245, 250
Japanese Sociology, 256
Journal for Equity in Health, 210
Journal for Transdisciplinary Research in Southern Africa, 255
Journal of African Economies, 114
Journal of Agrarian Change, 90, 240
Journal of Agricultural Cooperation, 114
Journal of Agricultural Economics, 116
Journal of Applied Behavioral Science, 194
Journal of Asian and African Studies, 236
Journal of Business Economics Statistics, 88
Journal of Democracy, 117
Journal of Development Economics, 145, 236, 279

Journal of Development Studies, 42, 115-16
Journal of Economic Growth, 278
Journal of Economic Literature, 278
Journal of Economic Perspectives, 144, 279
Journal of Epidemiology and Community Health, 279
Journal of European Social Policy, 88
Journal of Experimental Psychology, 143-44
Journal of Financial Economics, 143
Journal of Human Development and Capabilities, 162
Journal of Human Resource Management, 255
Journal of International Development, 194
Journal of International Women's Studies, 88, 90
Journal of Labor Economics, 144
Journal of Opinion, 237
Journal of Peasant Studies (JPS), 89, 236, 238, 240
Journal of Political Economy, 89, 144, 238-39
Journal of Politics and Law, 62
Journal of Public Health Policy, 210
Journal of Social Development in Africa, 62, 115
Journal of Social Paradigm Studies, 240
Journal of Social Policy, 143, 257
Journal of Social Science Medicine, 209
journals, 143, 210
journeys, 4, 78
JPS. *See* Journal of Peasant Studies
Judicial Reforms, 162
jurisdiction, 233

K

Kassa, 96, 107, 115
Kassie, 112
Katja Hujo, x, 4, 29
Katy, 191
Katz, 179, 181-82, 194
Kaunda, 56-58, 62
Kenneth, 21, 46, 49, 55, 58
Kebede, 112

kebele, 95-97, 110
Keefer, 92, 115
keen, 56, 245
Kelboro, 116
Kelemework, 96, 107, 115
Kelly, 118
Kenaw, 113
Kendal, 167
Kendall, 177
Kennett, 89
Keno, 112
Kent, 177
Kenya, 7, 9, 11, 22, 26, 28, 55, 87, 147-63, 174, 259-81
Kenya Institute for Public Policy Research and Analysis (KIPPRA), 279
Kenya Integrated Household Budget Survey. *See* KIHBS
Kenya National Bureau, 266-67, 279-80
Kenya National Bureau of Statistics (KNBS), 263, 266-67, 279-80
Kenyan context, 261
Kenyan data, 271
Kenyan households, 260
Kenyans, 153
Kenyan study, 265
Kenya's Gini, 278
Kenya's inequality, 261
KES, 267
Kessler, 122, 143
Keswell, 249, 254
Ketsela, 96, 107, 115
Kevane, 67, 87
key, xi, 15, 20, 32, 47, 52, 56, 60, 66, 72, 73-74, 83, 85, 124, 126, 136, 149, 150, 152, 153, 166, 209, 261, 265, 275-76
played, 57
Keynesian approach, 31
Keynesian model, 30
Keynesian paradigm, 30
Keynesian policy approach, 30
Keynes's discovery, 30
keynote address, 13, 25, 39, 235
keynote chapters, x
keynote lectures, 3

KIPPRA (Kenya Institute for Public Policy Research and Analysis), 279
KIPPRA Discussion Paper, 279
Kipruto, 279
Kirby, 143-44
Kirinyaga, 275
Kironde, 167, 177
Kisumu, 274-76
Kitui, 275
Kjetil, 95, 110, 118
Kling, 123, 144
Knack, 92, 115, 119
Knapp, 167, 177
KNBS. *See* Kenya National Bureau of
Knowledge and Demand for Social Insurance, 131
knowledge and expertise, 157
knowledge and material support, 159
knowledge bank, 180
Knowledge Base, 143
Knowledge Broker, 114
Knowledge Gap, 116
knowledge of labour regimes, 23
knowledge of labour regimes and transborder, 23
knowledge of social insurance, 6
Knowledge of Social Security and Monthly Income, 130
Knowledge of Social Security by Age, 129
Knowledge of Social Security by Firm Size, 131
knowledge production, 26
knowledge resources, 159
knowledge systems, 23
knowledge transfer, 149, 158
knowledge workers, 124
Knowles, 113, 118, 183, 194
Kofo, 192
Kolawole Omomowo, 179
Konrad Adenauer Foundation's Conference, 178
Kontext, 41
Korean Experience, 236
Korean War, 264
Kostas, 182, 194

KouyatÈ, 150, 163
Kozel, 216, 219, 237
Kpessa, 59, 62, 177
Kredit, 42
Krishna, 92, 115-16
Kristie Drucza, 91
Kronde, 167, 177
Kropotkin, 179, 181-82
  Peter, 181
Kumar, 184, 195
Kumarian Press, 237
Kwame Nkrumah, 21, 28, 46, 51
Kwame Nkrumah's Politico-cultural Thought and Policies, 61
KwaNdangezi, 195
Kwarts, 63
Kwekwe, 234
Kwerepe, 49, 62
Kydd, 236
Kyomuhendo, 115

L
Laakso, 22, 27
Labor, 116
laboratories, open, 4
Labor Economics, 144
Land Reform and Civil Society in Contemporary Zimbabwe, 239
Land Reform and Redistribution in Zimbabwe, 238
land reform and social policy, 9
land reform and transformative social policy, 214
land reform in Zimbabwe, 72, 215, 227
Land Reform in Zimbabwe, 238
land reform programme, 8, 221
Land Reforms Consumption, 88
Land Registration, 87
land resource, 85
Land Rights, 86, 89-90
  unequal, 66
Lands Officer, 220, 223
Lands Officer for Goromonzi, 221
Lands Officer in Goromonzi, 228
land tenure, 223, 226
Land Tenure Center, 87

Land Tenure in Sub-Saharan Africa, 87
land tenure in Zimbabwe, 226
land tenure issues, 74
Land Tenure Reform, 86
land-tenure studies, 66-67
land tenure system, 220
land to non-resident, 223
Land Use Policy, 87
Lane, 145
Lang, Peter, 41
Langa, 247, 255
language, 1, 4, 23
Lannoy, 243, 246-47, 255
Larbi, 34, 41
large-scale commercial farms
  See LSCFs
  twenty-five former, 219
large tracts of land, 81
Last, 116
Lateinamerika, 42
Latest Stats, 193
Latham, 167, 177
Latin America, 33, 42, 142-43, 147, 163, 238, 261
laudable achievement, 207
Lavers, 6, 12, 149, 162
Lavis, 150, 163
law enforcement, 51
Legality and Legitimacy of NGO Participation in International Law, 178
legal structure, 182
legislation, 16, 18, 45, 84, 228, 253
legislations and values, 18
legislators, 154
legislature, 153
legitimacy of NSAs, 168
legitimation, 14, 17, 22-23
legitimation component, 22
legitimation strategy, 22
legitimisation, 156
legitimise, 5, 19
legitimising, 48
legitimising foundation, 48
Leibbrandt, 249, 254
Lema, 20-21, 27-28

Lemma, 93, 107, 116
Leonardi, 117
Lesotho, 35
lessons, 43, 47, 84, 90, 162, 166, 172, 195, 198, 202, 208-9, 235-36, 240
Lessons Learned, 208
Lessons of good social policy, 240
Leta, 91, 116
levels of care, 202
levels of income inequality, 260
Levine, 99, 116
Levtov, 249, 256
Lewin, 194
Lewis, 69, 88, 248, 254
Lewis Henry Morgan Lectures, 254
Liberalisation, 90
liberation, 18
  total, 54
Liberation Movement, 57, 239
library.fes.de/pdf-files, 61
Lickert scale, 136
Liebman, 122-23, 144
Lieres, 100, 113
life chances, 45, 50, 59
  accessing, 45
life circumstances, 93
life-cycle, 2, 30, 32
Life-cycle Consumption, 144
Life Cycle Continuous Investment, 62
life-cycle theory, 124
life expectancy, 134
Life Insurance and Annuities, 143
Life-Long Learning, 171
life risk, 126
Lifetime and Intertemporal Choice, 143
light, 50, 174, 190, 201, 265
light on key patterns of inequality, 265
limat budin, 95
limitations, 7, 29-30, 37, 98, 109, 117, 184, 260, 266, 271
  potential, 266
Limited Liquidity and Anomalies in Intertemporal Choice, 143
limited notion, 18

limited notion of inclusive development, 18
Limited Social Assistance, 62
limited time period, 32
limited work experience, 245
Limpopo, 177
Lin, 54, 62
Lindegger, 247, 255
literature debates, 101
literature on group membership, 91
literature on group membership in Ethiopia, 91
Literature Overview, 67
Literature Review, 123, 255
literature-scoping, 12
Little Bit Soft, 255
Lit Verlag, 118
live births, 198-99
lived experiences, 74, 82, 184
Livelihoods and Pro-Poor Growth in Rural Sub-Saharan Africa, 90
livelihoods perspective, 67
Livelihood Sustainability, 239
livelihood trajectories, 214
Livermore, 50, 62
Liverpool, 12
Liverpool University Press, 12
livestock in response, 232
livestock in response to shocks, 232
livestock in response to shocks and deprivation, 232
livestock market, 232
livestock production, 232
Livestock Production Extension Officer, 232
livestock products, 232
Livestock Survey, 225, 240
Living, 90, 267
LMICs, 197
Loan Clubs, 194
loans, 111, 186, 192, 199, 267
 informal, 100
 short-term, 101
local administration, 97, 102-5, 110
Local Development, 177

Local Development Studies, 118
local goals, 24
locality, 9, 241, 261, 271-72, 275-76, 281
locality to aggregate inequality, 272, 275, 281
local names, 184
local population, 54, 263
local priorities, 25
local producers, 159
local producers of knowledge, 159
Local Solutions, 119
location, 4, 18, 36, 66, 75, 93, 111
location of women, 75
Loewenstein, 124, 144
logic, 30, 135, 244
 cold commercial, 108
 injecting market transactional, 8
 practical, 167
London, 25-27, 62-63, 86-87, 90, 113-15, 117, 162-63, 177, 194-95, 236-37, 239
London and Cape Town, 238
London and New York, 115
Longman Greens, 62
Long-Term Developmental Perspectives, 153
Long Term Observations, 236
Long-Term Perspective, 278
long-term perspective study, 211
long-term strategy, 206
loose and baggy, 167
Lopez-Calva, 261, 279
Lorenz curves, 260, 278
Los Angeles, 194-95
Lost in Translation, 89
lottery basis, 111
love and support, 192
Lowder, 113
LSCF owners, 223
LSCFs, seventy-five, 220
LSCFs (large-scale commercial farms), 213, 219-20, 226, 230
Lucky, 190-91
lump sum, 53
Lund, 37, 41, 69, 87

Lungu, 55, 58, 61
Lusaka, 63
Luttmer, 122-23, 136, 144
Luxton, 86
Lwanga-Ntale, 241-42, 253, 255

M
MacAuslan, 236
Machakos, 274-76
machinery, 58
 national policymaking, 7
machinery leasing, 110
macroeconomic constellation, 31
Macroeconomics, 279
Macroeconomics of Human Insecurity, 86
Makusha, 247, 257
Makuwira, 7, 11, 166-69, 171, 173, 175, 177
Makuwira situates, 7
Maladjusted African Economies and Globalisation, 237
maladjustment, 2
Malaria, 24
Malawi, 163, 165-66, 170-71, 174
 inclusive, 170
Malawian citizen, 170
Malawi Disabilities Act, 171
Malawi Disability Sports Association (MADISA), 170
Malawi Inclusive Education Policy and International Convention, 171
Malawi National Association, 170
Malawi National Association of the Deaf (MANAD), 170
Malawi Union, 170
Malawi Union of the Blind (MUB), 170
Malaysia, 55
male, 77, 91, 97, 109, 225, 255
male breadwinner ideology, 248
male breadwinner in South Africa, 9
Male Breadwinner Myth, 241-57
Male Caregiving in South African Palliative Care, 254
male care work, 248
male focus group, 83
Male Grain Marketing Systems, 115

Male-headed Household Group Membership, 106
Male-headed Household Respondents, 97
male-headed households. *See* MHHs
male household members, 69
male participation, 85
Male Participation in Reproductive Work, 83
Mambo Press, 236
Mamelodi, 183-84
MANAD (Malawi National Association of the Deaf), 170
management, 23, 163, 175, 194, 203
 active demand, 30
 post-harvest, 231
management industry, 16
Management Science, 144-45
Manchester, 63, 86, 163, 255
Manchester Centre, 86
Manchester University Press, 63
Manda, 259, 265, 278-79
Manderson, 255
Marsabit, 274
Marsabit counties, 274
Marsh, 151, 158, 162
Marshall, 215, 227, 237
Martin, 86
Marx, 67
Marx's analysis, 67
masculine constructions, restrictive, 249
Masculinities, 247, 254-55
masculinities, constructed, 242
masculinity, 248
masculinity studies, 247-48
Mashonaland, 214
Mashonaland Central, 222
Mashonaland East, 222
Mashonaland West Province of Zimbabwe, 237
Masiye, 57, 62
Mason, 13, 27
massive expansion of access to education and healthcare, 5
mass reorientation, 48
Mastewal Printing, 114

Index 305

Masvingo Province, 73, 226
material, 18, 60, 111, 155-56, 159, 171, 228, 230
material and socio-economic circumstances, 60
Material Life, 195
maternal mortality, 95
Maternal Mortality Ratio (MMR), 199
maternity, 30, 50, 122, 205
Matero Economic Reforms, 56
mathematical properties, 265
Mathenge, 265, 279
Mathieu, 85, 88
Matondi, 86, 89, 215, 225, 237
matric certificate, 246
Matrix, 263
Matthews, 169, 177
Mau Mau, 264
Maundeni, 49, 62
Mauritius, 35
Mavedzenge, 239
Maware, 73
Maware A1 Farms, 77
Maximum, 280-81
Max Planck Yearbook, 63
Mazhawidza, 225, 237
Mazowe District, 236
Mbilinyi, 20, 27-28
Mbuthia, 279
McCord, 149, 163
McGill-Queens University Press, 86
McNally, 71, 88
Measurement and Decomposition of Inequality by Education Level, 272
Measurement and Decomposition of Inequality by Locality, 272, 281
measurements of inequal
Metaferia, 118
Meyer, 85, 87, 247, 255-56
Meyiwa, 247, 255-56
MFP-03, 153
MGCSD-01, 154
MHHs (male-headed households), 5-6, 78-79, 83, 91, 102, 105-6
Mhondori-Ngezi District, 228

microcredit, 37
Micro-Dynamics, 162
microeconomic, 31
Microeconomic Approach, 279
Microeconomic Approach to Development Policy, 279
Microeconomic Determinants of Demand for Social Insurance, 144
microfinance, 92, 112, 195
micro-level, 74
Micropolitics of Mining and Development, 42
measures and decomposition of inequality, 272-74
Members' Attitudes, 113
Mènages, 143-44
MenCare, 249, 255
MenCare Advocacy Publication, 255
mengistawi budin, 95, 97
Menkir, 112
mentoring, 246
Mercy, 178
merit of informal social protection, 101
Merouani, 6, 10, 122-23, 125-45
Meru, 275
middle-income countries, 41, 55, 94, 197
middle schools, 53
Midgley, 49, 62, 169, 177, 181, 194
Midlands, 222
Migrant Laborers, 255
Migrant Laborers in Mozambique and South Africa, 255
migration, 24, 90
Mijadala, 26
Milanovic, 263
militancy, 45, 55
military dictators, 54
military dictatorships, 21
Military Downsizing Programs, 145
Military Medical Scheme, 206
Millennium Development Goals, 32, 86, 194
model farmer, 96, 98
Modeling Myopic Decisions, 144
model in terms, 31

model in terms of social development, 31
models and actors, 30
models in sub-Saharan Africa, 41
models to new state visions, 34
Modern Challenges, 117
modernisers, 21
modernising, 60
Modern Italy, 117
Modernity, 240
Modernity in Zimbabwe, 240
modes, 23, 72, 77-78, 80-81, 220
    dominant, 33
MoFED (Ministry of Finance and
    Economic Development), 116
Mogues, 92, 116
Moher, 61
Molteno, 55, 63
Mombasa, 273-75
Moodley categorises, 185
Moore, 244, 250, 254, 256
Moral Crusaders, 177
Morales-Gomez, 25-26, 61
Morrell, 247, 249, 255
Morris, 56, 62
mortality, under-five, 198
Moses, 62
Mosse, 99, 116
mothers, 59, 82-83, 85, 242
Mothers, Lone, 257
mothers
    self-employed, 188
    single, 186
mounting uncertainty, 37
movement, double, 182
Moyo, 75, 86, 89, 173, 177, 213-15,
    220-21, 223, 233, 235, 237-39
Mozambique, 255
Mozambique and South Africa, 255
MP-01, 154
Mpedi, 100, 117
MPhil Dissertation, 115
MPs, 154
MUB (Malawi Union of the Blind), 170
Mugabe, Robert, 174
Mujeyi, 238

Mukora, 81, 85, 87
Mulema, 116
Mullainathan, 144
Mulligan, 142, 261, 279
multi-disciplinary inquiry, 29
multi-ethnic landscape, 5
Multifaceted Perspective, 113, 115, 118
multilaterals, 167
Multinational Corporations (MNCs), 35
multi-page.pdf, 211
Multi-Party Elections, 118
multiple developmental, played, 47
multiplicity, 17, 19, 23
multivariate analyses, 75
Mulungushi Reforms, 56
Mundt, 99, 119
Munga, 9, 11, 261-81
Munga address, 11
municipal authorities, 203
municipalities, 34
Municipality, 194
Munyai, 189-92
Murambinda, 239
Murehwa, 222
Murisa, 215, 238-39
Murithi, 279
Murunga, xii
Musembi, 152, 161
musha, 9, 228-29
musha/ekhaya, 228
mushrooming, 167, 170
mushrooming of NSAs, 167
Mustapha Akanbi Foundation, 61
Mutanga, 73, 89
Mutegi, 279
Muteyo, 73
Muteyo Communal Areas, 77
Mutoko, 222
Mutopo, 67, 89, 215, 224-26, 229, 238
mutual acquaintance, 92
mutual aid, 179-82, 185, 195
Mutual-Aid Associations/Activities, 181
mutual-aid groups for social wellbeing,
    181
mutual aid in co-operation, 179

Index 307

mutual aid in co-operation for survival, 179
mutual aid in co-operation for survival and security, 179
Mutual-benefit societies, 182
mutualism, 182
mutual obligation, 8, 183
mutual support, 111, 180, 182, 184-86

N
Nacer-Eddine Hammouda, 121
Nafula, 265, 279
Naidoo, 243, 245-46, 255
Naidu, 71, 75, 80, 84, 89
Nairobi, 26, 114, 116, 255, 273-74, 279-80
Nairobi County, 275-77
NASASA (National Stokvel Association of South Africa), 185
Natal, 195
nation, 20-21, 48, 59-61, 237-38, 240
National Accounts, 263
national association claims, 185
national average, 98
national budgets, 154
national bureaucrats and politicians, 147, 153
national character, 57
national characteristics, 48
national coalitions, 158
national coalitions of social protection, 158
national debt, 52
National Democratic Revolution, 238
national development efforts in Ghana, 48
National Development Plan, 35, 152, 155, 255
National Extension Program, 115
national governments, 34
National Health Insurance in Nigeria, 209
National Health Insurance Scheme. *See* NHIS
National Health Insurance Scheme of Nigeria, 210
National Health Insurance Schemes of Nigeria and Ghana, 210
National Health Security Act, 205

National Health Security Office designs benefit packages, 205
Natural Region, 85
Natural Resource Perspectives, 86
Natural Resources Policy Analysis Network Discussion Paper, 237
nature, 11, 14, 20, 23, 36, 39, 148, 152, 168, 173-74, 181, 184-85, 248
nature and reason, 14
nature and search for African solidarity, 20
Nature of Group, 97
nature of political regimes, 23
nature of politics, 174
nature of regimes, 173
nature of social policymaking, 11
NC, 254
NCVO, 114
Ndangwa Noyoo, 45
NDC Governments, 62
Ndirangu, 265, 279
Nduna, 256
Negotiated Politics of Social Protection in Sub-Saharan Africa, 12
neighbourhood, 111
neighbours, 48, 92, 99, 111, 189, 230
neoclassical, 30
Neocolonialism, 235
Neocosmos, 226, 238
New York and London, 237
NGO-led support complements, 109
NGO Participation, 178
NGO Rights, 114
Nicholas, 201, 210
Niedzwiecki, 154, 162
Nigeria, 8, 15, 22, 61, 198-99, 201-2, 208-11, 245
    post-independence, 198
Nigeria and India, 245
Nigeria Medical Journal, 210
Nigerian Freedom, 27
Nigerian healthcare financing, 199
Nigerian health insurance scheme, 11
Nigerian Journal of Clinical Practice, 211
Nigerian model of SHI, 197
Nigerian people, 200

Nigerian population, 201, 208
Nigerians, 197, 201
Nigerians and reducing out-of-pocket health expenditure, 8
Nigerian Social Health Insurance Scheme, 8
Nigerian Social Health Insurance System, 197-211
Nigeria's National Health, 198
Nigeria's National Health Insurance Scheme Programmes/Plans, 200
Nigeria's NHIS, 208
night watchman state, 1
NiÒo-Zaraz´a, 12, 35, 42, 149, 163, 169
Nisbet, James, 237
Nitsch, 29, 42
nius kebele, 95
Nixon, 201-2, 210
Njieassam, 67, 89
nking-and-new-institutions, 254
Nkrumah, 21, 27-28, 51-54, 61
Nkrumah era, 58
Nkrumah's government, 53-54
Nkrumah's personality, 51
Nnamdi Azikiwe, 21
Noble, 248, 257
Non-Drug, 144
non-state actors work, 168
non-traditional forms, present, 24
non-work-related illnesses, 205
Norad, 27, 195
Norad Report, 195
Nordic Africa Institute, 176, 238
Nordic African Institute and Institute of Development Studies, 27
North African, 241
Northampton, 162
North-Eastern regions, 273
Northern Ethiopia, 12
Northern Ghana, 86
Northern Kenya, 148, 152
northern parts, 48
Northern Rhodesia, 48-49
Northern Rwanda, 194
Northern Uganda Social Action Fund, 115
Nowacka, 79, 82, 87

Noyoo, 49-50, 55, 57, 63
Noyoo and Boon, 3, 5, 10, 47-63
NPOs, faith-based, 251
NPOs (non-profit organisations), 242, 249-53
NPOs in terms of funding and legislation, 253
NPO Sonke Gender Justice, 251, 253
NPO type, 250
NPP and NDC Governments, 62
NSA approach, 176
NSA discourse, 166
NSAs (non-state actors), 7, 11, 40, 72, 165-69, 171-78, 242
NSAs and governments, 176
Ntombi, 191-92
Ntshongwana, 248, 257
Nugent, 239
number, large, 17, 34, 81, 85, 149, 154

O

Oaks, 236
OAU (Organisation of African Unity), 20, 172
Obafemi Awolowo, 21
Obasan, 199, 201, 210
Obstacles to Women's Land Access in South Africa, 87
occupations, 202
occupied senior government positions, 57
Ochiai, 250, 256
ocialreproduction-theory, 86
O'Connor, 71, 89
ODA (Official Development Assistance), 35
Odedokun, 259, 279
Odeyemi, 201-2, 210
ODI-IKM Working Paper, 162
ODI Working Paper, 117
Oduro, 100, 117
OECD (Organisation for Economic Co-operation and Development), 89, 167, 216
OECD bias, 216
OECD-centric, 8
OECD Development Centre, 87, 114

Index

OECD Development Centre Working Paper, 114
OECD donors, 167
OECD donors channel, 167
Officer, 232
offices, 144, 157
 regional, 251
Official Development Assistance (ODA), 35
officials, elected, 151, 155
offspring, mixed, 57
Ogunbekun, 198, 210
O'Hearn, 182, 195
Okpani, 197, 201, 210
Okwuosa, 211
O'Laughlin, 224, 238
Old-Age Crisis, 43
old age grant, 249
old age pension, 126, 134, 141, 244
 monthly, 188
Old-age Pension System Reforms Moving, 143
Older Persons Cash Transfer programmes, 148
Old Issues, 236, 279
Old resettlement farms, 225
Old Theories, 255
Oleche, 279
Olinto, 261, 279
Olukoshi, 22, 27
Omomowo, 7, 181-95
Omoruan, 8, 11, 199-211
One-in-Five model, 95, 98
one-party states, 21, 58
One-Person, 45
one-sided industrialisation strategy, 58
on/ethiopia-poverty-assessment, 119
One-Vote, 45
online, 143
online tutorial, 123
Onsomu, 265, 279
ontologies, individualistic, 84
Onwujekwe, 211
Ooh, 191
OOP, 197

OOP payments, 199
Orenstein, 151, 161
Organisational Form Matter, 114
organisational rules, 182
organisation and management, 23
organisation and management of knowledge, 23
organisation and management of knowledge and knowledge systems, 23
organisation documents, 152
Organisation for Economic Co-operation and Development. *See* OECD
Organisation of African Unity (OAU), 20, 172
organisation of work, 23
organisations, 23, 91, 150-52, 155-56, 158, 160, 167-70, 172-73, 182, 200, 204
Ownership of Time-Saving Household Consumer Commodities, 81
Ownership of time-saving household consumer items, 5
Ownership of time-saving household gadgets, 81
owners of livestock, 9
Oxfam, 96, 117, 195
Oxford, 28, 62, 89, 113-14, 117, 161, 163, 177-78, 195, 239
Oxford Development Studies, 90
Oxford Handbook, 177
Oxford Handbook of Africa and Economics, 62
Oxford University, 113-14
Oxford University Press, 28, 43, 62, 161, 177, 194, 211
Oyo State, 210

P

pace, 46, 59, 208
package, 166, 189, 202, 205
 limited-benefit, 202
 reward, 53
package and share, 189
Pakistan, 110
Pakistan and Ethiopia, 110
Pal, 162

Paldam, 92, 117
Palgrave Macmillan, 12, 26-27, 42, 61-62, 88, 163, 177-78, 195, 208, 210,
Pan-African Education Programme of Free Education, 53
pan-Africanism, 20, 53
Pan Africanism, 173
Pan African Medical Journal, 210
Pandolfelli, 116
Pankhurst, 114
Pan Macmillan, 254
Pantheon Press, 43
Paper Development Economics Group, 115
Paper Number, 89
paradigmatic change, 150
Paradigms, 239
paradoxical, 166
parameter, 260
    income aversion, 260
    weighting, 271
parastatals, 56-57
parentheses, 268, 272-73, 275, 281
Parenting, 256
parenting, positive, 251-52
Parenting Practices Following, 257
parents, 53, 189-90, 204
Parents of Disabled Children Association in Malawi (PODCAM), 170
Paris, 87, 89, 143-44
Park, 263
parliament, 95, 152, 154, 157, 159
parliament buildings, 21
parochial confrontation, 108
participants, 32, 124, 152, 154, 157, 184, 188, 226, 233
    Patrilineal Customary Land Tenure Systems of Sub-Saharan Africa, 87
Patriotic Front, 214
pension choice, 125
Pension Coverage, 145
pensioners, 125, 190, 204
pension insurance, 141
pension plans, 124-25, 129
Pension Provider Survey, 124

Pension Provisions, 144
Pension Reform, 41
pension retirees, 126
perspectives africaines, 42
perspectives and experiences, 74
Perspectives of Direct Beneficiaries, 255
perspectives of women, 74
persuasion, skilful, 158
persuasive narratives, 151
pervasiveness, 23
Pesando, 79, 82, 87
PLAAS Policy Brief, 237
PLAAS Working Paper, 236
Plagerson, 248, 255
planning, 55, 115, 163, 170, 182, 209-10, 280
planning of collective consumption, 182
PLRC, 225, 238
plunder, significant, 45
pluralism, 19
pocket, 187, 192
PODCAM (Parents of Disabled Children Association in Malawi), 170
Polanyi, 31, 43, 108, 117, 179-80, 182, 195
Polanyi's Double Movement, 41
polemical debates, 214
police officers, 57
policies, 15-18, 30-31, 33, 41, 49-51,
policy, xi, xii, 4, 6, 7, 9, 10, 11, 14, 15, 16, 22, 24, 31, 35, 39, 43, 47, 59, 62, 66, 79, 84, 87, 89, 90, 93, 96, 114, 115, 117, 119, 122, 123, 147, 148, 149, 150, 151, 152, 153, 155, 157, 158, 159, 160, 161, 162, 163, 166, 172, 177, 181, 195, 210, 215, 216, 217, 240, 250, 275, 276
political, 6, 10, 12, 14, 15, 21, 22, 25, 28, 29, 38, 46, 49, 51, 56, 61, 62, 63, 75, 87, 89, 98, 104, 106, 107, 110, 112, 117, 118, 143, 144, 147, 149, 151, 154, 158, 160, 162, 166, 168, 169, 177, 178, 179, 195, 200, 214, 218, 221, 235, 238, 239, 254, 256, 278

Index 311

politicians, 147, 153-55, 157, 159-60
politicisation, 96
    local, 110
politicisation arguments, 107
politics, 6, 13, 19, 23, 27, 41, 43, 62-63,
    for Development in Tigray, 117
Politics of Nation-Building in Sub-Saharan Africa, 62
Politics of Preternatural Space, 239
Politics of Promoting Social Cash Transfers in Uganda, 12, 27
Politics of Promoting Social Protection in Zambia, 12, 28, 163
Politics of Scaling, 163
politics of social policymaking, 4, 30, 40
Politics of Social Protection Expansion in Low Income Countries, 162
Politics of Social Protection Expansion in Low-Income Countries, 12
Politics Right, 42, 163
Politikon, 254
Politique Nationale, 206
Politiques, 143

Polity Press, 41, 237, 254
Polokwane, 177
polycentricity, 23
polygamous, 79, 82-83
Pomeroy, 147, 162
Pooled resources, 185
poorest countries in Africa, 58
poorest group of countries, 95
poor knowledge of social security, 139
poor women, 66, 194
popular measure of inequality, 271
population, 2, 8, 11, 23, 26, 32, 35, 50, 52, 125-26, 200-206, 208, 269, 271-74
population access, 199
population census, 263
population census data, 266
population coverage, 199, 201, 203-4, 208
population coverage in Germany, 208
Population Distribution by Health Insurance Plans, 207
population Lorenz curves, 278

population proportion, lower, 272, 276
population sectors, 215
population segments, 208
population share, 274
population subgroups, 260-61, 266, 271
Portsmouth, 255
Presidency, 255
president, first, 49
Presidential Input Scheme, 233
Presidential Land Review Committee, 225, 238
pressure, 147, 149
    Preternatural Space, 239
Pretoria, x, 3, 40, 63, 180, 183, 255-56
prevailing norms and values, 181
prevention, 227
    comprehensive, 172
Preventive Health Behavior, 143
prices, 172
    declining commodity, 58
    deflated, 268, 271
    high monopoly, 57
    international petroleum, 198
    plummeting copper, 57
Primary Health Care, 209
primary source of data, 151
Prime Minister's Office, 95
primordial loyalties, 60
Princeton, 117, 163
Princeton University Press, 117, 163
principles of social insurance, 202
prison inmates, 200
Prison Notebooks, 162
private contractors, 167
private foundations, 24
    powerful, 24
private funding in social insurance, 37
Private Healthcare in Nigeria, 210
private health expenditure in Nigeria, 199
Private-sector employees, 204
    privatisation, 31, 34, 61, 167, 247
privatising, 31
probability, 123, 134, 139
probability of demand for social insurance, 139

problems, 30, 32, 115, 122, 152, 157, 166, 168, 189, 192, 194
productive strategies, 39
Productive Transformation, 88
productivist, 4, 37
productivity, 4, 16, 31, 33, 36, 52, 108-
Productivity Impacts of Informal Labor-sharing Arrangements, 116
professional domain, 16
professionalisation, 16
Profile Books, 115
profits, 55, 185, 230
pro-government, 22
programmes, 32, 34, 36, 49-50, 56, 147, 153-55, 157, 159-60, 200, 213-15, 220-21, 223-24, 233, 245
  educational, 171
  emancipatory, 19
  flagship, 217
  initial, 15
  key postcolonial, 20
  massive developmental, 52
  monolithic neopatrimonial, 214
  nationalist, 19-20
  neoliberal, 4
  post-independence modernisation, 34
  small-scale microlevel, 156
  social, 19
proliferation, 186, 202
Prominent examples, 32, 41
prominent norms and values, 183
Promised Land, 239
Promondo and Sonke Gender Justice, 256
Promote Growth, 43
promoters, 148
Promoting Social Cash Transfers, 12, 27
Promoting Social Protection, 12, 28, 163
Promoting Women's Access, 87
promotion, 24, 112, 151, 155-56, 159, 227
Promundo and Sonke Gender Justice, 249
propensity, 101, 259
Propensity Score Matching, 88
prophylactic, 3
prophylactic social-protection, 10

Pro-Poor Growth in Rural Sub-Saharan Africa, 90
Public social infrastructure provision, 85
Public Social Policy Development and Implementation, 209
public spending on education and healthcare, 46
public work beneficiaries, 112
Publishers, 239
Pulling, 279
punishment, 122
  corporal, 252
Pure Life Cycle Hypothesis, 143
pursuit, 148, 150-51, 194
pursuit of interests, 148
Putnam, 92, 99, 115, 117
Putting Citizens' Voice, 117

Q

QEH Working Papers, 114
Qualitative, 236
Qualitative Report, 112
qualitative research, 183, 195
qualitative studies, 74, 248
  quality education, 59
quality healthcare, 8, 206
quality healthcare services, 11
quality of social reproduction, 186, 193
Quality Public Healthcare, 257
quality services, 2, 37
Quantifying Women, 118
Quantitative, 236
quarter, 16, 243, 256
Quarterly, 177
Quarterly Journal, 194
Quarterly Journal of Economics, 115, 142, 144, 194
Quarterly Labour Force Survey, 256
Quarterly Labour Force Survey Quarter, 256
questionnaire, 74, 125
  experimental, 125
  structured, 73
questionnaire survey, 142
questions, 30, 37-39, 94, 97-98, 108, 112, 124-28, 133, 142, 148, 169, 172, 178

R

Rabe, 9, 11, 242-43, 245-57
race, 16, 54, 79, 243
Race Relations, 240
racial ladder, 54
racial privilege, 56
Racial Studies, 62
Radical Approach, 177
Raftopolous, 237-40
Rahmato, 92, 96, 99, 111, 117
Rai, 80, 89
rainfall, 85
Rajani, 20, 27-28
Rajasthan, 116
Ramaswamy, 118-19
Ramoelo, 73, 89
Randomisation, 96
random sampling technique, 96
Ravallion, 74, 88, 263
Ravan Press, 195
Rawlings, Jerry, 59
Razavi, 68, 72, 80, 84, 89, 250, 256
RDP (Reconstruction and Development Programme), 245
reactionary, 154
readings, making, 215
Reagan, 166, 178
　Ronald, 166
Reconstruction and Development Redistribution Strategy, 245
redistributive effects, 60, 183
Redistributive Land Reform in Zimbabwe, 89
redistributive nature, 220, 226, 234
Redistributive Reform in Post Settler Zimbabwe, 238
Reduce Poverty, 118
reducing out-of-pocket health expenditure, 8
Reducing Youth Unemployment, 255
Reimbursement, 205
reinforcing, 33, 68, 101, 181, 193
reinforcing and contradictory impacts on society, 33
reiterate, 18, 249

Relatedness, 255
Relational Approach, 116
Relative Contribution, 273-75
relatively higher levels of income inequality, 276
relatively high rankings, 274
relatives, 111
　male, 225
relevance and merit of informal social protection, 101
Relevancy, 86
reliability, 74
relief funds, 203
religion, 18, 90, 100, 107, 111
religious devotion, 107
Religious Values in Extending Social Protection, 117
Remaoun, 142-43
remedial action, 216
remittances, 24-25, 37, 100
Resurgence, 238
retail, 22, 56
Re-thinking Africa, 176
Rethinking Land, 238, 240
Rethinking State and Nation, 237
retirement, 122, 124, 126, 137, 141, 143
retirement pension, 122
retirement plans, 6
Retirement Study, 142
Retraites, 144
retrenching, 1
Retrieved, 254, 256
Re-turn, 90, 240
revenue bargains, 38
revenue mobilisation, 38
revenues, 38-39, 197, 202, 207
review, 41, 47, 70, 78, 89, 113, 118, 145, 148, 236, 238-39
Review-Based Comparative Analysis, 210
Review of Experience of Social Health Insurance, 211
Review of Recent Knowledge-To-Policy Literature, 162
review of women, 78
Revised Version, 210

Revisiting, 239, 256
Revisiting Social Policy in Ghana and Zambia, 45
revisits, 47, 247
Revue Canadienne d, 12, 86, 145, 161, 193, 235, 254
Revue Interventions ...conomiques, 41
Rhodesia, 57, 235
Rhodes University, 236, 238
Richardson, 214, 238
richest, 271
Ridgeway, 68, 89
Rieger, 145
Riesberg, 204, 209
Rift Valley, 273-74
role of public education, 10
role of public education and design, 10
role of regimes, 173
Role of Regimes in Shaping, 173
Role of Religious Values in Extending Social Protection, 117
Role of Rural Organisations, 119
Role of Social Capital in Development, 116
role of social policy in nation-building, 15
Role of Social Risk Management in Rural Producer Organisations, 113
Rural Resettlement, 237
Rural Resource Portfolios, 118
Rural Services, 119
Rural Sub-Saharan Africa, 90
rural/urban, 66, 222
Russell, 179, 194
Russell Sage Foundation, 87
Rustichini, 259, 278
Rutherford, 189, 214, 238-39
Ruwa, 222
Rwanda, 95, 197, 202, 206-8, 210, 261-62
Rwanda Community Based Health Insurance Policy, 206
Rwanda Ministry, 206
Rwanda National Health Insurance Policy, 206, 210
Rwandan residents, 206
Rwanda's population, 206
Rwanda's population distribution by health insurance coverage, 206

S
Saarbrucken, 144
Saavedra, 261, 279
Sabates-Wheeler, 114, 155, 163, 219, 226, 236
Sacco, 214, 227, 239
Sachikonye, 214, 239
Sadomba, 214, 239
Saez, 143
safety, 50
    citizen, 24
    personal, 227
safety nets, 31-32, 43, 49, 58, 228-29, 241
    promoted, 155
safety nets and market-based schemes, 31
Safety Net to Springboard, 43
SAGE, 194-95, 236, 239
Sage Publications, 27, 62, 177, 236
Sahara, 67
Saharan Africa, 161
Sahile, 6, 10, 93, 95, 97, 99, 101, 105-19
sale, 229, 232
Salt Lake City, 88
SAM (Social Accounting Matrix), 262
SAM and population census, 263
Sam Moyo African Institute, 219
Sam Moyo African Institute for Agrarian Studies (SMAIAS), 219
Sam Moyo's Research Methodology, 239
Samoei, 279
SEWA Cooperative Federation, 115
sex, 97-98, 109, 111, 125, 243, 280
sex in South Africa, 243
Sex Roles, 86
sex trafficking, 24
Sexual Socialisation in South Africa, 254
Shafir, 144
Shamva, 222
Shaping NSAs, 173
Shapiro, 142
share, 9, 56, 99, 111, 189, 191, 220-21, 253, 270-74, 281
share care work, 249
sharecropping, 100
shared destiny, 61

Index 315

shared norms and values, 10
share household work, 83
share of expenditure, 265, 269
share of land, 220
sharing reproductive work, 83
Sharma, 42
Shaw, 197, 201-2, 210
Shearer, 150, 163
Shefer, 247, 255-56
shelter, 71, 185, 227-28, 234
    availing, 228
SHI (Social Health Insurance), 197, 199, 201, 203-4, 209-11
Shiferaw, 97, 112
Shifting Gender Dimensions and Rural Livelihoods, 238
Shifting Politics of Citizenship, 238
SHI in Germany, 203
SHI model, 203
shocks, 36, 50, 92-93, 100-101, 108, 155, 232
    external, 9
    minor, 229
Shocks and Asset Dynamics in Ethiopia, 116
Shona culture, 228
Shona culture marriage grants, 226
Shona Peoples, 236
shop, 114, 187
Shorrocks, 265, 279
shortages, 54
    repeated food, 112
shortcomings, 32, 215
shortfall, 81
    major gendered, 81
Short Run, 255
short term financial difficulties, 112
Social, 1-5, 7-17, 22, 25, 29, 30-47, 49, 50, 52-55, 57, 59, 60, 62, 66, 67, 68, 69, 71-75, 77-86, 88, 89-94, 97, 98, 99, 101, 102, 103, 107, 108, 109, 110, 112, 113, 115, 117, 118, 119, 121-126, 128, 129, 130, 131, 135, 136, 140-145, 150, 156, 161, 162, 163, 165, 166, 169, 171, 173, 174, 175, 177, 179, 180, 181, 182, 184, 186, 190, 193, 194, 195, 198, 204, 205, 208, 209, 210, 213, 215, 216, 217, 218, 219, 227, 229-237, 240, 241, 242, 244, 247, 249, 251, 254, 278
South African, 182, 185, 242-43, 245-47
South African Case, 241
South African Families, 256
South African Female Cash Transfer Recipients, 255
South African Goldmine Industry, 256
South African Institute of Race Relations, 240
South African Journal, 254
South African Journal of Political Studies, 254
South African literature, 185
South African NGO, 171
South African Palliative Care, 254
South African Perspective, 117
South African population, 244
South African Research Chair, 3, 13, 25, 66, 161
South African Review, 254
South African Review of Sociology, 161, 209, 235, 254
South African state, 243, 245
South African Township, 255
South Africa's Child Support Grant, 254
South Africa's Fathers, 257
South Africa's Hybrid Care Regime, 254
South Africa's National Development Plan, 245
South Asia Economic Journal, 115
South Asian, 115
South Co-operation, 63
South-East Asian Societies, 256
Southern Africa, 33, 35, 57, 86, 236, 238, 248, 251, 255
Southern Rhodesia and South Africa, 56
South framework for social policy, xii
South Korea, 55, 218, 236, 250
South Korean Developmental Success, 236

sovereignty, 48, 240
Soziale Sicherung, 41
Sozialpolitik, 42
Sozialversicherung Reformen, 42
sozioʻkonomische, 42
space, xi-xii, 1, 18, 23, 160, 172, 174, 219, 227
  democratic, 4, 23
  exilic, 182
  existing, xi
  intellectual, 182

T
TAAM (The Albino Association of
TAC (Treatment Action Campaign), 171-72, 250, 257
Tachgayint Wereda, 118
TAC strategies, 172
Tade, x, 13
Tade Aina, 39
Tadesse, 112
tails, lower, 260, 276
Taita Taveta, 274
Taiwan, 218, 250
Taking Responsibility, 43
Talampas, 197, 204, 211
Tambulasi, 151, 163
Teddlie, 219, 239
teenage years, 248
teeth, 189
Teevan, 184, 194
Tegegne, 113-14
Tekwa, 10, 67-90
Tekwa's contribution, 5
Tello, 189
Tembo, 57, 62
temperatures, hot, 73
temporary relief to households in times, 155
temporary relief to households in times of distress, 155
Tendances, 143
Tendencies, 238
Tendler, 169, 178
tensions, 13, 15, 87, 166, 169, 175, 253

Tenure, 90
Tertiary Social Health Insurance Programme (TSHIP), 200
Tesema, 107, 116
Tesfaye, 112, 116
Teshome, 92-93, 96, 99-101, 111-12, 118
Thailand, 197, 202, 204, 208-9, 211
Thailand and Rwanda, 197, 202, 208
Transformative Social Policy and Inclusive Development, 24
Transformative social policy and innovation, 27, 195, 237, 255
transformative social policy approach emphasise, 226
transformative social policy approach in Ghana and Zambia, 60
transformative social policy concept, 217
transformative social policy context, 242
transformative social policy discourse, 253
transformative social policy for inclusive development, 3
transformative social policy for inclusive development in contemporary Africa, 15
transformative social policy for inclusive development in twenty-first century Africa, 3
transformative social policy in Africa, 13
Transformative Social Policy in Small States, 89
transformative social policy interventions in inclusive development, 25
transformative social policy model, 36
Transformative Social Policy Perspective, 65, 90
Transformative Social Protection, 236
transformative tool, 59
Transformed forms, 24
Transformed Maize Productivity in Ethiopia, 112
Transforming Rural Livelihoods in Zimbabwe, 237
transition, 174, 201, 209
  political, 34
Transitional Development Plan (TDP), 55
Transition Countries, 42

Index 317

Transition Period, 209
transnational, 24
transnational action, 148
Transnational Actors and Policymaking in Ghana, 162
Transnational Gender Perspectives, 255-56
Transnational Ideas, 12, 162
transnational organisations advocating, 147
transnational policing, 24
Transnational Social Policies, 25
Trans-National Social Policies, 26
transparency, 54
transport, 52, 57-58, 77-78
transportation, 22, 56
transporting, 81
transport subsidy, 246
traps, 84
treason charges, 49
treatment, 179, 182, 250, 266
Treatment Action Campaign. *See* TAC
treaty, 49
trend analyses of inequality, 260
Trend Analysis, 89
trend assessments, 261
trend assessments of inequality, 261
trend in income inequality, 266
trends, 6, 42, 87-88, 107, 115, 210, 238, 245, 253, 266
Trends in Income/Expenditure
trust, 8, 53, 91, 99, 101, 109, 111, 119, 182-83, 185, 189-90
  Trust and ROSCA Membership, 194
Tschirgi, 61
Tsegy, 113
tsewu, 226, 229
TSHIP (Tertiary Social Health Insurance Programme), 200
Tsikata, 65-67, 69, 83, 87, 90, 224, 240
TSP. *See* Transformative Social Policy
TSP deploys, 4
TSP network, 40
TT/C-01, 155
tuberculosis, 24, 250
Turkana, 274

Turkey, 55
Turner, 67, 86
Turning Private Voluntary Organisations, 178
Tvedt, 168, 178
Twentieth Century, 194
twenty-first century, 2, 5, 18
  new, 40
two spheres, 68
Tyne, 256
types, 91-93, 95, 97, 99, 101, 104-5, 108, 110, 173-75, 182, 184-85, 248, 250, 253
  donor-funded, 250

U

Uasin Gishu, 274-76
UCS (Universal Coverage Scheme), 204-5
UDI (Unilateral Declaration of Independence), 57
Uganda, 12, 27, 95, 115, 174, 195, 262
Ughasoro, 211
Ujamaa, 46
  espoused, 46
UK, 25-27, 41, 86-87, 90, 113, 115-16, 119, 145, 162-63, 177-78, 195
UK and New York, 86
ultimate goal, 166
Umwelt, 42
unaffordable access, 50
unaffordable luxury, 82
UNAIDS, 176
UNCTAD (United Nations Conference on Trade and Development), 66, 90
underdevelopment, 216
underemployment, 30
undernourishment, 94
underperforming, 94
underpinning, theoretical, 180
Understand Globalisation, 26
understanding, 13, 15, 25, 29, 36, 109, 113, 147, 150, 160-61, 169, 175-76
  better, 108, 168, 175
  ideological, 202
  unified, 68

318 Social Policy in the African Context

Understanding Equality in Zimbabwe, 240
Understanding Exilic Spaces, 195
understanding gender, 110
Understanding Gender Equality in Zimbabwe, 225
Understanding Mutual Benefit Societies, 194
Understanding Nation-Building, 48
understanding of policy networks, 150
Understanding Policy Decisions, 162
Understanding Social Capital, 118
Understanding Social Capital and Middle Eastern Women, 112
underwriting, 84
UNDP (United Nations Development Programme), 14, 28, 56, 58, 63, 87, 95, 118
unearth, 260, 269, 276
UN-ECA, 278, 280
unemployed people, 245
unemployment, 9, 11, 50, 53, 58, 126, 182, 243
   persistent, 252
Unemployment and State Interventions in South Africa, 243
unemployment figures, 242-43, 253
   high, 245
unemployment rate, 243
   expanded, 243
   official, 243
unemployment rate by sex in South Africa, 243
unemployment trend, 243
unequal distribution of reproductive work, 80
UNESCO, 171, 178
UNESCO International Literacy Prize, 178
Uneven Development, 176
UNICEF, 147
UNIFEM, 87
UNIFEM Southern African Region Office, 87
unification, 48
Unilateral Declaration of Independence (UDI), 57
uninsured people, 203

uninsured respondents, 131
Union, 22
UNIP, supported, 57
UNIP (United National Independence Party), 49, 55, 58
UNIP government, 57-58
UNIP government and Kaunda, 56
United Nations Law, 63
United Nations Publications, 28
United Nations Research Institute, 3, 29, 43, 181, 195, 239-40
United Nations Research Institute for Social Development. *See* UNRISD
United Nations University, 26
United Nations University-WIDER, 114
United States, 125, 142-43
universal access, 199, 206, 208
   guaranteed, 198
universal coverage, 197-98, 201-4, 206, 209, 211
   high, 207
universal coverage agenda, 208
Universal Coverage and Social Health Insurance, 211
Universal Coverage Scheme (UCS), 204-5
Universal Declaration, 200, 211
universalhealthcoverageday.org/welcome, 209
Universal Health Coverage Forum, 210
Universal Health Coverage in Rwanda, 210
Universal Human Rights, 62
universalism, 1, 62
Universitas Forum, 119
Université, 143
Université Panthéon-Sorbonne, 144
Université Paris-Est Créteil, 143
universities, 53, 59, 61, 171, 190
University, 55, 87, 143, 177
University College, 53
University of Birmingham, 113
University of Bonn, 116
University of Cape Town, 256
University of Chicago Press, 12, 113, 116, 143

Index 319

University of Edinburgh, 237
University of Ghana, 53
University of Johannesburg, 256
University of Limpopo, 177
University of Manchester, 86
University of Manchester Centre for Growth and Business Cycle Research Discussion Paper Series, 86
University of Minnesota Press, 87
University of Nairobi, 280
University of South Africa, x, 3, 25, 234, 256
University of Sussex, 236-37
University of Warwick, 89
University of Western Cape, 236-37
University of Wisconsin, 87
University of Zambia, 55
University of Zimbabwe, 87
Unlocking, 255
Uppsala, 27, 176, 238
uptake, 147, 151, 160, 210, 252
   social-insurance, 10
Urban, 222, 268, 270-72, 281
urban areas, 22, 171, 205, 221, 223-24, 229, 265, 271
urban areas of Ethiopia, 171
Urban Black Township, 195
urban contexts, xi
urban inequality, 9, 265, 268-69, 276-77
urbanisation, 23, 277
urbanising effect, 277
urbanising effect on inequalities, 277
urban population, 23, 278
Urban Self-Help, 195
Urban South Africa, 195
urban townships in South Africa, 7
US, 123-25, 128
USAID, 178
USAID Amap Financial Services Knowledge Generation, 113
USD, 2, 228-30, 233, 278
user fees, 199
User Manual DASP, 278
US Federal Reserve Board's Survey, 124
USSR, 209
Utas, 176

Utete, 238
utilisation, 51, 97, 99, 143
   judicious, 200
Utility, 145
Utz, 48, 63
Uzochukwu, 201, 211
Uzumba Marimba, 222

V

vagaries, 2, 59-60, 183
validity, 74, 169
Valuation, 144
Value Added Tax (VAT), 38
value in Ethiopia, 101
value of cash, 128
value of informal groups, 108
value of self-discipline, 189
value of universal policy approaches, 37
value of ZAR, 185
Van Bastelaer, 116
Van Beek, 13, 28
Vandemoortele, 262-63, 266, 277, 280
Vanek, 69, 87
Van Ginneken, 263
vanhu vasina musha, 228
Van Praag, 143
Van Staveren, 66, 69, 87
variables, 76, 78, 121-22, 125-28, 136, 140-41, 160, 267, 280-81
   Variation Inflation Factors, 137
variations, 7, 250, 261, 266, 268, 271
varied interpretation, 98
varied literature, 18
varied marital statuses, 74
varieties, 20
   wheat, 97
Vassileva, 158, 162
VAT (Value Added Tax), 38
Vaughan, 96, 112, 118
vegetable producers, 231
vegetables, 189, 229-32
   leaf, 229
ventures, 24, 194
Verhoef, 183-85, 195
Verma, 67, 90

Vermeulen, 144
Verpoorten, 118
Verpooten, 101
Verschraegen, 101, 118
Vervuert Verlagsgesellschaft, 42
VGSIP (Vulnerable Group Social Insurance Programme), 200
victorious, emerged, 55
Vietnam, 201, 211
viewpoint, 157, 169
viewpointmag, 88
Viewpoint Magazine, 88
VIFs, 137, 140
VIHEMA, 170
Vihiga, 275
villages, 97, 234
Vinci, 93, 119
violence, 24, 245, 247, 251

W

Wacquant, 92, 113
Wagenigen University, 239
Wageningen University, 115
wages, 33, 53, 219, 253
   low, 182
wage subsidy, 246, 257
Wagner, 143
Wajir, 274-75
Walid Merouani, 121
Walker, 162
Walt, 150, 163
Wambugu, 259, 278-79
Wang, 122, 125, 127, 139, 145
Wanyama, 149, 163
Wanyeki, 66, 90
war, 219, 249
   wider, 172
Warburton, 210
Ward, 73-74
   rural, 73
Warner, 124-25, 145
war veterans, 204
War Veterans in Zimbabwe, 239
War Veteran Vanguard, 239
Warwick, 89

washing, 71, 76
washing machines, 73, 75, 81-82
Washington, 43, 117-18, 163, 178, 209-11, 256, 279-80
Washington consensus policies, 32
Washington DC, xi, 27, 43, 113, 115, 119, 280
Way Forward, 60, 115
WBI Development Studies, 210
WDR, 86
WEAI (Women's Empowerment in Agriculture Index), 91
weakening of public infrastructure investment in Zimbabwe, 5
weaknesses, 58, 109, 260
   minimise, 219
   structural, 2
Weak NGO sector, 174
Weerdt, 114
Wegary, 112
weight, 74, 158, 267, 269, 271-76
Weinbren, 181, 195
Weisbenner, 122, 143
welfare, 8, 11-12, 16, 21, 27, 33, 50, 55, 65-66, 72, 215, 217
   collective, 155
   economic, 83
   human, 169
Western hemisphere, 31
Western Quarterly, 61
Western Shoa in Ethiopia, 118
Western Society, 194
West Pokot, 274
Westview Press, 87
Weyland, 152, 154, 163
Wharton School Research Paper, 143
Wheat Adoption and Impact Survey, 97, 102-6, 109
wheat farmers in Ethiopia, 6
Wheat Improvement Center, 96
whistles, 191-92
Whitehead, 66-67, 90, 224, 240
White-settler Capitalism, 238
White Settler Capitalism, 239
WHO (World Health Organization),

Index 321

197, 199-200, 209, 211
WHO Regional Office, 209
wider group of people, 153
WIDER Working Paper, 12, 27-28, 162, 278
Widner, 99, 119
WIEGO, 37, 255
WIEGO Working Paper, 255
Wieland, 116
WIID (World Income Inequality Database), 263, 280
wind, 61, 170, 227
windows, 158, 173
Winners & Losers, 61
Winters, 161
Wirtschaftskrisen, 42
Wisconsin, 87
Within-county, 275
Within-group, 272, 281
within-group component of inequality, 272
Wits University Press, 255
Witwatersrand, 87
wives, 82-83, 90, 98, 225
WMS (Welfare Monitoring Survey), 263-64, 266-68, 270-71, 279-80
Wnuk-Lipinski, 13, 28
Wodon, 63
Wolof, 21
woman, 79, 190, 226
   married, 190
   unemployed, 189
woman access, 226
woman heading, 98
women, 5, 65-69, 71-75, 77-87, 90, 95-96, 98-99, 103, 107-12, 129, 132, 134, 187-88, 224-26, 229, 236-37, 243, 247-49, 251-53
   adult, 248
   divorced, 98
   economic infrastructure, 81
   empowered, 107
   increased, 66
   pregnant, 200, 243
   reproductive-aged, 95
   rural, 84

rural Ethiopia, 92
social assistance regime privileges, 9
social reproduction theory positions, 69
subjugated, 224
widowed, 98
working, 69
world, 69
women access land, 226
women and children, 249, 252
Women and Land, 87
Women and Land in Africa, 90
Women and Land in Zimbabwe, 237
Women and Land Redistribution, 224
Women and Land Tenure, 87
Women and Wasta, 112
women and youth, 173
women benefit, 99
Women-headed Households, 238
women in A1, 79
women in Africa, 224
women in FHHs, 79
Women in Informal Employment Globalizing, 37
women in male-headed households, 5, 78
women in MHHs, 83
women in parliament, 95
women in resettlement areas, 78, 80
women in resettlement areas to unpaid care work, 80
women land beneficiaries, 79
women landowners, 225
Women Matter in Agriculture, 237
women on housework, 80
women on unremunerated social reproductive work, 81
women's access, 90, 234
   increased, 66
Women's Access and Rights to Land and Gender Relations, 90
women's access to land, 234
Women's Access to Land and Relations in Tenure, 90
women's army, 96, 112
Women's association, 97, 102-4, 111

informal, 111
women's association membership for women, 107
women's confidence, 108
Women's Cooperatives and COVID-19, 115
Women's Development Army, 116
women's empowerment, 28, 91, 190
Women's Empowerment in Agriculture Index (WEAI), 91
women shifting, 82
Women's involvement, 71
Women's Land Access, 87
Women's Landlessness, 87
Women's Land Rights in Sub-Saharan Africa, 90, 240
Women's Land Rights in Zimbabwe, 237
Women's Legal Right of Access, 87
Women's Legal Right of Access to Agricultural Resources, 87
women's participation, 70
  increasing, 112
women spending, 78-79
women's rights, 66, 84, 90
women's rights to land, 66, 84
Women's Struggles, 89, 238
Women's Time Allocation, 86
women to escape, 84
women to traditional roles, 80
Woodbridge, 116
wood collection, 75-76
Woolcock, 92, 99, 119
Worby, 214, 240
work, 10-11, 23, 68-71, 78-79, 81-83, 87, 122-23, 125-26, 151, 156, 190, 215, 226, 234-35, 255
  analytical, 265
  caring, 85
  community-related, 245
  domestic, 36
  farm, 79, 82
  ground-breaking, 181
  important, 21
  invisible, 66, 75, 84
  legal, 251
  perpetual, 15
  policy, 29
  productive, 66, 71, 78, 80-81, 83, 85
  reconciling, 70
  solid, 54
  unskilled, 252
  waged, 68, 247
World Bank and International Monetary Fund, 58, 199
World Bank Group, 27, 113, 115, 117, 119, 163, 210-11, 235, 279-80
World Bank-inspired Social Risk Management, 219
World Bank Policy Study, 211
World Bank Publications, 43
World Bank Risk Management Framework, 30
World Bank's categorisation, 168
World Bank Study, 63
World Bank UniversitÈ Laval, 278
World Bank View, 237
World Development, 42, 88-89, 113-15, 163, 194, 278
World Development Indicators, 262
World Development Report, 117, 211
World Health Organisation, 200
World Health Organization. *See* WHO
World Health Report, 211
World Health Statistics, 211
World Income Inequality Database (WIID), 263, 280
World Institute for Development Economics Research, 26
world market conditions, 40
world of increasing fractures and inequalities, 40
World Politics, 113, 162
World Social Protection Report, 62
World Social Security Report, 143
World Summit, 32
World's Women, 86-87
Worshipping Meles, 114
Wright, 248, 257
Wrobel, 144

Index

X
Xanadu, 221
Xhosa, 185
Xhosa People, 195
Xu, 260-61

Y
Yablonski, 161
Yah, 187
Yale University Press, 238
Yao, 26
Yates, 210
Yawitch, 230, 240
years, 58, 97, 102, 104, 111-12, 123-24, 126-27, 132-36, 138-39, 169-73, 190, 199-200, 229-30, 244, 264-65, 267, 272, 280-81
Years of Advancing Gender Justice, 256
Yeboah, 66, 88
Ye Meles Amlko, 114
Yeros, 213, 235, 238
Yi, 33, 67, 70, 90, 216-17, 223, 226-27, 233, 236, 240
Yin, 184, 195
Yngstrom, 67, 83, 90
younger, 23, 134, 248, 252
young people and children, 251
Young people and unskilled people, 252
youth, 65, 111, 171, 173, 243, 245-46
youth and children, 171
Youth association, 97, 102, 104-6, 111
Youth Unemployment, 255
Youth Wage Subsidy, 245, 255

Z
Zaire, 21
Zak, 92, 119
Zambia, 5, 12, 16, 28, 40, 42, 45-49, 54-55, 57-63, 163
    ruled, 58
    transformed, 58
Zambia and Ghana, 5
Zambia Human Development Report, 63
Zambian Copper Belt, 34
Zambian economy, 56
Zambian governments, 48
Zambianisation, 56-57
Zambians, 55-56
    young, 55
Zambia's colonisation, 54
Zambia's Copper Mines, 61
Zambia's economy, 56
    mismanaged, 58
Zambia's First Republics, 58
Zambia's post-colonial history, 57
Zambia's support, 57
Zamchiya, 214, 240
ZANU, 214
ZAR, 185, 187-88
ZCCM, 58
Zed Books, 12, 90, 115, 237-38
ZEF Working Paper Series, 116
Zeira, 259, 279
Zenebe, 118
Zewde, 117
Zimba, 57-58, 63
Zimbabwe, 5, 8, 11, 66, 72-73, 81, 84-85, 87, 89, 174, 177, 213-40
    organised rural, 213
Zimbabwe Agriculture, 235
Zimbabweans, 174
zimbabweland, 239
zimbabweland.wordpress, 239
Zimbabwe National Statistics Agency, 240
Zimbabwe Newsletter, 235
Zimbabwe's affiliation, 174
Zimbabwe's agrarian structure, 213
Zimbabwe's Fast Track Land Reform, 237
Zimbabwe's Fast-Track Land Reform Programme, 238
Zimbabwe's Land Question, 239
Zimbabwe's Land Reform, 90, 239
Zimbabwe's Land Revolution, 239
Zimbabwe's Unfinished Business, 237-38, 240
ZIMSTAT, 225, 240
Zittoun, 148, 163
zoom, 30, 35
ZS, 110
Zvimba, 234

www.ingramcontent.com/pod-product-compliance
Lightning Source LLC
Chambersburg PA
CBHW070808300426
44111CB00014B/2451